THE PRIVATE LIFE OF NAPOLEON

BY THE AUTHOR OF

THE SECOND EMPIRE

NAPOLEON: SOLDIER AND EMPEROR

ST. HELENA

EUGENIE, EMPRESS OF THE FRENCH

THE KING OF ROME

THE PRIVATE LIFE
OF
NAPOLEON

❧ ❧ ❧

OCTAVE AUBRY

TRANSLATED FROM THE FRENCH BY
ELISABETH ABBOTT

J. B. LIPPINCOTT COMPANY
PHILADELPHIA AND NEW YORK

CONTENTS

PART ONE: YOUTH

PART TWO: MANHOOD

PART THREE: THE POLISH LOVE

PART FOUR: MARIE-LOUISE AND THE KING OF ROME

EPILOGUE: EXILE AND DEATH

INDEX

ILLUSTRATIONS

Author's Preface

MY PURPOSE in writing this particular book on Napoleon has been two-fold. In the first place I have tried to emphasize his character, to develop his psychology as it was revealed in the course of his daily life. But above all I have sought to show the influence which the sentiments of that man, who was a son, a brother, a husband, a father and a lover, had on the orientation of his political career. Historians of the past have not always attached sufficient importance to the acts and circumstances surrounding the private lives of great men. The historian of today is more aware of human realities: he looks for the motives and justifications of a man's achievements in the man himself. This method rounds out history; it also makes history more exciting by bringing it closer home to us.

Personal considerations played a major rôle in the destiny of Napoleon, more perhaps than in that of any other great man. It was Turreau, the husband of one of his early mistresses, who brought his name forward on that evening of the 12th of Vendémiaire. It was largely because of Josephine that Barras persuaded his colleagues in the Directory to give Bonaparte command of the army in Italy. Without his brother Lucien, Napoleon would have come to grief on the 19th of Brumaire and would have been lost then and there. As Emperor, his blind affection for his clan led him into violating Europe that he might place a crown on the head of every Bonaparte, one after the other. Again, in memory of his youthful love for Désirée Clary, he allowed Bernadotte, his avowed enemy, to mount the throne of Sweden. Marie Walewska's pregnancy decided the matter of his divorce. His second marriage inclined him to over-confidence in Austria. One might even go so far as to say the birth of the King of Rome produced in him that lack of mental balance that was to eventuate in the war with Russia.

During the campaign of France he wrote to Marie-Louise and, in an impulse of imprudent solicitude, revealed his plan of strategy. That letter was intercepted and, falling into Blücher's hands, resulted in the Allied attack on Paris and hastened the day of his first abdication. His premature and hurried escape from Elba was motivated by his desire to rejoin his wife and child. And finally, in later years, a prisoner in his ocean gaol, every one of his public acts was to be prompted by his affection, his hope, that centered solely around the little prisoner of Schönbrunn. If Napoleon had not been swayed by sentiment in those decisive moments of his life, his story would have been very different—and so would ours.

His enemies have tried to picture him as a mere automaton, a shrewd calculator without a soul. "He is neither kind-hearted nor violent," Madame de Staël said of him. "Neither gentle nor cruel as are most people one knows. He neither hates nor loves. In his eyes he is the only one who counts. Everybody else is a mere cipher. . . ." There speaks the malice of a woman of genius. Mme. de Staël erred in good faith no doubt, but she erred. Napoleon could hate as passionately as he could love, and his fellow-beings were infinitely important to him. Like all men, he knew by turns pity, anger, jealousy, friendship, bitterness, love—and to an intense degree, for he was extremely nervous and high-strung. Master over such a vast power and clever mathematician though he was, he had to resort to manipulations, to close calculations, in order to manage his Estate. He fought too many wars—on that point everyone agrees—and that was the cause of his downfall. But he fought less from a love of fighting than from necessity. All of his wars, with the exception of the war in Spain and, to a certain extent, the Russian campaign, were forced upon him by England and her allies. One often finds a touch of sadness, a note of regret in that great soldier, that conqueror accused of being drunk with power. His report on the Battle of Austerlitz ends with the words: "Never was there a more horrible battlefield. From the midst of vast lakes still rise the cries of thousands of men who are beyond help. It makes one's heart bleed. . . ." A strange song of triumph for a conqueror! The day after Wagram he rode out over the plain to make sure that all of the wounded had been picked up. Wherever he came upon a wounded or a dying man he would stop and speak to him and send him help. Caesar, even Alexander, had been more unfeeling.

The reader will find no footnotes to vitiate whatever strength and simplicity this story may have. However I have not set down a single word of Napoleon's that is not authentic and that does not derive from the best sources—and God knows how numerous they are. That unequaled wealth of source material is the chief difficulty which the historian of Napoleon has to encounter, for each source must be checked and carefully selected.

I may be criticized for omissions—and rightly so. I neither have been able nor have wished to set down any but the most significant facts, those that form the very essence of that prodigiously varied and tumultuous life. Though I admire Napoleon's magnificent qualities, in particular his energy, his love of order, his marvelous industry, I have tried to present, as well, his more questionable traits, and in their true light. French history tends more and more toward objectivity. It is, in fact, the very condition of its present rebirth. The chief merit of this study lies therefore, in my estimation, in its impartiality.

Part One

YOUTH

I

Childhood

A GIANT MOUNTAIN lashed by the waves, or rather a range of high peaks, daughter of the Alps, with soaring headlands, sharply indented bays and great masses of rocks merging in close embrace with the sea—that is Corsica. A harsh, free land, untouched by influences from the outside world, a land whose sons serve her only because they love her.

"Before you come in sight of Corsica," Napoleon once said at St. Helena, "you can smell its perfume." Even through winter storms, lashed by drenching spray, while still some miles at sea, one catches the mingled fragrance of lavender, thyme and the turpentine tree, which in summer, under that burning sky, turns the whole island into a pungent bonfire.

Certain places call forth memories that fill and exalt the soul. Corsica retains a kind of emanation of the genius she secreted. Over that land still hovers the shadow of that mighty life that soared aloft into the sky of Europe only to plunge back into the depths of the Atlantic, like those Perseids that, on certain evenings, illumine the edge of our world, only to vanish again after centuries of rushing through an unknown universe. . . .

1775: the citadel of Ajaccio. A tawny acropolis towering high above the sea. The setting sun, dipping toward the horizon, seems to gild earth, sky and water in its death-agony. Near the crenelated rampart, astride an ancient Genoese gun so hot that the greenish-bronze metal burns his skin, sits a boy of six, legs dangling, eyes fixed upon the sea. He looks small, almost emaciated. His arms and legs are thin, but his body is stocky, his chest rounded like a barrel, his head enormous. The dry salt winds have deepened the tan of his olive complexion. Reddish-brown hair, blowing in the breeze, falls over his eyes, that change from blue to gray in the glare of the sun. When he is angry—and that is not seldom—they look black.

As on many other days, he has been fighting with the rowdies who swarm about the waterfront and has been shouting in a voice already loud, already nasal. He has scratched his hands and legs and torn his clothes on the thorns of the cactus that bristles over the rocks on the shore. Then, having driven off his assailants, he has climbed all the way up to the citadel—that stern and martial spot against which the surf booms and breaks into spray. There, by himself, the boy likes to sit silently watching the sun sink toward the shores of that vast France which, as he knows, has conquered his island, and which therefore, young as he is, he hates with all his heart.

There he will linger till nightfall in the hope of escaping his mother, Signora Letizia, who often waits for him at home at the top of the stone staircase and punishes his truancies with a brisk and vigorous hand. That mother is the only human being he admires, the only one of whom he is afraid.

The Casa Buonaparte of those days was very different from the house now shown to tourists in Corsica. Burned down by the Paolists, it was rebuilt at a time when the family fortunes had taken a turn for the better. The original house in which Napoleon was born, and where he passed the first years of his life, was an old, ramshackle affair with narrow windows opening, on the one side, on an unpaved street that smelled of spoiled oranges, and on the other, on a little garden of the darkest green. There was one old servant, Caterina, with whom Mme. Buonaparte shared the housekeeping tasks—and they were not light. A husband, four children—the youngest, Marianne, just out of the willow cradle—and, added to all that, the comings and goings of large family connections, of a Corsican clan. Fortunately, young as she was, Letizia Buonaparte had a head on her shoulders. An early portrait, unsigned, that today hangs in her bedroom, shows her at that time with a long, pale face, enlivened by a dash of rouge, two nondescript eyes lacking in sparkle, and thin lips that were even then beginning to droop at the corners. A strong-willed woman, frugal, orderly, hard-working, almost illiterate, but beautiful in her simple gowns, at once a patrician and a homebody, an aristocrat and a peasant —as are all the women of her class and of her country. She counted every penny: she had to. The family exchequer was slender and her husband extravagant.

That husband, Charles Buonaparte, loved adventure and a good time. On his father's death he had become the ward of his Uncle Lucien, archdeacon at the Cathedral of Ajaccio. He studied law at Corte, then went as far as a doctorate at Pisa. But he was much less interested in the paltry lands he had inherited from his family than in politics—not a lucrative profession in those days.

Charles Buonaparte was a tall, slender man with a pleasant if somewhat pimply face. He wore a wig shaped like a horseshoe, was fastidious about his dress and cut a fine figure in his silk and embroidered velvet coats. Side by side with Pasquale Paoli, leader of the National Party, Buonaparte fought bravely for the independence of his island. In that savage fighting Letizia followed her husband on horseback and, though already large with Napoleon, managed to escape from the French after the defeat at Ponte Nuovo. Fording the beds of rushing torrents, she took refuge in the mountains, hiding out in thickets and caves and living on goat's milk and cornmeal cakes. Again and again bullets whistled past her head. She would have been quite capable of firing a shot herself. Letizia Buonaparte had thoughts only for her family and for Corsica. She bowed the knee to no one save God. But when Paoli fled to England and Louis XV offered the insurgents an amnesty, she was among the first to see the wisdom of going over to so strong—too strong—a conqueror, and she returned to Ajaccio to give birth to her son.

Yielding perhaps to his wife's influence, as well as to the advice of his friend, Laurent Giubega, chief clerk of the Estates of Corsica, but above all following the dictates of his own ambition, Charles Buonaparte wormed his way into the inner circle about the French General Marbeuf and lent his aid in the slow and ungrateful task of pacification. He was among those Corsicans who, to use the language of the newcomers, "had placed

themselves frankly in the king's hands." The conquerors showed
Buonaparte marked favor. Governor Beaumanoir and Quartermaster Pichon trotted little Napoleon on their knees. Marbeuf
and Mme. Boucheron, the wife of the tax-collector, stood godfather and godmother to little Louis, Napoleon's younger
brother. Thanks to Marbeuf, Charles Buonaparte was appointed
king's counselor and assessor at Ajaccio. He was made manager
of a mulberry nursery in the silk industry and of a marsh rec-
lamation project. Finally, as a member of the Estates of Corsica,
he formed part of the delegation that "went ashore" in 1776 to
pay homage to Louis XVI and to lay the needs of the new prov-
ince before him. Buonaparte returned home completely dazzled
by the Court of Versailles and more inclined than ever to support the "French party," even to become its leader, for he could
now see whence honors and posts would be likely to fall. The
French liked Charles Buonaparte for his tact, his polished manners, his knowledge of their language and customs. Was he not,
like his wife, of a good and ancient family? The Buonapartes
were counted among the leading citizens of Corsica and were
Florentines by origin. Banished, they went first to Sarzana, then
to Ajaccio. In those vapory eras they lived like little feudal
barons. At Bocognano and Bastelica where their olive groves
and sheepfolds lay, they could count on numerous henchmen—
tough ones too. Through their family alliances they were assured of support throughout the length and breadth of the
island. In Charles Buonaparte, Count de Marbeuf had gained a
recruit by no means to be despised.

Charles Buonaparte was almost always on the go, in quest of
money or amusement, or following up some intrigue or some
litigation. Intelligent to be sure, but of no great judgment, his
vivid imagination was always involving him in some scheme or
other. He was, however, a persistent lobbyist and never took
"no" for an answer. He had a genius for promoting projects
and petitions. Old Archdeacon Lucien often went to Letizia's
aid with advice and sometimes, miser though he was, with his
purse. Confined to his bed with the gout, the old man kept

the family books. The Buonapartes were counting on his money
to give the children their start in life.

Enemies of the Buonapartes soon began to accuse Letizia of
being too kind to M. de Marbeuf. Napoleon, so the gossip ran,
was the result of that friendship. An absurd slander! Napoleon
was already well on the way before Madame Letizia had even so
much as laid eyes on the general. When, later, she was introduced to Marbeuf, she showed him merely the courtesy due an
honored guest, a friendly and powerful patron. Poor Letizia, so
little of a coquette, so constantly absorbed in her household
tasks, her mending, her washing! Her austere beauty was not of
the kind to attract an elderly nobleman who, while something
of a lady's man to be sure, was an habitué of the Court and must
have found the women of Ajaccio very countrified. Moreover,
as her entire life proves, no woman ever had a higher sense of
her duties than Letizia Buonaparte. She loved and respected her
husband, she put up with his escapades in silence—she was never
unfaithful to him.

She could teach her two eldest boys, Joseph and Napoleon,
nothing but dialect. She knew little Italian and no French at
all, so she sent them to a nun's infant school. Napoleon did
not work much there. At the age of five he took a liking to a
little schoolmate named Giacominetta. Because his socks were
always falling down around his heels the other boys used to
run after him singing:

> *Napoleone di mezza calzetta,*
> *Fa l'amor a Giacominetta.*

From there he was sent to the Jesuit school, where Abbé
Recco taught him to read. Napoleon was to remember that
school to his dying day. The children sat facing each other in
two groups—the Romans and the Carthaginians. Above each
group hung a flag. Joseph sat under the standard of Rome,
Napoleon under that of Carthage. This greatly annoyed him
for, though he had not learned much as yet, he must have heard

vaguely about the Punic defeat; so by dint of working on the good Abbé he managed to get himself transferred to his brother's flag—the flag of the victors.

Joseph was a quiet, well-behaved lad, eighteen months older than Napoleon. But time and again the young Napoleon would make his elder brother do his lessons for him while he dashed off to roam the countryside or to eat *poppetti* (meat cakes) at the home of his wet nurse, Camilla Ilari, who was fonder of him than of her own son. Napoleon was sly, unfair, domineering. He would beat Joseph, scratch him, bite him—then run and complain of him to their mother. On rainy days the two boys played in a large bedroom at the top of the house. Joseph would draw jumping jacks on the wall, but Napoleon, whose father had bought him a drum and a wooden sword, made sketches of soldiers in battle line. When he was nearly eight, he began to show a decided flair for sums. His family had fixed up a board hut for him on the flat roof of the house and there, safe from any intrusion on the part of Joseph and their younger brother, Lucien, he would betake himself to scribble figures to his heart's content.

The boy had a sweet tooth. His grandmothers, Mme. Buonaparte and Mme. Fesch—his two *minannas,* as he called them, his aunt and godmother, *zia* Gertrude Paravicini, and his godfather, Laurent Giubega, often gave him cakes and jams. That did not prevent him from swapping his cheesecake with a soldier for a piece of hardtack and eating it on the street. His mother would scold him and he would answer that as he was going to be a soldier too, he had to get used to eating that sort of bread. To be a soldier—that was his one idea! And he would gaze enviously after the French officers in their smart blue and white uniforms whom he met on the streets of Ajaccio.

Though he was fond of his *minanna* Fesch, he liked to make fun of her. Bent almost double the old lady would hobble along leaning on her cane, with Napoleon behind her mimicking her limping gait. When his mother caught him at it and tried to whip him, he would run away. The next morning when he came to get his mother's kiss, she would push him away and

he would think they were quits. But at night when he climbed
upstairs to bed his mother would follow him, close the door,
and administer a spanking all the harder because it had been
delayed.

Once on a holiday their miller-farmer from Bocognano came
to the Buonaparte house with some young horses. Napoleon
waited till the man was ready to leave, jumped astride the live-
liest of the colts and galloped all the way back to the farm,
pursued by the peasant, who expected every moment to see the
boy break his neck. Before going home the child watched the
mill work and calculated the exact amount of wheat it ought to
grind in a week's time. When the farmer took him back to
Ajaccio, he said to Signora Letizia, "If God grants the young
gentleman a long life he is sure to become the greatest man in
the world."

Such were the stories, gilded with the radiance of her youth,
that Madame Mère loved to repeat to her reader, Rosa Mellini,
in the last years of her life. Her old hands would tremble as she
talked and a tear would trickle down from her unseeing eyes
as she thought of that troublesome little boy whom, secretly, she
had always loved the best. . . .

On his return from France Charles Buonaparte applied for a
scholarship for Napoleon in a military school. Joseph he intended to send to a church boarding school. Through Marbeuf,
both of those favors were readily obtained. What better way for
the King of France to rally the Corsican élite to his standard!
M. de Buonaparte produced the requisite proofs of nobility and,
setting out again for Versailles, on December 15, 1778, took with
him his two eldest boys and his young brother-in-law, Fesch.
Traveling through Tuscany and Piedmont, they came to Aix,
where Fesch entered the seminary, then went on to Autun,
where the two boys were placed in school. Joseph was to study
the classics under the supervision of the bishop, Mgr. de Marbeuf, a brother of the Governor. Napoleon was to remain there
several months to perfect himself in French while waiting to
enter the military school at Brienne.

The new life into which the two brothers were now plunged was a sudden and drastic change for them, but they seem not to have suffered greatly. Napoleon did not get on with his new schoolmates: they made fun of his first name pronounced in the Corsican fashion and nicknamed him *Paille au nez*. In a letter that has recently come to light, his French teacher, Abbé Chardon stated that the boy was inclined to be serious and brooding. "One day," wrote the Abbé, "Napoleon happened to be in the study hall with some other pupils who began to tease him about the capture of Corsica and accused the Corsicans of cowardice. Napoleon listened with that stolid expression so characteristic of him. But when they were through, that lad of nine and a half flung out his little arm angrily, shouting that if the odds had been only four to one the French would never have taken Corsica, but that they had come ten to one. I was standing beside him and I said to him, 'But you had a good general in Paoli.' His face fell. 'Yes, sir,' he answered. 'And I wish I could be like him.'

"He was a very talented boy," added the Abbé, "quick to grasp ideas and to learn. When I gave him a lesson he would fix his eyes on me, open-mouthed. But when I started to summarize what I had said, he stopped listening and, if I took him to task, he would answer coldly, even haughtily, 'I know it, sir.' "

Napoleon spent three months and twenty days at that school. In May, 1779, he was obliged to take leave of Joseph and enter Brienne. The two boys felt the separation keenly. Joseph burst into sobs. Napoleon struggled hard to keep a dry eye. And yet, of the two, he was the one who suffered more.

Napoleon was not quite ten years old when he entered that school in Champagne where everything seemed hostile to him: the countryside bleak, rainy; the buildings gloomy; the discipline harsh; the lessons dry; his schoolmates ill-natured. The teachers were twelve Minims, good souls but with little learning. They were assisted by a number of laymen, among them one Pichegru, who was to be heard from later.

The school numbered from one hundred to one hundred and fifty pupils according to the years. The boys wore a blue uniform with facings, lapels and collar of red, black breeches and white stockings. In winter they had an overcoat of the same cloth and the same color. They ate in a huge refectory with their masters. The food was fairly decent: for dinner, soup, boiled meat, an entrée, dessert; in the afternoon, bread and fruit; for supper, roast, an entrée or salad and dessert. There was plenty to drink—a little wine diluted with a lot of water. Each pupil slept in a separate cell opening on an endless corridor. The cells were small—six feet square—and furnished with a narrow camp bed and a small washstand. The boys were locked in at night.

Cut off from everything he loved best, his family, his island, the warm southern sun, Napoleon turned melancholy and bad-tempered. His schoolmates made fun of his short stature, his poverty, his strange ways. They did not like him. He was too different, too foreign. Frenchmen really like their own kind only: instinctively they turn from faces and temperaments they do not know. To escape their persecution the little Corsican took refuge in his memories, resorted to dreams. He wrote to Joseph, to his parents. But he never complained, he never asked to be taken back home whatever may have been said to the contrary. He was too proud for that. Bending his young shoulders to the task, he summoned all his courage, he possessed his soul in patience, he waited.

Among so many indignities, the worst seemed to him the insults to that conquered land of which, more than ever, he felt himself a part.

"I hope to free Corsica one of these days," he did not hesitate to say. "The fate of an empire often rests on a single man."

Pompous words for a child. Paoli was still his hero, his model. His sole ambition was to follow in his footsteps—but with better luck. How he loved Corsica! And how he hated that victorious and haughty France that held him prisoner! "I shall do all the harm to you French I can," he said angrily to young Bour-

rienne with whom he had struck up a friendship because
Bourrienne was poor too and because he "took to mathematics
like a duck to water."

Napoleon flung himself wholeheartedly into his studies.
Work alone could help him to rise above the jeers and repri-
mands, would put him in a position to aid his family, to
reach that rank of leader to which, even at that early age, he
believed he had been born. He was weak in Latin. It was a
waste of time, he thought, to read and write a dead language. If
a man wanted to know the masterpieces of the past, there were
plenty of good translations at hand. What use could Latin be to
him in later years? A soldier, he thought, had no need of it. He
chose instead to learn French, and it appears that the Minims
offered no objection.

Father Dupuy, who taught him grammar and French literature, not only gave him advice, but gratuitous private coaching.
Napoleon was excellent in the sciences. He had a flair for pains-
taking research and for the abstract problem. His teacher,
Father Patrault, a good geometrician, was proud of him.

He had drawing lessons from M. Courtalon. To tell the truth,
he drew badly. It took him some time to make a neat figure and
a plan of fortification. In fencing he was fair. As for dancing, he
seems not to have acquitted himself so badly, for in 1781, at the
public exercises of the school he was one of the seventeen pupils
chosen to take part in a contra-dance.

Pacing back and forth along the avenue of lindens, or sitting
in his room of an evening, he would become absorbed in the
study of geography or history, ancient history in particular:
Tacitus, Suetonius, Titus Livy—but above all, Plutarch.
Nothing gave him so much comfort, so much encouragement
as the example of noble lives. He envied those men tensed, exalted by love of country, giants even in their mistakes or in their
shortcomings. He was intoxicated with the grandeur of the
ancients and so deeply that he was never wholly to get over that
form of inebriation. In spirit he lived in Sparta and in Rome.
Like the Gracchi or Brutus, he dreamt of becoming a republican hero.

Little by little he grew accustomed to the school—no doubt in spite of himself. The principal, Father Berton, hit upon the happy idea of dividing a piece of ground among the resident pupils in which each boy could have a little garden of his own. Bonaparte enjoyed this pastime. He had never lost his country boy's love of plants and flowers. He now compelled two of his schoolmates to give up their portion, added it to his own and, with great care laid out a narrow strip of land, well walled in and equipped with a bower of the sort known as a green arbor. There, far from the noise and games, he would often withdraw to read and to dream. . . . He was extremely jealous of this retreat, admitting none of his comrades but Bourrienne, and the latter only on occasion. When, to tease him, the boys would come and interrupt him, he would rush at them in a rage, fists balled. "Even at that age," he was to confide in later years, to Mme. de Rémusat [Josephine's lady-in-waiting], "I had the feeling that my will must triumph over the others and that anything that appealed to me must be mine. We did not really like each other at school. It takes time to make real friends. . . ." However, at recess, he played ball, robbers, hide-and-seek, prisoners' base. He had his share in hazing the form-masters. A seed of rebellion was growing in him. . . . He was seldom punished. One day, however, ordered to eat his supper on his knees in front of the refectory door, he obeyed. But almost immediately the humiliation brought on a nervous attack and he was seized with such violent vomiting and convulsions that the principal was obliged to let him off.

In the end, through sheer force of character, Napoleon won the esteem of a number of his teachers and conquered the hostility of his schoolmates. Among the latter he made several friends, though they never became intimates: chief among them Bourrienne, then Gudin and Nansouty, for whom, in later years, he was to do many a good turn. He had few pleasures. He was not received at the Château of Brienne. Once a year only, at the Feast of St. Louis, he and his comrades were allowed to play in the park. Vacations were unknown in those days; but from the 15th of September to All Saints' Day, the boys had only one class a day, spent long hours playing games and taking walks, in slow files, along the highroads and across the fields. Sometimes they would stop for a glass of milk and a piece of whole-meal bread at Mother Marguerite's, an old peasant woman who lived in a little thatched hut in the heart of the woods. Napoleon preferred to spend the afternoon in his cell or in his little garden.

He won prizes, which were presented to him by the Duke of Orleans and the latter's beautiful friend, Mme. de Montesson. The winter of 1783 was unusually severe and snow was piled high in the school yards. Napoleon suggested to his schoolmates that they dig trenches and build a little fort. Dividing into two camps, the boys fought a wild and impassioned battle. Napoleon commanded the siege. Two weeks of pure joy at the price of frosted noses, blackened eyes and severe colds! But from that day no one ever thought of teasing "little Buonaparte" again.

In an age when libertinism was rampant in military schools and the "nymphs" of Brienne were as famous as the "unmentionables" of Tournon, Napoleon held himself scornfully aloof. His very nature, chaste but virile, protected him from such youthful errors. With him the mind ruled the senses.

He had not seen his family for five years. The journey was too long and too costly. But in July, 1784, M. de Buonaparte arrived in France to place his daughter Marianne in Saint-Cyr, where he had managed to get her admitted as a pupil, and seized the opportunity to visit Joseph at Autun. There he picked up Lucien, who had joined his elder brother the year before, and took him on with him to Brienne. Napoleon was very happy to see his father. In the few days they spent together, he discussed the future of the family with him. An authoritative manner, stern words, piercing glances—at fifteen the boy was already reasoning like a grown man. His father was ill, seriously ill. Suffering from stomach trouble and greatly depressed, Charles Buonaparte unburdened himself to this son, in whom he saw the future guardian of the family. Joseph had changed his mind about becoming a priest and now wanted to be a soldier.

Napoleon was worried. Joseph had a literary turn of mind: he knew nothing about mathematics. What sort of officer would he make? He was soft, easy-going. Much better for him to read for the bar. . . . So argued the young Napoleon. M. de Buonaparte admired that precocious maturity. On leaving Brienne he went up to Paris to consult a physician, but returned almost immediately to Corsica, taking Joseph with him. Lucien, that "gay, lively, overgrown, scatter-brained child," who at the age of nine knew French perfectly, was left with the Minims. Napoleon paid no attention to him beyond scolding him harshly. Lucien was hurt at such long-distance protection and was never to lose the bitter memory of it.

Nevertheless, at heart, Napoleon loved his brothers as he loved his parents. But he would have been ashamed to show his affection. He was a man, a soldier, born to command: he must be above emotion.

The school observed strict religious practices: prayers morning and evening, low mass every day, high mass, vespers and assembly on Sundays. But the older pupils, tinged with the unbelief of the age, spread an atmosphere of scepticism throughout the school. They made fun of the Minims who, to tell the truth, seem to have been somewhat lax in their duties. The boys calculated that it took Father Berton exactly nine minutes to say mass and Father Guérin, who was old and slow, thirteen. As for Father Château, he was at his best in the masses for the dead, polishing them off in four minutes and a half.

By the time he had finished his studies Napoleon was still undecided what course to follow. Should he be a sailor or go into the artillery? Keralio, the inspector of schools, had destined him for sea duty. Mme. Buonaparte suffered tortures of anxiety. In her letters she tried to dissuade her son from a career in the Navy. But she need not have worried. Fate was to decide the matter—and in the way she wished. A new inspector selected Napoleon for the artillery. In September, 1784, he was appointed "gentleman cadet" and left Brienne to enter the Military School at Paris.

That little cadet must have been well pleased as he traveled on the canal-boat that took him to the capital with four of his comrades, Comminges, Dampierre, Castres de Vaux and Laugier de Bellecour. He saw the future opening before him. And yet, when it came time to leave, he was sorry to say goodbye to Brienne. After all, he had not been unhappy there. That modest Champagne school had been one of the necessary way-stations in his life; throughout his whole career he was to refer to it with pleasure, even with emotion. He was to promote and heap favors on every one of his schoolmates from Brienne.

The school he now entered was situated in a palace, the noblest perhaps of those designed by Gabriel. Napoleon was shocked by the luxury in which those future officers lived: two-course meals, an endless number of servants, an expensive riding school. He would rather have had them "eat hardtack, brush their coats themselves and clean their own boots"—in short, have a sterner preparation for a soldier's career.

The training covered a wider field and was of better calibre than at Brienne, where, to tell the truth, certain of the masters were actually illiterate. But in the year he spent at the Champ de Mars, Napoleon, though still studious, showed progress only in his particular line. He was brilliant in mathematics, but his handwriting was still an illegible scrawl, his spelling uncertain, and he had forgotten the little Latin he had known. As to horsemanship he was wretched. "He's just an idiot," declared Bauer, his German professor. Others, however, were struck by his dignified bearing, the willful expression on his face, the heavy weight of his glance upon one. Domairon, his literature teacher, said of his strange, spirited style that it was like "granite heated red-hot in a volcano." Another teacher, L'Esguille, wrote: "If circumstances are favorable to him, this boy will go far."

Bourrienne had not come to Paris. But Bonaparte formed another and even closer friendship there. As instructor in infantry he had been given an old-timer, Alexandre des Mazis, who won him by his kindness, his mellowness. They soon became inseparable. On the other hand, from the very first day, he also made an enemy, the Vendéan, Phélippeaux, whom he was to meet again in a critical hour of his career at the siege of

Saint Jean d'Acre. Hostile in temperament as in thought, the two boys sat together in the study hall and kicked each other's shins black and blue.

Napoleon became involved in other quarrels. The *petits nobles,* the boys, like himself, who held scholarships, had fist fights with the sons of the aristocracy. "What blows I used to give in those days!" he was wont to say. Those warlike youths were seething with the ferments of the age. But there was no hazing at that school: the headmasters would not have tolerated it.

Napoleon seemed much more carefree and happy in Paris than he had been at Brienne. But the thought that he was about to be made an officer in a few months would have induced him to put up with anything. He annotated verses, and started to write a poem on the freedom of his island. The poem opened with a dream in which Corsica was portrayed as holding out a dagger to the slumbering Bonaparte, and saying: "Thou shalt be my avenger!" He recited that bit to his friend Laugier who could not restrain his laughter. Napoleon always talked of his country with jealous pride. On the flyleaf of a mathematics book he scribbled two rhythmic lines, in dialect: "Oh, Corsica, if thou hopest for a better fate from a just and friendly peace, thou wilt hope in vain." He scourged the French for their conquest in words of flame that earned him many a reprimand. "Sir," he was told, and not unwisely, "you are one of the King's cadets. You should remember this and restrain your love for Corsica, which is, after all, a part of France." At confession, which the cadets were obliged to attend every month, the chaplain reprimanded him for his opinions. Napoleon leapt to his feet, shouting in a loud voice: "I did not come here to talk about Corsica and it's not the business of a priest to read me a lecture on that point."

His repartees were often harsh. When Mgr. de Juigné, Archbishop of Paris, visited the school to attend confirmation exercises, he expressed surprise at the name Napoleon which, he said, he had never seen in the calendar. To which young Bonaparte retorted that as the year had only 365 days, there were any number of saints who had not been able to find a place there. The prelate smiled. In later years Napoleon was to recall that smile and to heap favors and honors on Juigné in his old age.

In March, 1785, Joseph informed his younger brother of the death of their father. Charles Buonaparte was only thirty-nine years old. Accompanied by Joseph and his brother-in-law, Fesch, he had gone to Montpellier in search of better medical treatment. Suffering from a cancer of the pylorus, he lingered for several months. Mme. Permon, a Corsican who had known Letizia and who had settled in Montpellier, nursed him in that last agonizing illness. As he lay dying he called for Napoleon. "Where is my son?" he kept asking. "He will take care of me, he will save me." He was buried in the Church of the Cordeliers. Mme. Permon took Joseph to her home and he set off shortly afterward for Corsica.

Though Napoleon gave no sign of his emotion—his letters at that time were cold and stilted—he suffered keenly. He had loved that irresponsible father whose weakness his implacable young eyes had not yet pierced. From that moment he considered himself, if not the head, at least the actual support of his family, shouldering the burden of protecting them, of relieving their financial distress and, wherever he could do so, of bettering their fortunes along with his own.

Napoleon took his final examination in the presence of the famous Laplace, a kindly, ceremonious figure in a black frock coat, his eyes protected by a shade. He had boned up so well on his "Bézout" that he passed forty-second among fifty-eight, a very honorable grade after one year of school. In later years he was to recall with pride that on September 1, 1785, "aged sixteen years and fifteen days," having asked for a post that would take him nearer his family, he was appointed second lieutenant in the La Fère artillery, in garrison at Valence. He was the first Corsican to graduate from the Military School.

II

Lieutenant Bonaparte

An OFFICER of France at sixteen! Never, in all the heyday and brilliancy of his after life, was Napoleon to taste so great a joy. As ruler of Europe he was to recall, with twinkling eyes, the huge yellow diligence (*turgotine*) and then the canal-boat in which he and Des Mazis journeyed to Valence. On his arrival he found lodgings with an elderly spinster, Mlle. Bou, who kept a little café and rented out rooms. For three months Napoleon, like his comrades, was compelled to pass through all the grades of the service: first as gunner, then as corporal, finally as sergeant. He mounted guard and was officer of the day. In that way he was initated into the life of the troop. A fortunate regulation: Lieutenant Bonaparte would know how to get along with the French soldier.

When for the first time he put on his uniform—a blue coat with a turned-down collar, trimmed and faced in red, blue trousers, plain epaulet decorated with a lozenge of gold and silk—he felt repaid for all those slow and difficult years when it sometimes seemed as if he were buried alive. That coat, which would always be to him, "the most beautiful in the world," opened the future for him. What would he be? A general in France or the liberator of Corsica? Fate and his own energy were to decide.

He lunched on meat pie from the bakery, washed down with a glass of water, but he dined at the lieutenants' table, at Gény's, at the inn of the Three Pigeons. The obliging Mlle. Bou ironed his shirts and mended his cuffs and jabots. His superior officers were kind to him, in particular his lieutenant colonel, the Vicomte d'Urtubie, and his captain, Masson d'Autume. "The Service was like one big family," he was to say in after years; "the officers were extremely fatherly and the finest, worthiest men in the world, pure gold, but too old because peace had lasted a long time. The younger officers made fun of them, for sarcasm and irony were the fashion of the day, but they worshipped them and did nothing but give them their due."

His relations with his brother officers were courteous, but he was on particularly friendly terms with Des Mazis and the latter's elder brother, who was already a captain in the regiment. He attended the corps dinners prepared at Faure's, at the *Ecu de France*, went to small parties given by the officers to the townspeople, and danced at St. Barbara's ball. He took a number of walking trips and climbed the Roche-Colombe and the Chartreuse de Bouvante. "I like to get up above the horizon," he said.

That little lieutenant began to make connections for himself in the social life of Valence. Marbeuf had given him an introduction to Mgr. de Tardivon, the abbé of Saint-Ruf, and through the latter he was received in the most delightful houses —Mme. du Colombier's, Mme. de Lauberie de Saint- Germain's, Mme. de Laurencin's. Sometimes he went to the Colombier's country house at Basseaux, walking along the highroad for three and a half miles, singing choruses. Mme. du Colombier, a cultured elderly Lyonnaise, was "mad about him." She was always urging him to have a good time, to lead a less austere life. "My mother has too many burdens already," he told her, "and I owe it to myself not to add to them by my extravagances, particularly when they are forced upon me by the stupid folly of my comrades." The good lady predicted a brilliant career for him.

When Bonaparte confided to her his ambition to write a "History of Corsica," she gave him a letter to Abbé Raynal [the eminent historian and philosopher]. Later, during the Revolution, she was to say to him: "Whatever you do, don't fly the country. It is easy enough to get out, but one never knows whether one will get back." To which Napoleon retorted that he would rather owe a marshal's baton to his country than to strangers.

She had a daughter, Caroline, a young and charming girl to

BIRTHPLACE OF NAPOLEON
Ajaccio, Corsica
From the Drawing by Eric Pape

NAPOLEON BONAPARTE
STUDENT AT BRIENNE
From the Statue by Rochet

whom Lieutenant Bonaparte paid some attention. On certain forenoons, they picked cherries and ate them, pelting each other with the stones just for the fun of it. But soon Caroline married an elderly officer, Bressieux, who took her away to Lyons. Napoleon may also have felt a slight flutter for Mlle. de Lauberie. She was to prefer her cousin Montalivet—they were both to come into his life again in the prosperous days of the Empire.

That little Corsican with the slender hands, the olive complexion, was still virgin. Those young girls touched his shy imagination, stirred his pulses. Though he flirted with them—they did not take him seriously and made fun of his awkward manner and his emphatic speech—he never indulged in vulgar diversions. His panacea was study. After all, he still had so much to learn. He realized the inadequacy of his education at Brienne. He would have to study more intensely, fill out the gaps in his knowledge. As he bent over his books in his bare little room furnished in massive oak, he could hear the noisy laughter of drinkers and the click of billiard balls from the café below. His purse was light—seventy-three francs a month as pay—and he had to be very economical. If, now and then, there was any money left, it went to buy or borrow books at Aurel's, the bookseller, whose stalls, tucked away in the "house of the Heads," faced his window. While his comrades caroused or took shopgirls out to picnic on the greensward, young Bonaparte read, annotated and wrote with unflagging zeal, with fiery passion.

Above all he steeped himself in Rousseau. The dry quips, the scintillations of a Voltaire repelled him. But the man from Geneva who had aroused a generation with his orchestrated doubts, his sentimental cries of love, his hymns to virtue, his dreams of a society that would be sweet, equal and free—Rousseau, the prophet and lawmaker of the future, Rousseau the tormented, the maligned, he understood, he loved. Had not Rousseau made himself Napoleon's mentor by declaring openly for Corsican independence and aspiring to become

Corsica's law-giver? Rousseau, he thought, was a kindred soul. Poor as he was, Napoleon had no mirror in which to see his own face. His hollow cheeks, his staring pupils, would have warned him that his was a soul of a different calibre, more ruthless, more orderly, the soul of a leader. Napoleon was not and never would be a philosopher. Though his spirit could still wing its way to the clouds—he was so young—he was soon to take his stand on reality.

Rousseau became the dominating influence in that laborious apprenticeship at Valence. Bonaparte devoured the *Contrat social, Émile,* the *Nouvelle Héloise,* the *Confessions,* dissecting them, imitating their phraseology. For his "History of Corsica" he jotted down at random a few biting comments: "Frenchmen, not satisfied with robbing us of all we held dear, you have even corrupted our morals." "Corsicans managed to throw off the Genoese yoke while still observing all the rules of the law. They can do the same with the French." One would have sworn that his tirade on suicide came straight from the pen of Jean Jacques:

"Ever alone, though surrounded by men, I come home to dream by myself and to give full rein to the keenness of my melancholy. Which way does it turn today? Toward death . . ."

Was that mere ranting? One cannot be sure. A man as sensitive as Napoleon naturally had his moments of despair. "What can one do in this world?" he asked. "As long as I have to die some time, would it not be just as well to kill myself?" What other course for an ambitious soul that sees a world closed before it? A life that did not offer immediate power and fame was too long for him. But once his anguish was set to paper, the poisonous mists cleared and he began to hope and to believe in his star again.

His thoughts were not always so tense. He was deeply absorbed in his profession, applying himself conscientiously to his studies, his officer's training. But the combined worries of family and country weighed constantly on him, and he looked forward impatiently to the moment when he would see them both again. At last, after a fortnight at Lyons with his company, where he helped to put down a workers' rebellion, he was granted a six months' leave. He set out at once for Aix, pausing only at the seminary to embrace his uncle Fesch, and young Lucien, who was just out of Brienne and now studying for the priesthood. On September 15, 1786, Napoleon stepped ashore on the quay at Ajaccio.

What a welcome that was! After an absence of eight years he found all his family gathered together in the old home to greet him: his mother, beaming at him from under her black hood, *minanna* Buonaparte, *minanna* Fesch, the latter leaning more heavily than ever on her cane, great-uncle Lucien, his aunts, his good old nurse, and all the friends and hangers-on who had a place at the Buonaparte fireside. He kissed little Louis and trotted on his knees Paulette, Maria-Nunziata and Jerome—all born since he had left the island. Paulette was his favorite—a coquette, roguish, enchanting, a little beauty even at that age. He laid himself out to win her, played her childish games with her. Toward those children who looked up to him in admiration, he was always tender, responsive, always ready to lend an attentive ear.

In those first weeks he put aside all thoughts of business and, giving himself up to the pleasure of revisiting old and beloved scenes, reveled in the sunshine of his native land. Never had that country seemed so beautiful to him. . . . His feet wandered back along the paths of his childhood. From dawn to dusk he roamed the outskirts of Ajaccio, lingering for hours in the olive groves, under the great green oak of Milelli, at Bocognano, at Salines, or in the vineyard of the Sposata. He wandered through the golden *maquis,* rambled across fields already abloom with autumn crocuses, strolled beside the sounding sea toward which the sun was dipping. Many a time he did not go home till the moon was pale in the sky. Sometimes, losing his way, he would even spend the night in a shepherd's hut. That Corsican land enchanted him: there at last he found himself again. Stripped bare, unsullied and forsaken, Corsica penetrated his very pores, roused his hidden energies. They were so alike, those two. After years of exile he became one with his native land, yielding himself up to her influence with a wholehearted abandon he was never to know again.

At home, after the first novelty had worn off, he plunged into the business of straightening out the family affairs. In a few days he had relearned all the dialect he had forgotten—for officer though he was and proud of his epaulets, he still bowed to his mother's authority. Ever since the death of Charles Buonaparte, the family had been living in very reduced circumstances. Madame Letizia managed to scrape along without money by pinching and by living on the products of the farm. The rare *écus* that turned up from time to time were promptly confiscated by Uncle Lucien, who tucked them away under the straw mattress on which he lay bedridden by gout. Joseph was away at Pisa studying law in the hope of becoming a judge. Napoleon helped the old priest keep the family books, acted as secretary to him and as agent for the sale of the harvest, looked after the upkeep of the farms and supervised the shepherds. Those powerful patrons who had once been the mainstay of the family were all gone now: Marbeuf had died recently; Boucheporn, the tax-collecter, had returned to France. The government of the island was in the hands of strangers. Absorbed in those family cares Napoleon asked for and obtained an extension of leave. He remained in Corsica a whole year. In September, 1787, his petitions for indemnities for the mulberry nurseries being still unanswered, he set out for Paris to besiege the government offices there.

He took a room at the Hôtel de Cherbourg, rue du Faubourg-Saint-Honoré, then, like his father before him, hastened to Versailles. He had the temerity to ask for an appointment with the prime minister, Loménie de Brienne, and he gave the clerks no peace. The matter dragged on. Between times he called on his sister Marianne at Saint-Cyr and strolled about the streets of Paris. He roamed the boulevards, gaped at the show-window displays, went to the Théâtre Français, and the Italiens, paced the arcades of the Palais-Royal. It was in that rendezvous of idlers, gamblers, rascals and prostitutes that he had his first adventure with a woman. A sordid, fleeting moment! His mania for writing made him promptly jot down a portrait of her under his smoky hotel light. To Napoleon at eighteen everything was a subject for study, an opportunity to analyze emotions, his own as well as others'. "I went out on the Boulevard des Italiens," he writes, "and was striding along under the arcades of the Palais-Royal, so absorbed by the usual intensity of my thoughts that I did not even feel the cold. Once my imagination had cooled off, however, I became aware of the sharpness of the season and went into the arcades to get warm. I was standing at the threshold of those iron doors when my glance, wandering about, fell on a young girl. The hour, her figure, her extreme youth, left no doubt in my mind as to her profession. I looked at her. She halted—not with the usual air of command, but with a manner wholly in keeping with the charm of her person. I was struck by that in particular. Her shyness encouraged me and I spoke to her. . . . Yes, I spoke to her! I, who am more convinced than anyone of the odiousness of her calling and have always felt myself sullied by a mere glance. . . . But when I saw her pale face, her frail physique and heard her soft voice I had not a moment's doubt. 'Either,' I said to myself, 'this girl will be useful to me in the study I wish to make, or she is just a stupid fool.'

" 'You must be cold,' I said to her. 'How can you bring yourself to walk in these arcades?'

" 'Oh, sir, hope keeps me going. I have to finish my evening.'

"The indifference with which she uttered those words, the mechanical response touched me and I fell into step beside her.

" 'You don't look very strong. Don't you find your profession very tiring?'

"She shrugged her shoulders. 'One must do something, monsieur!'

" 'True, but isn't there something that would be better for your health?'

" 'No, monsieur. One must live.'

"I was delighted. At least she was answering my questions—a success that had by no means crowned all the attempts I had made."

He asked about her life and she told him her story good-naturedly. An officer had seduced her. . . . She had not seen her own family for over three years.

After that moment of unbending, she suggested going home with him.

"What for?" asked Bonaparte.

"Well, we can get warm and you can satisfy your hunger."

"I was far from turning saint. I had led her on so that she would not run away when she found herself cornered by the argument I was holding in store for her, counterfeiting a moral scruple which I intended to show her I did not have. . . ."

The account breaks off here. Weariness, modesty? Perhaps! The stoic he would have liked to be had weakened for a second, but he quickly got hold of himself again. As is the case with many young men, Napoleon's first experience in love left him nothing but a feeling of sadness and disgust. He never saw the girl again. In fact as the result of that brief encounter he was, for a long time, something of a misogynist and studiously avoided having anything to do with women.

In spite of his petitions and lobbying, the affair of the mulberry nurseries had not advanced one iota. Living in Paris was expensive. Lieutenant Bonaparte was obliged to rejoin his regiment. However he again asked for leave and, having obtained it—in those days the army was strangely lenient—he turned his face toward Corsica. He arrived there on New Year's Day, 1788.

Never had the Bonaparte household been so poverty-stricken. Signora Letizia was doing all the work herself. She had written to Joseph asking him to bring her a servant-girl from Pisa, for she could not stand the strain any longer. "I should like a woman of a certain age, not too young," she wrote. "If she will not do the washing, I do not mind, but she must do all our cooking, she must know how to sew and how to iron and she must be obedient. That is what I should like, for ever since the trouble with my finger I have not been able to sew a stitch."

Napoleon again wrote out claims for the mulberry nursery and the salt marshes, but with no great success. He gathered material for his "History of Corsica," even outlining several portions of it in the rustic hideaway which he pompously called his "Milelli study." Poverty merely intensified his national patriotism. Though he was eating the bread of the King of France, he made no effort to hide his anti-French feelings. Invited to dine one day with the artillery officers at Bastia, he insulted them by his harangues on the "Corsican nation," even going so far as to accuse the Commandant, M. de Barrin, of delaying the assembly of the Estates.

"He does not know Corsicans," cried Napoleon. "He will find out what they can do."

One of the officers was annoyed.

"Would you draw your sword against the representative of the King?"

Bonaparte did not answer, and shortly afterward withdrew. The officers barely nodded to him.

In contrast to this anti-French sentiment, he boasted openly of his esteem for England, flaunting it before the public in a "Letter from Theodore to Walpole," a fragment found among his unpublished papers, and in his *Nouvelle Corse,* in which the hero speaks of the French as "tigers, monsters, thugs."

Napoleon spent another six months on the island before he was at last obliged to leave—he would either have to hand in his resignation or return to his regiment again. That regiment had left Valence and was now stationed at Auxonne, an ugly little town surrounded by swamps made by the river Saône. There Bonaparte rejoined his brother officers and his gunners. His quarters were in the barracks, on the second floor of one of the wings. It was not long before the damp climate began to tell on him and he came down with a fever that lingered for three or four days, left him for the same length of time, only to return again. Both officers and men suffered from the epidemic. Napoleon lost weight and grew very weak. It was some months before he fully recovered.

As soon as he was better he entered the artillery school, which was commanded by the Brigadier General du Theil. The general was struck by the young man's precocious talent, took a great fancy to him and ordered him to build a number of works at the proving grounds. In spite of Bonaparte's junior ranking, Du Theil made him a member of the research committee. The young officer spent his leisure walking about the town, alone or with Des Mazis and two other lieutenants, Villarceaux and Julien de Bidon. With these friends he was expansive, cordial, talkative. Sometimes, in the midst of an argument, his comrades would see him stop and begin drawing geometrical figures on the road with the point of his scabbard. In the evenings he would sometimes go to play lotto with Lombard, the mathematics professor, at Pillon d'Arquebouville's. Pillon was in charge of artillery. On those occasions Bonaparte would carry Mme. Lombard's work-bag for her.

He formed a firm friendship with Naudin, Commissioner of War, who had lived in Corsica for fifteen years, and with Captain Gassendi—a friendship which was later to make the fortunes of both men. His relations with the other lieutenants were friendly, even on a familiar footing. He went to all their gatherings and shared their pranks. It was Napoleon who drew up the bylaws of the "Forage Cap" of the La Fère regiment, statutes of a little society formed for the purpose of maintaining an esprit de corps among the younger officers and of preserving the traditions of courtesy and "fair play."

His brother officers played a few tricks on him, such as spiking his guns on the eve of a review. Fortunately Bonaparte noticed it in time, repaired the damage and had the laugh on them. On another occasion, however, he quarreled with Lieutenant de Bussy. The latter occupied the room above Napoleon, played the bugle incessantly and kept Napoleon from working. In the end Bonaparte lost his temper. Meeting De Bussy on the stairs one day he observed:

"You must find bugling very tiring, my dear fellow!"

"No, not at all," replied De Bussy.

"Well, it is certainly tiring to others."

"I am very sorry."

"It would be better if you went farther away where you could bugle to your heart's content."

"I can do as I please in my own room," retorted De Bussy stiffly.

The two young cocks looked each other up and down.

"One might give you a doubt or two on that point," replied Bonaparte.

"I do not think anyone would dare to—"

The quarrel would certainly have been settled on the dueling grounds had not the "Forage Cap" intervened as arbiter. Bonaparte was ordered to be more amenable and De Bussy was advised to practice his bugling only when he was certain not to disturb his neighbor.

On one occasion Bonaparte was placed under twenty-four hours' arrest—the reason is not known. In the room where he was interned, he found a dusty *Digeste* in an old cupboard, took down the pamphlet and read it through to the end. And such was his memory that years later in the Council of State when the discussion turned on articles of the Civil Code, he was able to cite with perfect accuracy entire passages of Justinian to the astonishment of all present. To such a mind everything is of profit.

It was his habit to retire early to his room and pore over his books. He was not satisfied to be merely a good artillery officer. He had a natural aptitude for politics: his main interest was in the government of men, with its maxims, its motives, its methods. History taught him the forms of societies. But he was not content to rest upon theory. He insisted upon the practical, the exact detail. Army, navy, diplomacy, finance, business, with facts, dates and figures—no matter what the material he always tried to inform himself on all the essentials. So he checked, annotated, made résumés in his notebooks of a vast number of works: Montesquieu, Rollin, Mably, Mirabeau, Marmontel, Buffon. He studied the history of the Arabs, of the Turks, of Prussia, England, Switzerland. He steeped himself in Abbé Raynal's eloquent rubbish. He spent long hours over Lacroix's "Geography," learning for the first time of the existence of "St. Helena, a small island in the Atlantic, an English colony." After he had written those words, perhaps in a moment of distraction, perhaps because he had been interrupted, he left the page blank. . . .

His interest in literature was equally keen. Ought he not to develop a style, to study philology if he would have a better command of words? He reread Corneille, Racine, Voltaire. Nor did he overlook novels. Restif's *Le Comte de Comminges,* and *Les Contemporaines,* amused him; he went mad over *Paul et Virginie* and the *Chaumière indienne.* His head was so crammed with books that he could not refrain from talking about them to his comrades—frequently to the point of boring them to death. In his enthusiasm his southern accent became more noticeable than ever. At times he lost his way in a maze of words, but more often than not his ideas were provocative, his language strong and marked by a touch of originality. Des Mazis used to tease him.

"See here now," he would say, "aren't you made like other men? What's the use of all this undigested learning? What difference does it make to me what happened a thousand years ago?"

Des Mazis was a handsome youth, madly in love with an Adélaide whom he expected to marry. Bonaparte upbraided him for his "weakness." He himself had nothing but scorn for such dalliance.

"Just a lot of big words that mean nothing, as usual!" cried Des Mazis. "What do I care for your State and its secrets? You are impossible today! You have never put up such a pitiful argument. . . ."

"Chevalier," shouted Bonaparte passionately, "do not limit that noble soul and that once proud heart to so narrow a sphere! You—to grovel at a woman's feet! Better to make the saucy minxes fall at yours!"

Des Mazis burst into a roar of laughter. Bonaparte shrugged his shoulders and stalked off to his room. Perhaps on that very day he made the following note on love: "I consider it detrimental to society, to the individual happiness of men—

in fact I am convinced that love does more harm than good and that it would be a kindness if some guardian angel would rid the world of it."

He was not to think so always.

He wrote copiously but so hastily, so badly, that often he could not decipher his own scrawls. Chiefly he wrote reports on ordnance, sending rough, kindly Du Theil a "Note on Bursting Bomb-Shells" that amazed the general by its clear logic and clever computations. But he soon returned to his own writings. Plagiarizing Filippini, he slaved over his book on Corsica which he intended to dedicate to Necker. He gave it to Father Dupuy, his former master at Brienne, to criticize—the latter advised him to soften the tone in speaking of France. For relaxation he dashed off a number of short stories: "The Count of Essex," "The Prophetic Mask," mediocre tales dry and bombastic, but with here and there a line that gleamed like pure gold.

"Work is my only refuge here," he wrote in July, 1789. "I do not dress from one week to the other and since my illness I sleep very little. It is incredible! I go to bed at ten o'clock and I get up at four. I eat only one meal a day."

His thoughts, first expressed by Rousseau and Raynal, but colored by his personality and nationality, were the thoughts of a conquered hero who refused to accept defeat, a hero who was biding his time, an enemy of tyrants, a republican. The following notation was found among his notebooks: "Outline for a memoir on the power of kings: Examine the circumstances of the usurped power which the kings of the twelve monarchies of Europe enjoy. Few would be found worthy to reign."

He came out boldly for an uprising of the masses against despots. True glory, he believed, was not won by conquests, but by love of country and good will toward men. He was roused to indignation against abuses, castes, privileges. He believed in natural kindness, in the supremacy of right. He declared himself against fanaticism. He had lost every shred of religious faith. Like his mother he still made and was always to make the sign of the cross in the Italian fashion, murmuring "Jesus!" when he heard something that grieved him or roused his indignation. But he had ceased to believe in a vague, diffused God. He was opposed to ritual in the name of logic and he cursed the power of priests over souls. "It is a fact," he wrote, "that Christianity, even a reformed Christianity, destroys the unity of the State." For him the State was all.

Such were Napoleon's thoughts when the first sparks of the Revolution began to sputter, that Revolution born in large part from the principles laid down by his beloved Rousseau. The moment he realized that the probable consequences would be the overthrow of a political organization which he considered outworn and the birth of a new order, how could that officer of twenty fail to hail it as the dawn of a new world? Along with an impassioned ideology, it brought him the promise of freedom for his native land and, for himself, a chance to play a rôle commensurate with his worth. "An equality which would raise me above the rest of men, was something I could not resist," he confessed.

And yet in April, 1789, when he was sent with his gunners to re-establish order at Seurre, where agitators had murdered two wheat merchants, and he came in contact for the first time with rioting, his deep sense of authority and discipline was aroused. He handled the situation firmly but without harshness and dispersed the mob by shouting:

"Let all decent citizens go back to their homes. I shall fire only on the rabble."

The streets emptied at once.

Rumor had it that for two months past he had been seen everywhere in that little Burgundian town with the wife of the cashier of the salt store, with a farmer's daughter at whose house he went to drink milk and, finally, with the lady of the house in which he lodged on the rue des Oies. This seems scarcely probable when one recalls his shyness toward women at that period. The stories were undoubtedly exaggerated.

On his return he found Auxonne greatly upset by events in

Paris. The Assembly of the States General, the opposition of the Third Estate to the Monarchy, the fall of the Bastille—all had stunned the people. On July 19th the populace rose in revolt, invaded and sacked the offices of Transport and Tolls. They were brought to order with difficulty and only at the point of the gun. However the La Fère regiment was already siding with the rebels. On August 16th, the regiment mutinied and compelled the Colonel to hand over the black bag. The gunners divided the money and, coming back from the taverns, insulted their officers.

Bonaparte was furious. In thought he was no longer in Auxonne, but in Corsica. What were they doing down there? Were his fellow-countrymen going to take advantage of that crisis? What a chance for his family, for him, to get ahead!

He wrote to Paoli, who was still his idol and who, thanks to the rebellion, was to return to the island in triumph. In his letter Napoleon showered fulsome praise on the old leader, hoping by this means to prevail upon him to make him his lieutenant.

"General, I was born as my country lay dying. Thirty thousand Frenchmen, spewed up on our shores, drowning the throne of Liberty in oceans of blood. Such the hateful spectacle that first met my eyes. . . . Slavery was the price of our submission: now, crushed beneath the triple weight of soldier, lawyer and preceptor our fellow-countrymen live despised. . . ."

Paoli did not reply. That silence disturbed Napoleon. The time soon came when he could stand it no longer. He had to go back to Corsica. In France the old order was giving way, everything was slipping its moorings. Napoleon seized his opportunity and asked for a leave. The moment it was granted he set off for Marseilles with a trunk full of books. At Valence he stopped to call on his friends. The abbé of Saint-Ruf, with whom he discussed the Revolution, said to him in jest:

"Monsieur de Bonaparte, at the rate things are going every man will have his turn at being king. When yours comes, try to get along with the Christian religion. You will never regret it."

Laughing, the young man answered that if ever he were to become king, he would not fail to make the Abbé a cardinal.

At Marseilles Napoleon called on Raynal, receiving praise and encouragement from him. His "History of Corsica" might well contribute to the liberation of his little country. Bursting with pride and dreams young Bonaparte set sail for Ajaccio.

III

Corsican or Frenchman?

THE MOMENT he arrived in Corsica Napoleon realized that nothing had changed. People had no idea what was going on in France, and events there had had no influence on the island government. But minds were in a ferment; men were arguing passionately. It did not take Napoleon long to grasp the rôle he had to play. The field was free. The age belonged to youth and daring. With the help of Fate—and he counted tremendously on Fate—why should he not carve out a proconsulate in Corsica for himself? To rule his land with the help of his clan! At that moment he could envisage no more desirable future. Wasting no time, he called on his friends, and stood around talking with them on the streets, followed everywhere by the ragtag and bobtail of Ajaccio. On his initiative the patriots adopted the tricolor cockade and founded a club.

His two brothers, Joseph and Lucien, aided him. Though Joseph considered himself the head of the family—and was always to do so—he bowed before the imperious sway of his younger brother. Joseph had been admitted to the bar, but had not yet pleaded a case. He had a good education and spoke Italian and French equally well. Lazy, good-natured, but cautious and stubborn, he was very vain and never doubted that Napoleon was working in the first place for him alone. His birthright, as well as his ability, he thought, entitled him to the cream of profits, the finest posts. If he embraced the popular cause it was less from inclination than from self-interest. His advice, it must be added, was always on the side of moderation.

Lucien, still a young boy, was all fire and flame. Home from the seminary where his quick wits had not prevented him from turning out poor work, he had an adventurous turn of mind and, perhaps even more than Napoleon, a flair for politics.

The capital of Corsica at that time was Bastia. That was where the struggle must be carried. Napoleon hastened thither and proceeded to turn things upside down. The rebellion was spreading step by step, like careless fires lighted in the stubble and fanned by a summer wind.

That was the moment when Paris finally turned its attention toward the distant island. At Mirabeau's suggestion the National Assembly had incorporated Corsica into the rest of the "French Empire." It now called home all the outlaws who had fought for her independence.

Towns and villages, ablaze with lights, acclaimed France and chanted Te Deums. Napoleon was carried away on that wave of popular enthusiasm. Only the day before he had been wholly Corsican: today he saw himself as a Frenchman. "France has taken us to her bosom," he cried. "From now on we have the same interests, the same anxieties. We are no longer separated by a sea." Whereupon he draped the Bonaparte house with a streamer bearing the words: "Hurrah for the Nation! Hurrah for Paoli! Hurrah for Mirabeau!"

He served as a simple private in the Ajaccio National Guard. He attended the innumerable secret meetings that preceded the legislative elections—he backed Joseph in them and though, according to the law, the latter was too young, he was made a voter. Delegates from all over Corsica gathered at Orezza. Paoli had been hailed by the National Assembly as a hero and had announced his return. Napoleon was eager to go to Orezza to attend the meetings and to welcome the hero. Pleading illness he asked for another furlough on full pay. His health, it was true, was wretched. He had had a relapse of fever while walking with his brothers in the salt marshes. But a nervous energy kept him going. On horseback he rode to Orezza with Joseph, pushed his brother into the limelight and urged him to make speeches.

Then at last Paoli came to Bastia. The sight of his tall figure, his manly face, his deep blue eyes, his white hair, roused the people to a long cry of love. The whole island went over to him in a body. He was granted plenary powers, both military and

DESIREE CLARY
QUEEN OF SWEDEN

LETIZIA BONAPARTE, MADAME MERE
From the Portrait by Gérard

civil. Napoleon had always admired Paoli extravagantly from afar, but he thought him old and tired, when, bearing greetings from Ajaccio, he met him on the very spot of the Corsican defeat at Ponte Nuovo. However the *Babbo* was his leader, his master. The children of Charles Buonaparte, Paoli's old and loyal friend, could do no less than range themselves at his side.

Paoli received him coldly. To the old hero, Napoleon was the son of a turncoat, a youth educated by France, who was now trying to hang on to his coattails—and he looked upon him with deep distrust. He considered him ruthless and dangerous. However, to keep him in check, he flattered him. "Oh, Napoleon!" Paoli is supposed to have said to the young man. "There is nothing modern about you. You are all Plutarch."

Back again in Ajaccio, Napoleon lingered on though his leave was up. At the Globe, the Ajaccio club, he read a rhetorical and scathing denunciation of Paoli's rival, the Corsican deputy, Buttafuoco. Lieutenant Bonaparte's pamphlet was applauded; the club voted to have it printed.

A few days later, after being twice delayed by winds along the coast, Napoleon set sail again for Auxonne, this time taking with him his young brother, Louis.

In spite of his long absence he was cordially welcomed by his regiment—with the exception perhaps of the Royalist officers who found fault with him for his Jacobin leanings. He lived with his brother in a scantily furnished bedroom and study in the Lombards' house, rue Vauban. The child Louis—he was only thirteen—slept in the study on a thin mattress. Between them they had only three francs a day for food and lodging. Napoleon refused all invitations and never set foot in a café any more. Locking his door on poverty, as he himself put it, he did the housework and cooked their meals, which often consisted only of a bowl of soup. Sometimes he would pretend that he was not hungry and would content himself with a crust of dry bread. He looked after his brother tenderly, giving him lessons and even teaching him the catechism for his first communion. At other times, his patience exhausted, he would box little Louis' ears. But he loved the boy and was pleased with his progress. He intended to make an officer of him like himself. In a letter to Joseph he wrote with charming pride:

"He will be excellent material. He is a hard worker, as much from inclination as from pride, and he is chock full of sentiment. . . . All the women of this town are in love with him. He has acquired a charming little French manner: he enters a drawing-room, bows gracefully and asks the customary questions with the seriousness and dignity of a man of thirty. There is no doubt about it, he will be the best of the four of us. It is true that none of us will have had such a fine education."

During the winter of 1791, Napoleon frequently went skating in the moats of the fortifications with a number of his brother officers. On one occasion, perceiving that it was near the dinner hour, Bonaparte began to unbuckle his skates. Two officers skated up to him.

"Come along," they urged. "Let's have one more round."

Bonaparte hesitated, then said:

"Sorry, but I really must go."

The two young men skated off. All of a sudden the ice cracked under them and they disappeared. That evening Bonaparte was shocked to learn of their deaths.

Meantime Joly, the printer at Dôle, had been setting type for his "Letter to Buttafuoco." Napoleon and Louis used to leave Auxonne at four o'clock in the morning, walk all the way to Dôle to correct the proofs and return to Auxonne later that same morning, having covered sixteen miles in all. As soon as the famous letter appeared in print, Bonaparte sent several copies to Paoli, at the same time begging the latter to furnish him with material for his book on Corsica. The *Babbo* answered by return post—a categorical refusal in which he warned young Bonaparte that "history is not written in the years of youth." He had no time, he said, to open his boxes and look up the documents. The young lieutenant from Auxonne was stunned. Was it possible that Paoli, his father's friend, the great patriot to whom both he and his brothers were devoted, could turn him down so coldly? He did not destroy the book that was so harmful to France, but hid it away in the bottom of his trunk. Through some strange bit of good luck, he was never to finish it.

Heated controversies brought him into conflict with several of his comrades who were partisans of the old régime. Two of them threatened to throw him into the river one day. They accused Napoleon of spreading new-fangled ideas among the noncommissioned officers and the men in the regiment. It is true that he did read the most advanced newspapers to his men, that he recommended an alliance between the army and the masses and that he went about agitating like a real demagogue. Nor did he hesitate to make his opinions public even when he went to Nuits to attend the marriage of his friend, Gassendi. Among the guests were a number of officers from his regiment. Gassendi was a Royalist, his father-in-law a patriot. Bonaparte defended the father-in-law's ideas passionately. For a moment politics overshadowed marriage. That same evening as a guest in the wealthiest house in town and completely surrounded by aristocrats, he again broke a lance in honor of the nation. For days the town buzzed with talk about that obscure little soldier who had set himself up as a champion of the people's rights.

Just at that time the War Department began to reorganize the artillery and, as the result of various promotions, Bonaparte was moved up to the rank of first lieutenant. To his great regret, however, he was obliged to quit the La Fère regiment for the Grenoble regiment which was stationed at Valence. He left behind him in Auxonne a number of real friends he was never to forget.

Taking his brother with him, Napoleon returned to Valence, where he settled again in his old room at Mlle. Bou's and ate his meals at the Three Pigeons. Left to the care of the landlady, Louis soon found a companion of his own age in the son of a notary, François Mesangère, who was to attach himself to the younger Bonaparte's fortunes and to profit by his rise in the world.

Many of Napoleon's former acquaintances had disap-peared. The abbé of Saint-Ruf was dead—he had not been able to wait for his cardinal's hat. Mlle. de Laurencin had married. But Mme. du Colombier and the amiable Caroline welcomed him joyfully at their country house. Napoleon quickly made friends with Sucy, the War Commissioner, and with Lieutenant de Montalivet.

Shortly after his arrival he allowed his name to be put up at the "Society of the Friends of the Constitution," a group affiliated with the Jacobins of Paris. The speech he made before that group caused a sensation. At Valence even more than at Auxonne the officers seemed to be divided in opinion—a number of them were to emigrate after the flight and arrest of the King at Varennes, to avoid swearing allegiance to the National Assembly that had taken the sovereign's place. Bonaparte was one of the first to take the oath. He went about disapproving in loud tones of emigration and demanding the trial of the King. As a result his soldiers looked on him with favor—the population was 100 per cent revolutionary. "This country," Napoleon wrote to his friend, Naudin [Commissioner of War], "is full of fire and enthusiasm." He confessed that he fell asleep "with my mind filled with great public matters," and, apologizing for the scrap of paper, he added: "The southern blood that flows in my veins is coursing with the swiftness of the Rhône."

He would like to have been in Paris in those critical hours, attending the meetings of the Jacobins. In a letter to his uncle, Archdeacon Lucien, in which he asked for money, he struck a curious note:

Send me three hundred francs. That ought to be enough to take me to Paris. There, at least, a man has a chance to get ahead, to overcome obstacles. Everyone tells me I would be a success there. Would you hold me back for the lack of a hundred *écus?* . . .

The miser evaded the request. Bonaparte, at Valence, champed at the bit. Seated before his little table in the embrasure of the window, he could be seen constantly bending over his books or covering vast quantities of paper with scribblings from his quill pen. At Auxonne he had hit upon the idea of presenting a memoir in the competition opened by the

Academy of Lyons on the subject of "What Truths and Emotions is it Important to Inculcate in Men for their Welfare?" He now set to work on it. Departing for the first time from Rousseau's principles, he declared that man was made to live in society and that, endowed from the beginning of the world with intelligence and emotions he had always known love, pity, friendship, gratitude, respect. Man could attain happiness only through courage. "There is neither virtue nor happiness apart from strength and energy." With freedom, man must have equality before the law. He must also have a certain amount of property. But let him take care to avoid ambition. Ambition had led Alexander, Cromwell and Louis XIV astray and had caused rivers of blood to flow. Was Bonaparte hypocritical when he expressed those opinions? No. He was not speaking for himself: he was thinking only of the masses from whom, even then, he considered himself set apart. . . .

That memoir was the first important work of the instinctive author that Bonaparte was. In it one finds a vagueness, a certain grandiloquent nonsense, but also precocious wisdom and sparkling beauty. Those forty pages offer passages of striking originality on the subject of the human heart and on the spectacles of nature. They are replete with the spirit of that young lieutenant —virile, enthusiastic, argumentative, but with an underlying sensitiveness that no one suspected in him. Bonaparte was satisfied. He hoped to carry off the prize—twelve hundred francs, which would be a great help to him. But his memoir was rejected. The great minds of Lyons found it "mediocre, disconnected, poorly written." All very true—but it dripped genius like honey from a comb.

Genius! Bonaparte had uttered the word all unaware that it would one day be applied to himself. And referring to the lot of a leader, he wrote prophetically: "Poor fellow! I pity him. He will be the admiration and envy of his fellow-men—and the most miserable of them all. The equilibrium is disturbed. He will lead an unhappy life. . . . Men of genius are meteors destined to blaze that they may light up their eras."

A sudden flash of prescience! In those few lines Napoleon traced the orbit of his life.

The Constituent Assembly was about to disperse. Elections to the Legislative Assembly were in order. Napoleon wanted to return to Corsica to support Joseph's candidacy and to make sure that he himself was given a high rank in the organizations of volunteers. He was granted a three months' furlough, thanks to General du Theil, who was still his friend in spite of his radical views. "That lad has great possibilities," the old soldier said of him. "We shall hear from him one of these days."

The moment he arrived Napoleon hurried off to Corte, where elections were in progress. There the Bonapartes ran afoul of Paoli's animosity: the old leader managed to have every one of his own candidates elected. Joseph was eliminated from the delegation. The two brothers returned to Ajaccio in time to be present at the deathbed of Archdeacon Lucien.

Pious though he was, the old man had insisted upon dying unattended by a priest. "Letizia," he said to his family, "I die happy in the knowledge that you are surrounded by your children. Joseph can manage your business affairs. You, Napoleon, will be a great man (*tu, poi, Napoleone, sarai un omone . . .*)."

The little fortune he had struggled so fiercely to increase made the Bonapartes fairly comfortable. They bought national property. With Joseph off to Corte again, Napoleon took over the leadership of the clan, no one in the family daring to offer any opposition. "We never argued with him," Lucien was to relate. "The slightest criticism annoyed him and the faintest opposition threw him into a rage." The money was useful in other ways too. By dint of intrigue and even of force, Napoleon succeeded in getting himself appointed lieutenant colonel in the National Guard in which so far he had been only adjutant. Great was the rejoicing that day among the Bonapartes, and the house re-echoed to music and song.

Intoxicated by that success, Napoleon then made a bad blunder. He tried to seize and occupy the citadel of Ajaccio with his battalion of volunteers. But the garrison held out, the popu-

lation turned against him. Shots were fired, blood flowed. Paoli
sent commissioners who imposed a truce. Condemned by the
majority of his fellow-citizens, disavowed by Paoli, Napoleon
made up his mind to return to France. There his conduct had
already been reported and he was in danger of being removed
from the army or perhaps even worse. Present, he might have a
better chance to weather the storm. And he returned to Paris
as swiftly as possible.

"I arrived here yesterday," he wrote to Joseph on May 29,
1792. "For the time being, I have taken a room at the hotel
where Pozzo di Borgo, Leonetti and Peraldi are living—the
Hôtel des Patriotes hollandais, on the rue Royale. It is too expensive, however, and I shall move tomorrow or the day
after. . . .

"Paris is in the greatest state of upheaval. It is swamped with
foreigners, and malcontents are extremely numerous. For three
nights now the city has been lighted all night long. The National Guard, which has remained at the Tuileries to guard the
King, has been doubled. . . .

"Keep on the good side of General Paoli. He can do everything and he is everything."

He redoubled his efforts at the War Offices to have the Ajaccio
affair quashed and also to obtain his reinstatement in the artillery—because of his prolonged absence he had been struck off
the lists. He called on his sister Marianne at Saint-Cyr, dined at
the Permons', and renewed his friendship with Bourrienne, his
former comrade from Brienne, with whom he moved into lodgings in the modest Hôtel de Metz, rue du Mail. Both young
men were very poor, both dreamt of fantastic speculations on
Exchange that would replenish their lean purses. They talked
about renting houses under construction and subletting them.
But the owners demanded guarantees and they could not
furnish them. They also had some idea of going into business
with Fauvelet, Bourrienne's brother, who had become the head
of a "National Auction," a kind of pawnshop with a salesroom
attached.

All these plans came to nothing. But what of that? Bonaparte
had more than enough to keep him busy with political events.
The Revolution was gathering momentum and getting out of
hand. War had been declared against Austria: the Girondin
ministry had been overthrown, the Legislative Assembly was
tottering. Each morning it seemed as if it would be overthrown
by riots. "This country is being riddled in every sense by the
most rabid parties," he wrote to his eldest brother. "It is difficult to get the thread of so many different plans. I don't know
how it will all come out, but it looks very much like revolution."
There spoke his love of order. Moreover his recent experience
in Ajaccio had disgusted him with the masses. The morning of
June 20th, which paved the way for the downfall of royalty,
served only to confirm him in his horror of that mud that was
spurting from the gutters. He was with Bourrienne at an eat-
ing-house on the rue Saint-Honoré when they saw a mob of five
or six thousand men, in rags and tatters, rush out from the direction of the Halles shouting insults and obscenities and march
on the Tuileries.

"Let's follow them," suggested Bonaparte.

They went out on the pavement along the river and from
there caught a glimpse of Louis XVI as he appeared at a palace
window with a red cap of the revolutionaries on his head. Bonaparte flew into a rage.

"*Che coglione!* What a fool!" he growled. "How could they
have let that scum get in there? They ought to have turned the
guns on four or five hundred of them and cleaned them out.
The rest would still be running."

He despised the King's weakness and considered him lost.
But, soldier that he was, if he had been given a chance for
action, he would have stood by the government. On June 22nd
he wrote: "On the one side we have M. de La Fayette, most of
the officers in the army, *all decent people,* the ministers and the
department of Paris: on the other, the majority of the Assembly,
the Jacobins and the rabble. . . . The Jacobins are fools without
any sense. . . ."

A few days later, on July 3rd, in a brief moment of weariness he dashed off the following lines to Lucien or to Joseph:

"The men at the head are a poor lot. One must admit that, seen at close quarters, they are hardly worth the trouble one has to take to win their favor. . . . The French are an aged people, without ties. Every man looks to his own interest and is determined to have it by dint of slanders and holy horrors. . . . All that sort of thing kills ambition."

In that noisy, rioting Paris, Napoleon came and went, listened to everyone, looked at everything. To be sure, he tried to elbow his way to the front, but in spirit he was still in Ajaccio. His thoughts, his real interest, were for Corsica alone. He advised Joseph to make ready to defend their house. He was afraid of blunders on the part of Fesch, who had got himself appointed vicar-general to the conforming bishop of Ajaccio, and of young Lucien's wild pranks. At seventeen the latter considered himself a leader of the opposition and dreamt of nothing but kidnappings and wholesale murders. The boy was already manifesting open opposition to his elder brother's views. With curious impudence he wrote to Joseph: "I have always detected in Napoleon an ambition that, while not altogether egotistical, is nevertheless greater than his love for the commonweal. I honestly believe that in a free State he would be a dangerous man. . . . He strikes me as having every tendency to being a dictator."

Meantime Napoleon had been reinstated in his branch of the service and, in addition, had been promoted to a captaincy. Increasing emigration had created a need for officers, and the army could not afford to be too exacting. The Ajaccio affair was squelched. It was never to be reopened again.

When Paris learned of the Duke of Brunswick's manifesto, popular excitement rose in intensity. On August 10th [1792], Bonaparte saw the old monarchy fall.

From his vantage post at Fauvelet's on the Carrousel, he witnessed the heroic defense of the Swiss Guards. After the King had gone to the Assembly and the palace had been given over to the mob, he ventured into the gardens.

Never in later years, were any of his battlefields to efface the memory of those garden paths heaped with the bodies of the dead and dying. He was just in time to prevent a man from Marseilles from killing a Swiss.

"Man of the South!" he cried. "Let us save this poor fellow!"

"Are you from the South?" asked the murderer.

"Yes."

"All right, then we'll let him go. . . ."

After that saturnalia of anarchy he felt the need of recovering the remnants of military discipline. Better for him to fight on the frontier, side by side with his comrades, and to trust to the chances of war to further his own advancement than to go back to intriguing on the island where his enemies were in the saddle and where he could look forward only to street fighting or guerrilla warfare. However he did not return to the army. Family matters prevented him or at least served as a pretext. The school at Saint-Cyr, where Marianne was being educated, was about to be closed, the pupils being put out on the street with only ten sous a mile to get them back to their homes. Marianne was now calling herself Elisa, a name then much in vogue. She was a tall, slender girl of fifteen, a typical French girl, with aristocratic manners. Napoleon could not think of letting her take that dangerous journey alone, nor could he keep her in Paris in those September days when throats were being cut at the Abbaye, at the Carmelites, at La Force, at the Châtelet, at Bicêtre, and where all the rivers were red with blood. Instead he set out with her for Corsica on that long journey he knew so well, stopping for a few hours in Valence, where Mlle. Bou and Mme. Mesangère met them and brought them a basket of grapes. At Marseilles, no boat! They were obliged to wait almost three weeks. When at last they arrived in Ajaccio, they were faced with a keen disappointment. Joseph, who had been intriguing for a seat in the Convention, had failed miserably and had been able to pick up only a modest job as judge of the court.

That failure on Joseph's part was the result of Paoli's enmity. Napoleon left for Corte to have it out with the old leader. The

interview was stormy. Paoli was surprised to see him back again.
What was he, after all—a captain in the fourth artillery, or a
lieutenant colonel in the Corsican volunteers? He could not
hold both posts. He must make up his mind and take his choice.
Bonaparte lost his temper, even going so far as to threaten Paoli.
When he returned to Ajaccio and informed his family, Joseph
intervened and for a time passions were assuaged. The Corsicans were preparing an expedition against Sardinia. Napoleon
was to go at the head of his volunteers. He joined his family in
welcoming Admiral Truguet, leader of the division that was to
share in the attack, and Sémonville whom the Republic had sent
as ambassador to the Sultan and who was to act as adviser to
Truguet. Never, even in the days of Charles, had the Casa Bonaparte known such a brilliant assembly. There was dancing almost every evening. Elisa flirted with the Admiral; Paulette
with his officers. Louis and little Jerome ran up and down the
shore with young Montholon, Sémonville's son-in-law.

However, the Sardinian venture was to fail, through the in-
competence of the leader, Colonna Cesari, and the insubordination of the sailors on the *Fauvette*. In vain did Bonaparte, who
commanded the artillery, turn his guns on Maddalena. The
order to re-embark was given. The guns were lost and they all
but had to leave an entire company of grenadiers behind.

Paoli had lent but half-hearted support to this hazardous expedition. When a commission sent by the Convention and
headed by his rival, Saliceti, arrived to organize the defense of
Corsica against the English fleet, they found him hostile to
them, already almost a rebel. Had Paoli's long sojourn in England won him over to the English? There is no proof. But he
had joined the Revolution solely in the hope of gaining independence for Corsica and he found it more tyrannical than the
monarchy. Moreover, he was thinking of retiring from public
life. That was the moment when Lucien Bonaparte, who had
followed Sémonville back to France as his secretary, foolishly
touched the match to the powder-keg. Before the club of
Toulon, he accused the old leader, denouncing him as a tyrant
and a traitor. The club sent a petition to the Convention and

the latter, acting too hastily on Cambon's proposal, ordered Paoli's arrest.

Step by step the island rose in rebellion. The peasants rushed to arms to defend the *Babbo*. The Bonapartes were horrified at Lucien's madness. "I have dealt our enemies a death blow. . . ." the braggart wrote to his brothers. "You did not think me capable of that!" Measuring Paoli's power, the Bonapartes saw themselves stripped of their possessions, driven from Corsica, ruined. "If Uncle Lucien were alive," said Napoleon, "his heart would bleed at the thought that his sheep, his goats, his cattle were in danger and he would be clever enough to find a way to calm the storm." He himself tried to appease the Paolists by having the Ajaccio club vote a declaration in favor of their idol. At the same time, to make sure of a refuge for himself, he tried again to take the citadel of Ajaccio, using both trickery and force. The town, as well as the country, was against him. On his way to Bastia to confer with Saliceti, he was surrounded by a company of Paolists. He managed to escape by night—though with the greatest difficulty and thanks to the loyalty of his shepherds at Bocognano.

Hiding for a while in a grotto, Bonaparte finally took refuge in the house of his cousin, Levie, a former mayor of Ajaccio. The order for his arrest had gone out. Gendarmes arrived at the house. Levie misled them and sent them off. That very evening Napoleon escaped in a boat, rounded the coast and, after warning his mother: "Make ready to leave! This country is not for us!" he mounted a horse and galloped to Bastia. At first Madame Letizia demurred. Given a choice she would rather have stood a siege in her own house, gun in hand. But a relative, Costa di Bastelica, persuaded her to flee, and she set out for Milelli accompanied by Fesch and her children. The very next day her house in Ajaccio was robbed and burned. The Consulta of Corte outlawed Saliceti and declared the Bonapartes in disgrace and banished in perpetuity.

At Milelli, defended by her shepherds, the courageous woman stood her ground for several days. But little by little the mountaineers drew closer about her. Again as in the days of the

War for Independence, she was obliged to flee at night through jungles and over rocks to reach the coast. At last she came to the Tower of Capitello, where, stoical, with never a tear for her misfortune, never a reproach for Lucien, she waited for the help Napoleon had promised to send.

From then on Napoleon thought only of revenge. No more mincing of words with Paoli now. He persuaded Saliceti and his two colleagues that he must first take Ajaccio. With the three deputies and Joseph, he embarked four hundred infantrymen and some twenty gunners on a frail corvette, a few lighters. Then going aboard a *chebek* Bonaparte sailed at the head of the flotilla. First, however, he put in at Capitello where he picked up his family and sent them in the *chebek* to Calvi to the home of their old friends, the Giubegas.

For the third time Napoleon tried to take Ajaccio by surprise—for the third time he failed. Disembarking on the beach at Orbitello, his troops fired a few rounds without any result. The patriots of Ajaccio should have risen to defend their city—they did not budge.

Napoleon returned to Calvi and rejoined his family in the Giubega house. His sisters, Elisa and Paulette, looked after the housekeeping and took turns in the kitchen preparing the "sweet course" for dinner. Joseph was paying court to pretty Annette Giubega, but her family thought him too poor to be her husband. As the Paolists were drawing near Calvi, the Bonapartes dared not prolong their stay. Moreover Corsica was to all appearances lost to them. There was nothing left but France. They were already French in feeling. Fate now flung them into her arms. On June 11, 1793, feeling sad at heart, they all set sail for Toulon.

From the deck of that storm-tossed ship carrying him toward the coast of Provence, Napoleon gazed back for hours at a time at the white peaks of that island which gradually merged with the sky. He had dearly loved that little country he had tried to free and from which, today, he had been banished. His thoughts were always to dwell on Corsica with a special tenderness. But he had made his choice: there was no going back. For a long time he had been fervently, passionately, whole-heartedly Corsican. Now self-interest, anger and a tremendous, bewildered admiration that formed the basis of so many new hopes and dreams, combined to make him feel French—he wanted to be French only, from now on. The civil wars and clan feuds in which he had been embroiled helped him to a better understanding of the grandeur of a country that proudly proclaimed its freedom to the world and which, in its weakness and in spite of the disorder resulting from the collapse of its military effectives, was defying a Europe in arms, with the certainty of winning.

Napoleon was never to see Paoli again. In the years that followed, the *Babbo* went over to the English, was compelled by them to leave the island and was to end his turbulent life in London. But, in 1799, he was to applaud Bonaparte as the destroyer of the Republic of Genoa, the age-old enemy. "It was a Corsican who dealt the death blow," he was to cry. And later, dazzled by the apotheosis of that young follower whom he had treated as a callow youth, *un ragazzo inesperto,* the old man was to pay him a touching compliment: "We have won our liberty through one of our fellow-countrymen who has avenged all the insults to our land with so much honor and glory. No longer is the name of Corsica held in scorn and we shall see other sons of ours appearing on the European stage, for they will have the ambition, the talents and the shining example of Bonaparte before them."

At that time Napoleon and his brothers were to speak of Paoli only with respect. The First Consul would have liked to summon him to his side. "It would have been a real triumph for me," he said. Though circumstances and his own ambition had placed him in the opposite party, he could not forget that Paoli had been the hero of his youth and that, in those troubled years when his genius was biding its time, trying to find itself, he could have conceived no greater honor than to be like him.

IV

Désirée Clary

HOMELESS, PENNILESS, without a country, Madame Letizia took shelter with Louis, Jerome and her three daughters in a little house at La Valette, a village at the gates of Toulon. Her only means of livelihood was the meagre charity granted to Corsican refugees and she lived in great poverty, Elisa and Paulette even going to the village fountain to wash their linen. After a month of this dreary existence the Bonapartes moved on to Marseilles, staying at first with friends, the Clarys. Soon thereafter they were assigned to quarters in the house of an émigré and from that moment their situation began to improve. Joseph set off for Paris, where he haunted the lobbies of the Convention. Thanks to his clubs, Lucien obtained a place as clerk of stores at Saint-Maximin at a salary of twelve hundred francs.

Napoleon had returned to his regiment at Nice. The brother of his former chief, Jean du Theil, was his commanding officer. Du Theil had noticed young Bonaparte at Auxonne and recognized his ability. He accordingly made him his adjutant, ordered him to have the coastal batteries prepared for defense and then sent him to Avignon to buy powder. Bonaparte found the whole region under arms. The Federalists of Marseilles had taken over the city of the Popes, and Carteaux was attacking with the troops that were still loyal to the Convention. Napoleon witnessed the fall of Avignon, but took no part in it, an attack of fever obliging him to keep to his bed for several days. To pass the time—inaction was torture to him—he wrote out a sixteen-page description of the latest events, in dialogue form in which he denounced the people of Marseilles, praised Carteaux's soldiers, and burned incense before the *Montagne*. His pamphlet—for that was all it was—was published by Sabin

Tournal, the printer of the *Courrier d'Avignon,* under the title of *Souper de Beaucaire.* It is one of his most meticulous essays, emphatic in style and showing clear evidence both of his precocious military judgment and his desire to count in the camp of the victors. Though the pamphlet made not the slightest impression on the public, Bonaparte sent it to the Convention, to the members on service in the South and, finally, to Carteaux.

That insignificant general was a former portrait painter who had been transformed in three years through the mere chance of Revolutionary days into a commanding officer in the army. He had been ordered to recapture Toulon, which because of its hatred for the Convention had gone over to the English. Dommartin, who commanded the artillery, had been wounded in a recent engagement. Saliceti and Gasparin, the two deputies whom the Assembly had sent to keep an eye on Carteaux, happened to be in Marseilles at that moment. Joseph had come with them—they had made him Commissioner of War, a lucrative position. Undoubtedly Joseph sized up the situation, saw the opportunity and sent word to Napoleon to join him at once. Saliceti knew Napoleon well and, at his instance, the two deputies invited young Bonaparte to replace Dommartin. He accepted the offer, though apparently without any realization that that historic moment was to mark the beginning of his meteoric career. On a clear, sunshiny morning in September, Napoleon appeared before the gates of Toulon.

From the first, Napoleon realized that, to take the town, he would have to destroy L'Eguillette, a fort commanding the harbor. Saliceti agreed with him and, to lend more weight to Napoleon's decisions, appointed him major in charge of a battalion. In spite of that, Carteaux hesitated to follow his advice. As a result Carteaux was forced to resign his command, Saliceti and Gasparin replacing him with Dugommier.

Dugommier was an old soldier of imposing appearance, a Republican but a stern disciplinarian, and he had full confidence in Bonaparte. Together they were to carry out Napoleon's plan. The English General O'Hara was taken prisoner.

Fort Mulgrave fell. In that engagement Bonaparte showed extraordinary bravery. Though wounded by a bayonet-thrust in the thigh, he snatched the sponge from the hands of a dying artilleryman and insisted upon firing the cannon himself. As a result he contracted the itch from which he was not to recover for years. Fort L'Eguillette was evacuated. On December 18th [1793], the English abandoned Toulon under full sail.

For Bonaparte that day marked the beginning of glory. He had put his whole soul into that siege and, thanks to him, Toulon had fallen. In agreement with Barras, who had been present during the action, Saliceti and Robespierre the younger promoted Bonaparte to the rank of brigadier general, a promotion confirmed shortly afterward in Paris.

In those three months of siege Bonaparte had made the acquaintance of several officers whose names were to be linked with his through life—Desaix, Marescot, Leclerc, Suchet. They were more than acquaintances: they were friends such as he had never known before. Those men were not only associated with the dreams of his youth, they had also been with him under fire. Nothing binds men so closely as to face death together. At Toulon Bonaparte discovered Marmont, Muiron and Junot. He liked them and thought highly of them. They adored the ground he walked on and for a long time were to live only to serve him. Promoted to a captaincy, Marmont refused to leave Bonaparte. Sergeant Junot used to take down Bonaparte's orders in his beautiful handwriting on the breastwork of a battery. A cannon-ball bursting near him, spattered his paper with mud.

"Good!" he laughed, "I won't need any sand to blot it with."

For that gallant jest, Napoleon was to heap honors upon him. No matter what Junot did, Bonaparte was always to forgive that magnificent youth, so irresponsible, but so warm hearted.

He appointed Muiron, a brave man with a fine face, his chief of staff and not even death could put an end to their friendship. When Muiron gave his life at the bridge of Arcole to save his General, his memory was to live on in Napoleon's heart. And toward the end of Napoleon's life, when he considered changing his name to ward off misfortune, Muiron's was the name he offered to assume.

He returned to Marseilles to see his family. After so much suffering and anxiety, Madame Letizia could at last draw a breath of relief. Napoleon maintained the little household on his pay and rations. Decorated with the surname Brutus, Lucien was less constant in his attendance at the Saint-Maximin storehouse, (now known as Marathon), than at public meetings. At nineteen, as president of the revolutionary committee, that tall, gawky, near-sighted rogue ordered the citizens of Marathon imprisoned as suspects. Many years later he was to confess that "people whom I would blush to have anything to do with now—convicts, thieves—had become my boon companions." On the coast he was known as the little Robespierre. There he lodged with an innkeeper named André Boyer and was on the best of terms with the latter's sister, Christine. In May, 1794, he was to marry the girl—to the great dismay of his family, who promptly severed relations with him.

Napoleon appointed Louis on his staff with the rank of second lieutenant. In the spring, while engaged in arming the coastal batteries, he moved his mother and sisters to the Château Sallé, near Antibes. The "château" was only a little cottage, where the Bonapartes kept house in the rustic style to which they had been accustomed in Corsica. Elisa read novels and played the fine lady, while Paulette raced about the fields, and stole artichokes and figs. Armed with a hop-pole, their neighbor, the terrible M. Bastide, would frequently give chase. Paulette would laugh in his face, scale fences and climb up to the attic under the pink tiles to hide away in the great mounds of hay.

Joseph had stayed at Toulon with Saliceti and Chief Commissioner Chauvet, his new patron, with whom he had become great friends. After the failure of a brief engagement against the English fleet, he returned to Marseilles where he had recently announced his engagement to Julie Clary, eldest of the Clary sisters. The Clary family had made a fortune in silk and

soap. In the days when the Bonapartes were poor, the Clarys had
been of great help to them. Later when M. Clary died, his sons-
in-law emigrated, and his sons, denounced before the Revolutionary Tribunal, were awaiting confiscation of their property
—perhaps even death on the guillotine—Joseph Bonaparte went
to their aid and rescued them. Using his influence with Saliceti
and Robespierre the younger, he managed to have Etienne
Clary freed; he stood sponsor for the family before the Jacobin
authorities. Julie's tender heart was touched by those services as
well as by Joseph's handsome face. Tall, well-built, with regular
and attractive features, Joseph Bonaparte had the manners of a
gentleman. He came of a good and ancient family and called
himself by the title of "Count." How could any young girl help
falling in love with that handsome youth who seemed to have
a great future before him? Julie was short, homely and awkward
in her movements, but she was kind and clever, with a disposition both headstrong and docile. Joseph was not in love with
her, but he was eager to settle down—and the Clary fortune
tempted him. His mother and sisters all urged the match. In
August, 1794, a few days after the 9th of Thermidor, he allowed himself to be married.

The collapse of the Incorruptible was to interrupt Napoleon's climb to power for a brief moment. He had been ordered
by Ricord and Robespierre the younger to hasten secretly to
Genoa, there to estimate the forces of the country before launch-
ing a new campaign. He returned from that mission to be arrested and imprisoned in the Fort Carré at Antibes. His papers
were seized.

The truth of the matter was that Saliceti had suddenly turned
against him and, with his colleagues Albitte and Laporte, had
signed the order for his arrest. Was it a Corsican's grudge against
one of his followers who was gaining too much power? More
likely Saliceti was merely thinking of his own skin, tacking and
veering in the gale that had been unleashed against anyone,
near or far, in any way connected with the Robespierre faction.
Sitting in his cell from where he could look out at the sea, Na-

poleon managed to keep a level head. He wrote to the Convention justifying himself. Junot offered to arrange an escape. Napoleon replied: "Men may be unjust toward me, but it is enough to know that I am innocent. . . . Do not make any move, therefore. You would only compromise me."

Ten days later, his fear or his bitterness forgotten, Saliceti ordered Napoleon's release—though he did not take him back in his employ. Napoleon was kept busy drawing up the plan of operations that were soon to be started against the Austro-Sardinians. After that he was sent to Piedmont to follow the staff of the Army of Italy—as an impatient observer. A few days later the enemy was defeated and withdrew. Cairo was taken.

In Cairo Bonaparte met a woman who was indirectly to influence his career. Turreau, a member of the Convention, had returned to the army to join Saliceti and had brought with him his young wife, Félicité, the daughter of a Versailles surgeon. Citizeness Turreau was a pretty, vivacious little woman with "fair hair, wit, patriotism and philosophy." Bonaparte found her delightful, and the young officer, thin, pale, and badly dressed as he was, seems not to have been displeasing to the lady—a fact she promptly set herself to prove to him. Theirs was a brief love story, the fleeting love of revolution and war. But the frivolous young wife knew how to throw sand in her husband's eyes and, as a result, Turreau was always to keep a pleasant memory of the "little general" and was to come to his aid in a crucial moment.

For five months Bonaparte was busy making ready the expedition that was to recapture Corsica from the English. His mother and sisters had returned to the Château Sallé and he often went there to see them. Joseph's wife had joined them, and there, too, Citizeness Turreau sometimes appeared—when she knew she would see Bonaparte or some of the young officers on his staff. Those were happy days and evenings in that glorious Provençal spring. Grave and dignified, Madame Letizia presided over many a gay dinner table. Hard times seemed very far away.

All the same, those hard times were to come back again. On March 3rd, accompanied by Louis, whom Turreau had made a lieutenant, Junot (now a captain), and his aides-de-camp, Muiron and Marmont, Bonaparte embarked on the brig *Amitié*. They were never to reach Corsica. Admiral Martin was stopped by the English squadron. Courageous but wholly lacking in discipline, his crew maneuvered badly. The *Ça Ira* and the *Censeur* were captured. The French fleet fled to the Juan Gulf. Bonaparte was again without a command. However, despite the fact that Scherer's report blamed his "overweening ambition," Bonaparte was assigned to the Army of the West under Hoche and put in command of artillery. He set out for Paris, taking with him Louis, Junot and Marmont.

In Marseilles at the Clarys he again saw young Désirée, Madame Joseph Bonaparte's sister. In spite of her sixteen years Désirée Clary still looked like a little girl, with her narrow chest, her slender hands and feet. She had dark hair and soft black eyes, set off by a pretty skin, a deliciously upturned nose and a rosebud mouth in a smiling countenance. As the young general entered her mother's drawing-room on the rue des Phocéens, Désirée raised her soft black eyes to his in a long, deep gaze. He noticed her emotion, was deeply touched and made no effort to hide it. Napoleon envied his brother's good marriage and would have liked to follow his example. His own fleeting affairs had convinced him that he could find complete happiness only in marriage. Fundamental in him was the Corsican's love of home and family. Why should he not marry Désirée? He stopped teasing her and treating her like a schoolgirl and began to talk to her, doubtless more of himself, his plans, his dreams, than of her. The young girl's pale cheeks flushed. She smiled at him. She had admired and loved him the very first time she saw him. Though she would not admit her love, neither could she conceal it. He begged for an answer (his time was short) and, encouraged by Joseph and Julie, the young couple became engaged. The campaign in the West was about to begin. It would therefore be impossible for Napoleon to marry at once, but Désirée promised to wait for him—they would write to one another. In the autumn they would certainly meet again. . . . When Bonaparte left Marseilles his little fiancée slipped into his hand a medallion of hair, which he carried in the inside pocket of his tunic next to his heart.

The journey to Paris was by no means dull. With his brother and his friends the young general loitered along the way, stopping in Châtillon at the house of Marmont's father, looking about the neighborhood for land that Joseph might purchase with his wife's money. In that charming little provincial society Napoleon forgot war and politics for a few days to chat with the ladies, dance and play lotto.

In Paris the four young men took an apartment together in the Hôtel de la Liberté, rue des Fossés Montmartre, for seventy-two francs a month. They were obliged to be economical. The Prairial coup d'état had driven their friends from power. Albitte, Saliceti and Ricord had been arrested. Bonaparte himself was under suspicion as a follower of Robespierre, and was received with scant courtesy by Aubry, the old captain of artillery. Aubry was a member of the Committee of Public Safety and in charge of the War Department—therefore all-powerful. He had never seen action and had got himself appointed general at the stroke of a pen. No wonder, therefore, that he considered young Bonaparte's advancement scandalous and, removing him from his own branch of the service, assigned him to the infantry.

"You are too young," he declared. "You must give the old fellows a chance."

"A man ages quickly on the battlefields," retorted Bonaparte. "And I have just come from one."

His reply displeased the general. Bonaparte protested in vain against the persecutions of an idiot who was still further debased by political passions. Should he hand in his resignation? But Aubry might not be in power more than a few weeks. The government was constantly shifting. The best thing for him would be to mark time. To avoid rejoining, he pretended illness and asked for an extension of time. By that means he could stay on in Paris at the heart of events. Had he left he would have been obliged to fight the Chouans, who were Frenchmen after all. "I am ill," he wrote to Joseph, "and as a result am obliged to take a two or three months' furlough. When I am quite well again I shall see what I can do." As a matter of fact he was really suffering from a nervous breakdown brought on by his disappointment, his fears for the future. Penniless, he tramped the streets, wandered from office to office seeking protectors not only for himself but also for his brothers. Barras remembered the good work he had done at Toulon and helped to get his furlough extended. He renewed his friendship with Fréron [a member of the Convention], who had paid court, and a very passionate one, to Paulette at Marseilles. At times he was disgusted at having to seek help and would wait outside of some rich man's house, while Junot went inside to make the request for him. Marmont had gone off to the Army of the Rhine taking with him Louis, who had managed to get a place in the artillery school at Châlons. Napoleon was entirely alone save for Junot—much against the wishes of the latter's family, for that matter.

"Who is this general?" asked Junot's father when his son gave up his career to follow Bonaparte. "Where has he served? No one knows anything about him!"

However, that father gave Junot a small allowance which the latter, good fellow that he was, often shared with his leader. The poverty-stricken general and his poverty-stricken aide used to wait impatiently for the allowance from Montbard. If they were too hungry, they would dine at Bourrienne's (he had married), or at the Permons' in the Hôtel de la Tranquillité, rue des Filles-Saint-Thomas.

Bonaparte would suddenly appear at Mme. Permon's house accompanied by Junot.

"Mme. Permon," he would say. "Our ships did not come in. I am bringing you a dinner guest."

Lively, bustling Mme. Permon was always surrounded by Corsicans—Arrighi, Arena, Moltedo, Chiappe among others. She took them all in, offered them pot luck and even sheltered the outlaw, Saliceti, for a few days. At that time Bonaparte was again quarreling with Saliceti. Though he guessed his hiding-place, he did not betray him.

From her window, little Laure Permon, a sly, homely child,

would often see Bonaparte cross the courtyard on his way up to her mother's apartment. She nicknamed him Puss-in-Boots. "He walks with an awkward, unsteady gait," she wrote. "From under an ugly round hat which he wears pulled down over his eyes, hang two sparsely powdered 'dog's ears' that fall to the collar of his iron-gray redingote. He never carries gloves and wears ill-shapen shoes that are always unpolished. . . . His emaciation, his yellow complexion, give him the appearance of a sick man. However, let a word, a thought stir him, and his eyes sparkle, his face changes and when he smiles that boyish smile that shows his white teeth, he is actually handsome."

At times his idleness, his poverty, were too much for him. He would become discouraged. "I care so little for life," he confided to Joseph, "I have so little interest in it, that I am continually in the state of mind of a man on the eve of battle who senses emotionally that, when death is near at hand to put an end to everything, it is folly to worry. All of which teaches me to brave Fate and, if this goes on, I shall end by not stepping aside when a carriage drives past." At other moments he would get hold of himself again, his spirits would rebound. Energy, hope were so strong in that soul that, like mighty winds, they blew away the clouds of despair.

Désirée wrote him tender letters in which she now called herself Eugénie to please her fiancé: "You might have written a line to your good little Eugénie who has been so desperately unhappy since you went away. . . . You know how much I love you, don't you? And yet I could never express what I really feel for you. Absence makes no difference in the emotion you inspire in me. My whole life is yours." She worried about his health: "It was not good when you left here. Take care of yourself for the sake of your Eugénie, who could not live without you. . . . Send me your likeness as soon as possible. It will be a great consolation to your sweetheart."

He answered the letters, had a miniature painted and sent it to Joseph. "Give it to her if she still wants it," he wrote to his brother. "Otherwise keep it for yourself." When the young girl was obliged to interrupt her correspondence to accompany her mother and sister to Genoa, he complained: "To get to Genoa one must have to cross the river Lethe, for Désirée does not write to me any more. . . ." He protested a number of times to Joseph, whose letters were matter-of-fact and devoid of news. "I believe you did not mention Désirée on purpose. I do not know whether she is still alive." He begged him to obtain her family's consent—he had thought them somewhat lukewarm since his disgrace. And going straight to the point he concluded: "This Eugénie matter must either be consummated or broken off. I await your reply impatiently."

Always inclined to confide his emotions to paper he wrote the story of his idyl—much distorted to be sure—in the form of a novelette called "Clisson and Eugénie." He himself was Clisson and already the glorious hero of many brilliant exploits. Clisson marries Eugénie, rides away at the head of his troops and leaves her. He is wounded in a victorious battle and sends word to his wife by one of his young officers. The latter pays court to Eugénie. Is the young wife unfaithful? Perhaps. In any case she stops writing to her husband. Clisson, who thinks he is stronger than he is, cannot endure this desertion. In the midst of battle he dashes off a few lines to her: "Farewell, you whom I chose as the arbiter of my life! Farewell, companion of my happiest days! At twenty-six I have exhausted the ephemeral joys of fame, but in your love I have tasted the sweetest emotion of a man's life. The memory wrings my heart. May you be happy and think no more of your wretched Clisson. . . ." Entrusting the letter to an aide-de-camp, he "flings himself headlong into the mêlée and dies, riddled by a thousand bullets. . . ." This novelette dramatized to an exaggerated degree the anxiety that Désirée's silence had aroused in him. At heart he did not doubt her. Désirée was not the girl to go back on her word. Even after several setbacks, he still expected to marry her.

"How lucky that rascal of a Joseph is!" he would often sigh. However, love or, if you will, a serious infatuation, could not separate him from his family. He looked after his mother and sisters and ran errands for them. He wrote a touchingly effusive letter to Joseph, who was at that time in business with the

Clarys, promising to get a consulate for him. "No matter what position Fate has in store for you, you know very well that you cannot have a better friend or one who more sincerely desires your happiness. . . . Life is a fleeting dream that vanishes. . . . We have lived together for so many years that our hearts are as one. . . . As I write these lines I feel an emotion such as I have seldom known in my life. . . . I cannot go on with my letter." . . . A tear or two trickles down on the page.

Though disappointed in Lucien, he overlooked the latter's political indiscretions and his ridiculous marriage to procure his release when that young man was arrested at Saint-Chamans and apparently in real danger. Bonaparte not only went to endless trouble to have him set free, but—by some miracle—he also managed to dig up enough money to send for him to come to Paris.

One evening as Bonaparte was walking with Junot in the Jardin des Plantes, the young man asked for Paulette's hand. In those beautiful evenings at Antibes, Paulette had apparently not shown herself averse to him. Junot, poor fellow, was madly in love with her. Bonaparte replied gravely that he would have to postpone any question of a marriage.

"I cannot write to my mother to make this request," he said. "After all you will have an income of twelve hundred francs, which is all well and good. But you have not got them yet. Your father is in excellent health and will make you wait a long time for that inheritance. When all is said and done, you have nothing but your epaulets. . . . As for Paulette, she has not even that much. Come now, let's add it up: you have nothing, she has nothing. What is the total? Why—nothing, of course. So, you see, it is impossible for you to get married at present. Let's just wait a while. . . ."

And as Junot, saddened, bowed his blond head, Bonaparte added:

"We shall have better days, my friend. Yes, we shall have them even if I have to go to another part of the world to find them."

Convinced that the government offices were hostile to him,

weary of never getting anywhere, he was actually thinking of leaving France. The Sultan was asking for officers to build up his army. Why should he not offer himself? And at once his imagination began to run away with him. That plan would bring him closer to Désirée—one of her brothers-in-law, Antoine, was already in Constantinople; and the Clarys, alarmed at the constant disturbances in Marseilles, were thinking seriously of moving there too. Bonaparte, therefore, wrote to Joseph on August 20th: "If I asked for it, I could get permission to go to Turkey as a general of artillery sent by the government to organize that branch of the service for the Grand Seigneur. The pay is good and I should have the very flattering title of 'Envoy.' I shall make you consul and shall take Villeneuve (Joseph's other brother-in-law) along as engineer." He also wanted to take Junot, Marmont and Muiron with him, thus reuniting his friends in an interesting and profitable post, sheltered from the storms of the West.

Meantime the inept Aubry had resigned his place at last and Bonaparte was able to approach his successor, young Doulcet de Pontécoulant. The latter was struck by Bonaparte's air of assurance and assigned him to the geodetic service of the Committee of Public Safety. In an empty room on the fifth floor of the Pavillon de Flore, Bonaparte spread his maps out on the floor and set to work outlining the plan of campaign for the armies of the Alps and the Army of Italy. He showed such mastery of his subject that Pontécoulant was loath to let him go and proposed him for a promotion in his own branch of the service. Bonaparte was radiant. At last his talents were being recognized, someone appreciated him. The line of his destiny, obscured for a while, again stretched out before him. He promptly moved to the rue de la Michodière while waiting to take a house on the rue des Marais opposite Bourrienne's apartment. "That house opposite you, with my friends, and a cabriolet—and I shall be the happiest of men," he exclaimed. But he rejoiced too soon. Pontécoulant had no sooner left the Committee of Public Safety than the artillery board took its revenge. Letourneur made a pretext of Bonaparte's repeated refusal to go to the Vendée as Corporal of infantry (*brigadier d'infanterie*) and, on September 18th, stripped him of his rank.

That was a gross injustice. Bonaparte had been requisitioned in due form by Pontécoulant. But though he raged, Napoleon did not despair. In those days of political chicanery he knew that to get back in the saddle again all he needed was a powerful advocate. Grabbing up an old hat he rushed over to the rue de Chaillot to see Barras.

V

Citizeness Beauharnais

EVER SINCE Thermidor, Barras had been one of the arbiters of a régime which, now that it was no longer held together by fear of danger, was slowly falling to pieces day by day. He was a tall man, with noble features and powdered hair that waved loosely about his temples. He carried his chest high, like a sergeant-at-arms, under the military redingote embroidered in gold—a cross between a general's uniform and that worn by members of the Tribune. In that ragtag and bobtail world into which his own vices and the Revolution had dragged him, among those crooked politicians, those rascally soldiers, those desiccated financiers, those women who sold themselves, he still retained the manners of a gentleman. He never forgot that he had been born a vicomte and had had his place in the King's carriages.

He listened to Bonaparte: he did not like him very much and he did not trust him—all the more so perhaps because the Corsican humbled himself before him and flattered him. But Toulon had shown what the little fellow could do. Tomorrow he might be useful to a man who would not have been at all displeased to govern France as Protector until the day when he could hand her over to the Bourbons. So he encouraged Bonaparte. He must be patient. They would have him reinstated in the army, they would find a post for him.

On several occasions Barras had invited him to La Chaumière, the home of his beautiful mistress, Mme. Tallien. In that circle Bonaparte was shy and so eager to please that his natural awkwardness came all the more to the fore. Unaccustomed to such gatherings and temperamentally unsuited to them, he stared in amazement at that strange and noisy crowd that milled about him in the vast salon decorated like a Greek

77

temple: members of the National Convention in their exotic uniforms, officers decked out in wide tricolor sashes, dandies in blond wigs and long-tailed coats—yellow, pink or green—with black collars, women in flowing Grecian or Roman robes, *merveilleuses* in tunics of gauze slit to the hips, with high waists that left their breasts bare. To the strains of imitation country tunes they danced, laughed, made love, transacted business. After so much bloodshed, so much terror, men and women alike were seized with a frenzy for living, for enjoying life to the full. From their bursts of excited laughter, their extravagant dress, their lavishness, their bold morals, it would seem as if now that they were at last sure of keeping their heads, they were actually trying to defy the guillotine that for two years had been the real dictator of the country.

In that fashionable throng that rubbed elbows with him and jostled him about without so much as a glance in his direction, Bonaparte drew himself to his full height, tried to appear less humble. And yet the thin, straight line of his mouth and the nervous impatience with which every now and then he wrung his patrician hands, were anything but humble.

Though he despised himself for being there, he went back again and again, even tried to worm his way into the good graces of those influential women, those important men: Tallien, the first to raise his dagger against Robespierre; Cambacérès, ceremonious, puffy-eyed, looking in his white judge's wig like one of those wax figures at the Musée Curtius; Carnot with his button-nose; Fouché, red-eyed, pale as treason; the former Abbé Sieyès, enigmatic, sententious, the mole of the Revolution; Ouvrard, the commissariat-official, an intriguer *par excellence*, who shared everything with Barras—even to his mistresses. There too came Hoche, a colossus with stern features, who had just crushed the royalists at Quiberon; the artist David; the poet Arnault; the musician Méhul; and noble, impetuous Talma, who had brought tragedy to life again by portraying real men living and suffering on the stage instead of puppets. There, too, were all those elegant heads that had escaped the guillotine: Citizeness Hamelin, lascivious creole with olive complexion and eyes like black diamonds; Citizeness Krudener, pale, fair-haired Livonian; Citizeness Beauharnais, widow of the general, a former president of the Constituent Assembly; Citizeness Récamier of the Greuze face, she who looked like a vestal maiden in her tulles and ivory satins.

Country lad though he was, Bonaparte recognized instinctively that these women were different from those he had seen so far. Through them he came in contact for the first time with the luxury, the wit, the elegance of Paris that was constantly being reborn in spite of poverty and crime. Those women reigned through beauty, caprice, desire, intrigue. They were the real masters of the hour.

"The women are all over the place," he confided to Joseph. "One sees them at the play, on the promenades, in the libraries. You even find the pretty creatures in the scholar's study. Of all places on earth Paris is the only one where they deserve to hold the helm. Moreover the men are crazy about them. . . ."

To tell the truth those women did not waste their glances on General Bonaparte. What was he to them? They could scarcely have given a name to his face in that crowd of satellites that followed in their train. Though he was merely one of many he did not despair of winning the brilliant and incomparable Thérésia Tallien to his cause. One word from her would drag him from that obscurity into which he had fallen. One evening he appeared again at her house, determined to speak to her. His uniform was shabby, worn at the seams, for the quartermaster's department had refused him cloth for a new one. He would ask her to intervene in his behalf—a slender pretext but one that might touch her, might rouse her interest in his poverty— she was said to be kind.

As she passed on Barras' arm making the rounds of the drawing-rooms like a sovereign, under the brilliant glare of the chandeliers and followed by a murmur of adulation, he stepped forward and bowed low before her. She was a tall woman. Her ample muslin gown, draped over her generous bosom, fell in long pleats like a peplum. Two exquisitely shaped arms held a scarf of purple cashmere. Her black hair piled high on her little

head set off her warm Spanish coloring. She looked like a high
priestess of pleasure and easy virtue.

Her large coffee-colored eyes took stock of the young officer
bowing before her. He looked thin, sickly, but his voice had a
sharp, authoritative ring. Though she did not like him, she was
struck by a sort of mysterious charm that emanated from him.
She began to talk to him. Yes, she would speak to Quartermaster
Lefeuve, who was under obligations to her. The General should
have the cloth for the coat he wanted. Then she went on to
speak of Corsica, of Toulon, and promised to see that he was
given a square deal. Exhilarated by that welcome, Bonaparte
became expansive, gay, bold, even flirtatious. He turned fortune-
teller. Taking first Mme. Tallien's hand, then, one after the
other, the hands of all those ladies who pressed about him in
a little group, he began to prophesy and predict all sorts of
delightful nonsense. But he went too far when he told Hoche
that he "would die in his bed." The general would have flown
into a rage had not Citizeness Beauharnais, his erstwhile mistress, cleverly retorted:

"What is so surprising about that? Did not Alexander die
in his?"

On that same evening no doubt Bonaparte talked at length
with Talma, in whom he found a reflection of his own deep
admiration for the great monuments of Athens and Rome. The
actor was a handsome man of thirty, with an expressive face, a
lithe and graceful bearing. He had dash, warmth and style. The
soldier and the actor seem to have taken a liking to each other,
for, a few days later, Talma sent the general some books, and
they dined together several times at the Frères Provençaux.
When he was not working in the evening in his bedroom under
the light of his Argand lamp, Napoleon would go to the theatre
to applaud the actor in his leading rôles. Thanks to the passes
Talma procured for him, he was a frequent attendant at the
Théâtre Feydeau and even at the Opéra.

He was at Feydeau on the night of the 12th of Vendémiaire
[October 4, 1795] when the rumor spread that the Royalist sec-

tions had revolted against the Convention. Ordered to disperse them, General Menou had capitulated in the face of the rioting mob. The Assembly saw itself overrun. Immediate danger lent it courage. It removed Menou and appointed Barras in his place.

Bonaparte left the theatre and, as if by instinct, went straight to the Tuileries, where the Convention was in session. As he waited for events to break, he paced the dimly lighted corridors and kept his ears open.

Barras, who had been invested with full power, now found himself in an embarrassing position. Clever enough to recognize his own inadequacy in such a serious crisis, he would have liked to summon a general of artillery to his aid. Among the members of the Convention about him, several names had been mentioned. Turreau, the former commissioner, was the first to bring forward the name of Bonaparte. Barras thought he could trust him. Fréron, who was hoping to marry his sister, pretty Paulette, backed him enthusiastically.

"Go and fetch him," Barras ordered.

The moment Bonaparte entered the room Barras offered him the post of second in command of the army. The young man hesitated, took time to collect his thoughts. He felt instinctively that his future was at stake. He did not like the Convention. But at that moment the Convention was France.

Now that Corsica would have nothing of him, France was all he had left to serve. He looked to her for everything.

Casting aside his scruples he took the plunge.

"I accept," he said.

He was given carte blanche and promptly went into action. By dawn he had reassembled men, cannon, guns, ammunition. That evening he mowed down the royalists with grape-shot on the steps of Saint-Roch. The rebellion died during the night.

The Convention was not slow to reward its savior. On the 24th of Vendémiaire [Oct. 16, 1795] that general, yesterday unknown, whose name now re-echoed from one end of France to the other, was promoted to the rank of major general. On the 4th of Brumaire, he was named commander-in-chief of the Army of the Interior—in other words, military master of Paris.

Bonaparte established himself at general headquarters, rue Neuve des Capucines. Such a stroke of fortune no more turned his head than did the style of living it entailed. It was as if he had never known any other. However, he was quick to take advantage of it for his family and friends. He made Marmont, Junot and Louis aides-de-camp. He sent for Fesch to act as his secretary—Fain would substitute for him till he arrived. He saw to it that Joseph was given his post as consul, he had Lucien appointed Commissioner on Wars and he settled little Jerome in a good boarding school at Saint-Germain. Chauvet, Joseph's former employer, became quartermaster-in-chief; Ramolino, a relative of Madame Letizia's, was made the head of the commissary. He sent his mother and sisters "fifty to sixty thousand francs worth of cash, promissory notes, and furbelows." He looked after everybody and everything. Every day he went to see poor Permon, who was dying, comforted his wife and children and helped them "like a son and brother." His whole being exuded a goodness and kindliness that no one would have suspected in him. He interceded for Menou and had him acquitted. In disarming the sections, he proved to be both considerate and humane, allowing a number of suspects to escape. In the words of Laure Permon "he saved more than a hundred families from death." To relieve the extreme poverty of the masses he organized distributions of bread and wood.

The Directory had begun to function. Barras held full sway there. Bonaparte was now treating him almost as an equal. He went frequently to Barras' house, attended his sumptuous banquets, spent his evenings at the Chaumière where Thérésia Tallien now welcomed him as an   guest. The play in those salons was for high stakes.   ever sat down at the tables of *bouillotte* or twenty-one   other hand he was always to be seen hovering near the ladies, paying them compliments—somewhat labored ones, to be sure—and receiving their flattery. Among them all, the one who seemed to hold his interest was the *ci-devant* Vicomtesse de Beauharnais.

Born at Martinique and married too young, Josephine-Rose Tascher de la Pagerie had had an unhappy life with Alexandre de Beauharnais, general in command of the Army of the Rhine. Beauharnais had been guillotined under the Terror. She herself had awaited a similar death in the prison of the Carmelites where the friendship of Thérésia Tallien had kept her from despair. Together the two women had seen the dawn of Thermidor. They were never to forget it, though life might make them rivals or separate them. Since then, owing to circumstances, Josephine had led a rather casual, disorderly sort of life. After passing through various liaisons she had become the mistress of Barras and was still on intimate terms with him. Bonaparte did not know that. He mistook her for a "great lady" of the old aristocracy who had wandered by chance into a somewhat hit-or-miss society. She was well over thirty and she rouged to excess. But what grace in that long, lithe neck, that mysterious smile, those deep blue eyes that were often veiled with her long lashes, eyes that could laugh as well as grow heavy with languor. Her hair, chestnut with tawny lights, curled in ringlets on her forehead, giving her an air of delicious roguishness.

That girlish innocence hid a woman's guile; that frail appearance, great strength. Loving the good things of life—pleasure, luxury—she was as coquettish as a courtesan, as facile as a procuress, lied outrageously and had a natural taste for intrigue. Never spiteful, though capable of sharpness and even of treachery on occasion, she was loyal to her friends without, perhaps, permitt͏ loyalty to predominate in moments of danger. Citize nais was always beautifully dressed in flowing past ffetas, a gauze scarf, held together by a cameo, vei s that were still firm and small. All the details of ere exquisite, from the coiffure with its silk ribbon to the light satin slippers fastened with a buckle of chiseled gold or bar of pearls. Such elegance abashed the country lad that Bonaparte still was at heart. It was beyond his comprehension.

That clever woman of the world was charming to everyone, but she took particular care to please him. That young general who was so well seated in the saddle might be useful some day. Josephine had been supplanted by Mme. Tallien in Barras' affections. She was, moreover, burdened with two already half-grown children. Penniless, save for the negligible sums that fell to her through the kindness of men of power—contracts for supplies, a few poor investments—and with all that improvident, letting promissory notes slip through her slender little hands, she was worried about the future. Sometimes she even thought that if she could not find a protector she would have to return to Martinique, there to end her life, old and forgotten. To stay on in Paris and enjoy her giddy whirl, she wrapped herself like a clinging vine around Barras' good nature, Thérésia's friendship. Thanks to them, like an adventuress in folly, she sought to open new paths for herself here and there.

At her invitation Bonaparte called on her in the little house on the rue Chantereine which she rented from Julie Carreau, the wife of Talma. The villa, neo-Greek in style, stood by itself in the semi-suburban quarter of the Chaussée-d'Antin, at the end of a narrow passageway between two gardens. It had an entrance floor with four high windows and a low attic. The drawing-room where Citizeness Beauharnais received the general was decorated in white woodwork, set off by a frieze in half-relief, in Pompeian style. The furnishings were anything but harmonious: easy-chairs and old-fashioned armchairs displayed their worn velvets side by side with a brand-new lemon-yellow divan, a sumptuous Cupid or a beautiful Renaud harp.

In that house Bonaparte met a number of aristocrats, friends of his hostess: the elderly Marquis de Caulaincourt, the Duc de Nivernois, M. de Ségur, former ambassador to Russia; also Mme. Renaudin, Mme. de Beauharnais' aunt. The latter had arranged Josephine's first marriage and now frequently came to her aid with her purse and her advice. They were, however, the only women present. Mme. de Beauharnais' unconventional way of life kept others away. But of this Bonaparte was unaware. He thought that he was seeing a group of the old aristocracy that had frequented the Court, and that society amazed and impressed him. Those gentlemen addressed him with such a condescending air. Sometimes in their eagerness to exchange memories, they would forget the Jacobin general and exclaim: "Let's go for a stroll at Versailles!"

Notwithstanding Josephine's attentions, her handclasps, her languishing glances and her pretty laughter, Bonaparte may at times have been repelled by the people around him, remnants of a world that was dead and done for. In any case he would sometimes stay away for days at a time. Mme. de Beauharnais would pursue him coquettishly, sending him brief notes in her flowing handwriting. He would come running to put himself at her disposal again. He was already on the verge of loving her. But he was still writing to Joseph: "Kiss your wife and Désirée for me." Désirée—he still thought of her, but the young girl's face had faded in his memory. Beside the beautiful ladies of Paris she seemed far too countrified. That long period of waiting, that silence, had told on him. He was in a hurry to be loved, to have a wife of his own, someone who could receive at his side and look after his household. By a strange reversal he even went so far as to propose marriage to Mme. Permon, a charming woman to be sure but twenty years his senior. She laughed at him and refused. Bonaparte appears to have been annoyed and for a long time he would not forgive her for having shown herself to be wiser than he.

Josephine, however, had made up her mind to win him. M. de Ségur said to her one day: "That little general might well become a great man." She had been struck by those words. As she had to have a protector why not find one in Bonaparte? Then and there she began cleverly to lay siege to him. She insisted that he devote to her every hour he could spare from his duties and she knew how to make those hours exquisite. She talked politics, business; she took an interest in his career; she gave him advice with just a touch of friendly solicitude. He was deeply moved, and he began to consult her on every point.

Naturally she never confessed her own worries. He thought she was rich and she managed to encourage him in that illusion.

In spite of his habit of command and that sense of authority that he seems to have had from his cradle, in Josephine's presence Bonaparte became as timid as in the days of his obscurity. He would wait anxiously for a word, a glance, a sign from her. He loved her with his heart and with his senses—he loved everything she was and everything about her. He even thought Fortuné charming, that little red mongrel with the body of a weasel and the nose of a pug that followed Josephine about everywhere, snarling and growling and manifesting an aversion to intruders. Fortuné had bitten him once, but Josephine had apologized so charmingly! That little dog had been her constant companion at the Carmelites. She had even smuggled out notes under his collar to her defenders in those gloomy days that seemed to have no morrow. To please Josephine the general tried to please Fortuné.

He had now lost all power of reasoning and let himself go in a sort of mad intoxication. He was twenty-seven—a wild, chaste Corsican who knew nothing about women, about their coquetry, their wiles. She was short on brains and frivolous, but so expert, so caressing. . . . How could he help falling at her knees, if that was what she wanted?

And one evening he fell. A dinner for two, long kisses on an ottoman, a key turned in the lock. . . . Josephine was no prude and Napoleon was urgent. That embrace so entranced him that he forgot everything that had gone before. The next morning he wrote to her:

"I awake filled with thoughts of you. Your image and the memory of those intoxicating hours last night give me no peace. . . . Ah! Last night I learned that the image I had of you did not do you justice.

"You leave at noon. I shall see you in three hours. Till then a thousand kisses, but do not give me any in return, for they set me on fire!"

She smiled, amused, flattered. That impetuous young lover was not at all displeasing to her. Not that she understood or was ever to understand that tense, sharp spirit that she would never be able to satisfy. To her love was merely a profitable game. But never in all her experience had she found such flaming passion in any man. Beauharnais had seen in her merely a novice to initiate, Hoche nothing but a docile mistress, Barras a companion in hours of love. That earnest, passionate love with which Bonaparte enveloped her as with an incense can hardly be said to have turned her head, but it did save her from promiscuousness, it consoled her for the scorn she had suffered, it restored her childish trust in life and in the future.

What was that indolent but shrewd daughter of the Isles to make of that new lover who, so everyone said, was destined for high places? A husband? He was six years younger than she, but did that matter to a man in love? That marriage would ensure her a distinguished position; it would help her to set up her children in life. Barras was urging her into it with all his might. Delighted to be rid of a suppliant who was frequently importunate he intended through Josephine to secure Bonaparte's loyalty and lasting devotion for himself. As a major argument he promised the Creole that, if she would follow his advice, he would obtain the chief command of the Army of Italy for the general as a wedding present. That command had been Bonaparte's dream. For the past two years he had been drawing up and perfecting a plan of campaign for that army. The path to glory would thus be opened to him—and through love.

To Bonaparte himself, Barras talked common sense, personal interest. Mme. de Beauharnais "had something of the old régime and of the new." Moreover she would "Frenchify" him completely. Through her he would take a great stride forward in the social world which, now that the whirlwind had passed, was settling back into its place again. Bonaparte did not need that lecturing. He himself was eager to join his life to Josephine's. He begged her to give him an answer. She temporized and caressed him, only to find him each day more impatient. Notwithstanding the advantages she was weighing, she still hesitated to take the final plunge.

" 'Do you love him?' you will ask me," she wrote to a friend. "Well . . . no . . . 'Then he is repulsive to you?' . . . No, but I am indifferent and I do not like that . . . I admire the General's courage, his vast store of knowledge, his keenness of wit, but I am frightened, I admit, by the dominance he seems to exercise over everyone about him. . . . If, after we are married, he should cease to care for me, would he not remind me of all he has done for me? . . . What would I do then? I should weep. . . ."

No doubt too she was afraid that the General's family might refuse to receive her, that they might inform him of her questionable past. . . . As a matter of fact Joseph and Lucien had tried to open their brother's eyes. But Bonaparte would not believe them: Josephine had been able to blind him. He actually believed that there had never been anything between her and Barras but a business and friendly relation. The times were so free! Josephine may perhaps have been imprudent, but compared to a Tallien or a Chateaurenault she seemed to him as artless, as ingenuous as a child. Moreover he was convinced that she loved him—she had given him such marvelous proofs of that love . . . kisses that could not lie. True, he suffered several attacks of jealousy, but each time Josephine managed to dispel his fears. She nipped slander in the bud and silenced it with a word. Sometimes the artful minx would even turn on him and accuse him. Bonaparte would defend himself hotly:

"So you thought I did not love you for yourself! . . . Ah! Madam, I would have changed indeed! How could a soul so pure harbor so base a thought? I am amazed. Less, however, than at the emotion that, in spite of myself, brought me back to your feet the moment I awoke, and without the slightest bitterness. What is your strange power, incomparable Josephine?"

With Napoleon urging her to consent and Barras negotiating between them, Josephine yielded at last. On the 9th of February she allowed the banns to be published. Three weeks later the Directory appointed Bonaparte commander-in-chief of the Army of Italy.

The marriage contract, which was drawn up by Josephine's notary, M. Raguideau, was a most unusual one. The notary was mistrustful and warned his client against any pooling of property. Who was this little general? A military mushroom that had sprouted overnight and might dry up on the morrow. "The cape and the sword," no name—and what sort of future? He would prefer an army contractor for her. Napoleon overheard a few words of that advice as he was waiting in the study. Eight years later he was to avenge himself on the notary by summoning him to the Tuileries on the eve of the Coronation and "condemning" him to be present at the ceremony at Notre-Dame. As she was not obliged to show proof of her fortune in the document Josephine, who was particularly well provided with debts, did not fail to lay claim to imaginary property. Napoleon could therefore cherish the illusion that he was marrying not only a woman of noble birth, but a woman of wealth. After all, what did it matter? At that moment, even had she been in the gutter, he would have married her. When the document was drawn up the future husband first declared that he "owned no furnishings, nor any personal property other than his wardrobe and his military accoutrement. . . ." But on reading over those lines he thought that they made him appear too poor, so he had them struck out. Josephine cheated on her age. With Martinique in the hands of the English, it was impossible for her to produce her birth certificate. She therefore made herself out four years younger, while Bonaparte, perhaps as a gallant gesture, added eighteen months to his age. He presented his fiancée with a little sapphire ring—a very modest one. On the wedding ring he had engraved the two words: TO FATE.

On the evening of March 9, 1796 (the 19th of Ventose, Year IV), at the city hall on the rue d'Antin, in the assembly room of the old Mondragon mansion which at that time was being used as a marriage bureau, Josephine and three witnesses, Barras, Tallien and Calmelet, were waiting for Bonaparte. Barras fidgeted and looked at the clock. Tallien made jesting remarks. Wrapped in a gray cloth coat, Josephine held out her thin satin slippers to the fire and rested her chin on her hand. There was no smile on her face now. Behind his desk, Mayor

Le Clercq had fallen asleep with his head resting against the back of his chair.

Ten o'clock. Had Bonaparte forgotten? Had he gone back on his word? Or had he been detained by preparations for his departure for Italy?

Suddenly there was the sound of hurried footsteps, a clanking of swords on the stone stairs. The General entered, somewhat out of breath, followed by Le Marois, his aide-de-camp. He saluted and, scarcely taking time to apologize, strode over to Le Clercq and shook him by the shoulder.

"Come, sir, hurry up and marry us."

Le Clercq stood up and read the marriage service by the light of the flickering candles. The vows were exchanged, a firm "yes" from the General, a murmured "yes" from Josephine. The bride and groom signed, the witnesses signed. Josephine held out her cheek to the witnesses in the Republican style. Then the General departed with his wife in the barouche she had obtained through Barras from the former royal stables to replace the carriage that Beauharnais had lost with the Army of the Rhine.

The following day, at Josephine's request, they went to visit her two children, Eugène and Hortense, at their Saint-Germain boarding schools. Eugène was fifteen years old, a tall, slender boy with a handsome though somewhat weak face. Hortense was still a little girl, a trifle awkward in the uniform worn by Mme. Campan's pupils, but she had pretty eyes, beautiful fair hair and a sheep's profile which she had inherited from her father. Both of the children received the General coldly. Eugène had not met him before—the story of a visit to Bonaparte to reclaim Alexandre de Beauharnais' sword that had been seized at the time of the disarmament of the sections, is nothing but a legend which developed through popular fantasy in later years. Hortense had seen him at a dinner at Barras', and she had gone home and wept. In the children's eyes their mother was making a mésalliance. Bonaparte had no idea of that aversion. He himself was overflowing with friendship for them and had assumed full responsibility for their futures.

One more night in Josephine's arms, a day of feverish work, and that evening Bonaparte climbed into the post chaise with Junot, Louis and his friend Chauvet. He waved a fond farewell to his wife as she stood on the steps. She had promised to rejoin him as soon as he had his army well in hand. Leaning out of the carriage he watched her out of sight as he galloped away toward Italy, eager for a glory that in spirit he was already spreading at her feet.

For weeks he had not thought of Désirée. Informed by Joseph of the marriage, the poor girl maintained a sorrowful silence till the day when, from an overburdened heart, she wrote a letter which Napoleon was to receive in Italy after his first victories:

"You have made me unhappy for the rest of my life and I am still weak enough to forgive you for everything. So you have married. . . . Poor Eugénie has no right to love you and to think of you any longer. You, married! No, I cannot get used to that thought. It is killing me. . . . I shall show you that I am more faithful to my promises. . . . In the midst of your happiness, do not forget Eugénie and pity her fate."

Dreamer that he was, he must have held that humble letter in his hands for a second. And then he let it fall again on his table among his maps and plans. Alas! He had wounded that loyal heart deeply: it would take her years to get over it. He knew that he was in the wrong—he admitted that. But Fate that was always to play such an important rôle in his life, had spoken there again. Had he married that young girl and had children by her, with his career, history would have been very different. He could not know that then. Nevertheless he was always to feel a special tenderness for that forsaken fiancée, an indulgence, a desire to do everything to make her happy and to help her to forget his desertion. He would have liked to marry her to Duphot, but the latter died. After Désirée married Bernadotte, he was to stand godfather to her son; he was to lavish honors, property, riches on her, to shut his eyes to the enmity, the intrigues, the treachery of her husband. He was to make that dangerous Béarnais whom he hated, a marshal, a prince, even to allow him to become King of Sweden. Désirée was to be a queen and in the downfall of those thrones built by Napoleon, she alone would keep her crown. But at the bottom of her heart, no matter what she said, one could never be sure that she had forgiven him.

VI

Josephine's Unfaithfulness

BONAPARTE TRAVELED toward Italy, obsessed by the image of a woman who did not love him. He wrote to her daily at every halt.

"Every moment takes me farther from you, adorable one. . . . You are constantly in my thoughts: my imagination becomes exhausted wondering what you are doing. . . ."

From Nice, where he was organizing the troops that had been given him for an army, worn out with hard work and anxiety he flung her a cry of jealousy: "If the day should ever come when you find that you do not love me any more, tell me so. At least I shall know how to deserve such misfortune. . . . Josephine! Josephine! Remember what I told you: Nature has given me a strong and determined soul; she has formed you of lace and gauze. Don't you love me any more?" From Porto Maurizio: "Farewell, farewell, I go to bed without you, I sleep without you. I implore you, let me sleep. For the past few nights I felt as if I held you in my arms. A happy dream, but—not you!"

His friend Chauvet died. That loss saddened him. Mentally bowing his head on Josephine's shoulder he dreamed aloud: "What is the future? What is the past? What are we? What magic fluid surrounds us, hiding from us the things most important for us to know? We pass, we live, we die in the midst of wonders. . . ."

Victory! He was eager to win a victory that he might see her again the more quickly, that she might be proud of him. And his genius performed the miracle: Montenotte, Millesimo, Dego, Mondovi, the Austrians cut off from the Piedmontese, Italy split open like a ripe fig, the King of Sardinia begging for peace—all that in seventeen days, with lieutenants ready to revolt at the first setback, with soldiers cursing as they pointed to their hollow stomachs and their bare feet, but all of them exhilarated, united, kindled anew by the flame of Bonaparte's spirit. He sent Junot back to Paris with twenty-one flags at the same time ordering him to bring Josephine with him on his return. "The ghastly hardships and your absence—that is too much at one time. . . . You will come, won't you? You will lie here beside me, on my heart, in my arms, your lips on mine! Oh, take wings, come! come! *Un baiser au coeur et puis un plus bas, bien plus bas.*"

He was suffering from fever, had a cough and was losing weight. His aching forehead longed for his wife's tiny, cool hands. He had been completely faithful to her. In Cairo his officers had brought a magnificent Piedmontese beauty to his tent, but he had scorned her. He had rejected La Grassini, whom the whole army adored for her singing, and who had offered herself to him. It was Josephine he wanted, Josephine and no other—and he waited for her.

Josephine, however, had no desire to join her husband. Where better than in Paris could she enjoy the brilliant life that Bonaparte's sudden rise to fame had brought her? Greedy for adulation, she saw herself acclaimed with cheers as she drove along the boulevards in her carriage, when she entered her box at the theatre. Notre-Dame des Victoires they called her as in earlier days they had called Mme. Tallien Notre-Dame de Thermidor. She still kept up her friendship with Barras and was seen constantly at his receptions and his balls. She herself began to entertain frequently, giving spicy, unconventional dinners where the guests screamed with laughter. She had become the mistress of Murat, who had just brought the Cherasco Convention to the Directory. She did not find it hard to yield to that muscular soldier whose black eyes shone like gems in his pale, rather flat-nosed, face. But that was destined to be only a passing affair. She had already begun to deceive him with Charles, a young lieutenant from the Army of Italy who had been sent to Paris by Leclerc on a mission and had lingered on in the capital.

Hippolyte Charles was a trim, dark-skinned, black-haired

little Dauphinois with beautiful teeth, knowing eyes and a pleasing personality. He was always well groomed and wore elaborately trimmed, tight-fitting uniforms that showed off his fine figure to advantage. When he entered the army in 1791, his superior officers dubbed him *"L'Eveillé"* ["Wide-awake"] and he deserved that nickname. Gay, loquacious, with an inexhaustible store of puns, he was also extremely witty. He had made himself the Man Friday of Citizeness Bonaparte's household, ran innumerable errands for her to her tradespeople and in particular entertained her by his whimsical speech, his nasal twang and his droll gestures. "He is my court fool," Josephine was often heard to say.

One shadow only darkened that round of pleasures for the Creole—her husband's letters. Every three or four days they arrived by post or by special messenger, for Napoleon never missed an opportunity. Not an officer, not a merchant, not a consular agent journeying from Italy to France who did not bear a letter for the rue Chantereine. And what letters! Anguished cries that were often smothered in sighs lest he frighten her away. "If you loved me, you would write to me twice a day. Instead, you have to gossip from ten o'clock in the morning with the *petits messieurs* who call on you, and then listen to the idle chatter and the stupidities of a hundred whippersnappers till one hour past midnight. In countries where there are such things as morals, everyone is at home by ten o'clock at night, but then in those countries a wife writes to her husband, she thinks of him, she lives for him only. Farewell, Josephine, you are a monster I cannot explain. . . ."

Between a report to the Directory on the conduct of the war, orders to his generals, an ultimatum to an Italian prince, harassed, his teeth chattering from chills and fever, he poured out on paper that love which was tortured and exaggerated by her absence. Sometimes the intensity of his passion alarmed him. On several occasions, passing his hand across his forehead, he said to Berthier:

"I cannot think clearly any more . . ."

He waited for his wife's arrival anxiously, but the pretexts she offered one after the other for postponing her journey, found him blindly credulous. One in particular sent him into transports of joy: Josephine thought that she was pregnant. In a letter to his general, Murat confirmed that belief. When the news reached him, Napoleon turned to his officers a face bathed in tears. He would have embraced them all had it been possible. . . . Instead he pulled himself together and resumed his usual air of reserve, his clear, keen glance. A few days later he made a triumphal entry into Milan to which the victory of Lodi had paved the way. He wrote to Josephine:

"I am longing to see how you look when you are carrying a child. That must give you an imposing air of majesty which I think must be very attractive. . . . Farewell, *mio dolce amore*, farewell, beloved. Come as quickly as you can to hear all this good music and see this beautiful Italy! . . ."

His joy was quickly dimmed. Josephine sent word through Murat that she was very ill—another pretext. Bonaparte was beside himself with anxiety. On the 26th of Prairial he wrote from Tortona:

"I hear that you are ill, that you have called three physicians in attendance. . . . Since that news reached me I have been in a state that beggars description. . . .

"First of all, you must forgive the crazy, senseless letters I have written you. . . . My darling, think only of your health: sacrifice everything to your rest. You are weak, delicate and ill, the weather is hot, the journey long. I beg you on my knees, do not expose so precious a life to danger. Short as life is, three months will soon pass . . . three months more without seeing each other. . . ."

That thought actually set him raving:

"Without you, without you, I am no longer of any use here. Let him who will, love glory, let him who will, serve his country, my soul can bear this exile no longer and when my dear love is ill and suffering I cannot coldly prepare for victory. . . . A hundred times I have been tempted to take the post chaise and hasten back to Paris, but the honor you esteem restrains me

against the dictates of my heart. Take pity on me and have someone write to me!"

The next day he unburdened himself in a letter to Joseph:
"My wife whom I love best in all the world is ill. . . . I implore you to tell me what the matter is, how she is getting on.
For the sake of our ties of blood and the tender friendship that
has united us from childhood, I beg of you, do everything you
can for her, do for her what I would glory in doing myself. You
are the only man on earth for whom I have felt a true and lasting friendship. Send me some comforting news. . . ."

To be sure, no woman could ask for a better or more fervent
lover! But how naïve the poor soldier was, how annoying his
passion!

"Bonaparte is a very fine man," Josephine sighed, "but I do
not understand him."

No, she did not understand him and she never would—until
it was too late. Those heartbreaking notes, those marvelous letters, were merely a nuisance to her. The stupid fellow! Why
could he not leave her alone in Paris? She was so popular there!
She was having such a good time!

She did not stop to think that her present happiness, her
luxurious style of living, the halo that surrounded her, all came
from that man who was risking his life day after day on the
Lombard plains. By giving her the name of Bonaparte, which
she honored so lightly, he had set her upon a throne. She owed
everything to him and she did not even realize it.

In the end Bonaparte's faith was troubled by doubts. Josephine's prolonged silences, her rare and hastily written notes,
the stubbornness with which she persisted in remaining in Paris
while continuing to announce her early arrival, finally aroused
his suspicions. One morning the glass over the miniature he always wore broke. He turned very pale and, superstitious as he
was, exclaimed to his aide-de-camp:

"Marmont, my wife is either very ill or else she is untrue to
me."

Josephine had forgotten him. She was shallow. She loved society more than her husband. . . .

"A day will come perhaps," he wrote from Pistoia, "when I
shall see you, for I do not doubt that you are still in Paris. Well,
that day I shall show you my pockets filled with letters that I
have not sent you because they were too foolish. *Mon Dieu!*
You who are so adept at making men love you without loving
in return, tell me, how does one fall out of love? I would pay a
pretty price for that remedy. . . . I scourge myself by reciting
your faults day after day in the hope that I can cease loving
you—but I only love you all the more! Well then, my adorable
little mother, I am going to confess my secret: mock me as you
will, stay on in Paris, have lovers and let the whole world know
it, never write a line—and I shall only love you ten times as
much. If that is not madness, delirium, fever, what is it, pray?
And I shall never get over it! Oh! Yes, by God! I *will* get over
it!"

His grief and bitterness increased from day to day. He grew
nervous, irritable. The slightest mistake exasperated him. He
made severe demands on his troops, set his officers' nerves on
edge. To forget his own sorrow, he flung himself headlong into
work.

Jealousy tortured him to the point where he was ready to give
up everything—army, conquest, fame—and hasten back to Paris.
Then at last Barras took fright. To prevent a catastrophe he
called Josephine to order and, with Joseph's help, obliged her
to set out for Italy. "Her grief was extreme," writes Arnault.
"When she saw that there was no chance of avoiding it the poor
woman burst into tears and sobbed as if she were going to the
torture." On June 26th, after a farewell dinner at the Luxemburg, Barras put her in the coach with Joseph and Junot, her
maid, Louise, and her dog, Fortuné—not to mention that rascal
of a Charles. The journey was long, the lovers purposely lingering on the way and having a most wonderful time.

Not till the beginning of July was Bonaparte certain that
Josephine had left Paris. Then all suspicion, all bitterness, were
wiped away. If she came to him, it was because she loved him.

How unjust he had been to accuse her of indifference! He hurried Marmont to Turin to inform the King of Sardinia that Bonaparte would be grateful to him if he would receive his wife with special honors. He ordered double relays all along the road as far as Milan—an honor due only to a sovereign. Finally, as the supreme mark of his tenderness, he turned his back on all his worries—the siege of Mantua that was dragging on interminably, the second Austrian Army that was drawing near under command of Würmser, the intrigues of the small Italian states that were only waiting for the French Army to have a reverse in order to fall upon them in their turn. Jumping into a post chaise, he hastened to Milan.

Josephine had already taken up residence in the Serbelloni Palace. He spent two days with her—two days of embraces, kisses, solemn promises. Then he hurried back to the battlefield. The campaign was reaching a decisive point. Würmser had swooped down from the Tyrol with 80,000 men to set Mantua free. For a moment, with Massena beaten at Castelnuovo, it looked as though Bonaparte might be forced to evacuate the Milanese. However, he could not bring himself to that step without making a fight for it. In that terrible hour when his destiny, his very life were at stake, he did not miss a day in writing to his wife. "I implore you, show me a few of your faults: be less beautiful, less gracious, less tender, in particular less kind; above all never be jealous, never weep. Your tears drive me mad. . . ."

He wrote again from Castiglione on the 3rd of Thermidor, with difficulty concealing his anxiety as to Josephine's relations with Charles:

"I am sending you some Florentine taffetas with which to make a pretty skirt. You can wear it on Sundays and on days when you wish to look specially nice. But that is not all—I am going to send you another beautiful crêpe gown. . . . By this time you must know Milan very well. Perhaps you have found that lover you came to look for. . . . By the way I hear that you have known for some time—and very well indeed—the gentleman you recommended to me for a certain mission. If such a thing were true, you would be a monster. What are you doing

at this hour? Are you asleep? And I am not there to breathe
your breath, to gaze on your beauty and to overwhelm you with
my caresses! Without you the nights are long, empty and sad.
. . . *Adieu, belle et bonne, toute incomparable, toute divine.
Mille baisers amoureux, partout, partout.*"

On August 5th, he defeated Würmser at Castiglione, took
Verona and established headquarters at Brescia. His first act
was to send for Josephine. She answered his call reluctantly.
They spent a day and a night together—then Würmser came
down again from the Alps with his reformed regiments. Bonaparte sent his wife back hastily to Milan under the escort of a
squadron. Josephine wept and moaned in terror. He saw her to
the carriage, clasped her to his heart a last time and murmured:
"Go! Würmser shall pay dearly for the tears he has made you
shed."

On the way back Josephine suffered a real fright. Her carriage
was fired on by a troop of Uhlans, and two of her horses were
killed. She was obliged to borrow a peasant *carricolo* and flee
to Peschiera. At last, after seeing several bullets ricochet against
her escort, she returned to the Serbelloni Palace.

That adventure gave her food for thought. She was well aware
of the uncertainties of war. Bonaparte might cover himself with
laurels, but he was also at the mercy of a defeat. She herself was
now beyond the age of risk and aspired only to security. She held
it against Bonaparte for being nothing more than a commander
who had been lucky but who, tomorrow perhaps, might be a
fugitive.

To distract her thoughts, she opened her drawing-rooms
again, was seen at receptions, and went off to spend two days on
the shores of Lake Como with Charles and Mme. de Saint-
Huberty. She was very friendly with that intriguing woman,
whose sharp wit amused her. Moreover, through her connections with the princes, Mme. de Saint-Huberty might some day
be a valuable support should the Bourbons ever return to the
throne. Josephine was still a Royalist at heart and, like her
friend Barras, she did not believe that the Republic would last.

Meanwhile her husband was fighting, defeating Würmser again and shutting him up in Mantua. That victory delighted Bonaparte less than his hope of seeing his adored wife again. He sent her a hasty note:

"In a few days now we shall see each other. That is the sweetest of rewards for my hardships and sufferings. . . .

"Adorable Josephine, one of these nights your doors will be flung open with a great crash, as if a jealous lover were entering, and I shall be in your arms. . . ."

Josephine replied vaguely. She had thoughts only for Charles. Thin, exhausted, Bonaparte lay on his lonely camp bed panting for love:

"Good God! How happy I would be if I might be present to see you dress—little shoulder, little white breast, elastic but so firm, and above it an exquisite little face with a handkerchief tied around it *à la créole,* sweet enough to eat. . . ."

Underneath the jesting, the delight, his anxiety was visible. "What do you do all day long, Madame?"

That was his constant refrain.

What was she doing? Frivolous, elegant, Josephine was laughing and having a good time, making her entrance at the Scala like a queen, giving receptions that lasted into the wee hours. Meanwhile Bonaparte was meeting with reverses. He had only a handful of tired and discouraged men. His officers thought that he was done for. He himself had a moment of discouragement. At Verona, in the chilly night that turned the Scaliger Palace into a sepulchre, he sat alone with his maps, shivering with anguish and cursing that cowardly government that had failed to send the promised reinforcements and was condemning so many brave men to death. . . . But let Berthier, who knew his secret thoughts, open the door, and the man immediately gave place to the leader. He would wave his major general to a seat, dictate an order for a daring, unexpected maneuver which, five days later, after terrible reverses, was to culminate in the crushing of Alvinzi in the swamps of Arcole. In that battle Bonaparte almost lost his life. His friend Muiron was killed trying to shield him with his body.

Putting spurs to his horse Bonaparte dashed for Milan. Josephine was not there. Accompanied by Charles, she had set out for Genoa where the Senate was giving a reception for her. She knew that Bonaparte was expected, but the Creole had no idea of waiting for him by the fireside like a nice little middle-class wife. She did not intend to miss an opportunity to enjoy herself, to receive the adulation she adored. In that empty palace where a pretty disorder spoke eloquently of her recent presence, Napoleon sat consumed with bitterness and grief. At last his eyes were opened. Josephine did not love him any more—if she had ever loved him. Their marriage had been just another adventure for her. To such a marriage he had sacrificed Désirée, who loved him!

He bowed his head, resigned himself. But he was still too attached to his wife to reproach her. Sitting alone in their bedroom he penned those lines, the most pitiful that wounded love has ever inspired:

"Surrounded by pleasures and activities as you are, it would be wrong of you to make the slightest sacrifice for me. . . . I do not wish you to change your plans or the parties given in your honor. I am not worth the trouble, and the happiness or unhappiness of a man you do not love can be of no interest to you.

"Farewell, wife I adore! Farewell, my Josephine! May Fate concentrate all sorrow and suffering in my heart, but may it grant my Josephine happy and prosperous days. . . . I shall open my letter again to send you a kiss. . . . Oh, Josephine! Josephine!"

The blow had been so severe that he was taken ill on getting out of the bath and suffered a congestion in his head.

One more glance at those frills and furbelows the wretched woman had left behind her, and the poor man returned to his army. There was nothing left him now but to amass glory. He defeated Alvinzi at Rivoli, he took Mantua, he made a treaty with the Pope at Tolentino. He was not merely a leader now, he was a diplomat. Ever since the day when all Italy had acclaimed him as its liberator, and in particular since Arcole, his mood had changed. Or rather his mind had suddenly developed, matured, settled, his ambition had sprouted vast wings. In later years he was to say that he "already saw the world rushing past beneath him as if he were being wafted away in the air."

He closed his eyes to his wife's "flightiness." He did not want to know whether that "flightiness" concealed more serious faults. Moreover she had been quick to find excuses, to humble herself, for she was beginning to be afraid of him. Charles had been cheating far too obviously in the matter of supplies. He was denounced and Bonaparte ordered his arrest. Napoleon despised those thefts and intended to make an example of them. For a few hours Charles was dangerously close to the firing squad. Josephine saved him by subtle maneuvering. Dismissed from the army and sent back to Paris, he was to lose no time in getting on his feet again.

Citizeness Bonaparte deeply missed her cavalier servente and accomplice. Ever since her arrival at the Serbelloni Palace he had acted as a go-between for her in many transactions. He had directed toward her the lavish gifts with which cities and princes, mindful of treaties that would presently determine the status of Italy, sought to buy her influence. Boxes of medallions, cameos, pearl bracelets, diamond necklaces, paintings, statues, watches—a storehouse of treasures which Josephine hid away in two little attic bedrooms so that Bonaparte would not see them when he came home.

He still loved her. . . . He still worried about her, about her illness, which she exaggerated, about her boredom, which she did not conceal. She was eager to return to Paris: he begged her to be patient. He sent for Eugène to come to Milan so that she might be less lonely in her round of pleasure-seeking. He continued to write to her whenever he could snatch a moment from so many cares, and his letters were still very tender. But the disillusionment in Milan had left its mark. From that moment he bore a wound in his heart, a disenchantment that was little by little to divert his passion into more discreet channels.

The French Army crossed the Tagliamento and threatened Vienna. Bonaparte signed the Loeben peace preliminaries with

the Austrians. While waiting for peace to be concluded, he hastened to the Château of Mombello, eight miles from Milan, and
settled there with Josephine and the entire Bonaparte family,
whom he had summoned from Marseilles.

Though she had been whisked from poverty to great fortune,
Madame Letizia seems to have evinced no surprise at that
sudden change in her estate. Dressed in black and sparing of
words, she hid her natural timidity beneath an air of dignified
pride. Out of consideration for Napoleon, she was polite to
Josephine, but at heart she despised her. Before leaving Marseilles she had married Elisa to Felix Bacciocchi, a Corsican captain, thirty-five years old and a rather stupid fellow. Napoleon
was opposed to the marriage—his mother and sister over-
ruled him. However, when they arrived he forgave them.
He himself arranged a marriage for Paulette with Leclerc, the
second in command on his General Staff, a man for whom he
had great respect and whom he had been pushing forward ever
since the days of Toulon. Paulette was only sixteen. Beautiful,
charming, ready for any folly, she had of late given Napoleon
much worry. She had engaged herself to Fréron and had practically given herself to him. Napoleon had not forgotten how
much the former member of the National Convention had
helped him at the beginning of his career, and he would have
been willing enough to oblige him. But let that lovely creature,
fashioned like the nymphs of Primaticcio, marry a vicious old
man who had been accused of misappropriations, even of crime!
No, he could not do that. He refused to sanction the plan,
even though his mother had approved of it. Paulette held
out. She insisted upon marrying the choice of her heart and
she wrote him passionate letters, all horribly misspelled. But
time and distance—as well as her famous brother's prestige—
gradually softened the rebel. In the end she yielded and accepted the handsome fair-haired officer who had fallen in love
with her when she was only a girl and who was still under
her spell. Junot was now out of the question. He was too fickle
and had already consoled himself in the arms of Louise Com-
point, Josephine's maid. The marriage of Leclerc and Paulette

was celebrated at Mombello before a priest. At Bonaparte's order he also blessed the union of Elisa and Bacciocchi.

As the result of Napoleon's constant insistence at the Directory on behalf of his brother, Joseph had become an important personage. When the English became alarmed by the victories in Italy and abandoned Corsica, Joseph returned to Ajaccio and, acting on his own initiative, managed to get himself elected as a member of the Council of the Five Hundred. That however was only a beginning. The General's prestige was soon to net him an ambassadorship to Rome. Napoleon had no wish to rise to power alone: he intended to raise his entire family up with him.

Young as he was, Louis had been made a captain. But that once good-natured lad had turned moody, sullen. The gay life in Milan had undermined his health to such a degree that he was never to recover entirely. To distract him Bonaparte sent him off to carry the news of peace to the Directory.

Lucien was still stubborn, still self-assured, but even his many escapades had been unable to discourage his brother. He had been commissioner for the Army of the North but, thanks to Napoleon, was transferred to the Army of the Rhine and thence to Corsica. In Paris he had made friends with Barras, Carnot and Mme. Tallien, even going so far as to call the latter "my adorable sister." Napoleon did not trust Lucien. He did not want him in Italy. But he had already acknowledged his marriage and by assuring him a sufficiently lucrative and important post at Bastia had given him a chance to prepare the way for his re-entry into politics. Lucien was confident that he would rise to the top in no time at all.

Caroline, a tall girl for her fifteen years with a beautiful rose-petal almost transparent complexion, and Jerome, a rather dull schoolboy who had been taken out of his boarding school for a few months, had become great friends with Eugène de Beauharnais. Napoleon had conceived a real affection for Eugène on account of his polished manners and his sweetness of disposition, and had made him his aide-de-camp. Those three young people were always up to some prank or other and, with Paulette, were the life of the castle.

Bonaparte also had two friends with him: the poet Arnault, a frail man and a fluent orator who had entered the army as commissioner of war but whom the General had rejected because he "found him too honest for that rascally job," and Bourrienne, his comrade from Brienne, who had shared those difficult days in Paris with him. Bonaparte made Bourrienne his secretary. The latter was a miserable character, the essence of intrigue and greed. In the end he was to exhaust Napoleon's kind indulgence.

The entire General Staff was assembled at Mombello: Berthier, whose gray head had been turned by beautiful Mme. Visconti; distinguished Marmont; that amazing Junot wearing a bandage on his head to conceal the wound he had received at Rivoli; Augereau, looking like an old recruiting sergeant; silent Soult; restless Lavalette; Duroc with the eyes and shaggy hair of a dog; and passionate Murat who, even in those days, was given to wearing exotic uniforms. And mingling with those intimate friends, those soldiers, in a constant coming and going were Austrian diplomats, envoys from the Pope, from Venice, the lesser princes of Italy, the scientists Monge and Berthollet, the artists Denon and Gros—in short, almost an entire court. Bonaparte had unconsciously acquired the tone and the manners of a sovereign.

Every evening a table of forty covers was laid in the great tent that had been set up in the park. The menu was somewhat Spartan in its frugality, to be sure: soup, a boiled dish, an entrée, salad and fruits, with only one wine, and that one mediocre— instead of silver dishes, pottery. Without Paulette's gay jests and Caroline's laughter, which a glance from their brother quelled every now and then, boredom would have hung heavy over that long table. The neighboring farmers were permitted to peer in at the doors, some even making so bold as to wander about the room. Had it not been for the Ça Ira which a military band was playing in her ears, and that officer without any gold braid beside her who drew himself up to listen to the Marquis de Gallo, the negotiator for Austria, the former Vicomtesse de Beauharnais might have imagined herself at a dinner of the King, in that Versailles of which she spoke so gladly and where she had never been received.

Clever woman of the world that she was, she played her queenly rôle to perfection. Ever since Charles's departure, frightened perhaps, or won over in spite of her natural flightiness by that charm, that strange ascendancy that Bonaparte exercised over everyone with whom he came in contact, she had given up "indiscretions." She welcomed the incessant flood of visitors with gracious words that made each guest think himself the favored one. Toward the Bonapartes who disliked her as she well knew, but whom, as she also knew, Napoleon would always have around him, she consistently displayed an outward courtesy. She was always solicitously attentive to her husband, made the most charming of homes for him and was ever ready with suggestions that might divert and relax his mind. She fought shy of subjects that might depress him, silenced evil tongues, avoided storms of abuse, and showed everyone a smiling face. Never weary, in spite of her natural indolence, she was always ready to walk or drive, to talk or keep silent, or to wait patiently. A connoisseur of good food, expert at ordering a meal or arranging a reception, she was an easy, gracious hostess, tactful, unaffectedly attentive, creating about her an atmosphere of gentleness and elegance to which Bonaparte was extremely susceptible. He thought of her as the splendor and the elegance in his life. That was what held him most now. Not that he was averse to love-making. Josephine was clever enough to see to that. At times they would appear in the morning with heavy circles under their eyes like any newly married couple. But even with those fragrant arms about his neck, even under the spell of those expert kisses or lulled by that birdlike voice, Napoleon now kept a clear head—he remained master of his soul.

Josephine was well aware of that. She was not a very intelligent woman, but no woman could have been more sensitive. However, she was not worried. What could she do with that romantic love, those moonlight vows, those tears, those rages, that repentance? That sort of thing was all too outdated. Was Bonaparte less solicitous in his attitude toward her? Well, that was merely because he was getting used to her. After all they had been married sixteen months. Forbearance, friendship, she thought, were the best fruits of marriage.

Fortuné, her snappish little mongrel, to whom Bonaparte had once sent kisses "notwithstanding his bad temper," was not there now to annoy the General. He had attacked the cook and the latter's mastiff had choked him to death. The Creole had mourned him deeply. To all appearances Bonaparte sympathized keenly with her. But Josephine soon replaced her pet with another pug-nose, afflicted with the same defects. One day Napoleon, out walking, noticed the cook, who jumped back into the bushes at sight of him. Bonaparte called to him.

"Why are you running away from me?" he asked, smiling.

"General, after what my dog did, I was afraid my presence might offend you."

"Your dog! Have you lost your dog?"

"Excuse me, General, but he does not come into the garden any more, especially now that Madame has another one."

"Let him run about all he wants," cried Bonaparte gaily. "Perhaps he will get rid of this one for me too."

Accompanied by the Bacciocchis and well provided with money, Madame Letizia had gone back to Ajaccio. Napoleon encouraged that journey by giving her a commission to "put the ancestral home of the Bonapartes in a habitable condition." Joseph had already begun work on the restoration, which Madame Letizia was to continue with the greatest joy. Mme. Clary, Joseph's mother-in-law, sent her the necessary furniture from Marseilles. Napoleon may have thought that in such troubled times the family might find a refuge there. In any event his mother looked forward to spending her declining years in her old home, where she could lead a fuller, richer life among her old friends.

That departure was far from displeasing to Josephine, but she knew better than to show it.

In those beautiful Lombard summer days the guests of Mombello would often take long walks beside the shores of Lake Como or Lake Maggiore. After a supper at Isola Bella they would hear Grassini's rich contralto in the songs of Monteverde floating out on the clear night air. In those happy interludes Bonaparte seemed to cast aside all care. He became gay, simple, affectionate. No trace of vanity in him. But most certainly a deep pride buoyed him up. He felt that he was soaring on the wings of fortune. He had no definite plans, he trusted in the future—he was happy.

VII

Egypt

AT LAST, after months of delay, Austria signed the Treaty of Campo-Formio. Bonaparte set out for Rastadt, where the terms for the peace with Germany were to be arranged. Josephine did not accompany him. She, who had once been so eager to return home, now lingered in Milan with Eugène, allowing herself to be entertained first in Turin, then in Lyons. She had met Charles again and he had ridden with her in her carriage to within three halts of Paris. She did not rejoin Napoleon in the little mansion on the rue Chantereine, now known as the rue de la Victoire, till the day before Talleyrand, the Minister for Foreign Affairs, flung open the salons of the Hôtel Gallifet in honor of the conqueror of Italy. A triumphal reception of a sumptuousness unknown after those years of revolution! All Paris crowded into those salons, from the Directors, whom Bonaparte had helped to keep in power during Fructidor, to the *ci-devants* who were more and more resuming their places in society and who thought they saw in the young leader a new Monk, the future restorer of the monarchy. To all Napoleon was the man of the hour, the necessary man. All were impressed by him, the more so perhaps because his modest demeanor caused supporters and enemies of the régime alike to suspect him of deep and devious designs.

He made his entrance at eleven o'clock with Josephine on his arm. Napoleon wore the coat embroidered with the green palm leaves of the Institut, to him the most flattering of the many tributes paid him by the great bodies of State. Josephine was in a yellow Grecian tunic embroidered in black and adorned with precious cameos. Walking backwards Talleyrand cleared the way for them. Bonaparte followed, at first amid a deep silence, more poignant than any acclamation. He seemed to be embarrassed by it, deeply moved. He blinked his eyes under the glare from the chandeliers. Respectful hands reached out and touched him. He heard a young girl cry: "Mama, *c'est un homme!*" A low murmur rose and ran down the double line of guests that swayed forward as he approached, and the words were always the same: "There he is! There he is!" He tried to smile, but his heart was beating too loudly and his lips would not obey.

He bowed, held out his hands, but he did not recognize anyone. And yet they were all there—all those he had left behind when he went off to Italy. How they had changed! But no, he was the one who had changed! In those two years the "general of the streets," the man who was Barras' favorite, had become the hero of a nation. Never did glory more sudden pierce the sky of France. Milan had welcomed him as a prince, but Paris, where he would have liked to appear as a plain citizen, showed him that evening the true measure of his greatness. He seized Arnault by the arm, tried to draw him aside. The music blared out again, the dancing was resumed. Bonaparte stopped to speak to Mme. Permon, the friend of his poorer days, and to little Laure whom he had often trotted on his knee. The latter was now a young lady. She must have remembered his teasing, for she blushed in embarrassment in her white crêpe gown. Then he moved on to talk with Barras, with Cambacérès and with Fouché.

He tried to avoid Mme. de Staël, but could not do so. Tall, broadshouldered, with a huge turban on her head and a laurel branch in her hand, she pushed her way toward him through the crowd like a high-masted vessel towing a tiny launch—Arnault, who was to present her to the General. For months she had been deluging Bonaparte with letters in which she wrote disparagingly of Josephine and flung herself brazenly at his head.

"That woman is crazy," he said to Bourrienne. "A set of brains, a phrase-maker, to compare herself to Josephine! I do not intend to answer. . . ."

That evening, going up to him she offered him her laurel wreath. He refused.

"We must leave some for the Muses," he said gallantly enough.

She overwhelmed him with praise. He evaded her, tried to break off the interview. She insisted, angling for a compliment.

"General, what sort of woman could you love most?"

"My wife."

"That is obvious. But what sort of woman would you hold in the highest esteem?"

"The one who looked after her household best."

"Granted. But whom, after all, would you consider first among women?"

"The woman who produces the most children, Madame."

Those brusk replies were a direct hit at Necker's daughter and put her in her place. Bonaparte had no intention of embarrassing himself with an Egeria. Corinne might be a genius, but she irritated him, he did not like her. He turned on his heel and walked away. Later, Mme. de Staël was to make another effort to win him, even going so far as to flatter Josephine. She was never to succeed and, having failed to win his love, she made up her mind to hate him.

A month passed. Bonaparte lived in the greatest seclusion, seldom mingling with the official world. He attended the meetings of the Institut, but more often he remained at home on the rue de la Victoire, working over his books and his maps. He received a few intimates: his brothers, his officers, several political friends. But he was bored. He was afraid that his glory might grow dim.

"Nothing is remembered long in Paris," he said to Bourrienne in one of those moments when he was bored by inaction. "If I stay idle much longer, I am lost."

And yet he had only to appear in public to be greeted with shouts and cheers.

"Bah!" he exclaimed sadly. "The people would run to cheer me just as enthusiastically if I were on my way to the scaffold."

A brief inspection of the ports on the north had convinced him that that was not the moment to risk an invasion of England. He therefore hit upon the idea of threatening the route to India by conquering Egypt, thus forcing the stubborn enemy to his knees. For that matter, the Orient had always stirred his imagination. He was obsessed by the memory of Alexander, of Caesar. He would have liked to follow their footprints in the mud of the Nile, to build a Mediterranean empire for himself. . . . His preparations were carried out quietly but in detail. It was not merely a question of waging war, but of setting up a state, another France, which he could expand by pushing back the desert.

Before he departed he set his private affairs in order. He had brought back three millions from Italy with the tacit consent of the Directory, money accruing chiefly from the mercury mines at Idria. Those millions he entrusted to Joseph as treasurer of the family, charging him to invest them in real estate and to pay Josephine a pension of forty thousand francs in quarterly instalments.

Citizeness Bonaparte did not look with favor on that arrangement. It placed her at the mercy of a brother-in-law from whom, as she well knew, she had nothing to expect. Her collection of jewels was magnificent, in particular those given her by the army purveyors and the Italian princes, of which the General knew nothing. She had also brought back a number of valuable paintings. But one cannot live on jewelry and works of art alone. Josephine had no money, and her debts had a way of steadily increasing. While still at Mombello, she had given orders to have her Paris hôtel redecorated and refurnished. Bonaparte paid the bills. He purchased the house which they had formerly rented. But he was alarmed by his wife's extravagance and relied on Joseph to control it.

He intended to send for her to come to Egypt if the campaign permitted. She was not eager to go, preferring to enjoy her new-found liberty in Paris. Smiling, she went with Bonaparte to see him off. They dined at Barras' house, appeared with him at the Théâtre de la Nation where Talma was playing Macbeth, and then set off in a huge berlin with Bourrienne, Duroc and Lavallette, the latter married only a few days before to the charming Emilie de Beauharnais. Eugène had gone on ahead and was waiting for his stepfather at Toulon.

On the 30th Floréal [May 19, 1798], Napoleon sailed on the *Orient*. The harbor was filled with ships. An immense crowd swarmed about the docks. As the ship pulled out, to the roar of saluting cannon and the sound of martial strains, Josephine waved her scarf in farewell to her husband and her son.

Nelson had been informed of the departure of the great French fleet for an unknown destination, and set out to overtake it—in vain. His vessels were scattered by violent storms. Meantime Bonaparte lay outstretched in his cabin on the bridge in dread of the seasickness that racked him at intervals. He tried to forget his impatience on those endless summer days by reading or having long talks with Monge, Laplace, Berthollet or Admiral Brueys. He made Arnault his librarian.

"Don't lend anything but novels," he told him. "Keep the histories for me."

But in the next breath he was horrified to find that the men about him cared for nothing but light reading.

"What have you there, Bessières? A novel. And you, Bourrienne? A novel. Berthier is falling asleep over *Werther*. Backstairs literature!" he would scold. "Arnault, in future give them nothing but history. Men should not read anything else."

One day when he was more bored than usual, he sent Duroc to fetch the poor librarian.

"Have you anything to do?"

"Nothing, General."

"Neither have I. Let's read, that will keep us both busy."

"What do you wish to read? Philosophy, politics, poetry?"

"Poetry."

"Would Homer do?"

"He is the father of all. Very well, let us read Homer. Besides, I do not know the *Odyssey* very well. Let us read the *Odyssey*."

Giving orders to admit no one, Bonaparte settled himself on the sofa to listen.

Arnault read the first canto: Penelope's suitors, the customs of ancient Greece amused the General. But for all that he was disappointed. Was that all there was to Homer? Such simplicity offended his taste, ever more inclined toward the grandiose.

"And you poets call that sublime!" he cried. "What a contrast between your Homer and my *Ossian!* Let us read a little *Ossian.*"

He picked up a handsome, gilt-edged book from the table beside his bed and began to read in his loud, slightly hoarse voice.

He read badly and too quickly, slurring over the words. In his emotion he stressed the words so dramatically that what had at first been sublime became ridiculous. At moments Arnault could hardly restrain his laughter. The session was a long one: he deserved much credit for keeping a straight face.

History and poetry were precisely the forces that lured Bonaparte toward the Oriental dream. His imagination, which they nourished, formed the counterpoise to his gift for realism, to strike a balance that was long admirable and which—not until he reached the peak of his career—was to have that upset that would hasten his fall.

In the evening he gathered about him what he called "his Egyptian Institute," scientists, artists and Orientalists who had followed him. He would suggest subjects for discussion, as a rule dealing with astronomy, the revolutions of the globe, the various types of governments, or war, religions. . . . Under stars that shone brighter in nights that became bluer the farther south they sailed, refreshed by the breezes that whistled in the rigging, Napoleon listened to those scholarly voices, he himself giving fresh impetus to the talk or putting an end to the argument with a penetrating and decisive word.

On July 2nd, after six weeks at sea, Bonaparte set foot on the sands of Alexandria. That same day he was in command of the city. He immediately set out for Cairo, marching under a burning sky. The Arabs had filled up the wells. The troops suffered and complained—the desert that stretched before them seemed strewn with their frustrated hopes. Even the officers were discouraged. Bonaparte upbraided them harshly. But at sight of the minarets of Cairo and the white masses of the Pyramids lying golden in the sunshine, their hearts rose again. Brandishing his sword, the General, all smiles, galloped ahead of his troops, encouraging them with spirited words which, according to legend were: "Remember, soldiers, forty centuries are watching you from the tips of those pyramids."

With the Mamelukes crushed and scattered, Bonaparte established himself in Cairo like a sultan. He began to organize, to build, to govern, just as he had in Italy. To cement his conquest he flattered the sheiks and set his scholars to work to make that conquest productive. "I spent the late afternoons discussing theology with the beys," he was to say to Roederer, "telling them that the god of Mohammed was the only god, that it was absurd to believe that three make one. . . . I always had seven pots of coffee on the fire. . . ."

Meanwhile Brueys allowed Nelson to destroy his fleet in the harbor of Aboukir. Bonaparte was the prisoner of his own conquest. "Well," he said, "either we shall die here or we shall come out of it as great as the Ancients." And he sent Desaix to subdue Upper Egypt while he himself set out for Syria to look for a way home.

Successes, the enjoyment of the power he wielded over that ancient land, did not prevent him from having his moments of depression. Several indiscreet remarks of Junot, perhaps also of Berthier, had killed his trust in Josephine. He knew that even before he had left France she had resumed her intimacy with Hippolyte Charles, that she was receiving him in her house, and that she had been seen with him at the theatre. At that very moment, no doubt, Charles was with her. . . .

On the 7th of Thermidor he wrote to Joseph:

"In two months I may be in France. I beg you to look after my interests. I have been much worried about my domestic affairs, for the veil has been completely torn away. You are the only one I have left on earth. . . . See that I have a country house when I get back, either near Paris or in Burgundy. I am counting on spending the winter there and going into seclusion. I am sick and tired of human nature. I need to be alone and rest."

Did the sad picture of Désirée rise before his mind's eye at that moment? There was a woman who would not have been unfaithful to him. . . . Now she had married General Bernadotte—a marriage of reason not of love—and Bernadotte was certainly not one of Bonaparte's loyal followers. However, he instructed Joseph to send his best wishes to his little friend of bygone days: "Wish Désirée all happiness—she deserves it."

For all of his bitterness he was still strong enough to be kind, even cordial, in his manner toward his stepson. Eugène reported this to the rue de la Victoire with respect that did not hide a word of blame: "He is kinder than ever to me. It is as if he were trying to show by his actions that children are not responsible for their mothers' faults."

Those letters were never to reach France. Seized by an English cruiser they were not to warn Josephine of her danger, nor to restrain her from that downward path toward which she was gliding.

So far Bonaparte had been faithful to her: he now began to think of amusing himself in his turn. He was neither turbulent nor dissolute, but he had, nevertheless, the passions of a young man. His officers urged him to enjoy himself as they did with the Circassian beauties from the harems of the Mamelukes. He sent for several of them, was promptly revolted "by their shape and their obesity" and sent them back again. It is possible that he may have had a brief affair with the wife of General Verdier, an amazon who could fight like a soldier. In any event, toward the end of autumn at the Tivoli in Cairo, a busy gaming resort, copied after the Tivoli in Paris, where one sipped sherbets to the strains of gay dance music, he noticed a small, fair-haired woman, extremely pretty, with a rose-leaf complexion—Mme. Fourès. She was always laughing and always surrounded by a group of young officers.

Pauline Bellisle, known as Bellilotte, had been a milliner

in Carcassonne when she married the nephew of her employer, Lieutenant Fourès of the Rifles. Shortly after the wedding, Fourès was ordered to Egypt. Bellilotte wanted to go along, so, in defiance of strict orders to the contrary, she put on men's clothing and stowed away aboard the vessel. Once in Cairo she resumed her skirts again. And so charming was she that the military authorities readily closed an eye.

Bonaparte had heard her story from willing gossips and it had delighted him. He spoke to her in that abrupt way of his that held a hint of tenderness and invited her to come to see him. She held out for several days, then, after promises, and handsome gifts, prepared to yield. Berthier thereupon sent Fourès off to Italy to carry despatches to the Directory. On the very evening of the husband's departure, the Commander-in-chief entertained the wife at dinner. He received her with dignified courtesy, and was devotedly attentive. But suddenly, feigning awkwardness, he upset a pitcher of water on her dress. Whereupon he took her into his bedroom to repair the damage —and they both remained there so long that the dinner guests were left in no doubt as to the true situation.

The next day a house near the palace of Elfi-Bey, where Bonaparte was living, was equipped and furnished for Bellilotte. Bonaparte fell more and more in love and went to see her every day. The young woman enchanted him with her pretty ways, her lack of constraint, her guileless charm and lively wit. He found her amusing. He felt relaxed in her presence, enjoyed her merry sallies and, to play up to her, displayed the high spirits of a young lieutenant.

Suddenly the husband returned. The English had captured him with his despatches and, to have the laugh on Bonaparte whose infatuation was well known, had landed him on the Egyptian coast "wishing him good luck." Marmont tried vainly to hold him in Alexandria. The poor fellow hurried to Cairo, rushed to his house, found Bellilotte gone and was not long in discovering her unfaithfulness. Now Fourès had a great admiration for his general, but he was not a complaisant husband. He ranted and raved and stirred up a fine hullabaloo. In the end Bonaparte decided to have his young mistress divorced. It was such an easy matter in those days! A few words pronounced by the commissary-in-chief and taken down in writing by a clerk—and the Fourès were freed of their bonds.

After that the lovers flaunted their affair openly. Surrounded by typically Oriental luxury, and wearing Bonaparte's miniature in a gold oval about her neck, Bellilotte received the General Staff at her home, doing the honors of the palace brazenly, even appearing beside the General in his carriage with an aide-de-camp on horseback caracoling beside the door. On several occasions Eugène served in that capacity—not a very fortunate choice. But he balked and in the end managed to be relieved. Wearing a military cloak and a plumed hat and riding a beautiful Arab horse with a tail so long that it touched the ground, the favorite would appear on the promenade. The soldiers stood at attention, saluting as she passed. "There goes our lady-general," they would say, laughing. They also called her "Cliopâtre" and "Our Sovereign of the East."

The times were very lax. Almost all of the generals had mistresses with whom they were living openly. Bonaparte had undoubtedly a better excuse than any of them. He had ceased to think of Josephine, was all devotion toward Bellilotte and had even promised to marry her if she had a child. But the ex-Madame Fourès showed no signs of losing her girlish figure. Speaking to Bourrienne, Bonaparte deplored that fact.

"What do you expect?" he said. "The little silly just can't do it."

When teased about it, however, Bellilotte replied:

"My word! It's not my fault!"

And laughed heartily.

Meanwhile, after a sojourn at Plombières, Josephine returned to Paris. There was no question now of a trip to Egypt. Since Aboukir, the English had been masters of the sea. With Charles ever at her side Citizeness Bonaparte amused herself as best she could: receptions, balls, the theatre, suppers with Barras or with Ouvrard, and their mistresses. When she was too weary, she went off to spend a few days at Malmaison, that charming property which she had just purchased through the intermediary of Isabey, from Lecoulteux de Canteleu, for 225,000 francs. As usual she had not paid over the money, but that did not prevent her from ordering extensive improvements. She sent for the Guidos, the Correggios, the Carraccios which the Pope and the princes of Italy had given her and had them brought to Malmaison; she adorned the salons with mosaics and rare pieces of furniture; she peopled the grounds with statues. It was not long before she became so fond of the place that she decided to make it her permanent residence. Often, of an evening, passers-by on the road would see Mme. Bonaparte in a long white gown, with a cashmere shawl over her shoulders and a lace scarf on her head, walking slowly along the moonlit paths, leaning on the arm of a young man—her son, of course, those simple souls would say. He would stoop and kiss her. She would kiss him in return, clasp him to her heart, and then move off with him into the shadows of the shrubbery.

Only the peasants could have believed that the young man at Malmaison was Eugène. Paris made no such mistake. Citizeness Bonaparte's brazen passion amused the gossips and idlers: it was grist to the mill for those who were jealous of the General.

How could Josephine have been so bold? Because she had no sense of responsibility, she was reckless. She had always lived for the pleasure of the moment, without thought of the future. In Bonaparte's presence she had affected a semblance of dignity of which, secretly, she was weary. Now that he was gone, she drew a deep breath, she let herself go, she forgot. Would that last? She did not know. Who could say whether Bonaparte would ever return. He had been gone for months now: his fleet had been destroyed, his communications cut, his army decimated by the plague. There had been several rumors of his death. And with the passing of time that event appeared to be far more likely than his return. But if, by some miracle, he should escape so many dangers and tread French soil again, Josephine felt without a doubt that she would be able to weather the storm and that the General's affection would triumph over his resentment.

Meanwhile, to keep up her ruinous style of living, she was obliged as before to resort to various expedients. Through Barras she had wangled a partnership for Charles in the Bodin Company, purveyors to the army. She had other resources at her disposal, too, commissions and profits on the sale of national properties, on war contracts, on the abrogation of sentences of exile. She had, moreover, a genius for turning her credit into cash, and in that already weakened Directory which was growing feebler day by day, that credit was still large.

The Bonapartes had broken off all relations with her, and Joseph had stopped her pension. That woman, he thought, was disgracing their name at the very moment when the family had risen so amazingly in the world. Lucien was a deputy from Corsica to the Five Hundred. Thanks to his gift of oratory he had become the leader of the Right and was talked of as President of the Assembly. Joseph had given him enough out of the funds turned over to him by Napoleon to buy Plessis-Chamant, the ancient fief of the Saint-Simons, as well as a house in Paris. Lucien now had horses, carriages and footmen. No one would have recognized in him the tall, gangling youth who had been so poverty-stricken two years before.

Joseph, too, had become quite as important a personage. He was the first of the Bonapartes to buy a house and lands—a magnificent place, the estate of Mortefontaine. As a former ambassador to Rome and a deputy from Corsica, Joseph was host and friend of the leading publicists, writers and scholars of the day—Benjamin Constant, Mme. de Staël, Cabanis, Roederer. He met the members of the Directory and the ministers as an equal. He was confident that sooner or later the need for men on the part of a government which was eating men up, would bring him into power.

Disowned by her husband's family, Josephine was looked at askance by those who did not believe that Bonaparte was lost forever in the desert and who were counting on his return to further their own interests. One evening at Barras' house, she found herself seated next to Talleyrand. He scarcely addressed a word to her, devoting his full attention to Citizeness Tallien, his neighbor on the other side. Once or twice he glanced at Josephine with that courteous disdain that marked him as a great gentleman among so many parvenues. Josephine was eager to clear matters up. She deliberately engaged him in conversation, mentioned Egypt and spoke of Bonaparte. The last letter she had received from him, she said, had been written seven months before. The minister murmured a vague reply and immediately turned his back and began to discuss politics with Barras and Cambacérès.

That warning from a man famous for his tact and the reliability of his information, opened Josephine's eyes. Realizing that she could expect nothing from Bonaparte's friends, she began to make overtures to Gohier, the President of the Directory. Gohier was an old roué who had married his cook. He was completely dazzled by Josephine, and advised her, if she did not want to break with Charles, to get a divorce and marry him. Marry Charles? Fond as she was of that handsome youth, Josephine hesitated. Charles was ten years younger. He was a gambler, he had no name and never would have. After having been Mme. de Beauharnais and Mme. Bonaparte, wife of a famous general, it would be a comedown to be plain Citizeness Charles! Josephine was extraordinarily vain: the opinion of the world, the value society set on rank and high office meant much to her.

In her indecision she turned to Charles himself for advice. He did not refuse to marry her, but he cannot be said to have shown much eagerness. In the end he managed to extricate himself from the predicament with a few merry quips. Josephine sighed a little and then she laughed. Charles would always be good fun, but he would not make a good husband.

She had no idea what Bonaparte intended to do. Meanwhile, he was moving toward Syria according to his plan. Doubtless even before he left Cairo the courier Hamelin had brought him

letters from his brothers in which they accused Josephine. He
made up his mind to open the abscess, to probe the wound.
Walking alone with Junot by the fountains of Messoudieh,
near El Arish, he again questioned his aide-de-camp about
Josephine's conduct. Junot, a clumsy chatterbox, poured out
the whole story. Now at last Bonaparte heard of his wife's past
defections. She had been the mistress of Murat, and of Bottot,
Barras' secretary—Bottot had merely been following in his employer's footsteps in this as in other things. Bonaparte pressed
Junot for more details and each reply cut him to the heart.
Several times he clasped his head and his face was contorted
with pain. Suddenly he left Junot and walked towards Bourrienne who was standing a little way off. Wild-eyed, hammering
out the words, he cried:

"Women! Women! . . . Josephine! If you had had any love for
me you would have told me all these things I have just learned
from Junot. There is a true friend! Oh, Josephine! . . . And I
am twelve hundred miles away! Oh, Josephine . . . how could
you betray me like that? A pest on them all! I'll wipe out that
race of nincompoops and fops! As for her—divorce! Yes, divorce!
A public divorce, with all the scandal. . . ."

Bourrienne was a staunch friend of Josephine's. He tried in
vain to dissuade him. Bonaparte would not listen. His last
illusions were dead. He knew her now as flighty, frivolous,
caring only for luxury and jewels and oversensitive to flattery.
He knew that she had given him only a lukewarm affection in
return for the passion that had swayed him in those early days
of their marriage. He had gradually become accustomed to
that thought and his own ardor had cooled somewhat. . . . He
had thought that they might establish some sort of a life together on that basis with a reasonable degree of happiness. . . .
Never, even in his blackest hours had he dreamt that she could
deceive him in such an utterly shameless fashion!

Bourrienne reminded him of his fame, urging that it was his
duty to preserve it from scandal.

"My fame!" Bonaparte cried. "What would I not give if only
the things that Junot has just told me were not true! . . . I shall

write to Joseph. He will take the necessary steps to have the divorce granted."

Did he write to his brother? Bourrienne boasted that he had persuaded him to give up the idea. In any event Napoleon seems to have come to a decision. He would tear up by the roots that treacherous tie that like a clinging vine bound him to her, he would stamp it under foot. Let other men keep silent and forgive—he could not. He was responsible for a soul—and that soul was France! Away over there on that arid soil of Egypt he heard, wafted toward him like a confused but passionate murmur, the invocation of a people, weary for its hero, that lined the opposite shores and stretched out its millions of arms toward the sea.

He advanced into Syria, took Jaffa, conquered Mount Tabor. But he failed before Saint Jean d'Acre, which was defended by Phélippeaux, his former comrade from the Military School, who had entered the service of the English. Bonaparte raised the siege with deep regret. "At Saint Jean d'Acre," he was often heard to say, "I missed my great opportunity." He returned to the Nile with an exhausted army that blazed a trail along the road with its dead.

Bonaparte had not taken Pauline Fourès with him on that harassing and dangerous campaign that lasted for three months. She was waiting for him in Cairo, however, and they resumed their life together. Things were going badly for him: the soldiers begged to be sent back to France, his officers were full of recriminations. Kléber, that rough, insubordinate soldier, obeyed commands only at the point of battle. But in the firing line the commander-in-chief was in full control again. The Turks were defeated once more on the beach of Aboukir.

From Europe not a word. Consumed with anxiety, Bonaparte sent a bearer with a flag of truce to the English Admiral Sydney Smith, hoping that under pretext of negotiating an exchange of prisoners, he might pick up some information. Smith surpassed his expectations by ironically sending him a package of newspapers. From them Bonaparte learned of the disasters that had befallen France in the past months: Austria and Russia again fighting on the side of England, Moreau defeated at Cassano, Jourdan at Stokach, Italy lost, and the enemy overrunning the frontiers as in the darkest days of the Revolution.

All night long he sat with his head in his hands, studying those newspapers. By morning he had reached a decision.

"My presentiment was right," he said to Bourrienne. "Italy is lost! . . . I must go back."

He could not linger in Egypt any longer. Kléber would be a sufficient guard for the country. To save the Revolution and France, as well as Italy his famous conquest, Bonaparte must return and seize the power. Who was there to prevent him now? Those Paris lawyers would scatter like so much smoke. His glory was still untarnished. Distance had even lent it added strength and brilliancy. He had only to reappear and all France would fall at his feet.

The Orient had disappointed him, but though he did not realize it, those fourteen months in Egypt had left an indelible impression. In the future he would always have inclinations and turns of thought that were not quite of the Western world. Contact with a servile people, the esteem he had come to feel for Mussulman customs, as well as certain bodily habits he had formed (such as the exquisite care of his person and the exaggerated use of baths) had made Bonaparte a different being. He had become completely fatalistic. More autocratic, more imperious than ever, he no longer looked at men—or women either—with the same eye as before. "I am disgusted with Rousseau," he was to say to Roederer, "since I have seen the Orient. The natural man is a dog."

At once he set about making preparations, and gave orders secretly to Berthier, to Gantheaume. He would try to run the English blockade. If he were taken prisoner the game would be up, but he accepted that risk—the stakes were too high. On the night of August 22nd, from a lonely beach of the Delta, he sailed with Berthier, Lannes, Murat, Marmont, Berthollet and Monge on board the *Muiron,* a small frigate that he had christened with the name of his friend who had died. They were followed by another frigate and two *chebeks*. On the horizon English ships could be seen cruising about. Some of the men around Bonaparte took fright.

"Don't worry," he said. "We shall get by."

And they did get by. But variable winds prolonged the journey and every time a sail was sighted, their hearts almost stopped beating. Thirty-seven days to Ajaccio! Bonaparte was consumed with impatience. However his whole island had come to meet him. From the front row in the crowd on the wharf at Ajaccio a woman in black held out her arms to him—his old nurse, Camilla Ilari. He clasped her to his breast. She presented him with a bottle of milk, saying through tears of joy:

"My son, I have given you my heart's milk, I have nothing to offer you now but my goat's."

Bonaparte was deeply touched.

"*Madre! Madre!* Mother! Mother!" he kept saying as he patted her hands.

Everyone was eager to claim relationship with him. But Napoleon soon had enough.

"What a visit!" he exclaimed. "What a bore! It's more than one can stand! Why, it's actually raining relatives!"

There was no wind and he was obliged to remain there eight days. At last he could set sail. On October 9th (the 17th of Vendémiaire) he stepped ashore at Fréjus. He was never to see Corsica again.

To her great chagrin Bellilotte had been left behind in Egypt. But, on such a hazardous venture, how could Bonaparte encumber himself with a mistress?

"I may be captured by the English," he told her. "You yourself ought to be more careful of my reputation. What would people say if they found a woman on board my ship?"

Bonaparte left her a thousand louis, and urged Kléber to send her off on the first ship. But the latter held Bellilotte prisoner and forced her to "yield to his wishes." No doubt he thought that he could be Bonaparte's successor in everything. Not until several months later could the poor "Cliopâtre" sail with Junot and several scholars of the Academy. Her ship, the

America, though a neutral vessel, was stopped by the English. When she was finally released and arrived in France, everything had changed. Bonaparte had become First Consul. Though he still remembered her with tender affection, he had no desire to see Pauline Fourès again. He ordered Duroc and Junot to look after her and give her large sums of money, and he married her off to a former officer, Ranchoup, whom he made consul at Santander. Bellilotte was to have many adventures and numerous lovers. And for many years she was to remain fresh and youthful in appearance. On numerous occasions, at the theatre or at balls, she tried to attract the Emperor's eye, but she never succeeded. One evening at a masked ball he spoke to her without recognizing her. At the time of the Restoration she was to make a number of journeys to Brazil, where she sold private cargoes, bought woodlands, and dreamed, perhaps, of joining one of those plots hatched in America to rescue Napoleon from St. Helena. Writing, knitting, always merry, surrounded by her monkeys and parrakeets she was to live to the ripe old age of ninety-two. Before her death, no doubt out of respect for the great memory, she burned all those tender and often passionate letters that Bonaparte had written to her in Egypt or in Syria in the days when she was known to all those young men who found her graciousness so disarming as "Our Sovereign of the East."

VIII

The Closed Door

ON THE EVENING of the 20th of Vendémiaire, Josephine was dining at the Luxemburg with the Gohiers, with whom she had become very friendly, when a state messenger arrived with word of Bonaparte's return. Rescued from sea and sands, welcomed in triumph at Fréjus, he had broken the required period of quarantine and was hurrying toward Paris.

At first Josephine was frightened. She had never expected to see her husband again and had been leading her life accordingly. To pull the wool over his eyes, to win him back, would mean a hard struggle, as she well knew. But she was not the woman to give up. She had weathered too many storms. Instinctively she faced the music and, seeing Gohier at a loss, tried to join forces with him.

"Mr. President," she told him, "do not be afraid that Bonaparte is coming back with any intent of destroying freedom. But we must work together to prevent a lot of no-accounts from getting control."

The "no-accounts" were Joseph and Lucien. The next moment she added:

"I shall go and meet him. It is important for me to get there before his brothers. They have always hated me. . . ."

The following morning she set out. The horses, provided by Gohier, carried her at a gallop along the road to Burgundy. At each relay she asked for news of Bonaparte. The General had not been seen. She pushed on to Lyons where she learned that Bonaparte had taken the other road—by way of the Bourbonnais. His brothers had met him.

Had she been there on his arrival, Josephine could have won him easily in his joy at being home again. His bitterness had grown less with the passing of time. But the moment the General appeared his entire family bore down upon him, accusing the absent wife and urging him to get rid of her without delay. Too conscious of her guilt to face him, they said, she had fled with Charles. Napoleon felt his anger sweeping over him again. He would send Josephine away. He would not even see her.

Bourrienne and Collot tried to soften him, but without any success. Collot was purveyor for the Army in Italy and during that campaign had placed his money continually at the General's service. Through Josephine's influence his affairs had prospered and he now came to her defense and pleaded her cause. That short, thickset man with the face of a mulatto, had not a trace of ingratitude in him. A bold speculator and a rival of the Ouvrards and the Récamiers, he spoke frankly to the General, who appreciated him and treated him with consideration. Having brought back only a few rolls of louis, Bonaparte foresaw that he would have need of the financier if he were to carry out his plans successfully.

"What!" cried Collot. "You intend to leave your wife?"

"Has she not deserved it?"

"That I do not know. But is this the moment for you to waste your time with such matters? Think of France! France has her eyes on you. France expects you to devote every moment of your time to her preservation. As soon as she notices that you are muddling about with family quarrels, your greatness will vanish and you will be nothing in her eyes but a Molière husband."

Bonaparte leaned against the mantelpiece in silence. Collot, he was thinking, is right. Then, suddenly, he stamped his foot and cried:

"No, my mind is made up. She shall not set foot inside my house again. What difference does it make to me what the world says? People will gossip for a day or two, on the third day they will forget all about it. Compared to the great events that are ahead of us what is a rupture with one's wife? Mine will not even be noticed. My wife will go to Malmaison. I shall stay here. The public is well enough informed. It will make no mistake about the reasons for her departure."

Carried away by his anger, he launched into reproaches, even insults. However, Collot kept his head.

"So much violence," he said, "merely proves to me that you are still in love with her. She will appear with a dozen excuses, you will forgive her—and everything will be all right."

"Who, me? Forgive her! Never! If I had any doubt on that point, I would tear out this heart and fling it into the fire."

He was gasping for breath, his hands clutching his hollowed chest as if he would tear it apart. . . . The moment Collot left, he called Gonthier, the maître d'hôtel, and ordered him to have Josephine's personal belongings packed and to leave them with the concierge, where she would find them on her return.

What, after all, was a wife's desertion at a time when a whole nation was at his feet? As he rode over to Gohier's house that same day he saw the streets filled with bared foreheads that were raised toward him. In that crowd were men of all ages, and all conditions, in all sorts of clothes: bourgeois, working-men, porters, peasants from the markets. Women and children too! Veterans of the wars of the Republic with bearded cheeks and ragged coats, waving their forage caps at arm's length. Many of them were weeping. All about him rose and fell like the beating of the sea, an immense, a terrible shout of applause:

"Hurrah for Bonaparte! Hurrah for the Little Corporal! Hurrah for the Egyptian! He has come back to save us!"

As he rode along, the crowd pressed back against the houses, leaving a narrow lane for him to pass. With one hand he held his little Arabian horse's bridle, with the other he waved his round hat. He now wore his hair close-cropped save for a few long strands that fell over his forehead. His thin, pointed face was burned by the sun of Africa. His body was flat, his shoulders narrow. But his steady eyes gleamed, his colorless lips were parted in a radiant smile. He wore a strange uniform: a redingote of olive-colored cloth, with high, red-leather boots. A Turkish scimitar with a gold knob hung from his belt by silken cords. A Mameluke, in purple velvet, with a green turban on his head, rode behind him.

As he passed, the double line that had formed gradually melted together behind him and the people of Paris, bare-headed, shouting, laughing, and singing the *Ça Ira* and the *Hymne des Girondins,* followed him in a procession through the streets.

Urging on coachman and postilions to their utmost, Josephine sped along the highway. She was desperately worried at the mistake she had made and the danger in which she now found herself. Along the road she had caught an echo of those frenzied ovations with which all France was welcoming the recovered hero. Every city was draped with flags, every town had erected arches of green leaves and hung out lighted lanterns in his honor. At night she passed by country dances where workingmen in their revolutionary jackets danced with girls in tricolor skirts in honor of Bonaparte. The soldier of fortune whom the *ci-devant* Vicomtesse de Beauharnais had thought she was honoring by giving him her hand was today the most famous man in Europe. He was, in actual fact, master of France. And that man was her husband, the husband she had jeered at. . . . Now that she was about to lose him, she realized what a great future stretched before him and measured, in contrast, the distress into which she would be plunged if Bonaparte should cast her off.

With whom could she spend the last years of her life? Charles was nothing but a puppet, Sieyès, Gohier who had courted her, would turn from her if her reputation were ruined by the scandal of a divorce. It would mean retirement, solitude, of which she had the greatest horror, she who had always lived in the midst of the great world.

And there would be poverty too. She had creditors without number, whom she appeased by small payments from time to time when they showed their teeth too much. How much did she owe? She herself had no idea. Perhaps a million francs. If Bonaparte divorced her, who would pay those debts?

And then, in the last analysis, there were her children: Hortense, almost a young lady—she was there with her, leaning back deep in thought against the cushions of the postchaise—and that genial, kindly Eugène, whose future had seemed assured by the General's patronage. By her conduct she would have ruined their lives—and yet she loved them. Her maternal love was, perhaps, her deepest emotion. . . .

Lights—Paris at last! The wide blocks of the highroad gave way to the narrow cobblestones of the streets. The carriage wheels seemed to turn faster and faster the nearer they drew to their destination. Josephine's fears grew by leaps and bounds. . . . It was eleven o'clock at night; the boulevard, feebly lighted. . . . Now she was in her quarter, the Chaussée-d'Antin. The rue de la Victoire. Her heart beat violently. What would she find? What awaited her there?

She was met by the concierge's embarrassed, almost insulting reception. The General had given orders that she was not to be allowed to enter the house. There were her trunks!

Treated like a housemaid who has been dismissed for theft, dazed, choking with emotion, she hesitated for a second. But the next moment she drew herself to her full height. She would attempt the impossible, she would fight to the very end.

Prayers, threats finally broke down the concierge's resistance. The gate was flung open, the carriage drove in and drew up in front of the steps. Gonthier came running, and Agathe, the chambermaid, both of them devoted to Josephine. In low tones they explained that the General had locked himself in his bedroom. Eugène was up in his attic bedroom. He was in despair. Instinctively Josephine moved toward the little staircase that led to the first floor. At the bedroom door she stopped and knocked gently. Silence. She turned the handle—the door was locked. Again she knocked. Then she called, softly at first, then louder, in a fond, plaintive tone.

Bonaparte did not answer.

She implored him to open the door. Someone had been setting him against her. If she could only see him, if she could only speak to him, she could explain everything.

Still no answer.

She began to weep, great, heartrending sobs—sincere for that matter—sobs that racked her and, on the other side of the door, also racked the man who had sworn that he would remain unmoved. Now, lying on his bed, he thrust his head under the pillow to shut out those dreadful sounds. Alas, he still heard them. . . .

Falling to her knees on the cold steps, she groaned, at intervals, like a dog in agony. The maid, Agathe, took her hands and tried in vain to lift her up.

Again she pounded with both tiny fists on that inexorable door. She implored Bonaparte to forgive her, admitted that she had done wrong—oh, nothing of any importance, just foolish little mistakes—swore that she was innocent, reminded him shamelessly of their embraces, their vows, their kisses. . . . If he would not forgive her, there was nothing left but for her to die.

Crouched on the threshold she huddled there in the silence of the night, limp, broken, past complaining, without a tear. Then, with an effort, she rose to her feet, feeling her way like a blind woman. It was no use, all was lost, she gave up, was about to leave . . .

At that moment Bonaparte burst into tears. The thought of Josephine stirred so many memories! He had loved her so much! She had been unfaithful to him, of that he had no doubt. Not even her terrible despair could shake that conviction. But his youth, his tenderness, his generosity all pleaded for her. Ten times he had been on the point of running to the door. But that would mean taking her back. . . . Could he do that after what his family had told him, after the resolve he had made?

A deep tenderness that remembered the delights of the flesh stirred in him, pleading for the guilty woman, seeking to attenuate her faults. But the next moment, he thrust it aside. He did not belong to himself any longer. He belonged to the nation. France had an interest in his honor. Impossible to be lenient now, impossible to forgive . . .

Disheveled, her dress soiled and torn, leaning on her housemaid's arm Josephine started down a few steps. Suddenly Agathe bent and whispered into her ear. Why did she not send the children? Perhaps he would listen to them.

They were there, Hortense and Eugène, on the attic landing, clinging to each other and hiding their pale faces as they shuddered at those terrible cries and wept at those anguished sobs. Agathe was right. It was the last chance—perhaps they might soften Bonaparte's heart. He had grown very fond of them, of Eugène in particular. If they would ask him to see her, perhaps he would give in. . . .

Standing outside of his door they begged him awkwardly, naïvely, but with all their hearts:

"Do not desert our mother, it will kill her! And what about us . . . what will become of us?"

Not a sound. Josephine, Hortense and Eugène looked at each other, discouraged. . . . Then suddenly, a step.

The key turns in the lock, the door opens . . . Bonaparte appears. He leans against the doorjamb, his eyes blinded by tears. He is as pale as Medusa. Josephine rushes to him with a cry and flings her arms about his neck, pressing her head against his shoulder. He breathes in the perfume of which he has dreamt so many lonely nights. Speechless, they stand locked in close embrace.

So once again he had yielded to his old infatuation—and after what a struggle! But even though he touched his lips to Josephine's forehead in response to her caresses, Napoleon had not lost his sober judgment. He had yielded out of pity, stirred by old memories—and not from love. Never again would he experience that passionate, impetuous love he had known at twenty-six! Josephine had killed it.

He brushed aside her explanations, her excuses. He did not believe them. "The soldiers of Egypt," he was to say one day, "are like those who fought the siege of Troy. Their wives have kept the same sort of faithfulness to them." But he forgave her— and for Josephine that was the essential. He forgave her unreservedly, generously, absolved her of all her past faults, but it was a forgiving, as Josephine was to discover later, that was not forgetting. Bonaparte showed her affection, friendship, even trust—or almost that. But from that dreadful hour there was a chasm between them that could never be bridged. The common plane on which they had moved in former days was obliterated. He who had once been so eager to please her, now spoke with an air of command and she who had formerly treated him with charming casualness now was filled with a real desire to obey. Appearances to the contrary, she was the vanquished, he was the victor.

The next morning when Lucien Bonaparte arrived to call on his brother, he found him in bed with Josephine, a Josephine younger, more alluring—she always kept powder and rouge at her bedside—who received him with charming grace. She had triumphed over the clan that had thought to be rid of her. But she was tactful in her triumph; she did not insist upon it. And to all intents and purposes the Bonaparte family bowed its head and resumed relations with the intruder which the public might have considered almost friendly. The political struggle that was about to begin was so great in magnitude and involved so many dangers, notwithstanding the favorable outlook, that all who were supporting Bonaparte felt the need of drawing close together around him.

To tell the truth France was no longer in the alarming state in which Napoleon had expected to find it on his return from Egypt. Masséna had defeated Souvorof at Zurich. Brune had forced the English to evacuate Holland. At home anarchy was decreasing. The rebels had surrendered. The Directory believed themselves out of danger, as they plainly showed by their attitude toward Bonaparte. Furious at his return, they had thought for a moment of accusing him of deserting his army and violating the quarantine. But they did not dare: the General was too popular. They received him therefore without a word of reproach, even going so far as to flatter him. Actually they had only one desire—to be rid of him. They suggested that he take command of a new army and reconquer Italy. Bonaparte refused, pleading ill-health as an excuse.

What he wanted, as those confident Jacobins all knew, was

the power they still held in their feeble hands. Every day a long procession of army leaders, high officials, members of the Institut, financiers, stood in line before the house on the rue de la Victoire. Collot lent him five hundred thousand francs, Talleyrand, Fouché gave him their support. However Barras still held back; Sieyès sulked; Gohier and his friend, Moulin, were still hostile; Moreau was hesitating. Bernadotte announced openly that he was ready to bar the way of his former general and, if the latter so much as made a move, he would lead him to the scaffold. Meeting followed meeting in Julie Talma's tiny mansion. Josephine was almost always present, forwarding her husband's plans with all the skill, grace and experience of a woman of the world, well versed in the ways of society and the life of intrigue. She acted as mediator and messenger, welcoming to her drawing-room, holding there, flattering and winning even those men she disliked or found boring, but who, as she knew, were useful to the great project.

At first those plans were fluid, tentative. Josephine and Fouché urged Bonaparte to join forces with his friend, Barras, but in spite of the favors he had received from Barras in the past, Napoleon disliked the idea. How could he inaugurate the new era side by side with the *roi des pourris?* Talleyrand and Lucien —the latter now president of the Council of the Five Hundred— advocated an entente with Sieyès. Bonaparte inclined toward their view. The coup d'état, which was pulled off in two days, was followed neatly by the 18th of Brumaire. But on the 19th, at Saint-Cloud, Bonaparte seemed near to failure. Greeted by the jeers of the Five Hundred, he managed to stammer a few awkward sentences. Lucien came to his rescue. At the head of a column of grenadiers, Murat drove the representatives from the house.

With Sieyès and Roger Ducos, Bonaparte was appointed provisional consul and, accompanied by Bourrienne, returned to Paris through the Bois de Boulogne at three o'clock in the morning. Silent, with eyes closed, he leaned back in the carriage, pretending to doze. . . .

At the rue de la Victoire he hurried up to Josephine's bedroom. She was in bed, and worried, though Fouché had already informed her of the success of the coup. He clasped her in his arms, then turned to Bourrienne and referring to events at Saint-Cloud, asked:

"Bourrienne, did I say many foolish things?"

"Quite a few, General."

"I would rather talk to soldiers than to lawyers. Those b—— frightened me. I'm not used to Assemblies. But that will come."

Late as it was, the three sat there talking, their nerves relaxed from the tension. Josephine urged them to reward her old friend, Gohier. Could they not do something for him?

"What do you expect, my dear?" said Bonaparte. "It is not my fault. He is a good fellow, but a fool. He does not understand. Perhaps I ought to have him deported."

At her protest, he laughed.

"Yesterday, of all days, he asked me to dinner! . . . And he calls himself a statesman. . . . Well, but we won't discuss it any more."

His thoughts turned to Bernadotte. The latter's underground activities and his deep enmity had given Bonaparte much anxiety. But Bernadotte was Désirée's husband, the father of her child. How could he take revenge on such a man? Aloud, to excuse his weakness, he said:

"Joseph likes him. I should have everyone against me. Oh! How stupid those family considerations are!"

He motioned to his secretary to leave them.

"Goodnight, Bourrienne. . . . By the way, we shall sleep at the Luxemburg tomorrow."

That night he slept only two hours. Not even Josephine's blandishments could hold him back. What was a mere woman to the man who had just espoused France?

Part Two

MANHOOD

I

The First Consul

FROM THE DAY when he came to power, Bonaparte grasped it with both hands. Power was absolutely necessary to him. It was his passion, it was his "art." In later years he was to confess to Roederer:

"I love power, but I love it as an artist. I love it as a musician loves his violin. I love to draw tunes, chords, harmonies from it." He got rid of his two colleagues and replaced them with men of his own choice, Cambacérès and Lebrun, men of standing whom he could count on to carry out his wishes. It was not long before his innate sense of pageantry, his desire to gild his dictatorship with the lustre of a former grandeur, impelled him to leave the Luxemburg and move to the Tuileries.

The removal was attended with pomp and ceremony.

"All this bores me," he remarked to Bourrienne, "but you have to put up a front. It is good for the masses."

To tell the truth, luxury had become such an unknown quantity in Paris that it was difficult to find carriages for the public officials. The Council of State rode in fiacres. The First Consul's carriage was drawn by six white horses, a gift of the Emperor Francis at Campo Formio. The crowds greeted it with rousing cheers. As Bonaparte drove through the gateway into the Tuileries courtyard he raised his eyes to an inscription that dated from 1792:

"Royalty has been abolished in France and will never rise again."

Mounting his horse he held a review of his troops—the battle-stained and glorious flags were carried past. Josephine stood at the windows of the Pavillon de Flore, surrounded by handsomely appareled ladies and waved her scarf. The First Consul bowed his head. The next moment, with a firm tread, he mounted the palace steps.

The apartments were uncomfortable and dark, "as gloomy as grandeur," Bonaparte said. Save for the brief reign of Louis XVI, the Tuileries had not been used since the days of Louis XIV. Since then it had been the assembly hall of the Convention and its committees; most of the furniture had been removed and the decorations were in ruins. The first thing Bonaparte did was to restore it to its former grandeur.

Josephine's apartments were on the ground floor, overlooking the garden. The Consul selected the King's suite on the floor above—an antechamber, two drawing-rooms, two studies, a bedroom and a bath. Bonaparte never used his state bedroom. Every evening it was his custom to descend the secret staircase that led to Josephine's apartments below, for he slept with his wife like any good little bourgeois.

"Well, little Creole," he said to her in jest the first night. "Come and get into your master's bed."

With an ingenuousness and an almost Republican simplicity, he promptly set up a princely establishment. But temporary arrangements were hateful to him. Walking with his secretary through the *galerie de Diane,* where a number of statues had just been placed at his order, he said to him:

"Bourrienne, it is not enough to be in the Tuileries. The thing is to stay here. Who has not lived in this palace? Rascals, members of the National Assembly . . . but look! There is your brother's house. Wasn't it from there that I witnessed the attack on the Tuileries and saw good King Louis XVI carried off? But don't worry. Just let them come!"

To emphasize the change of régime, his first act on arriving at the château was to give a reception for the diplomatic corps. Afterwards the diplomats went to the apartments below to pay their respects to Mme. Bonaparte as in former days they had paid homage to the Queen.

Josephine had no court as yet, but around a nucleus of her close friends, she had gathered a circle at first modest, then gradually increasing in size. She had gone to some pains to

bring the men of the old France who had formerly frequented
the rue Chantereine—Ségur, Caulaincourt, De Mun, Noailles—
into friendly and harmonious relations with the supporters of
the new régime, such as Cambacérès, Monge, Réal, Regnault,
Roederer, even Fouché. Her drawing-room was a no-man's-land
of good will, a rallying-point around the Consul. Bonaparte had
forbidden her to receive those former friends of doubtful reputation: Mme. Tallien and Mme. Hamelin. He chose instead as
her daily companions women of a very different and much
higher calibre—Mme. de la Rochefoucauld, short, hunchbacked
and kindhearted as well as extremely witty, and Mmes. de
Talhouët, de Luçay, de Lauriston, de Rémusat. He was concerned to create an atmosphere of dignity and decorum about
him in contrast to the laxness and cynicism of the Directory.
The *Moniteur* printed a note that emanated from Bonaparte's
study and was perhaps even dictated by him:

> In the month of December last, a large reception was held
> at the Luxemburg. Bonaparte ordered his servants to build up
> the fires, and even went so far as to repeat the order two or
> three times. Whereupon one of the servants took the liberty of
> pointing out that it was impossible to put more wood in the
> fireplace. "That will do," Bonaparte then said, raising his voice.
> "I wanted the place well heated, for it is extremely cold; be-
> sides, these ladies are almost naked."

The lesson went home. Fashions changed at once: bosoms
were covered, a lining was worn under chiffons and embroidered
tulles. Gowns were now made of heavy, rich satins. The women
of the Directory, like the dandies of that period, had vanished
from the scene.

Though Josephine held no official rank and was without ap-
parent influence, she played an important rôle in politics. She
was feverishly active in striking an ever increasing number of
names off the list of émigrés, many of them nobles of the former
Court. Delighting in her ostensible importance, she wrote mar-
ginal notes on petitions and made recommendations ad infini-
tum. The First Consul ordered his ministers to grant her any
favors she might ask. After all she would only be following out

his own wishes. What Bonaparte desired above all was to recon-
cile the whole of France. He restored the churches to the priests,
abolished the holiday of January 21st, pacified the provinces in
the west—Frotté was put to death there only because his pardon
came too late—and last, but not least, had Cadoudal brought to
the Tuileries.

The leader of the Royalists was a giant in stature. Rapp, who
introduced him into the salon where the First Consul was waiting to receive him, was afraid of an attempt on the Consul's life
and did not dare to close the door. From time to time he would
glance inside. The interview was long and stormy. Bonaparte
tried to win over the Vendéan by offering him a military command and talking to him of glory and of country. Stanch in his
faith, Cadoudal refused. He was apparently afraid of being arrested in spite of his safe-conduct. Bonaparte reassured him
nobly:

"You have the wrong slant on things and you are making a
mistake not to come to some agreement, but if you insist on
going back home, you are as free to leave Paris as you were to
come here."

After Cadoudal had left, he took Rapp to task.

"Why did you leave the door open?"

Rapp replied that he could not leave the Consul alone with
such a powerful and violent man.

Bonaparte drew himself up to his full height:

"Shame on you, Rapp! You don't mean that!"

And he set to work again.

That work was a gigantic task. But his life henceforth was to
be all work. Affairs of state absorbed his thoughts in a constant
tension, a sort of frenzy for governing.

"I am born and built for work," he sometimes said. "There
is apparently no limit to the amount I can do." Everything
passed through his hands: he saw everything, knew everything
that was going on, made all the decisions, supervised everything.
Not hastily and impulsively, but carefully, methodically, with
an attention to detail, a grasp of reality that fascinated all who
came in contact with him and bent them to his will. His

physician, Corvisart, who had been recommended by Lannes, won his confidence by curing him of the stubborn itch he had contracted at Toulon. When Corvisart forbade him to sit up too late, he shrugged his shoulders and remarked to Lucien:

"Poor Corvisart! He is everlastingly harping on the same old tune! But I have shown him, as clearly as two and two make four, that I really have to take the night to run my shop, for the day is not enough. . . . I should prefer more rest, but the ox is yoked, he must pull the plough."

What that ploughing was everyone knew. The same attention he gave to foreign affairs, finance, government, he also applied to the army, increasing it, reorganizing it, keeping it in good condition by constant training. He was unwilling to let them have the old white coats again. "Blood shows too plainly on them," he said. Every fifth day, in the courtyard of the Tuileries, he reviewed not only the consular guard, but all the regiments of France, sending for them in rotation the better to keep them in hand. He questioned the soldiers about their food, their clothing, had a lively retort for their sallies, and made them tremble with pride and devotion by talking to them of their victories. To those soldiers of France there was only one leader, one ruler—Bonaparte. Junot, who had recently married young Laure Permon, was often moved to tears as he passed along the ranks at the Consul's side.

"It is all running magnificently as if on wheels," he told his wife. "That man is a supernatural being!"

Toward five o'clock, Bonaparte would go downstairs to dine, sometimes stopping first at Josephine's apartment to tease her as she dressed. He considered himself an authority on lady's fashions. He would change the position of the flowers the hairdresser had placed in his wife's hair, fasten her necklace on her, make her walk up and down in front of him the better to judge the effect, even call in Hortense as a witness—and all in the utmost seriousness.

At other times when his thoughts were intent on some important matter, he would enter Josephine's room and, paying no attention to anyone, sink into an armchair.

"Not ready yet?"

Instantly Mme. Bonaparte would be on her feet. She was mad about jewels, she changed her gowns five times a day and she spent hours in front of her mirror rouging and making up her eyes, but she had one priceless quality: She never kept him waiting. He would offer her his arm and lead her into the salon where dinner was served. The guests were usually few in number, members of the family, intimate friends of the Consul's. Bonaparte frequently left the table before dessert was brought in. The meal was always too long for him.

"That," he said, "is indeed one of the corruptions of power."

Every tenth day he gave a banquet of two hundred covers which was served in the Galerie de Diane. Among the guests were members of the diplomatic corps, most of the ministers, a number of generals and colonels from the Paris garrison and many high officials. Everyone was bored. After coffee Josephine received her guests. Bonaparte never sat down, but walked about talking now to this person, now to that, breaking off a conversation abruptly, asking questions and making witty retorts. Suddenly he would call his secretary:

"Come, Bourrienne! We must get back to work."

Now and then, however, he would give himself a holiday. On those occasions he would put on a dark redingote and go out with Bourrienne for a "stroll around the town."

The two men would slip out by a side door and wander along the rue Saint-Honoré, where they would enter the shops and haggle over the price of a few worthless trinkets. Bourrienne would be the purchaser while Bonaparte talked politics "in a light, bantering tone." Turning up the edge of his collar to make himself look like a young man about town he would ask:

"Well, Madame, what is new today? Your shop seems to be doing a thriving business. You must see a lot of people here. What do they say about that buffoon of a Bonaparte?'

Many times in shops where business had picked up, the owners would turn on him furiously. Once he even had to escape on Bourrienne's arm to avoid the insults he had brought down upon himself by a remark disparaging to the Consul. That delighted him and for days he insisted upon relating his experience to everyone with whom he came in contact. On other evenings he would accompany Josephine and Hortense to the theatre. He considered it his duty to appear in public and encourage by his presence a renewal of national activity in every form. He attended the Opéra out of courtesy to his wife rather than from any personal liking for it. But he went to first nights at the Comédie française with the keenest interest. Whenever his friend Talma appeared in a new rôle, Bonaparte was there to applaud him.

Even before the coming of spring he found his real relaxation at Malmaison. Trees, flowers, the wide open spaces had always appealed to his passionate yet dreamy nature. There, too, he took the exercise which he considered so healthy for him—thin as he was in those days he was even then anxious not to put on weight.

He worked in the country just as hard as in Paris, but he could work out of doors in a tent set up on a ramp that led from his study to the private gardens. There he carried his maps, his books, his mail.

"When I am out of doors," he said, "I feel that my thoughts have a loftier trend, a wider scope. I cannot imagine how any man can work successfully beside a stove, cut off from sight of the sky."

In that cheerful, sunlit house he felt freer, more at ease. He had always dreamt of having a home of his own. He enjoyed furnishing it, embellishing it. He wanted to enlarge the gardens and he even went so far as to calculate the possible revenues from them. There were constant visitors—his mother, his brothers, his sisters; old friends and new: Talleyrand, Fouché, Cambacérès, Monge, Volney, Laplace, Arnault, Isabey, Talma. The Prince de Poix, M. de Mun and M. de Laigle rubbed elbows as equals with the officers of the General Staff. On Wednesdays, weather permitting, dinner was served in the park. If Bonaparte happened to be in a good mood and not too absorbed in affairs of state, he would suggest a game of prisoner's base. Taking off his coat he would dash across the lawn like a schoolboy, paying no attention to the rules of the game. All his lost youth would come back to him in those moments. When he fell, or tripped Hortense or Laure Junot, he would laugh uproariously. But one day when they were playing leapfrog, he turned angrily on Isabey who had mistaken him for Eugène and had dared to jump over him as he stooped down. Bonaparte rebuked him sharply. It infuriated him for people to become too familiar or to forget for a second that he was the master. But he did not bear a grudge against the artist very long. He had put him in his place—that was enough.

Now and then he played *reversi* at a round table in the drawing-room, and his cheating roused endless protests and merriment. On other days, half reclining on a sofa before an attentive audience, he would invent a weird tale or perhaps a ghost story that would make the ladies shiver with fright. He liked to imagine all sorts of ghoulish adventures. At such times his voice would take on a deeper note and he would accompany the story with expressive gestures, even shutting his eyes at the most lurid moment as if he himself were really afraid.

Occasionally the talk would ramble on with a real lack of restraint, Bonaparte not infrequently contributing a subtle jest, a pungent witticism. Of Mme. de Staël, he said: "That woman teaches people to think who would never dare to or who have forgotten how." Of Mme. de Genlis: "When she tries to defend virtue, she always talks as if she had made a discovery." Of Abbé Delille: "He drools wit."

Now and then they would give a play, the company consisting as a rule of the young people in the château, with the addition of Bourrienne and Isabey. They opened with *The Barber of Seville*, in which Isabey made an excellent Figaro and Hortense a charming Rosine. Then came *The Lover's Quarrel, The Unexpected Wager, The Heirs, The Scatter-brained,* as well as charades and farces. With his weasel-like face, Bourrienne was a frank success in the old-men rôles. The whole household attended those performances, Bonaparte and Josephine in the front row, with soldiers and servants filling up the back of the small drawing-room that had been arranged as a theatre at Talma's suggestion.

The Consul enjoyed himself hugely, criticizing the actors or paying them compliments as the case might be. He told Bourrienne that he ought to get up earlier in the morning to learn his part. Pompous Cambacérès would have liked to act too, and claimed that he had been a great success at Montpellier in his youth. They laughed at him and brushed him ruthlessly aside.

On certain evenings when Bonaparte chanced to be alone with his wife and stepdaughter—a rare occurrence it is true—he would invite Hortense to read aloud to him. She made rather a poor showing with *Atala*, stumbling over the unfamiliar names of places, plants and animals.

"Doesn't Mme. Campan teach you how to read?" asked the Consul.

At other times he gave her financial reports to add up. The poor child would lose her way in the columns of figures and mix receipts and expenditures. Bonaparte, who carried the figures in his head, teased her mercilessly:

"So Mme. Campan does not teach you how to count either?"

Glorious Malmaison days, when he was young, alert and strong, days in which Bonaparte tested his strength and prepared himself for the task ahead, days in which France drew a long breath, relaxed, felt her wounds close and heal. It was a sunrise, the most brilliant perhaps that any single man had ever caused to dawn and that a nation had ever known. . . . Everything had its use, nothing was superfluous. . . .

Bonaparte had tried to make peace with Austria, but his offers had been rejected. He therefore prepared for a decisive action. He would sweep down into Lombardy while Moreau was attacking on the Rhine.

On May 6th, full of confidence, he set out, accompanied by Bourrienne.

"I have many conscripts in my army," he said, "But those conscripts are Frenchmen. Did I not sweep Italy clean four years ago with an inferior force? The sun that shines on us today is the same that shone on us at Arcole and at Lodi."

He rested for three days at the convent of Martigny. He had a cold and did not leave his room except to go to the refectory to dine and once to walk in the monks' garden. After that he set out by way of the St. Bernard Pass. Wearing a gray redingote, and carrying his riding-whip in his hand, he chatted with the guide Dorsez as he rode up the steep incline. At the hospice he dined in a cell and visited the library, where he reread the passage on Hannibal in Titus Livy. In the evening he set out again. His army followed him, the artillery being brought up by hand. He captured a few towns that offered little resistance and, on June 2nd, cutting the Austrian lines, he reached Milan. On the 14th he joined battle with old Mélas at Marengo. At first it looked as if Bonaparte were going to lose. Victor fell back, Lannes was outflanked. But Napoleon could not bring himself to order a retreat and he marked time till evening. Then Desaix, hearing the roar of the guns, hurried up with fresh troops. At six o'clock that evening Bonaparte went into battle again. Marengo was taken by assault and the Austrians fled.

However, the death of Desaix turned the victory into mourning.

"I saw that he was very depressed," Bonaparte said, "and as there was a great deal of anxiety around me toward the decisive moment, I purposely got off my horse to show him that I felt quite confident and said to him: 'Let us sit down on the grass for a moment.' That was the moment when Desaix said to me: 'The cannon balls do not know me any more.' I mounted again and gave the order to attack. At the very beginning he was hit by a cannon ball . . . I have great faith in presentiments myself."

He restrained his tears with difficulty: "Why am I not allowed to weep?" he murmured.

On the 15th he signed an armistice, then re-entered Milan in triumph, half-smothered under the offerings of flowers.

In those brief days when he was reorganizing the Cisalpine Republic, negotiating with the envoy of the new Pope Pius VII, regulating a thousand affairs for France, he fell in love with

La Grassini. With her pure and powerful voice, her instinctive artistry, Giuseppina Grassini was easily the foremost singer in Italy. She was a tall woman, with a fine figure, a swarthy complexion, prominent features and cheeks that were already getting too plump, but she had wonderful, glowing eyes and magnificent hair. Nor was she lacking in wit, though of a somewhat heavy order. She had already had many lovers whom she dropped as the fancy seized her. Besides, true artist that she was, she cared nothing for money except as a means of gambling. Gambling was her great weakness—and she was never to get over it. She had always been a passionate admirer of Bonaparte and had tried unsuccessfully to attract his attention three years before. This time her singing captivated the Consul. Though not a musician, he had a deep love of music and liked to sing himself, particularly in the morning—and always off key. He enjoyed hearing La Grassini practice her songs. It took him out of the world of reality about him and steadied his nerves. She sang for him alone and he listened to her for hours at a time. One evening after a concert shortly before Marengo, she gave herself to him joyfully, ecstatically. The next morning, while she was at breakfast in Bonaparte's bedroom, with Berthier present, it was decided that she should go to Paris. The fourth bulletin of the Army of Italy announced the coming event, mentioning her name among the names of other artists in order not to arouse Josephine's suspicions.

La Grassini did indeed go to Paris. On July 14th, after much heralding and amid great pomp and lavish display, she sang a duet of Méhul's with the tenor Bianchi at the Temple of Mars (the Invalides). For many months she was to continue to be Bonaparte's mistress. Roustan, the Mameluke whom Bonaparte had brought back from Egypt, would admit her secretly at night to the little mezzanine apartment at the Tuileries, a replica of the Consul's official apartment directly above, and she would often remain until morning.

It was not long before Josephine was informed of the affair, for she had numerous and exceedingly clever spies. She moaned and wailed, but in private, where she would not be heard. After all it was only a passing fancy and would not last. And as a matter of fact La Grassini was already beginning to be bored in that house on the rue de la Victoire where Bonaparte had installed her and where he would have liked her to live in seclusion. She found that demand by far too Egyptian—and she proceeded to amuse herself with the violinist Rode. The Consul heard of it and flew into a rage. All of which did not prevent the singer from knocking at Napoleon's door from time to time for many years to come. She was always welcomed and was to receive many generous gifts.

Bonaparte returned from Italy in great haste. Paris gave him a rousing welcome and lighted up in his honor. But for all of that the Consul was worried. The German campaign had got off to a good start. Moreau had won at Hochstaedt and had conquered Bavaria. But negotiations with Austria dragged. On the very day that Desaix fell at Marengo, Kléber had been murdered in Cairo. Bonaparte did not like Kléber, who hated him. But with Kléber gone, who was there to defend Egypt? In Paris the situation had become precarious. Everything depended upon him, upon the safety of his life. And that life was threatened by plots. The Jacobins considered him a traitor. Arena and Ceracchi hatched a plot to assassinate him at the Opéra. They were arrested and executed. After them it was the turn of the Royalists. They had expected that sooner or later Bonaparte would place the crown again on the head of Louis XVI's brother. Even Josephine and Hortense, Royalists at heart, looked forward to a restoration of the monarchy. They did not believe that the new régime would last and they would have liked to see Bonaparte exchange his consular office for a great title conferred by the monarchy. They referred to it constantly and redoubled their entreaties. Bonaparte smiled. He called Hortense his little Vendéan. But in the end he grew annoyed:

"Those devilish women are crazy! They've had their heads turned by the Faubourg Saint-Germain."

At Lucien's suggestion Fontanes had written a pamphlet called "Parallel between Cǎesar, Cromwell, Monk and Bonaparte," in which the Consul was urged to carry out the will of the people and proclaim himself hereditary sovereign. The Royalists, disillusioned, lost patience. Cadoudal had been well provided with money by the English, to say nothing of his receipts from stage-coach robberies in the west of France where the Chouans had resumed their depredations. He now sent several of his henchmen to Paris to do away with Bonaparte. On the 3rd of Nivose, Haydn's *Creation* was being sung at the Opéra. The First Consul was expected to attend. After dinner, however, he sat down by the fire and showed no signs of leaving. Hortense and her mother, who were already dressed, tried to persuade him to go.

"It will be a relaxation for you," Josephine urged. "You work too hard."

Bonaparte closed his eyes and made no reply. In the end he consented to go, and entered his carriage with Berthier, Lannes and Lauriston. Mme. Bonaparte lingered while Rapp arranged her shawl for her, and did not leave till some moments later. At the rue Saint Nicaise the horsemen preceding the Consul found the way barred by a cart loaded with a keg. They shoved it over to the right. César, Bonaparte's coachman, impatient at the delay, whipped up his horses to a gallop. They had not gone more than two hundred yards when the barrel, which was filled with powder and shot, exploded killing twenty people and wounding sixty. Bonaparte's carriage was almost overturned and the panes of glass were shattered. But neither Bonaparte nor any of his escort was injured. Josephine's tardiness saved her. She did not reach the rue Saint Nicaise till after the explosion had occurred.

At the Opéra the rumor spread that a Paris district had just been blown up in an attempt on the Consul's life.

When Bonaparte, absolutely calm, entered his box, the house rose to its feet and greeted him with frenzied cheers. Josephine hurried in after him. Her face was drawn and she was in tears.

"What is the matter with you?" Bonaparte asked her. "What has happened? Why, nothing, nothing at all."

And while the cheers and applause continued all around him,

he listened quietly to Junot's report of the carnage that had
resulted from the attempt.

"How horrible!" he groaned in a sort of despair. "To kill so
many people just because they want to get rid of one man!"

At last he took his seat in the box. The tumult subsided and,
at a gesture from the Consul, the oratorio began. Bonaparte
did not wait for the end. He left the Opéra shortly afterward
and returned to the Tuileries.

So far he had controlled himself, but once at home, his anger
burst its bounds. Not for a second did he doubt that the explosion had been a fresh attempt on the part of the Republicans.
The great drawing-room on the ground floor was crowded with
ministers, generals, officials who had gathered to greet him.
Bonaparte paced swiftly up and down, exclaiming and gestic-
ulating violently:

"It was the Jacobins who tried to assassinate me! It was the
Septembrists, those filthy rascals who are always in open revolt
against every government. If they can't be curbed, they will
have to be crushed! . . ."

His voice, low as a rule but very sonorous, rose to a piercing
note with now and then sudden drops into hoarseness. In those
moments of rage his Corsican accent was very noticeable. Standing before the Consul, Fouché looked straight at him with his
corpselike eyes and announced coldly that it had been a Royalist
plot. Talleyrand, and Roederer in particular, blamed Fouché's
police. Fouché faced the pack. Josephine had been on friendly
terms with him for some time and now rushed hotly to his
defense. Bonaparte did not dare to dismiss him. But he ordered
him to draw up a list of the men to be outlawed—in which a
number of his Jacobin friends would figure. Though this was a
rank injustice, Bonaparte was not to pardon the outlaws when,
a few days later, Fouché triumphantly announced that the in-
ventors of the infernal machine, Cadoudal's agents, the Royalists
Saint-Régent and Carbon, had been arrested. However the
Consul restored Fouché to favor.

He did not trust Fouché as a man, but he valued his services.
No matter what the occasion, Fouché always proved to be far-

sighted, active and subtle. He knew men and he had an extraordinary skill in handling them. Though in power such a short time he had already managed to place many people under obligation to him and to build up a formidable system of espionage.

Talleyrand, the other head of the ministry, treated his colleague with an affectation of hauteur that dissolved into caresses the moment he felt the need of flattering him. A cripple from childhood, embittered because he had been forced to take orders and interested only in his own pleasures and his own profits, that former bishop who had betrayed his God and his king, cherished a profound disdain for mankind—with the exception of himself—though he was the paragon of corruption. A Monarchist by instinct and by education, he was urging Bonaparte to consolidate the dictatorial régime, whereas Fouché would have liked to keep the First Consul in the paths of the Revolution. Though he continued to pursue his own course, Bonaparte accepted their advice—he still had so much to learn—and sometimes followed it. He knew himself to be their superior in will power, in enthusiasm, in a quality of soul that set him apart in an age already rich in personalities, but, in spite of himself he was impressed by those two men and would always be impressed by them. They were both older than he—and that was a potent reason. Moreover he had known them as men of importance, already in high positions at a time when he was still a mere underling. They had given him notable aid on the 18th of Brumaire—had it not been for their connivance the coup d'état would have failed. They had initiated him into the mysteries of government politics. They owed him less perhaps than he owed them; he had not so much chosen them as kept them on—reason enough why he should treat them with consideration, why he should be so long-suffering.

His attitude toward Cambacérès, on the other hand, was altogether different. Cambacérès had also done Bonaparte many services—perhaps not such vital ones—but he had neither the intelligence of a Fouché nor the prestige of a Talleyrand. Flabby of face and of mind, the Second Consul displayed a sensuality that was not far from being a vice. His vanity and his greediness were constant subjects of ridicule. Bonaparte, however, refused to see anything but his good qualities—his discretion, his forethought, his perfect knowledge of law and civil government. Finding him thoroughly loyal, he trusted him completely. At Council Meetings Cambacérès scarcely opened his mouth, but alone with Bonaparte he overcame his shyness and talked freely. His clear, precise thought, his level-headedness, his sense of order, and his instinct for the practical made him the only deep, though secret, influence not only in Bonaparte's political career, but in his private life as well. To the very last Napoleon was always to look upon him as a friend: and in that he was not to be altogether mistaken.

II

Bonaparte and His Family

YIELDING AT LAST, Austria signed the treaty at Lunéville. Now that Bonaparte had given France political peace he was eager to give her a spiritual peace. Accordingly he drew up the Concordat with Cardinal Spina. There could be no social stability, he thought, without religion. Nor any happiness. If man ceased to look up to heaven, he would see only death.

"In every country," he said, "religion is useful to the government. One must use it to influence men. In Egypt I was a Mohammedan, in France I am a Catholic. The religion of a state should be entirely in the hands of the man who governs it. Many people urge me to found a Gallic church and place myself at the head of it. Those people do not know France. I could do that only if the Pope were to drive me to the limit, but I do not think he will."

"You remember, General," Bourrienne retorted, "what Cardinal Consalvi said: 'The Pope will do anything the First Consul wishes'."

"And he would be right. He need not think he is dealing with a fool. Guess what they are bringing up—the salvation of my soul! But to my mind the only immortality is the memory we leave behind us in the minds of men. . . ."

He refused to offer an example by complying with religious practices.

"Don't let them ask any more of me," he said. "They won't get it. They will never make a hypocrite of me."

In that delicate transaction he encountered the disapprobation and irony of a group of his associates. On Easter Sunday, 1802, Bonaparte drove to Notre-Dame with great pomp and ceremony in the carriage that had been used for the coronation of Louis XVI, with the new green and gold livery that he had chosen for the consular household, and the famous diamond, the *Régent,* set in the hilt of his sword, to hear the Te Deum sung in celebration of the signing of his agreement with the Pope. The congregation laughed, joked, talked aloud and even ate with a kind of ostentation that shocked him and caused him to frown several times. Bernadotte, Lannes and Augereau attended the service only on his formal order. When he asked General Delmas, a veteran of the Year II, what he thought of the ceremony, that old soldier replied:

"A fine funeral oration! All that was lacking were the millions of men who have given their lives to destroy what you are building up again!"

Bonaparte turned his back on him. Steeped as he was in the admiration of a people, the obstinate refusal of certain men to bow to his wishes seemed to him actually an offense. On that same occasion he resented the audacity of Mme. Hulot, Moreau's turbulent mother-in-law, who calmly usurped the place reserved for Josephine. For that act of insubordination Bonaparte was always to bear a grudge against her; nor did Moreau, whom he already mistrusted, gain by it.

Any hint of civil or military rivalry found him instantly on the alert. He was determined to remain sole master. On that score his brothers Joseph and Lucien caused him much anxiety. They would have liked to share in the power. Toward Joseph, Napoleon displayed great patience, even offering him the presidency of the Cisalpine Republic. But Joseph wanted more than that—a vice-consulate in France for instance. Napoleon refused, whereupon Joseph retired to Mortefontaine, followed by his friends who formed a sort of court around him.

At Fouché's instigation, Bonaparte removed Lucien from the post of Minister of the Interior after the affair of the "Parallel." Josephine feared above all that her husband might be aiming at a real sovereignty, which would perhaps lead him to divorce her. She seated herself on Napoleon's knees and, fondling his hair, murmured:

"Please, Bonaparte, do not make yourself king. It's that horrid Lucien egging you on. Don't listen to him!"

Bonaparte began to laugh.

"You are crazy, my poor Josephine! You get those tales from your old dowagers and your La Rochefoucauld. . . . Come! You are boring me! Don't bother me!"

Lucien, however, was stirring up trouble. He was talking too much; moreover he had become involved in several questionable deals in his ministry. Bonaparte made up his mind to send him out of the country. But he gilded his exile. Lucien was to be sent to Madrid as ambassador and the régime would close an eye to his methods of enriching himself in his embassy. The final conversation between the two brothers at the Tuileries was painful. When the Consul returned to the drawing-room his face was drained of color. All that evening he wandered restlessly about from one room to the other, unable to keep up a consecutive conversation. Lucien was much better at pretending—affecting a gaiety he did not feel, he asked Josephine and Hortense if they had any commissions for him in Madrid.

Caroline had married Murat. For a time Bonaparte had kept that handsome soldier in a state of semi-disgrace—had he not been too friendly with Josephine? But after Brumaire he had restored him to his favor. Murat was now a major general in command of the Consul's guard.

Caroline was young and lovely and she had been in love with Murat ever since the days at Mombello. Josephine encouraged them. She was looking for allies who might further her interests. But at the general's first formal request, Bonaparte confined himself to saying that he would think it over, and dismissed him.

That marriage did not suit him at all. Murat, he thought, was of much too plain a family. Moreover he was too quick-tempered. A brother-in-law like that might well prove embarrassing. He would have preferred Lannes, or, even better, Duroc.

"I do not like these love matches," he said. "Those young minds aflame listen to nothing but the volcano of imagination. I had other plans in mind. Who knows what sort of a marriage

I might be able to arrange for Caroline? She is a scatterbrained child and has no real conception of my position. A day will come perhaps when kings will sue for her hand. . . . One must let destiny fulfil itself. . . ."

Caroline wept, Josephine urged him to yield. Little by little the Consul's resistance weakened. One evening in his drawing-room, Mme. Bonaparte made a final effort, Hortense, Eugène and Bourrienne lending a hand.

"Murat," said Bonaparte, "is the son of an innkeeper. In the station in life in which fame and fortune have placed me, I cannot mingle his blood with mine. Besides, there is no hurry. I shall see later on."

They tried to show him how wonderful the love of two young people could be. Bourrienne also reminded him of Murat's conduct in Egypt.

"Yes, I admit," said the Consul, stirred by that memory, "Murat was superb at Aboukir!"

In the end he gave in and, in an abrupt reversal of mood, congratulated himself on having made such a decision.

"After all," he remarked to Bourrienne, "Murat and my sister are well matched and then, no one can say that I am proud or that I am looking for important alliances. If I had given my sister to a nobleman, all you Jacobins would have shouted that I was turning anti-Revolutionary. Besides, I am very glad my wife has taken an interest in this marriage—you can readily guess why. . . . Well, as long as that is all settled, I shall hurry things along."

He gave Caroline a dowry of forty thousand francs—the same that he had given Elisa and Pauline—and for a wedding gift presented his sister with a beautiful diamond necklace which he took from Josephine's jewel box, to that lady's lively displeasure. The marriage was celebrated quietly at Joseph's estate, Mortefontaine. Murat beamed, Caroline was radiant. The handsome and happy young couple set up housekeeping in the Brionne mansion.

The Bonaparte family felt no gratitude toward Josephine for

NAPOLEON BONAPARTE
FIRST CONSUL
From the Portrait by Gérard

JOSEPHINE AT MALMAISON
From the Portrait by Prud'hon

her many kindnesses. Daily, fresh quarrels broke out between the two camps. One evening at Mortefontaine as dinner was announced, Joseph offered his arm to his mother to lead her to the place of honor. Bonaparte stepped forward and, taking Josephine's arm, went in ahead of the guests and sat down at the table with his wife at his side. That was a lesson to Joseph, a warning to his family! As the wife of the leader of the Republic Josephine must have the first place everywhere. In the days that followed, the animosity increased. Madame Letizia sulked, his brothers affected icy exteriors, his sisters poked fun at the "Old Girl," as Pauline called her. Flanked by her natural allies, Hortense and Eugène, Josephine still held the upper hand. She lavished subtle attentions on Bonaparte; she was always near him at the proper moment.

But not for a second did she forget that that "position" she was defending so well was in danger. She was always afraid that Bonaparte might be killed in battle or assassinated, or even that he might become infatuated with a new love and, in his anxiety to make sure of his succession, divorce her. Should such a day ever dawn Josephine intended to be provided with a solid fortune, and she made an effort to accumulate large sums. But though she cheated with Bourrienne and with many others in a hundred different ways, she was not successful.

She received huge sums for her influence and intervention, real or supposed, in contracts for provisioning the army and in the restitution of property belonging to émigrés. She borrowed money from Ouvrard, and to Ouvrard giving meant getting something in return—Josephine was seeing him secretly though Bonaparte had forbidden her to do so. From Fouché she received a thousand francs a day for keeping him informed of the Consul's plans and intentions. Fouché, to be sure, checked her reports against those of Bourrienne, to whom he was paying twenty-five thousand francs a month.

But neither the income her husband gave her, nor her clandestine profits were enough for Josephine. She flung money out of the window—for gowns, jewelry, flowers, gambling, for Malmaison, as well as for numerous charities. She could not resist any temptation. She bought everything that was offered —laces, paintings, objets d'art—never asking the price, never stopping to think how she would pay for them. She was threatened with lawsuits—for money was scarce and her credit had run out. Fearing a scandal, Talleyrand made it his business to inform the First Consul. Bonaparte was furious. He despised waste in any form.

"Whether she confesses everything or not," he said to Bourrienne, "I am going to put a stop to it and I do not intend to begin again. But don't pay anything until you show me the bills of all those scoundrels—they are a bunch of crooks."

At first Josephine was delighted, but when she added up the total she was alarmed. Faced with over a million francs in debts she dared not confess to more than half that amount at first. Bonaparte was in funds at the time—he had just received a princely gift from the Senate in Hamburg—and he gave her six hundred thousand francs . . . enough to pay off the tradespeople who had added many fictitious items to their bills. The next day, however, Josephine was just as extravagant as ever. How could she avoid running into debt when she paid four thousand francs for a tulip bulb, owned six hundred gowns and ordered thirty-eight hats in one month only?

Be that as it may Josephine was laying up an important reserve for herself by adding to her collection of jewelry. She adored jewels and no sovereign in Europe ever possessed so many, such rare ones or such a variety. Nothing was too insignificant, nothing too costly, to be added to that collection. She knew that Poncier, the jeweler then in vogue, owned a string of pearls that had belonged to Marie Antoinette. She had him show it to her. It was worth 250,000 francs. Was that all? Josephine did not have even the first sou. She appealed to Berthier. The Minister of War was eager to keep in her good graces. Sniffling and biting his nails, he agreed to liquidate the debts of the hospitals in Italy and such was the gratitude of the creditors that the Queen's pearls soon found their way into Mme. Bonaparte's jewel box.

She was too much a woman to resist the temptation to wear

them on the first occasion. But how could she fool the Consul? He knew all her jewels. Unable to stand it any longer, she appealed to Bourrienne:

"Tomorrow there is to be a large reception. I simply must wear my pearls, but Bonaparte will scold me if he notices anything. I beg you, Bourrienne, do not leave me alone. If he asks me where the pearls came from I shall not hesitate to tell him that I have had them a long time."

As luck would have it Bonaparte did notice the pearls.

"What have you there?" he said to his wife. "You are very beautiful today! What are those pearls? I don't seem to recognize them."

"*Mon Dieu,* you have seen them dozens of times. That is the necklace the Cisalpine Republic gave me. I used to wear them in my hair."

"But it seems to me—"

"If you don't believe me, ask Bourrienne. He will tell you."

Bonaparte turned naïvely to her accomplice:

"Well, Bourrienne, what have you to say about it? Do you remember them?"

"Yes, General, I remember perfectly having seen them before."

Josephine drew a long breath. She was to wear the pearls for one month, then, attracted by another set of jewelry, to relegate them to her dressing table.

For some time she had been toying with the idea of marrying Hortense to one of the Consul's brothers, hoping by that move to strengthen her ties with the Bonaparte family and so make a divorce difficult. At eighteen Hortense was what her teacher, Mme. Campan, called "an accomplished young lady." Tall and slender, with long hands and legs and a graceful carriage, she had inherited the charm of the creoles from her mother. She was more intelligent than Josephine and had had a good education. She could draw, paint, write, sing, dance, play the piano and the harp, all with no real talent it is true, but easily and delightfully. She was affectionate and given to daydreaming, which did not, however, prevent her from enjoying a social life and holding her place gaily in the strangely assorted and brilliant circle in which her stepfather's fortune had placed her. She adored her mother, watched over her and her sense of the fitness of things; her youthful wisdom had often been of material aid to Josephine. Sometimes it almost seemed as if Josephine were her child. Hortense had no idea of her mother's revolutionary past. She thought that she had always been a great lady and that her father was a hero, a martyr. She had always felt that Josephine's second marriage had been a mésalliance . . . and at heart she was not very fond of the Consul. He frightened her with his loud voice, his strict orders, the tears he made her mother shed. She did not understand him, did not appreciate his genius, and she looked upon him as an intruder in their house as well as in the State. She dreamed of a husband who would be a member of the old régime and would bear a fine name. Her choice had fallen on Charles de Gontaut. But the young man's family disapproved of the idyl and packed him off to England. Hortense managed to survive. A few months later she fell in love with Duroc.

Duroc was twenty-eight years old, a handsome, well-built young man of good birth and the most polished manners. She liked his boyish earnestness and his frankness. He was the Consul's favorite aide-de-camp, his particular friend, and devoted to him body and soul. Hortense made repeated advances to the young man and he met her half way, though always with some reserve. Soon they were writing to each other. Bonaparte would gladly have given them his blessing, but Josephine was opposed to the match. Hortense struggled a little, then quickly wearied. She would take the husband her mother chose for her.

Josephine had thought at first of Jerome. But Jerome was frankly a bad lot and moreover he was too young. In any event the First Consul decided to make a sailor of him and shipped him off under Villaret-Joyeuse on the expedition to San Domingo. Josephine then turned her attention to Lucien, whose wife, poor Christine Boyer, had died the year before. Lucien had recently come back from Madrid, where he had lined his pockets at the expense of Spain. He had brought back paintings, diamonds and cash to the tune of millions. Josephine had always considered Lucien her principal enemy. Had he not offered Napoleon the hand of an Infanta during his embassy in Spain? The Consul had laughed about it with Volney:

"If I were free to marry again I would not go looking for a wife in a house that is about to collapse."

With his customary lack of discretion Napoleon told Josephine about that proposal. It did not tend to make her love Lucien any the more, but she found in it a new reason for trying to win him over. As soon as he arrived in Paris, she invited him to call and pushed Hortense into the limelight. Nothing definite—she was too subtle for that—but Lucien knew how to take a hint. By the same token he gave her to understand that he had no intention of marrying again—at least not in that direction.

That left only one of Bonaparte's brothers—Louis. Louis was now a colonel, and the Consul still considered him his favorite brother. Napoleon thought that if he needed an heir to carry on his great plan, no one could be better fitted to take his place some day than Louis, whom he had molded with his own hands.

Josephine urged him to make his intentions public, and she sang the young man's praises to her friends.

"Louis is a splendid fellow. Though there were some things I did not like when Bonaparte was away, I cannot help admiring him. He has a kind heart, a fine mind. He is very serious and is always improving himself. He loves Bonaparte the way a man loves his mistress."

Then she sounded out the Consul on the question of marriage. At first he was opposed. He had a deep affection for Hortense—but a purely paternal affection. The accusations brought against Napoleon by numerous pamphlets of having corrupted his stepdaughter are outrageous libels. As a Corsican and a home lover he had too strong a sense of family ever to dream of taking advantage of a young girl for whom he had assumed responsibility. He wanted her to have a good husband and he intended to give her one. Could Louis make her happy? He doubted it. Ever since the unfortunate experience in Milan his young brother's character had undergone a change. He had grown sensitive, peevish. As a matter of fact Louis did not show the slightest interest in Hortense. He had wanted to marry Émilie de Beauharnais, who had become the wife of Lavallette, and he could not forget her. Hortense, for her part, had small liking for Louis.

Some time passed. Louis went to Portugal, then to Barèges, where he nursed what was euphemistically spoken of as rheumatism. However Josephine was not idle. Little by little Bonaparte's prejudices were worn down. And when Louis returned to Paris in the autumn of 1801, relations between the two young people took a different turn. Though he was not in love with her, Louis found Hortense agreeable and quite charming. Lucien tried in vain to warn him—Louis liked the girl. Yielding to her mother's pleas, Hortense met him halfway. He was not a bad-looking young man—he had the beautiful eyes and the charming smile of the Bonapartes and he was a good conversationalist. They had a long talk one evening at a ball at Malmaison and shortly afterward, following an interview with his brother and Josephine, Louis came to the point. However, the First Consul must have regretted his move, for he promptly ordered Bourrienne to speak to Duroc.

"I should like him to marry Hortense. But see that he does it right away. I will give him five hundred thousand francs and make him commander of the Eighth Division. The day after the wedding he is to leave for Toulon with his wife and we shall live apart. I do not want any son-in-law around my house. Let me know this evening whether that is agreeable to him."

How did Bourrienne, that perfidious friend, acquit himself of his mission? He was jealous of Duroc's prestige and, though married himself, he had sighed for Hortense. There can be no doubt that he represented the Consul's invitation as a command. Duroc's pride was hurt.

"Let him keep his daughter," he cried, picking up his hat. "I'm off to see the wh——s."

Bourrienne ran to tell Bonaparte. That same evening, to her

great delight, Josephine was ordered to make everything ready for the marriage with Louis.

That marriage was celebrated on the evening of January 4, 1802 in the state apartments at the Tuileries. Hortense, very sad and fearing that her voice might tremble, pronounced her "yes" in too loud a tone. The consular family then adjourned to the little house on the rue de la Victoire, which Bonaparte had made over to the young couple. There, in the drawing-room on the ground floor, which had been transformed into a chapel, Hortense and Louis were married by Cardinal Caprara. At the end of the ceremony, Murat stepped up to the prelate and asked him to bless his union with Caroline, which had been merely a civil ceremony. Bonaparte had approved of Murat's request. But, in spite of Josephine's reiterated pleas and her tears, he had refused to have their own marriage consecrated by the Church. Was that his way of leaving the door open to divorce? Perhaps, but he was more particularly anxious not to give his soldiers the impression that he had "gone Church."

Though Bonaparte was so jealous of power that the slightest infringement threw him into a rage, he was curiously indifferent to money. He needed money and a great deal of it—in the Year X his expenditures were over twelve million, derived from public and concealed sources. He never saved a sou. He allowed his family and those friends whom he considered faithful to him to amass enormous fortunes, even helping them lavishly. The Bonapartes were the first to be provided for. Though Napoleon exceeded his usual extravagance in his gifts to his mother, Letizia could not forget those sudden reversals of fortune she had known in her youth. Provident soul that she was, she divided her money, investing it in various places, determined that if her luck should change, she would at least always have enough for a rainy day. Though she lived with her half-brother, Fesch, a sly, presumptuous chatterbox, in the house he had purchased on the rue du Mont-Blanc, she considered herself, if not the head, at least the heart of the family, exercised a firm control over her children and kept the family united. Lucien was her favorite and she defended him against Josephine and against Fouché. In spite of her sudden rise to fortune, her life was simple and dignified. She had lost none of her old-fashioned ideas, neither her sympathies nor her enmities, and she forced Napoleon and his ministers to find good posts for all her relatives and all her protégés from Corsica.

Joseph lived like a prince in the Marbeuf mansion in Paris and at Mortefontaine flinging money about with reckless extravagance—the many treaties Napoleon had allowed him to sign had lined his pockets. He persisted stubbornly in calling himself the head of the Bonaparte clan, and as such demanded full honors and perquisites. Lucien had purchased the Brionne mansion and was furnishing it and plastering the walls with old masters. He had consoled himself with a Marquise de Santa-Cruz whom he had brought back from Madrid. But he was soon to meet the widow of a bankrupt financier, Alexandrine Jouberthou, with whom he fell so madly in love that he took her to live with him and permitted her to do the honors of his house. The lady became pregnant: after the birth of their child, Lucien married her before a priest. At that very moment Napoleon offered him the Queen of Etruria, an ugly, misshapen dwarf, as a wife. Lucien refused. The Consul seems not to have held that refusal against him, for he made Lucien a senator like Joseph and even thought of appointing him governor of the Low Countries, with the rank of Archduke.

However, the two brothers were soon to clash—and seriously. Lucien had his marriage regularized before the civil authorities. Napoleon was furious.

"Lucien has married his slut!" he exclaimed.

He had hoped at least to keep the marriage secret. Lucien defied him, introducing his wife to the family while the Consul was absent on a journey to Boulogne. On hearing of this, Bonaparte flew into a towering rage, and in Josephine's presence accused Caroline and Hortense "of having given the name of sister to a woman who is not worthy of it."

"What!" he cried, not glancing in their direction as he paced feverishly back and forth in the drawing-room, "I try to restore morals and I have a woman like that brought into the family! I am the head of a nation and accountable not only for my actions but for the example I set. . . . The French are a moral people. Their leaders must be moral too. I have obligations and I mean to fulfil them. The man who does not go along with me is against me."

Lucien left Paris in a rage and returned to Italy. "I am leaving," he wrote to Joseph, "with hatred in my heart." Madame Letizia took up the cudgels for him and joined him in Rome.

Elisa continued to befriend Lucien, and in this she showed not a little courage. Her husband, Bacciocchi, was something of a fool, but Elisa was a woman of brains, intelligent, resolute, with an eye to her own interests. Though she was the least charming of the Consul's sisters, she had nevertheless the Bonaparte air of distinction, their regular features, black eyes and beautiful teeth. Moreover Elisa had much common sense. She had taken Fontanes as her lover, a pedantic man, a verbose flatterer, who was already in favor with the Consul. Elisa went to great lengths to further his career. Napoleon gave her large sums of money; and through his lavish gifts, she was able to buy the Maurepas mansion where she held a literary salon. She was also the patron of Chateaubriand whose *Génie du Christianisme*, published through official backing, had already distinguished him as the foremost writer of the day.

Pauline, or as her sisters called her, Paulette, had accompanied her husband, the courteous Leclerc to San Domingo. Yellow fever had decimated the army on the island, but in spite of danger and increasing difficulties Pauline had behaved magnificently. At a time when death was knocking at every door she gave balls and gathered up in her carriage wounded soldiers or people who had been stricken with the fever. Leclerc wanted to send her home, but she would not leave. The other Frenchwomen gathered around her and implored her to sail with them.

"You are afraid," she told them proudly. "But I am Bonaparte's sister. I am not afraid of anything."

When at last Leclerc came down with the fever in his turn and died, Paulette a widow and in poor health, returned to France on the *Swiftsure*, bringing with her her son, Dermide, and her husband's coffin strewn with her beautiful hair which she had cut off in her distracted grief. The First Consul welcomed her tenderly and did his utmost to distract and cheer her. She cheered up all too quickly. It was not long before she had bought the beautiful Charost mansion in the Faubourg Saint-Honoré and was having a wonderful time furnishing it. The beaux and dandies of the day were soon hovering around her, Decrès, the fat Minister of the Navy, entering the lists as a suitor for her hand. Bonaparte, however, would have none but the best for his sister. He thought of marrying her to Melzi d'Eril, Vice-President of the Republic in Italy. When Melzi hedged, Napoleon cast his eye on young Prince Camillo Borghese, owner of the largest fortune in Italy. Delighted to become a princess, Paulette accepted that handsome youth and married him at the end of her period of mourning. The First Consul gave her a dowry of eight hundred thousand francs.

Caroline and Murat, who owed their marriage to Josephine's intervention, at first remained close friends with the Creole and were assiduous in their attentions. Caroline was with Josephine on the evening of the attempted assassination on the rue Saint Nicaise. But after the birth of her first son, Achille, she joined Murat in Italy, where he had become commanding general. Intoxicated by his good luck, Murat treated the Italians with a high hand and took good care to line his pockets. With his income—both public and concealed—he bought the Thelusson mansion on the rue de Provence and enlarged his estate at Neuilly. He already had his eye on a vice-regency in Italy, but Napoleon was deaf to that appeal. However, Caroline was so attentive, she flattered her brother so charmingly that the First Consul finally gave Murat a post of the highest importance—the military governorship of Paris. Junot had previously held that position but had handled it so poorly that Napoleon had been obliged to remove him. The Murats lived on a magnificent scale: dinners, balls, concerts galore. The good Italian money flowed like a raging torrent. They were said to have the finest table and perhaps the gayest house in all Paris.

For ten years Fesch had been leading an almost scandalously worldly life, but now that the Concordat had been signed, he suddenly remembered that he was a priest. By dint of systematically robbing Church property in Corsica and buying and selling paintings in Italy he had amassed a fortune of a magnitude even beyond the suspicions of his nephew. Why should he not take orders again? That would be right in line with the wishes of the Consul, who detested unfrocked priests. The erstwhile vicar-general of Ajaccio was promptly showered with an avalanche of the highest ecclesiastical dignities: Archbishop of Lyons, primate of Gaul. Six months after he had been made cardinal, Bonaparte sent him to Rome as ambassador—an impossible choice even though Chateaubriand went along as his secretary. The Consul was blind to Fesch's faults. He should have known the man's ignorance, his base cupidity, his covert jealousy. But Fesch was one of his clan: that was enough. He believed that he was loyal and, not content with heaping honors upon him, he even put him in a position of responsibility.

With Jerome, the last born of his brothers and his favorite as a boy, Bonaparte suffered the keenest disillusionments. After returning from a cruise to San Domingo the flighty, extravagant but good-hearted youth led such a wild life that the First Consul shipped him off again to the Antilles.

"Now that you are an ensign," he wrote to him, "I cannot wait to know that you are on your ship on the high seas, following a profession which ought to be your path to glory. Were you to die young, I would be comforted, but not if you lived for sixty years, without making a name for yourself, useless to your country and having done nothing worth while. To live that way is not to have lived at all."

Those proud words had no effect on Jerome. He had no intention of dying—though he was brave enough for that matter— but he meant to have a good time first. All his life was to be one long quest for pleasure. He was bored on his ship, left his brig and went to the United States where, in Baltimore he fell in love with a pretty girl, Elizabeth Patterson, and married her. At that deliberate defiance, Napoleon broke off all relations with his brother, and cast the rebel out of the family. Madame Letizia and Lucien pleaded in vain for Jerome. If that young man did not obey his orders, Napoleon would refuse to see him again. Jerome was to obey in the end—but not for some time.

Bonaparte found more satisfaction in his stepson, Eugène, a cheerful, good-natured young man, now a colonel of the Guides. Eugène had been with him in all his campaigns, and with Bessières and Duroc was his constant companion. Toward his stepfather he was invariably respectful and discreet. He would never be a man of the first water, being essentially subservient in type—one of the reasons why Bonaparte liked him. The First Consul was to lavish favors on his stepson all the more generously because, of all the family, he was the one who asked the least.

In October, 1802, the Consul had to make up his mind to part with Bourrienne. His personal secretary had overstepped in his graft in army contracts. Bonaparte's patience was exhausted. He sent the swindler packing and replaced him by Méneval, a thin, sickly young man whom Joseph had recommended. That change was difficult for him.

"The First Consul," Méneval wrote to his predecessor, "was extremely sad last evening. He kept repeating: 'See how unhappy I am! I have known that man since I was nine years old.' . . . He went to bed with a heavy heart."

In Bourrienne, Josephine lost a very useful accomplice. Failing to have him reinstated in the First Consul's cabinet, she managed to obtain the post of Minister to Hamburg for him. And though Bourrienne continued his depredations, Napoleon closed an eye to his thefts—doubtless in memory of their days together at Brienne.

III

Revelry

NO SOONER WAS Mme. Bonaparte reassured about La Grassini than she began to suffer fresh anxieties. The Consul's familiarity with Laure Junot—easily comprehensible since he had known her as a child—gave Josephine cause for worry. To tell the truth, in the free and easy atmosphere of Malmaison that friendship had taken a somewhat equivocal turn. Mme. Junot was not beautiful: her skin was almost swarthy in contrast to the light gowns she wore, and her large nose and piercing eyes gave her somewhat the appearance of a bird. But she was young, sprightly and sparkling with animation. Beside her Mme. Bonaparte suddenly realized that she was growing old. Moreover Napoleon sometimes bullied his wife; he accused her in public of using too much rouge and powder, called her Countess Escarbagnas, [after the Molière comedy on snobs] annoyed her by shooting her ducks and swans as they swam in the pools, or clipped off rare blooms in her conservatories. At times he exhibited an almost childish mania for destruction. He would tease her roughly or openly express his regret at not having a child. Once when a couple of generals were present at luncheon, he offered to arrange a hunt for them in the park.

"A hunt at this moment!" cried Josephine. "You can't be thinking of such a thing, Bonaparte. All our animals are with young."

Bonaparte gave a bitter laugh. Turning to his guests he remarked crudely:

"Well, we shall have to give it up. Everything is prolific on this place, except Madame."

To enlarge Malmaison, of which he grew fonder daily, he purchased the Butard woods. The day after the sale he invited his wife to go with him to see the charming pavilion that had been built for Mme. de Pompadour. Josephine was suffering from a headache. She excused herself saying she would rather rest and sleep.

"Oh, come on! Come with us!" Bonaparte urged: "The air will do you good. It is a sovereign remedy for all ills."

Josephine did not dare to refuse again. She called for her hat and shawl and, with Mme. Junot, entered the barouche, which was driven by four horses. Bonaparte set out on horseback. He was in excellent spirits and galloped ahead, then dashed back to the carriage. Leaning down at the door he seized Josephine's hand, pressed it tenderly and was off again.

Mme. Bonaparte disliked driving—she was always timid. This time she was really ill, and she closed her eyes to shut out the sight of obstacles along the road. When they came to a steep bank over a stream, the postilion hesitated. Josephine took fright.

"I do not want to go to Butard by that road," she told the groom. And she ordered them to turn around.

Bonaparte galloped back to the barouche.

"What new whim is this?" he cried. Then, bringing his whip down on the postilion's shoulder, he ordered: "Go back the same way you came."

He himself rode to the stream, dismounted and waited for the carriage to come up.

"A good spurt," he said to the postilion, "then give them their heads and you will make it."

Josephine uttered a piercing shriek.

"Let me out! Bonaparte, for pity's sake, let me out!"

She clasped her hands and began to weep. The Consul shrugged his shoulders.

"That is pure childishness. You are going to cross—and in the barouche. Come!" he shouted at the postilion. "Didn't you hear me?"

Mme. Junot felt sorry for Mme. Bonaparte. Besides, she herself was pregnant, and she went to the rescue with her usual self-assurance.

"General," she cried, "I am responsible for the life of another. I cannot remain here. The jolt will be violent and might do me harm. You don't want to kill me, do you, General?"

"You are right. Get out!"

He held out his hand to her. The moment Mme. Junot had jumped down, he ordered:

"Pull up the steps and take the barouche over!"

"General! Mme. Bonaparte is ill. She has a fever. I implore you, let her get out."

He gave her a withering glance:

"Mme. Junot, I could never brook reproof even as a child. You can ask Signora Letizia. . . . Well, come along now! Let me help you across this terrifying river, this alarming precipice!"

With Bonaparte holding her arm, Mme. Junot crossed the stream on a few stepping stones. Bonaparte saw that the barouche in which Josephine sat, pale and trembling, had not moved. He brought his whip down on the postilion's back in a stinging blow.

"Well, fellow! Are you going to do as I say or aren't you?"

The postilion whipped up his horses. Lurching violently, the carriage crossed the stream. Josephine's eyes were red from weeping, her complexion was badly streaked. She felt so disheveled that she wrapped herself in her tulle veil and sobbed all the way to Butard. Bonaparte approached to help her out of the carriage. He was angry at himself and that anger increased as Josephine ventured to rebuke him for the kindness he had shown Mme. Junot.

"You are a silly little thing!" he scolded. "You know how I hate all those ridiculous jealousies. Come, kiss me and be quiet. You are very ugly when you cry. . . . I've already told you that."

Was there anything but friendship between the Consul and Mme. Junot? When she was alone at Malmaison, Bonaparte would wake her at five in the morning. Settling himself on the foot of her bed he would gossip with her and pinch her toes through the bedclothes. One morning he surprised her with Junot—who was supposed to be on duty in Paris and had come to Malmaison secretly and without permission.

"But, my God! General!" exclaimed that naïve soldier. "What are you doing in our wives' rooms at such an hour as this?"

The First Consul turned it off with an amusing jest and managed to extricate himself from the predicament. Junot was not punished for his escapade—perhaps Bonaparte had his own reasons for handling the young husband with gloves. However that intimacy was of brief duration. Mme. Junot returned to Paris and shortly afterward went to live in a country house at Bièvres, which the Junots bought with money the Consul had given them. After that, Josephine was always very friendly to her. She knew that she had nothing more to fear from that quarter.

She was to have much more reason to worry when, a little later, Bonaparte met Mlle. George, the young actress at the Théâtre-Français.

The theatre had always held a fascination for him. He was a southerner, from the shores of the Mediterranean—therefore a born actor, a talent that power and politics had helped to perfect. The stage was familiar ground to him. He did not care much for comedy, and Molière's philosophy was foreign to his temperament.

"He placed his characters in a setting where I would never have thought of going to see them in action," he said.

Marivaux's plays bored him. Beaumarchais irritated him—he thought him dangerous. He disliked irony, for he himself took everything seriously. Still a country lad at heart he mistrusted the wit of Paris, misunderstood its clash of words, its allusions that only men of versatile mind with a turn for satire could find amusing. As for farce, he despised it. To him the drama was a hybrid form of art—as a good mathematician he appreciated only clear-cut, definite forms. Like all the men of his day he worshipped tragedy. Its precise design, the cadence of the alexandrines, satisfied his craving for order and grandeur. That, he felt, was the plane on which he moved: it was an art worthy of him. Moreover he attached a moral value to it.

"Tragedy," he said one evening at Saint-Cloud, "should be

LOUIS BONAPARTE
KING OF HOLLAND
From the Portrait by Gérard

MLLE. GEORGE
After the Portrait by Champagne

rated higher even than history. . . . One need not be a poet to appreciate it. It is enough to know men and affairs, to have a certain highmindedness, to be a statesman. Tragedy warms the soul, lifts the heart. It can and should beget heroes."

He preferred Corneille to Racine though he invited Talma to give several performanecs of *Esther* and *Athalie* at Malmaison. But *The Cid, The Horaces, The Death of Pompey, Cinna* in particular, all swept him off his feet. He never tired of seeing them and always enjoyed them thoroughly each time. Corneille, he once told Mme. de Rémusat, had a flair for politics.

"Not very long ago I came to understand the ending of *Cinna*. At first I saw in it only a means of making the fifth act pathetic. However, clemency in and for itself is such a petty and miserable virtue when there is no policy behind it that the clemency of August, who suddenly turned into a gay young prince, did not strike me as a worthy ending for that beautiful tragedy. But I once heard Monvel speak the 'Let us be friends, Cinna,' in so suave, so wily a tone that I realized instantly that that gesture was merely the clever ruse of a tyrant and I approved as policy what I had found childish as sentiment. That line should always be spoken in such a way that of all who hear it Cinna is the only one to be misled."

He first noticed Mlle. George in *Iphigénie*. She was sixteen, but looked older, a tall, big-boned woman, with a classic beauty, a trifle cold and perhaps more imposing than charming.

The child of actors, she had played small rôles on provincial stages where her father was a director. The celebrated Raucourt heard her at Amiens, took her to Paris, gave her lessons and sponsored her début at fifteen, in the rôle of Clytemnestra at the Comédie-Française. Notwithstanding the intrigue worked up against her by the friends of Mlle. Duchesnois, Mlle. George scored a real triumph. Then, suddenly, she became the fashion. She was Lucien's mistress—and afterwards the mistress of a great Polish lord, Prince Sapieha.

Her sculptural form, built for tragic rôles, attracted Bonaparte's eye—unfortunately Mlle. George had big hands and feet which he dubbed *abatis canailles*. He sent Constant, his valet, to invite the actress to Saint-Cloud. The Consul talked with her, joked a little and made her tell him about her début. He forbade her to see the Prince again. With a sudden movement he ripped off the lace scarf that Sapieha had given her and trampled it under foot. The next day, at crack of dawn, he replaced it with an English scarf which Constant, most indiscreetly, stole from Josephine's wardrobe.

Informed at once of the situation Mme. Bonaparte at first tried to control herself. It would be just another affair like La Grassini, she thought. But soon Bonaparte's interest in Mlle. George went beyond caprice—he began to receive her two or three times a week at the Tuileries. They would often sit side by side in front of the fire, clad in the scantiest of attire, while he made her recount the latest news of the theatre or the gossip of the town. Her chatter amused him and he would laugh heartily. He called her Georgina, addressed her by the familiar *tu* and teased her unmercifully. The young woman's simple manner called forth the natural hoyden in him. But Mlle. George gave him back as boldly as he gave. When he pinched her or pulled her hair, she would run after him and chase him into the library. He would take refuge on the ladder that stood by the bookshelves and she would roll it the entire length of the room with Bonaparte clinging to it, almost falling, and shouting:

"You are going to hurt me! Stop, or I'll get angry!"

One day she appeared with a garland of white roses in her hair. Bonaparte put it on his own head.

"See, Georgina," he said, "how pretty I look in your crown! Just like a fly in the milk!"

He liked to sing the duet from *La Fausse Magie* with her— and heaven only knew how badly he could sing:

Vous souvient-il de cette fête
Où l'on voulut nous voir danser . . .

and he would caper about the room.

"Bonaparte's love was sweet," Mlle. George was to write later.

"He was never licentious." For her he was all devotion, all subtle kindness. One morning as he was walking with her in the woods at Saint-Cloud, he noticed that the young woman's light satin slippers were scratched by the leaves and twigs that covered the path. Bonaparte stooped and brushed the twigs away.

"I do not want you to hurt yourself," he explained smiling.

He became dependent on her, formed a real friendship for her. With her he could relax from the demands of power. She was restful—and she asked nothing in return. She herself was amazed at Bonaparte's generosity. He would sometimes press a thick roll of bank notes into her hands. She would take them, for she was a spendthrift. But her devotion was genuine. She admired the Consul; she loved the man.

In the end Josephine took fright, even going so far as to venture a few reproaches, to make a few scenes. She accused Napoleon and bewailed her lot. He tried to reassure her—but without success.

Unfaithful though Bonaparte was, it was undoubtedly less from natural inclination than because his wife had disappointed him in the first days of their marriage, because she had begun to age and he worshipped youth and beauty. Also all the men around him, everyone he knew, had a mistress, every woman had a lover. With the exception of Madame Letizia, who was always beyond reproach, and Louis, isolated by health as well as by temperament, everyone even in his own family was fickle, everyone carried on intrigues, everyone took his pleasures where he found them. Those Bonapartes were a hot-blooded lot like their father. Joseph neglected Julie for passing fancies without number. Lucien had love affair after love affair on the side. Elisa betrayed Fontanes constantly. Caroline was to have Junot as a lover, then Metternich, and many others. Paulette snatched up all the handsome men who came within her reach, in a frenzy that was to exhaust her and ruin her brilliant complexion. Was Bonaparte unfaithful? Yes, he too was unfaithful like all the others. "That has no importance," he was wont to say. Why should he stand on ceremony, a man surrounded by temptations, wooed by so many lovely eyes?

Josephine feared that one of those loves might gain a lasting hold and that she might be relegated to second place. Particularly if a child were to be born! That fear was constantly in her mind and she suffered the greatest anguish. Bonaparte had so often reproached her for the sterility of their marriage. She had enlisted Corvisart's aid—he was devoted to her interests—and in the end had managed to convince Bonaparte by a clever trick that that sterility was his fault. After all, had she not already given birth to two children? True, as a creole she might have reached the menopause at an early age, as Elisa and Pauline were always pointing out. But Corvisart gave her a drug that brought on her periods again. Beaming with delight, Bonaparte announced that fact one morning to his secretary. And for a time his hopes rose.

He still shared the same bed with Josephine. It was better for the Consul's personal safety, she insisted. She herself was a light sleeper and should an intruder enter the room, she could call for help. But on the nights when he received Mlle. George, Bonaparte did not go down to Josephine's apartments till very late. One evening she was left alone in her salon with her lady-in-waiting, Mme. de Rémusat. For some time she had made a confidante of Mme. de Rémusat—rather imprudently. But Josephine's suspicions had been aroused and in her anxiety she was almost beside herself. Bonaparte did not appear, sending word that he had to work. She did not believe him. She knew that he was with his actress in that private apartment he had forbidden her to enter. Finally she could not stand it any longer.

"Mlle. George is upstairs," she cried, "I am going to take them by surprise."

Mme. de Rémusat was afraid of a scene. She tried to dissuade her, but Josephine persisted stubbornly.

"Follow me," she ordered. "We will go up together."

The lady-in-waiting tried to get out of it. That sort of spying

was bad taste, she urged. If she stooped to that, Bonaparte's
wrath would rebound on her. Josephine would not listen to
reason. She accused Mme. de Rémusat of deserting her in her
hour of trouble and pleaded so wildly that the lady-in-waiting
finally gave in. One behind the other they climbed the dark
stairs that led to the Consul's apartment, Josephine in front, her
friend behind holding a candle. Before they reached the landing
they heard a noise. Mme. Bonaparte turned back, pale with
fright.

"It may be Roustan," she whispered. "Bonaparte's Mameluke. That villian is capable of choking us both!"

Pretending to be terrified, Mme. de Rémusat escaped, carrying
off the light with her, and returned to the drawing-room on a
run. Josephine followed, stumbling along in the dark. When
they were both in the large lighted room again, the two women
looked at each other's startled faces and burst into peals of
laughter.

In those moments of jealous panic Josephine lost all power of
reasoning. She lied, she heaped insults on her rival—a poor
defense against the danger that threatened. She insinuated that
Paulette was the Consul's mistress, and Caroline too without
a doubt. She had never been noted for decorum and she now
lost all trace of dignity: she supported the Royalists and stooped
to cheap slander, sparing no one, not excepting Madame Letizia,
even going so far as to say that "everyone knows that Bonaparte
is Marbeuf's son."

Shortly after that Bonaparte began to allow longer intervals
to elapse between Mlle. George's visits—perhaps to avoid giving
Josephine cause for grief, perhaps also to avoid becoming too
much involved himself. However, Mlle. George appeared at
the Tuileries or at Saint-Cloud just as frequently as in the past,
and was to receive valuable gifts from the Emperor up until
1808. That year she left Paris suddenly for Russia, saying that
she was going to marry Count Benckendorff. Rumor had it,
however—though proof is lacking—that she went there expressly
on Napoleon's order to captivate Czar Alexander and supplant

the current favorite, Mme. Narishkine, who was hostile to
France. In any event Mlle. George did not appear at the
Comédie-Française again until 1812.

Did Bonaparte fall in love with other actresses after Mlle.
George? He always denied it. Mme. Branchu, a singer of no
great beauty, but very fascinating, was said to have been one of
his loves. As for Mlle. Duchesnois, Mlle. George's rival, her story
is well known. That tragedienne had deep, soft eyes, a charming
figure, a musical voice, and an air of gentle sadness combined
with a delicious wit. Many people considered her ugly. Bonaparte sent for her. She was late and he began to work, as usual
becoming so interested in the task at hand that he forgot everything else. Constant knocked at his door and murmured:

"Mlle. Duchesnois is here."

"Tell her to wait. . . ."

And he bent over his reports again. An hour passed. The
actress began to grow restless. Constant half opened the door.

"Tell her to take off her clothes!"

Mlle. Duchesnois was ushered into the First Consul's bedroom, where she undressed and got into bed. Sometime later
Constant again ventured to disturb his master. Dawn was just
breaking. Bonaparte raised his head in surprise.

"Tell her to go away," he said.

And he did not leave his desk.

With Mlle. Bourgoing, it was a more serious matter. That
charming actress bubbled with gaiety. Her loud speech and
salty wit belied her big, innocent eyes. She was Chaptal's official
mistress, and the Minister of the Interior, who was beginning to
age, believed implicitly in her virtue. One evening as he sat
working with Chaptal, Bonaparte sent for Mlle. Bourgoing.
She arrived and was announced—and not secretly. Chaptal,
raging, picked up his papers and left. The moment he reached
home he sent in his resignation.

Did Bonaparte merely wish to open Chaptal's eyes? In any
event he did not detain Mlle. Bourgoing—and the actress never
forgave him. She declared open war on him and on her tours in

France and throughout Europe was unremitting in spreading all the unfortunate gossip, the epigrams, the harsh words that might insult or compromise the Consul and later the Emperor. He himself felt a strong aversion to her—and he was to give proof of that dislike later at Erfurt.

IV

The Emperor

THE PEACE OF AMIENS was broken as the result of misunderstanding and bad faith on both sides. Without stopping to declare war, the British fleet put an embargo on French ships. In reprisal Bonaparte arrested all the English in France and again began to consider the idea of fighting his mighty enemy on their own soil. In November, 1803, he assembled ships and regiments at Boulogne and inspected them, accompanied only by his aides-de-camp and by a palace chamberlain, Rémusat.

Rémusat fell ill and his wife hastened to Pont-de-Briques, a village where the First Consul had established his headquarters, to nurse him. As soon as he learned of Mme. de Rémusat's arrival, Bonaparte sent for her. She was a young and fairly pretty woman, with a lively and cultivated mind. He was a little mistrustful of her, but she was one of the consular household and, in moments of disagreement, had often acted as mediator between him and Josephine. With a winning smile he invited her to lunch and dine every day at his table.

"I have to keep an eye on a pretty young woman like you let loose in the midst of so many soldiers," he said laughing.

Sitting in that little room from where he could look across at Dover through his glasses, he talked to her of Josephine and of her annoying jealousy.

"Josephine worries much more than is necessary. She is always afraid I shall fall seriously in love. Doesn't she know that love is not for me? What is love anyway? A passion that thrusts the whole world to one side and looks only at the beloved. It is certainly not my temperament to cut myself off from others to that extent."

In the beginning Mme. de Rémusat was rather reserved. But

she soon thawed under the influence of their many tête-à-têtes. Bonaparte often confided in her: he liked to talk of his youth, to analyze his temperament, explaining that he was a dreamer and inclined toward melancholy. For her benefit he recalled the highlights of his career: Toulon, Vendémiaire, Italy, Egypt. In his opinion the Egyptian memories effaced all others.

"The time I spent there was the most beautiful in my life, for it was the most ideal."

On other days he would talk of literature, of which he spoke with an air of good-natured authority.

"Perhaps it is my fault, but there are some rules I cannot grasp at all. For example, I never notice what people call style, either good or bad. What strikes me most is the vigor of the thought. I liked *Ossian* from the first, but for the same reason that I like to hear the murmuring of wind and waves...."

Those conversations between that man of thirty and that young woman of twenty-two may perhaps have taken another turn. Mme. de Rémusat was always to deny it. But at Boulogne the General Staff had a good laugh at those secret meetings that took place under the very nose of the convalescent husband.

In the midst of so many activities Bonaparte still found time to write affectionate letters to Josephine. She replied and on a note that shows how much her feeling for him had changed in those last years:

"How grateful I am to you for giving so much time to your Josephine! . . . A letter is the portrait of the soul and I press yours against my heart. It did me so much good! I shall keep it always. It will be my consolation when you are away, my guide when you are near, for in your eyes I would always be your good, your loving Josephine who thinks of your happiness only. . . ."

The Consul returned to Paris. And so did Mme. de Rémusat. Josephine must have got wind of the affair. She looked anything but pleased to see her lady-in-waiting and even went so far as to complain to Bonaparte. He was annoyed and took delight in

leaving her in uncertainty. But those anxieties were soon forgotten in the press of greater worries. There was talk of nothing
but plots. Popular as the régime was in France, it was still at the
mercy of a violent attack. Fouché had lost his ministry but had
kept his spies. He warned the First Consul that "the air is full
of daggers." Royalists, Jacobins, disgruntled generals banded
together against that new monarchy which everybody felt was
in the offing.

English gold was to turn that restless excitement into concrete
action. Alarmed by the preparations at Boulogne, the British
Cabinet thought it expedient to get rid of the Consul. In
London, the Royalists Cadoudal and Pichegru equipped a small
force that was to fall upon him on the Malmaison Road. They
won over to their side—or thought they had won over—Moreau
who, if he should come to power in Bonaparte's place, would
prepare the way for the return of the Bourbons. Réal, as chief
of the consular police, got wind of the affair and arrested several
of Cadoudal's less important accomplices. They turned State's
evidence and disclosed the whole plot.

Bonaparte realized fully the gravity of the situation. After
a sleepless night in his study, he resolved to have Moreau arrested. The next morning Mme. de Rémusat found the First
Consul with Josephine. He was sitting beside the fireplace
dandling little Napoleon, the first child of Hortense and Louis,
on his knees. Eager to judge the effect it would make on the
public, he announced his decision. Mme. de Rémusat gasped.

"It will stir up a fine row," said Bonaparte calmly. "People
will be sure to say that I was jealous of Moreau, that it is vengeance and a thousand other things of the sort. . . . Me, jealous
of Moreau! . . . All I asked was to live on good terms with
him. I warned him that they were trying to come between us."

He rose and going over to his wife took her chin in his hand.
Josephine's eyes were red from weeping.

"You are crying, Josephine? But why? Are you afraid?"

"No, but I don't like what people are going to say."

"What can you do about it? I feel no hatred, no desire for
vengeance. I thought it over a long time before I ordered

Moreau's arrest. Of course, I could close an eye, give him time to escape—but then people would say that I did not dare to bring him to trial. I have the evidence. He is guilty. I represent the government—there should be no trouble about it at all."

After Moreau, it was Pichegru's turn, then Cadoudal's. The judicial investigation was prosecuted. But that was not enough. Cadoudal was waiting for one of the princes to come to Paris before making any move. Which prince? The Duc d'Enghien, it was said—though there was no proof. At that time the Duke was very close to the frontier, at Ettenheim, in Baden territory. Talleyrand urged the First Consul to have him kidnapped. Bonaparte made his decision in a council held on the 10th of March. Régnier and Fouché approved of the plan: Cambacérès and Lebrun protested feebly.

The Consul turned a scornful eye on Cambacérès:

"You are getting very saving of Bourbon blood!"

His anger, the anger of a nervous man, rose suddenly, blinding him, driving him to blunder.

"The Bourbons are trying to kill me like a dog. We'll see about that."

And he ordered Caulaincourt to set out for Ettenheim.

There seems to be no doubt that in his rage he had resolved to make an example of this affair. He was beside himself. He intended to strike such a tremendous blow that he would crush the traitors and murderers once and for all. In vain Josephine begged him not to make that mistake.

"You are a child," he said. "You know nothing about politics."

She blamed him for sending Caulaincourt, whose family had served the Condés. Napoleon cursed roundly:

"I did not know that, but anyway what does it matter? If he has compromised himself he will serve me all the better."

Josephine left the room in tears saying:

"Bonaparte, if you have your prisoner killed, you yourself will be guillotined like my poor husband, and this time I will be killed too as your accomplice!"

On the evening of March 20th, the Duc d'Enghien was

brought to Vincennes. A military tribunal questioned him at midnight. Savary was present. He had received explicit orders from Bonaparte:

"See that it is all over tonight and that the death sentence, of which there can be no doubt, is carried out immediately."

Convicted of bearing arms against France, the Duc d'Enghien asked in vain for an audience with the First Consul. He was shot by lantern light, without the consolation of a priest, and was buried in a grave which Harel, the commandant of the fort, had ordered dug that afternoon.

At Malmaison, all that afternoon and that night Bonaparte behaved very strangely. First Joseph and then Cambacérès urged him to pardon the Prince. Josephine and Hortense flung themselves at his knees. Even Caroline burst into tears. He made no answer. The dinner was sad and constrained. He tried to enliven it but without success. Afterward he went into the salon, and sitting down on the floor, began to play with little Napoleon. Glancing at Mme. de Rémusat he said to her abruptly:

"Why aren't you wearing any rouge? You are too pale."

The young woman stammered an excuse—she had forgotten to put it on.

He burst out laughing:

"That would never happen to you, would it, Josephine?" And he added: "There are two things that are very becoming to women—rouge and tears."

Later he sat down to a game of chess, but he played badly, haphazardly, disregarding the position of the pieces. Mme. de Rémusat was playing with him, but she did not complain. The others sat in deep silence around them. He began to hum and murmured the lines of *Alzire:*

Et le mien, quand ton bras vient de m'assassiner . . .

Mme. de Rémusat raised her head. He smiled. She thought he was preparing a scene in which he would yield to their pleas and revoke the sentence. And, though he did not admit it, Bonaparte had really had a change of heart. He had sent a special message to Réal ordering him to question the Duc d'Enghien first "on certain essential points." But Fate intervened. No doubt Talleyrand and Fouché had something to do with holding up that order. Réal was to say that he had not been wakened in time. However that may be, Savary, dullwitted policeman, hastened to carry out his order. The unfortunate prince fell under the bullets of the firing squad at the very moment when Bonaparte had made up his mind to pardon him.

The following day at eight o'clock in the morning, Savary arrived at Malmaison. The First Consul was at his desk. Méneval sat in an embrasure of the casement window writing at a little table. Savary announced that it was all over. Bonaparte, stupefied, fixed his piercing eyes on him:

"There is something back of this I don't understand," he said. "I am not surprised that the commission has passed judgment on the Duc d'Enghien's confession. . . . But that confession could not have been made until the trial had been held and that could not have taken place until after M. Réal had questioned him. . . ."

Savary replied that Réal had not appeared at Vincennes.

The First Consul could not restrain "a sudden movement of displeased surprise." He said again:

"There is something back of this I do not understand. . . . That is a crime and a useless one."

With a wave of his hand he dismissed Savary and sat plunged in thought. Méneval saw him pacing up and down the library with his hands clasped behind his back. He must have realized that Réal, bought by Talleyrand, had tricked him and that the men of Brumaire, had planned to compromise him by that murder and to keep him in their hands forever.

He sent for Réal. The latter arrived promptly. By this time Bonaparte had control of himself. His face was impassive as he asked Réal coldly for his report. He listened to the policeman's tortuous explanations without moving a muscle, then said:

"That will do."

Picking up his hat he went upstairs to his apartments, locked himself in and refused to see anyone for the rest of the day.

There is no doubt that at that hour Bonaparte was suffering a deep regret. But he dared not show that regret because he was a ruler and to his way of thinking a ruler must neither make mistakes nor allow himself to be tricked by his agents. In the face of the tragedy that horrified all Paris and distressed his wife and his friends, Bonaparte shrugged his shoulders and assumed entire responsibility for the murder before the Council of State. That night, while Talleyrand was giving a ball, the First Consul decided to appear at the Opéra. When he entered his box, his face was livid and Josephine at his side trembled. He stepped forward "looking like a man walking into the mouth of the guns." His attitude impressed the people. The customary applause broke out. He bowed, sat down, and the color came back to his face.

The affair of the Duc d'Enghien hastened the transformation of the Consulate into an Empire. Power was not enough for Bonaparte now: he had to have a throne. To make sure that his régime would endure permanently he must create a new dynasty. Fouché and Talleyrand approved. Cambacérès and Lebrun allowed themselves to be convinced. In his family, however, the First Consul ran up against more serious difficulties. If he were to become a hereditary sovereign he would have to ensure his succession. He would have liked to bestow it on little Napoleon, the child of Louis and Hortense, to whom he had become greatly attached. But first he had to obtain the renunciation of his brothers. Entrenched in his pride as the eldest, Joseph refused.

"I want all or nothing," he said to one of his close friends. "I shall go over to Sieyès, even to Moreau if necessary, or to any group of patriotic friends of liberty that may be left in France—anything to escape such tyranny."

Louis had become very extravagant and was leading poor Hortense a most unhappy life. In him, too, Bonaparte met the same opposition. For that matter Joseph had maliciously stirred up Louis against Napoleon "by reminding him of the gossip that had been current at the time of his son's birth." Cursing his brother's ambition, Louis even went so far as to wish for his death as the best thing that could happen to his family and to France.

"No," he said to Napoleon, "rather than renounce the royalty that is about to become our heritage, rather than consent to bow my head before my son, I shall leave France, I shall take him with me, and we shall see whether you dare to snatch a son publicly from his father."

Lucien hurried back from Italy and Napoleon had a painful interview with him. Lucien would have nothing to do with the succession if his children were to be excluded.

"My wife, my son, my daughters and I are all one."

Napoleon broke off relations with him. When, at midnight, the First Consul entered Josephine's room, he dropped into an armchair, sad and dejected.

"Well, that's over!" he exclaimed. "I have just quarreled with Lucien and ordered him out of my presence!"

Josephine, little hypocrite, spoke in praise of Lucien.

"You are a good woman," said Napoleon, "to intercede for him. . . ."

He rose and, clasping her in his arms, pressed his head against her shoulder.

"It is hard," he murmured, "to find such opposition to such great interests. There is nothing left for me but to stand alone. Well, I am sufficient unto myself—and you, Josephine, you will console me for everything."

Two days later, against the advice of Bernadotte, who kept urging, "Stick it out! Don't go away! He who leaves the game is lost!" Lucien returned to Italy.

In the end Napoleon was the one to yield. For the moment he gave up the idea of adopting his nephew. Joseph was to be made Grand Elector, Louis, Constable; and both of them were to be French princes and imperial highnesses. They were each to receive a million in revenues from special prerogatives, in addition to salary and other gifts that doubled the amount. Napoleon was extraordinarily generous: he bought Louis a palace on the rue Cerutti and a large estate at Saint-Leu, and installed Joseph in a magnificent mansion on the Faubourg Saint-Honoré.

Lucien and Jerome were excluded from the imperial succession because of their marriages and their rebellion. As for the sisters, they were not given any titles at first, though Julie and Hortense became highnesses through their husbands. Caroline took Hortense angrily to task:

"What! Your children are to be princes and heirs to the kingdom of France, and mine, their cousins, will be nothing at all! Never will I tolerate such an injustice!"

She was all the more infuriated because Napoleon openly showed his preference for Hortense's son. One day in the presence of the family, the First Consul, who was holding the little boy on his knees, said to the child:

"Do you know, little one, that you may be a king some day?"

Murat raised his curly head. His eldest son, Achille, was sitting beside him.

"And what about Achille?" he asked crudely.

"Achille?" replied Bonaparte. "Oh! Achille will make a fine soldier. . . ."

And bending over his little favorite he added—for he delighted in adding fuel to their jealousies:

"In any event, if you want to live, my poor child, I advise you never to accept any meals from your cousins."

Murat and Caroline were to find it difficult to forget that thrust.

With political obstacles smoothed out, the details of the new constitution drawn up, court appointments reapportioned, and Fouché re-established as Minister of Police in reward for his intervention, on May 18, 1804 the Senate, with Cambacérès at its head, went in a body to Saint-Cloud to pay its respects to the Emperor. On that bright spring morning the schoolboy of Brienne, the second lieutenant of Valence, now raised to the skies on the shield of his glory, was proclaimed hereditary monarch and the successor of sixty kings. He had expressed a desire to retain the name of Napoleon, which still rang so strangely in French ears. Joseph had advised him to do so, remarking that at least he would be the first emperor to bear that name. That, Bonaparte thought, was an excellent reason. Later he was to say to Las Cases that "that unknown, sonorous and poetic name" had been very useful to him.

Wearing the plain uniform of a common soldier, he received the homage, good wishes and acclaim as if he had always reigned.

Afterwards Josephine welcomed the Senate in her turn. She had not wanted that crown that a fortune-teller had predicted for her long before. She even saw in it a bad omen. Raised to that vertiginous height, her frivolous spirit lost its breath. She was afraid. For the rest of the day she remained in her apartments receiving only her children.

While the guests were assembling in the salon before dinner to await the Emperor, Duroc, now Grand Marshal of the palace, informed them of the titles by which they should address Joseph, Louis and their wives. Toward six o'clock Napoleon entered and greeted each in turn according to his new rank. He was radiant with joy. Josephine appeared to be quite at her ease. The Emperor's brothers seemed satisfied: Eugène, a light-hearted youth, talked and laughed as usual. Murat had been made a marshal that morning, along with seventeen other generals. But he felt that he had been given a very mediocre share. He stood about in gloomy silence, looking worried.

Hearing Napoleon mention the "Princess Louis" several times during the meal, Caroline could not restrain her tears. She swallowed large glasses of water in an effort to control herself, but her tears would not stop. Though so young and so lovely in her pink satin gown she sobbed as uncontrollably as a child. Elisa, more mistress of her emotions, set her pale face with the hard eyes and treated the ladies of the palace with haughty disdain. Napoleon glanced at his sisters now and then and smiled—not without malice.

He made no comment at the time, but the next day when the family gathered alone at dinner the expected scene occurred. Caroline ventured to ask "why she and her sisters were condemned to obscurity while strangers were loaded with honors."

The Emperor replied coldly:

"To hear you talk one would think that I have robbed you of the inheritance of our father, the late king!"

And he burst out with such insulting epithets that Caroline fell to the floor in a faint. Napoleon's anger vanished immediately. When his sister had regained consciousness he embraced her and murmured a few words of hope in her ear.

To have peace, to see them satisfied again, Napoleon ordered a notice inserted in the *Moniteur* the following day:

"French princes and princesses bear the title of Imperial Highness. The Emperor's sisters are to be addressed by the same title."

Madame Letizia was to be a highness too. She was to rank directly after Josephine . . . and was to be known as Madame Mère. All of them were given large pensions, with the exception of Pauline, who had become rich through her marriage. In 1804 Elisa alone received nearly seven hundred thousand francs. The inept Bacciocchi was made a senator. At first it looked as though Eugène had been forgotten. He had refused a post of grand chamberlain to stay in the army. But his stepfather soon made him a brigadier general of the Chasseurs, in other words, grand officer of the Empire, at a magnificent salary.

In that brand-new Court where etiquette was stiffened by a sort of military reserve, there was a constant ferment of bitterness, intrigues, quarrels of precedence, a rush to obtain important posts. Mme. Maret was disgruntled because she had to give precedence to the ladies of the palace. She espoused Caroline's cause and from that moment the Empress treated her with less favor. Mme. de Lavallette, Josephine's niece, shed tears because, not having an official title at first, she could no longer accompany her aunt to mass. Mme. de Rémusat, a stanch friend of Talleyrand, was working to further her own and her husband's interests. At times that whirlwind of petty vanities amused Napoleon, but more often it irritated him. At such moments, with a harsh word, he would crush to earth ambitions and jealousies.

Ten days after the proclamation of the Empire the trial of Cadoudal, Moreau and their accomplices began. Pichegru had killed himself in prison so opportunely that the police were accused of having strangled him. Moreau pleaded his own defense, with pride and self-respect. He was condemned to two years in prison. Cadoudal and nineteen others were sentenced to death.

At first Napoleon thought the prison sentence too lenient. He flew into a rage, then got hold of himself, became more generous and commuted Moreau's sentence to banishment. His military rival was to sail for America after disposing of his property, which the Emperor purchased at a high price with funds belonging to the police department. He gave the Paris mansion to Bernadotte and the estate of Grosbois to Berthier.

Josephine and Mme. de Rémusat intervened in favor of Armand de Polignac, who had been sentenced to death by hanging. At first Napoleon refused to receive the condemned man's wife.

"I shall not see her. . . . The Royalist party is full of imprudent young men who would keep on doing the same thing over and over again if they were not given a severe lesson to hold them in check."

And Mme. de Rémusat persisting, he asked:

"What interest have you in those people anyway? Your insistence is excusable only if they are your relatives."

He refused to consider the matter. But other efforts met with better results: the intervention of old Mme. de Montesson, who had bestowed a prize on Napoleon in the days at Brienne and had always found him very grateful; and also Talleyrand's pleas. Napoleon began to weaken. Mme. de Polignac was introduced into his presence as he was walking in the gallery of the château. She was a very beautiful woman. She flung herself at his feet and wept. Napoleon was deeply touched. As he raised her to her feet he said:

"Madame, it was *my* life your husband wanted. I can therefore pardon him." And he added bitterly: "How guilty those princes are who compromise the lives of their devoted followers but do not share their dangers!"

By his own admission Napoleon was averse to granting pardons, but he commuted the sentences of six of the condemned men. The others followed Cadoudal, the heroic Chouan, who died on the Place de Grève, shouting: "Long live the King!"

V

Josephine in Danger

ON THE 14th of July, Napoleon distributed the crosses of the newly founded Legion of Honor at the Invalides. The Empress appeared that day in a gown of pink tulle studded with silver stars and looked so charming that she far outshone the ladies in her retinue. Shortly afterward she left for Aix-la-Chapelle to take the waters, while Napoleon returned to Boulogne, where he spent a whole month tirelessly inspecting forts and batteries on the coast. Then he rejoined Josephine at Aix, and the imperial couple set out on their exhausting and triumphal journey on the Rhine, where they were greeted by the princes of Germany. That was the moment when a new and fleeting love came into Napoleon's life.

Mme. de Vaudey had been appointed lady-in-waiting on the recommendation of Lecoulteux de Canteleu, the former owner of Malmaison, who was still a friend of Josephine's, and she had accompanied the Empress to Aix. She was a beautiful creature, full of life and energy and extremely well connected. During the many festivities on the journey she was always exquisitely dressed, and, having decided to attract the Emperor's attention, she succeeded with the greatest of ease. Women usually embarrassed Napoleon, but he was sensitive to their advances. He joked with Mme. de Vaudey and paid a little court to her. She led him on—and finally yielded to his persuasions. Back again in Paris she was so bold in her manner toward the Empress that the latter's eyes could not fail to be opened. Moreover Mme. de Vaudey proved to be greedy, demanding—failings that Napoleon detested. She lived sumptuously at the château of the Tuilerie at Auteuil, gave innumerable receptions, and entertained guests who were anything but discreet. She was soon deeply in debt for she was not only a coquette, but a gambler. Twice Napoleon paid the bills she presented. But when she asked for another audience and he guessed her purpose, he ordered Duroc to send her away.

"I should never have enough money or enough good nature," he said, "to purchase so dearly what one can find so cheaply. Thank Mme. de Vaudey for her kindnesses to me and do not mention her to me again."

The lady-in-waiting then resorted to a very ordinary ruse: she decided to kill herself—first taking care to inform the Emperor of her intention in a touching letter that sent Rapp running to Auteuil. When the aide-de-camp arrived out of breath he found Mme. de Vaudey chatting gaily with friends over a gaming table. Informed by Rapp, Napoleon stopped her pension at once and forbade her to appear again at the Tuileries.

What was Mme. de Vaudey to Napoleon? A passing fancy, a mere caprice. The germ of another attachment had already been planted in Napoleon and was developing, the strongest, without any doubt, that he had known since the days of the first campaign in Italy.

Mme. Duchâtel was twenty years old—a slender blonde, with an aquiline nose, eyes of an unusual blue, and enchanting hands and feet. She was all grace, all elegance. She had a quick and richly furnished mind, she danced and sang like a professional and she played the harp delightfully. She could shine in conversation or listen equally well, and she knew how to bide her time and conceal her impressions. Gay and casual in manner she was really serious-minded; to all appearances gentleness itself, she was actually very firm. On occasions she could intrigue and compromise perfidiously for she was wholly feminine and in every court women have had to stoop to any means to maintain their positions. A bourgeoise by birth, she had acquired the manners of the most polished circles and, better still, that instinct which draws a woman to those circles and makes her shine there.

Napoleon thought highly of her husband. M. Duchâtel was Councillor of State and Director-in-chief of Registration, and in the dull routine of his duties he had rendered eminent services. He was one of those men who forged the administrative armor of the Empire! But age and work had banked his fires. In contrast to such a young wife, he seemed like an old fogey, almost an old man.

They first met in the last days of the Consulate at Saint-Cloud, whither the Consul had invited Duchâtel. Constant relates that in order to allay Josephine's suspicions, Bonaparte did not visit his mistress till all the castle was sound asleep. "He even went so far in his precautions as to make the trip between the two apartments in nightclothes, without shoes or bedroom slippers." Once Constant saw the day break before his master returned. Fearing a scandal he went to warn Mme. Duchâtel's maid. Five minutes later Bonaparte appeared. He was very much disturbed because he had caught one of Josephine's women spying on him from the end of the corridor. Constant immediately hurried off to warn the curious woman that she would lose her job if she did not hold her tongue. To avoid further surprises the Consul ordered his valet to rent a house on the Champs-Elysées, in the Allée des Veuves. There he and Mme. Duchâtel met frequently.

When the Empire was proclaimed and the posts at Court were increased, Napoleon made Mme. Duchâtel one of the eight new ladies-in-waiting, an arrangement that would facilitate their meetings. She did not accompany him on the journey to the Rhine, but the moment he returned their intimacy was resumed and strengthened.

Those were the days when all energies were directed toward preparations for the Coronation. Inspired by that love of the miraculous which always induced him to astonish people, Napoleon was eager to associate the Church with that ceremony. After protracted negotiations, and notwithstanding the scruples and fears that racked his pure and modest soul, Pius VII consented at last to come to Paris and crown the Emperor. A momentous event that rocked all France, nay even all Europe! Napoleon's family, however, looked forward to that ceremony with ill humor. They were indignant that Josephine should have a share in it. Joseph protested loudly, even going so far as to declare a divorce necessary. Napoleon brushed aside the suggestion impatiently. But the fact that it had been expressed—and Josephine was not long in hearing of it—threw the poor Empress into fresh terrors all the more alarming as she had recently been informed of the relations between Mme. Duchâtel and the Emperor. She had suspected something for a long time. But she had thought that her son Eugène, who had fallen in love with the young woman and was paying marked attention to her, was the lady's lover. As a complaisant mother she was gracious to Mme. Duchâtel and boasted of her charm and merits to everyone.

Josephine had managed to preserve those illusions until the Court settled at Fontainebleau, whither Napoleon had gone to welcome the Pope. But there she noticed an extraordinary change in the Emperor. Napoleon began to be charming, attentive, even gallant toward the ladies. What was behind all that? Was there a love affair in the wind? Josephine's suspicions first fell on Mme. Ney. She was very cool to her, treating her haughtily and scarcely addressing a word to her. Hortense had gone to school with Mme. Ney at Mme. Campan's. She now took her old school friend to task. The Maréchale protested her innocence. Yes, the Emperor had apparently singled her out for attention, but he had never talked with her more than casually. For that matter she was afraid of him and had scarcely answered him. And she directed Hortense's researches toward Mme. Duchâtel.

At last mother and daughter opened their eyes. Duroc was pointedly respectful in his attitude towards Mme. Duchâtel. Napoleon attended his wife's receptions so assiduously only because they offered excellent opportunities for tête-à-têtes with the lady-in-waiting. He came and sat beside the Empress at the theatre only when Mme. Duchâtel was in attendance. If he made up a table of cards he was sure to choose Mme. Maret, Mme. Duchâtel and Mme. de Rémusat as partners. As she sat chatting absent-mindedly with some dignitary or other at the

far end of the drawing-room, Josephine would watch with chagrin the Emperor talking volubly, to all appearances having a
very good time.

Exasperated by that conduct, the Empress sometimes braved
the advice of Hortense and Mme. de Rémusat and risked a scene
that came close to ruining her. At Saint-Cloud Napoleon occupied an apartment on the same level as the garden. Above it,
as at the Tuileries, he had reserved several rooms that were
reached by a private staircase which no one was allowed to use.
One morning the Empress went down to her drawing-room.
A few minutes later she saw Mme. Duchâtel come out. Convinced that Mme Duchâtel was on her way to join the Emperor,
Josephine took Mme. de Rémusat aside—in spite of various ups
and downs the latter was still the Empress's confidante.

"I am going to get to the bottom of this, and at once," she
said. "Stay here with my guests and, if anyone asks what has become of me, you are to say that the Emperor sent for me."

She hurried to Napoleon's study. He was not there. Climbing
the private stairs, she found the door locked, put her ear against
it, listened and recognized the Emperor's voice and Mme.
Duchâtel's. At that she knocked loudly and announced herself.
There was a long silence. At last the door opened. The state of
dishevelment in which the two lovers appeared, left Josephine
no illusions. She broke into reproaches, insults. Mme. Duchâtel
began to weep. Pale, his eyes black with anger, Napoleon burst
into such a violent rage that Josephine turned and fled.

Sobbing, gasping, she poured out the story of her discovery
to Mme. de Rémusat. That lady advised her to go back to her
own rooms and wait there for the Emperor.

A few minutes later there was a great uproar in the Empress'
apartment. Napoleon stormed into the room, furious, shouting
outrageous insults, smashing everything within reach of his
hands. Josephine sobbed loudly. When he had calmed down a
little the Emperor declared that he was "tired of such jealous
spying and that he had decided to shake off a yoke of that sort
and in the future listen to his political advisers who were in
favor of his taking a wife who could give him children." He

then left her and sent word to Eugène to come to Saint-Cloud and arrange for his mother's departure.

The moment Eugène arrived, Napoleon informed him of his resolve to get a divorce. He spoke awkwardly of "compensations." Eugène took the blow with great dignity. "At a moment when such a misfortune was about to befall his mother, he would accept nothing for himself. He would follow her in her retirement, even to Martinique, sacrificing everything to her need of consolation."

Grim, rigid, the Emperor heard him out, then dismissed him without a word.

Josephine's friends thought that she was lost and they did not dare to defend her. Even Hortense was silent. She herself had been so unjustly treated by her husband, and had no hope of a divorce that would set her free, that she was not far from wishing for one for her mother.

"I cannot interfere in any way," she said to Claire de Rémusat, who had come to Paris to break the news to her. "My husband has positively forbidden me to make the slightest move. My mother has been very imprudent. She is going to lose a crown, but at least she will have peace. Oh, believe me, there are women who are more unhappy!"

Mme. de Rémusat did not dare to show that she understood the allusion—Hortense never complained and she did not like to be pitied.

"Indeed," Hortense added, "if there is any chance of patching up this affair, it should lie in the influence my mother's gentleness and tears have over Bonaparte. We must leave them alone, avoid coming between them. And I advise you not to go to Saint-Cloud, all the more so as Mme. Duchâtel has mentioned your name and believes that you would counsel violence."

Poor Hortense of the gentle eyes! She was so wise. Harsh experiences had matured her. And truly, Josephine's sadness, her silent submission, were to calm Napoleon and to make him regret his decision. An even greater factor perhaps was the sudden outburst of joy from the Bonapartes and their open boast that the repudiation of the Creole was their work which they had plotted untiringly for years and years. The fact that they should belittle her, should try to trample her under foot, angered Napoleon and inclined him to defend her. Suddenly he changed his mind and gave up the idea of divorce.

"How could I send that good woman away just because I have become great?" he said to Roederer. "If I had been imprisoned or sent into exile, she would have shared my fate. Shall I now throw her over just because I have acquired power? No, I cannot do that. I have a man's heart—I have not been weaned by a tigress. When she dies I shall remarry and I shall have children. But I cannot make her unhappy."

One evening he took Josephine in his arms and announced that everything was changed, that he was not going to send her away. Of course, it would be to his interest to get a divorce. "But," he said, "I have not the courage to take the final step and if you show me that you are too unhappy, if you obey me in everything, I feel that I shall never be strong enough to compel you to leave me. . . ."

Then, the Pope having finally announced his intention of coming to France, Napoleon invited Josephine to prepare for the ceremony of the Coronation. She was to be crowned beside him. Crowned . . . that meant saved. At that moment she must have trembled with joy. . . . At last she could draw a free breath, she could relax, she could think of the future without fear. Crowned Empress of the French by the Pontiff, who could cast her down from the height to which she would climb?

The lesson Napoleon had given his family did not soften his animosity toward them. Joseph claimed that the coronation of his sister-in-law would damage his own interests. The Emperor referred to those ridiculous notions in a conversation one Sunday morning with Roederer, a great friend of Joseph. He poured out angry, violent words, at the rate of a mile a minute.

"Joseph has been my friend since childhood. I have never wanted him to have reason to complain of me at any time. But we must face facts. Joseph is not born to rule. I have risen by my own efforts; he has not advanced beyond the point where he was placed by birth. . . . Joseph thinks he is fit to command armies. If he had had any military genius he would have done what I did. As a child, Achilles ran to pick up the first weapons his eyes fell on. . . ." Tapping Roederer on the shoulder, he exclaimed: "I count you one of my friends, but you are a headstrong fellow, aren't you?" Then becoming excited: "What does Joseph want? What is he asking for? He does not want to be a prince. Well, does he think the State should give him two millions just to walk around the streets of Paris in a redingote and a round hat? I have sacrificed all my personal pleasures to make myself what I am. . . . Does he think he can dispute my power? I have built on rock."

Roederer tried to calm him. He assured him that Joseph was ill.

"Power does not make me ill! I grow fat on it. I am in better health than ever. . . . It hurts me that Joseph should dare to speak to me of his rights and his interests. It is like telling a man that he has been dallying with his mistress. My mistress is Power. I have worked too hard to win her to let her be stolen from me or even to suffer others to covet her. . . . I shall pretend to laugh at him, but just the same he has dallied with my mistress!"

His whole family was jealous of Josephine, of Eugène, of Hortense. He was thoroughly tired of hearing about it.

"My wife has diamonds and debts—that is all. Eugène has an income of less than twenty thousand francs. I love those children because they have always tried to please me. . . . Joseph's daughters do not even know that I am the Emperor. They still call me Consul. They think I am a monster, whereas when little Napoleon passes in front of the grenadiers in the garden he shouts at them: 'Hurrah for Nonon, the soldier!' I love Hortense, yes, I love her. She and her brother always take my part even against their mother when she flies into a rage over some girl or something like that. They tell her: 'After all, he is a young man. You are making a mistake. He has quite enough trouble—and he does so much for us!' . . ."

There was a knock on the door and Napoleon was informed that they were waiting mass for him. Roederer had been closeted with him for almost two hours. The Emperor strode back and forth in his study, his hands under his coattails, talking with that lack of restraint he evinced toward men he could trust, men to whom he opened his heart, showing them his perspicacity as well as his illusions, his strength of will as well as his weakness, his vigor as well as his pettiness. He bared his heart —the heart of a leader, but as he himself had said, the heart of a man.

"My wife is satisfied to play the Empress. . . . I have never loved her blindly. If I make her Empress it is only just. And I am above all a just man. They are always tormenting her, persecuting her. Only recently she humbled herself to the point of apologizing to Joseph. Yes, she shall be crowned! She shall be crowned, even if it costs me two hundred thousand men!"

He instructed Roederer to report that conversation to Joseph. And he added in summary:

"He would be called to my succession only as a precaution against the misfortune of falling into a regency. His wife does not have any more boys than mine does. But if she should give him one, I might prefer him to Louis' little fellow. I shall choose the one who shows the most talent. . . . Whether I have any children or not, the régime must go on. Neither Caesar nor Frederick had children. . . ."

VI

The Coronation

THE CORONATION had been fixed for the 2nd of December. The ceremonies connected with it were to be magnificent. From all over Europe crowds of eager spectators poured into France to witness that extraordinary pageant.

The Emperor sent to Corsica for his godchild, Faustina Poli, and his old nurse, Camilla Ilari. The latter, good soul, appeared at the Tuileries, decked out in brand-new clothes and not in the least intimidated as she chattered away incessantly in her dialect. Napoleon even arranged to have her received in private audience by the Pope. He was to keep her in Paris for three months and refused to let her leave until he had given her twelve thousand francs in lands and vineyards, among others the famous Sposata, where as a child he had helped to gather the grape harvest. He offered the family house in Ajaccio to his maternal relatives, the Ramolinos, on condition that they turn over their own house to Camilla Ilari.

The Court buzzed like a veritable beehive. Houses had to be assigned to princes and princesses, precedences established, the order of the procession arranged. David had already made a number of sketches to determine the positions of the principal actors in the ceremony—they were used later in his famous painting of the Coronation. Napoleon discussed costumes with Isabey and a whole nation of workingmen and women cut them out, sewed them up, embroidered them. Napoleon saw to everything, arranged everything himself. He ordered Josephine's jewelry, was present at the fittings for her gowns. He inspected the coats of dignitaries, the gowns of princesses. A number of rehearsals were held at Notre-Dame. And that there might be no mistake Isabey had even set up on a large table at the Tuileries several hundred leather figurines representing the Emperor, the Empress, the family and the high dignitaries in their proper positions according to rank.

The Pope was housed in the Pavillon de Flore where every attention was lavished upon him. He was a frail man, pale, with bright eyes and hair that was still black. His gentle, kindly manner surprised Napoleon and enchanted the people—so much so in fact that the Emperor became alarmed at the eagerness of the populace. On being informed of this Pius VII avoided frequent public appearances. That was a great relief to him. Ascribing everything to God, he had not the slightest trace of human pride.

At Fontainebleau Josephine confessed to the Pontiff that she had not been married in church. So far, she said, the Emperor had always rejected her pleas. Ever since the days in Italy she had been trying to conciliate the Pope, and she now found in this question of marriage a major means of consolidating her position. Pius VII saw in her desire only the natural reaction of a religious scruple of which he approved and he hastened to reassure her.

"Do not worry, my child," he said, "we shall arrange all that."

He brought up the subject at once with the Emperor. How could he give his blessing to a woman who was merely a concubine? Napoleon saw that he had been tricked: Josephine had forced his hand. But what could he do? Without a religious marriage, there could be no coronation. And the day for that coronation was at hand. To avoid a ridiculous scandal, he yielded. On the morning of December 1st, an altar was set up in Josephine's own bedroom. Without witnesses—Pius VII having granted the dispensation—the Emperor and the Empress were married by Cardinal Fesch. That same day Josephine made Fesch hand over the marriage certificate, which she carefully locked away.

On the eve of the most glorious moment in his career Napoleon could not be angry with his wife for the trick that had bound him to her in a new and stronger tie. He was in one of those moods of profound exaltation in which everything delighted him. As for her, she could not conceal her joy. The Emperor himself had fitted on her forehead the diadem she was to assume the following day before the eyes of all France. She told Mme. Junot about it with tears in her eyes. She forgot her jealousy, her animosity, and seeing him so well disposed, tried to soften his heart toward Lucien. But he turned on her angrily and she did not insist. Neither Lucien nor Madame Letizia, who had openly espoused the cause of that son in disgrace, were to attend the Coronation. His mother's absence hurt Napoleon deeply. He wanted people to forget it and he ordered David to give her the most prominent place in his painting that posterity at least might be deceived.

That night no one in the palace went to bed: everybody was waiting for the hairdressers of whom there were too few, everybody wrangled over them. Several of the ladies slept in armchairs. At break of day the crowds began to throng the streets and, in spite of winter weather, the windows along the route the procession was to follow were filled with eager spectators.

The Emperor rose late—at eight o'clock. Constant dressed him: white silk stockings embroidered in gold, short trousers and vest of white velvet, a coat of cramoisy velvet braided in gold along the seams, a short cloak of the same color, embroidered with laurel leaves and strewn with bees and, fastened with a diamond clasp, a cap of black velvet surmounted by white aigrettes and adorned with the *Régent*. Napoleon seems to have been annoyed at that costume, which was foreign to his taste, and he cursed the tailors.

"A fine thing this is, *Monsieur le drôle!*" he cried pinching his valet's ear. "But wait till we see the bills!"

Then he went down to Josephine's rooms. She was ready and very beautiful as she stood surrounded by her ladies in full court dress. She wore her hair in curls "in the fashion of Louis XIV." Her gown and long court train were of white satin, embroidered in gold and silver. She glittered with jewels. Though she was forty-one years old, she had made herself up with such art that she looked like a young girl and utterly eclipsed her sisters-in-law who, though sumptuously gowned, could ill conceal their bitterness.

At nine o'clock the Pope left the Tuileries and drove to the Cathedral. A chamberlain, perched on a mule and bearing a huge cross, preceded his carriage. The crowd stared in amazement and roared with laughter at that sight. Two hours later the sovereigns entered a glass and gold carriage, lined with white velvet and surmounted by eagles bearing a crown. Joseph and Louis occupied the seat facing them. The entire Court, brilliantly gowned, followed in magnificent carriages escorted by the handsomest cavalry officers in the army. As the procession moved at a walk to Notre-Dame along streets strewn with sand, bells pealed, cannon boomed, music blared and a roar went up as the continuous cheers of five hundred thousand spectators rent the air. The day was cold, but little by little the sun broke through the fog. All Paris beamed and sparkled.

At the Archbishop's palace Napoleon halted to don the imperial cloak. He looked very small under that mass of ermine and purple. His face, rigid with emotion, his eyes enormous, he seemed made of marble. But that marble lived, that marble saw, that marble, desiring to speak to Fesch, struck him on the back with his sceptre. And when Elisa, Pauline and Caroline maliciously dropped the Empress's train to trip her as she mounted the throne, he hurled burning words at them as they made their obeisances before him. Those Imperial Highnesses, who had washed their linen at the village fountain only ten years before, bowed their heads under that stinging rebuke. As he walked toward the Vicar of Christ, who awaited him, gentle and resigned, Napoleon turned to his elder brother and, as if he had had a sudden vision of their humble past rising behind his glory, whispered with boyish ingenuousness:

"Joseph, if only our father could see us now!"

Four hours of an exhausting ceremony, to the sound of great organs and violins playing the cantatas of Paer and Lesueur! Napoleon did not wish to be crowned by the Pope. He did not owe his crown to God, but to his sword. As soon as the Pontiff had anointed him, he forestalled any other move by taking a simple laurel wreath from the altar and binding it on his forehead like a Caesar of old. Then he moved down the steps toward Josephine. She knelt at his feet with clasped hands. Nobly, deliberately, he placed on her head the light diadem which made that woman, battered by so many storms and menaced by so much hatred, the first Empress of the French.

They dined alone that evening, while from below, the din of Paris, illuminated and rejoicing, rose to their windows. Never had Napoleon seemed more content. He insisted that Josephine must keep on her crown, he paid her the choicest compliments on her beauty and charm, on the good impression she had made. She was enraptured. At that moment, without any doubt, she loved him as she had never loved him before.

After dinner they received the members of the Court who had dined at the château with Duroc. Napoleon walked about among the ladies and paid them compliments with a gracious familiarity rare in him:

"If you are so charming, ladies, you owe it to me."

But a little later, when he had retired to his own rooms and Constant was helping him to undress, his thoughts took a serious turn. "To whom shall I leave all this?" the valet heard him say to himself.

The days that followed were one long succession of festivities —at the Champ de Mars where the Emperor distributed eagles to the army, at the Senate, the Legislative Body, the Ministry of War, at the Hôtel de Ville, at the Opéra where the marshals gave a ball in honor of the sovereigns. Napoleon was careless about concealing his attentions to Mme. Duchâtel and the quarrels with Josephine began again. At a reception at Berthier's, only the women were seated at supper. The Emperor made the rounds of the table of honor and, contrary to his usual habit, was particularly attentive to the Empress, taking her plate from the flunkey's hands and giving it to her himself. But he lingered long—far too long—beside Mme. Junot and Mme. Duchâtel. As the latter leaned forward to pick up a dish of olives, he handed it to her saying:

"You should not eat olives in the evening. It will make you ill."

Then he leaned toward her neighbor:

"And what about you, Mme. Junot? You don't eat olives, do you? You are quite right. And doubly right not to imitate Mme. Duchâtel, for she is inimitable in everything."

He spoke the last words tenderly with a glance that caused Mme. Duchâtel to blush. She made no reply, but lowered her silken eyelids. Though she had not overheard a word, the Empress guessed the whole situation. She was not wise enough to keep silent and she could not resist questioning Laure Junot.

"Was the Emperor praising your gown at Berthier's?"

Junot had just been appointed ambassador to Portugal and his young wife, to her great regret, was obliged to accompany him.

"Yes, Madame," she replied. "He mentioned my gown and my duties as the wife of a French diplomat."

"And did he also compliment Mme. Duchâtel on her gown?"

"No, Madame. He told her, as well as I can recall, that she must not eat olives in the evening."

"As he was giving her such good advice he should also tell her that it is ridiculous for a woman with such a long nose to play Roxelane . . ." She gave a harsh laugh, then picking up Mme. de Genlis' popular novel on Mlle. de La Vallière, she added: "There is a book calculated to turn the heads of all slender, blond young women. They all think of themselves as favorites. But we shall set them straight on that point."

This time too, Mme. de Rémusat tried to pacify her—it was wasted effort. The Empress dictated anonymous letters of an extraordinary venom, which the lady-in-waiting then burned, though protesting that she had delivered them. She set spies to watch the retreat in the Allée des Veuves which the Emperor visited in the evening. She even descended to making use of servants and tradespeople in her investigations.

Once again she overwhelmed the Emperor with her scenes, her tears. She declared that she would not permit Mme. Duchâ-

tel to enter her apartments. Napoleon lost no time in giving the
unfortunate Mme. de Rémusat a good dressing-down:

"If you don't approve of the inquisition the Empress is putting me through why have you not enough control over her to
keep her from doing it? She is humiliating us both by this constant espionage and she is giving her enemies food for talk. You
must see that she stops it: I shall hold you responsible for all
her blunders."

Though he would not admit it, Napoleon had fallen under
the quiet, but potent spell of the intelligent and sensitive woman
with whom he was spending most of his rare hours of leisure.
Mme. Duchâtel loved the Emperor sincerely and sought to serve
him to the best of her ability. She was, to all appearances, completely unselfish. Again and again she refused gifts of money for
herself and posts for her husband who had no idea of the situation—for that matter he would have been anything but a complaisant husband. But she took a long view of things and her
ambition was no less definite because hidden. She protected the
Murats, who were her ardent supporters and with whom she had
been close friends ever since Napoleon had begun to shower her
with attentions. Caroline was delighted when Murat was made
a prince and a grand-admiral. To keep the balance between the
Beauharnais and the Bonapartes, Napoleon gave Eugène the
title of Prince and made him Chancellor of State. Josephine felt
somewhat reassured inasmuch as, in a moment of confidence,
Napoleon admitted his infatuation for Mme. Duchâtel, adding
that "it was merely a passing fancy that would only become
greater if she worried about it, but that left to itself would die a
natural death."

On his order the Court moved to Malmaison in mid-February.
The weather was severe and the women shivered in their low-
cut evening gowns. But Napoleon, usually so sensitive to cold,
did not seem to notice it. Disregarding all comments, he would
walk for hours in the park with Mme. Duchâtel, Savary's wife
sometimes acting as chaperone. From her bedroom window
Josephine could watch them strolling along the garden paths.
But she did not dare to complain. Her sorrowful air, her obvious

suffering, seem to have softened the Emperor in the end. For
one thing, possession had lessened his passion for Mme. Duchâtel and, as he himself said, he could not bear to see "long faces
and wet eyes." One morning he appeared in Josephine's room
as she was dressing and sat talking with her with the same affection he had shown in the early days of their marriage. Yes, he
admitted, he had been very much in love, but just as he had
foreseen, his fancy had passed. With his usual lack of tact, he
described his love affair in its most intimate details and confessed that he had noticed "that she was trying to boss him" and
that Mme. Duchâtel had made "rather catty remarks" about a
number of people at court. And he wound up on a sudden impulse by asking the Empress to help him break off a liaison that
had grown distasteful to him.

Josephine was far from being hurt at such confidences. On the
contrary she considered them proof of her power over Napoleon.
Instead of trying to revenge herself on her rival she would set
to work to avoid any scandal. If the Emperor had changed
toward Mme. Duchâtel, she too would change: she would protect her during this transition period and defend her against
evil tongues and venomous glances. Napoleon thanked her and
embraced her. The Empress promptly sent for the lady in
question.

Josephine took a mild tone: Mme. Duchâtel had been somewhat indiscreet, she said, in fact she had very nearly ruined her
reputation. But she was scarcely more than a child, that was her
great excuse. In future she must just be a little more cautious
and the past would be forgotten.

The young woman received the lecture with great dignity.
Never losing her poise she protested that she had not deserved
such accusations. And she persisted in maintaining a consistently grave and dignified attitude before the Empress and before
the entire Court. Napoleon scarcely so much as glanced in her
direction and never addressed a word to her. He appeared to
have forgotten the whole incident, as if, with one sweep of the
sponge, he had wiped out the past. Mme. Duchâtel was deeply
hurt, but she never reproached him. Was he not the master?

She admired him and would love him always. .... The time was soon to come when the Emperor would be touched by that gentle attitude and would try to win her forgiveness. There were even to be recurrences of their love affair. Napoleon was to visit her house again at night, wearing a redingote and round hat and be driven by César in a coupé without armorial bearings.

On one of those visits, on which Murat and Constant accompanied him and waited for him in the carriage, he lingered so long with the young woman that his friends became alarmed. The Emperor's life had been threatened often enough for them to suspect that he might have run into a trap. Finally, as dawn was breaking, Murat could not restrain his impatience. Jumping out of the coupé, he had just grasped the doorknob, when the door opened and Napoleon walked out. He stared in astonishment at the man. Murat apologized and told him of his fear.

"What childish nonsense!" cried the Emperor. "What business is it of yours to worry about me so? Am I not at home no matter where I am?"

Those meetings were so carefully guarded that Josephine never learned of them. Mme. Duchâtel continued to refuse honors and favors. She accepted nothing from Napoleon, not even diamonds. Her husband served the Emperor well and Napoleon was to promote him according to his deserts. But Mme. Duchâtel did not even thank him for it. As in the heyday of the Empire, so in days of distress, she was to continue to grace the Tuileries with her charm and beauty. Though she was not the woman Napoleon loved best, she was to be the one he would have reason to esteem the most highly.

On April 1, 1805, the Emperor set out for Milan, where he was to receive the title of King of Italy. Josephine had begged so hard that she finally obtained permission to accompany him, but with a retinue reduced to the minimum.

He left her at Fontainebleau while he went off on a journey to Brienne. Now that he had risen to such heights he liked to revisit the place where he had spent his childhood, where he

had often been so sad and so lonely. Mme. de Brienne welcomed
him at the château. A tiresome chatterbox, she had already
asked a thousand favors and had never been refused one. He
walked with her in the park, where in bygone days the pupils of
the school had been admitted only on the Feast of St. Louis.
At dinner that evening the atmosphere at first was somewhat
strained. When a footman spilled a sauce on the table and spattered Napoleon, Mme. de Brienne was in despair. Her imperial
guest, however, laughed heartily. That broke the ice and the
evening was a huge success. The Emperor was all graciousness,
all good-nature.

That visit stirred so many memories! The very contrast with
his present position called them to mind. At dawn, the day
after his arrival, accompanied by Canisy, Mme. de Brienne's
nephew whom Napoleon had made his equerry, he rode out to
visit the former school of the Minims, now a ruin. To the
officers who caught up with him he pointed out the convent, the
lane of willow trees where he used to walk with a book tucked
under his arm, the location of the study rooms, of the dormi-
tories. . . . He thought it might be a good idea to rebuild the
school, but he saw that it would be too expensive a proposition.
Disappointed, he mounted his horse again and set off at a gallop
across fields and hedges, reveling in the swiftness of motion and
the keen morning air. On that excursion—according to Constant, who may have exaggerated the anecdote—Napoleon came
upon the hut in the midst of the woods where Mother Marguerite, the goodwife, used to sell the schoolboys milk. Mme.
de Brienne had assured him that she was still alive. He dismounted and went inside.

"Good-morning, Mother Marguerite," said Napoleon. "Aren't
you curious to see the Emperor?"

"Of course, my good sir," replied the old woman. "I am
very curious to see him. I am going to take Madame this basket
of eggs and then I shall wait at the château and see if I can't
get a peep at him. . . . I shan't see him so well nowadays as
when he used to come here with his comrades. He was not an

Emperor then, but even so, he used to make the others step around. . . ."

"What, Mother Marguerite! Do you mean to say you have not forgotten little Bonaparte?"

"Forgotten, sir? I am only a peasant, but I could have told you then that that boy would make his mark some day."

As Napoleon stepped into the full glare of the sunlight, the poor old woman recognized him and fell at his feet. He lifted her up.

"By the way, Mother Marguerite, I have a regular schoolboy's appetite. Can't you give me something to eat?"

Trembling, almost beside herself, she bustled about, trying to hurry and finding nothing. In the end she served him eggs and milk. When the meal was over the Emperor presented her with a wallet full of gold.

"Goodbye, Mother Marguerite, I shall not forget you."

And off he went at a gallop, covering in three hours nearly fifteen miles. He did not return to Brienne until he heard a shot fired by Caulaincourt, which was to be his signal of recall. His horse, exhausted, was breathing blood through his nostrils.

Napoleon asked Mme. de Brienne to sell him her land. The old woman stubbornly refused.

"Brienne means much to me . . ." he told her.

"To me, sire," she replied in her weak voice, "it means everything."

He did not insist.

Before leaving Brienne he stood gazing out over the wide sweep of land.

"This plain," he mused, "would make a fine battlefield."

Nine years later it was indeed to be one of his last battlefields, and one of the most tragic.

He spent ten days at Stupinigi, near Turin, then went on to Alexandria and from there to Marengo, where he held a review of his troops on the site of the battle, wearing, out of a strange affectation, the very uniform he had worn at that time and which he sent to Paris for—a long-waisted blue coat with tails, very much worn and even moth-eaten in spots, and a dusty old blackened hat. At his side hung the cavalry sword of the General of the Republic. He looked as if he had just stepped out of the year 1800. In his address to the army he spoke of Desaix with deep emotion.

After that he entered Milan and established himself in the Monza Palace. On May 5th he was proclaimed King of Italy. Josephine was present at the ceremony, but she was not crowned —an oversight that annoyed her vastly. Napoleon tried to please her by making Eugène Viceroy of Italy—for that boy of twenty-four a really magnificent début. But she complained at being separated from her son in the future. On that occasion Napoleon made a bitter rejoinder:

"If the absence of your children causes you so much grief, consider what I myself must feel! The devotion you show for them makes me all the more cruelly conscious of my misfortune at not having any myself!"

As a matter of fact he had not thought of Eugène as ruler over Italy in the first place, intending to offer it first to Joseph, then to little Napoleon, Louis' son. But his brothers' objections and the claims they put forward, caused him to abandon that plan. He then turned to Lucien—Madame Mère was urging them to make up their differences. Lucien would have liked nothing better than to be a prince, even a king, but he dearly loved his wife and, as he was still insisting upon having her received into the family, the negotiation which Fesch had undertaken was broken off.

"Let him forget me as I shall forget him," the Emperor told his uncle. "Let him stop writing to me. Let him wait for the moment when some murderer's dagger will end my life. He will then find in the weakness of others what my character and my influence will always refuse him."

Napoleon might lay his decision to "the interest of his people and his policies"—he had something else in mind. A bitterness, an inveterate mistrust of Lucien, whose usefulness he could not deny and whose ability he knew perhaps too well. He still loved him, for Napoleon never willingly slackened the ties that bound him to those of his own blood, but he feared Lucien's ambitions, he weighed his possibilities as a rival.

He turned therefore to Eugène, on whom he had already lavished honors to the indignation of the Bonapartes. The Murats at first said nothing. Caroline thought that the best way to obtain what she wanted was to flatter and cajole her brother. He had already given her the Elysée palace and many millions. But what was that compared to her dreams of a kingdom? Could not Napoleon do anything he chose, and was he not dismembering Italy as he pleased? After his reconciliation with Madame Mère, the Emperor had lavished honors on her too. Elisa was made ruler over Piombina, then over Lucca. As for Jerome, back in Europe again after two years of sulking and adventures, he had bowed the knee at last. The Emperor rebuked him severely and then forgave him. He made him a commander in the navy and, while keeping a tight rein on him, was thinking of taking him back into the family hierarchy and making him a prince, perhaps even, if he should mend his ways, a king.

On that journey through Italy where he traveled from city to city until the end of June, Napoleon stirred up another domestic storm.

Josephine had brought a new reader with her to Milan, Mlle. Lacoste, a frail, blond girl, with a pretty figure and a flowerlike face. The post of reader was a real sinecure, for the Empress almost never asked to be read to—she never read a book herself. But the young woman's charm and her poverty had won the Empress' sympathy. In the intimacy of that traveling Court, Napoleon had more opportunity to notice the young woman—first at the château of Stupinigi, then at Milan. Mlle. Lacoste offered no resistance and had already become an old habit to him when Josephine became aware of the situation and registered clamorous despair. Napoleon gave in and Mlle. Lacoste was ordered to leave. While waiting for the young woman's aunt to come from Paris to fetch her, Napoleon insisted that Mlle. Lacoste should appear at the Empress' evening receptions. In that way her disgrace would pass unnoticed and her reputation would be saved. But a mere reader at the Empress' reception—

that was a blatant breach of etiquette. However, Josephine was obliged to swallow the bitter pill. Napoleon quickly forgot Mlle. Lacoste, whom for that matter he rewarded handsomely. She married a banker with whom she lived happily, became a good mother and never appeared at Court again.

From Turin the Emperor returned to Fontainebleau with all possible speed. Josephine insisted upon accompanying him.

"You are sure you won't have a migraine?" Napoleon took care to stipulate. Josephine promised and she uttered no complaints though she was exhausted from the jolting of the carriage over the rough roads. They traveled like the wind, halting only at the relays to change horses and pour water over the smoking wheels, while the Emperor would mutter impatiently:

"Come! Come along now! We must be getting on!"

At the beginning of August the couple separated, Napoleon returning to the camp at Boulogne and Josephine going off to Plombières to take the waters. Corvisart was still hopeful that the treatment might restore her fertility. But Napoleon had lost all hope. Besides, he was beginning to wonder whether he himself might not be to blame. That doubt, which Josephine had instilled in his mind and which his brothers, Joseph in particular, fostered complacently, often returned to torment him. To Bourrienne whom he visited again before his departure for Italy, he confessed:

"The great torment of my life is that I have no child. I am perfectly aware that my position will never be assured until I do have one. If I were to fail in this, none of my brothers is capable of replacing me. Everything is foundation, nothing is finished. God only knows what would happen!"

VII

A Day in Napoleon's Life

THE DAWN OF the Empire found Napoleon in the full vigor of mind and body. With the exception of a few fairly frequent disturbances from which he still suffered, such as colds, hoarseness, boils, a slight touch of rheumatism, his health was excellent. Bourrienne, however, had already seen him place his hand on his right side and sometimes, of an evening, unbutton his vest and lean on the arm of his chair in evident pain. Of late years he had put on weight, but had not yet lost his figure. His arms and legs, his face had grown plumper. He had lost that sallow complexion, those prominent cheekbones, those hollow eyes, all the sharpness, the severity he had had as Consul.

At that moment he was handsome: his softened features often wore the serenity as well as the color of ancient marble. But his eye was still keen, he still retained that piercing glance that could on occasion mellow introspectively as if he withdrew into himself, to lose himself in the dreams of a poet, or the machinations of a gambler. And when he smiled that fresh, young boyish smile, his face seemed to be suffused with light.

A sort of magnetism emanated from him that cast a spell on all with whom he came in contact, whether comrades in arms like Lannes, Caffarelli, Junot, Duroc, Marmont, or older men of experience and wiles, with their own views and their own secret aims, like Fouché, Talleyrand, Cambacérès. His voice won them in spite of themselves—the ascendancy of genius perhaps, but also the effect of a very human, very direct personal appeal of which he himself was fully aware and which he exercised with an innate dexterity. He laid himself out deliberately to win them! His lack of restraint, his bluntness, even his gentleness were pure calculation. In his presence men forgot themselves, they bowed to his will. But away from him the magic failed and each man began to think of his own interests again.

He ordered his daily life with the precision of a mathematician. His habits never varied whether he was at Paris, at Saint-Cloud, at Fontainebleau or at Malmaison. Even in the country he took with him the things he would be most likely to need. He insisted upon having the rooms and furnishings of his country estates exactly like those of the Tuileries, his books even being arranged in the same order. His personal staff accompanied him wherever he went. "I am a creature of habit," he was wont to say. He detested any change in the people about him, often choosing to close an eye to faults rather than to remove his ministers, his generals, even his private servants, from their positions. Toward those servants, for that matter, he was always very lenient—he knew that with them there was no need to parade his rank or to weigh every act, every word with an eye to the outside world. Valets, ushers, page boys he scolded them all, often with sharp words, but he took an interest in their lives, in their needs, in their families. In their presence he was quick to forget his bad humor and when he had been unjust, he would atone for it with a friendly word, not seldom accompanied by a generous gift.

Constant had orders to wake him between half-past six and seven in the morning. He slept soundly, as usual without dreams, for he had that marvelous faculty of dozing off wherever he was and for as long as he pleased. He would waken promptly and generally in a good humor, ask Constant whether the weather were fine, then joke with him and tease him while he made him repeat the gossip of the château. The tittle-tattle, the servants' quarrels and intrigues, amused him.

He would have the window opened, for as a child of the sun he loved the morning air and light. Humming one of his favorite tunes, *Monaco* or perhaps *Malbrouk*, he would rise, put on his bathrobe, tie a bandanna on his head and sip a cup of tea or orange leaves. Immediately afterward he would go into his bath, which he insisted upon having piping hot. Méneval then read the despatches and the French newspapers. On mornings when he did not take a bath—a rare occurrence for he considered it a remedy against constipation from which he suffered constantly—he would sit down by the fire and glance through his mail, tossing on the floor anything that did not interest him.

His first physician, Corvisart, or Yvan his house physician, would then come in. Napoleon was very fond of Corvisart and always greeted him with an ironic phrase, to which the doctor would reply without turning a hair.

"There you are, you big bluff!" the Emperor would cry. "How many people are you going to kill today?"

"Not so many, sire," Corvisart would answer in jest. He was a broad-shouldered Champenois with white hair and sideburns, his chin almost hidden in his shirt frill.

Napoleon liked to tease him about medicine, declaring that it was all humbug and that he had no faith in it—which did not prevent him from taking with great regularity the drugs prescribed by the doctor, for he was much preoccupied with his health and in that respect something of a mollycoddle. He would also fire questions on weighty problems at the doctor.

"What is life? When and how do we receive it? Is it all anything but a mystery?"

Corvisart would answer to the best of his ability, not seldom wittily. Napoleon would laugh, tweak his ear and begin to shave. He preferred to shave himself while Roustan, the Mameluke, held the mirror for him; and he scrubbed his own face and hands with a brush. Constant then poured eau de cologne over his body and rubbed him down—a habit Napoleon had acquired in Egypt.

"Harder," he would often say to Constant, "much harder, as if you were currying a donkey."

He would walk about in front of the members of his household completely nude, without the slightest feeling of shame, like a Greek of old. The valet then dressed him—a flannel vest, a shirt of very fine linen, white silk stockings, shoes with gold buckles or short boots adorned with silver spurs, knee breeches of white cashmere, a waistcoat of the same material and, pinned on it, the decoration of the Legion of Honor. With that he wore the green coat of a colonel of the *Chasseurs,* with collar and facings of scarlet. Napoleon had adopted that coat when he first saw it in 1801, lying folded over a chair in his brother's house at Mortefontaine.

"Let me try that on," he explained. "That is a fine coat. I have never seen one I liked so well, unless perhaps it be my artillery uniform . . ." the artillery uniform, the one dearest to him, his first. . . .

On Sundays and at ceremonials he wore the uniform of the Foot Grenadiers. "A valet's man," he put himself into their hands like a child while they were dressing him, and whistled or chatted with Duroc, Méneval or such of his friends as had been waiting in the anteroom and whom he had ordered shown in.

Punctually at nine o'clock he would enter the salon where he held his morning reception. Princes of the family, cardinals, ministers, high officers, would be assembled in their brilliant uniforms. The Emperor would move from one group to the other, pausing to chat with each man of his particular interest. No real conversation: brief questions, concise replies, definite orders. When he had made the rounds, the Emperor would bow his head slightly and all would withdraw to make way for the audiences to follow. Standing in front of the mantelpiece, with his heels held out to the fire that burned brightly even in summer months, Napoleon would receive those who came to solicit favors. He never held out his hand. Impressive, his eye fixed on his visitor with that air of stern simplicity that genius often lends, he would listen in silence, without a sign, then dismiss him with a wave of his hand.

"There are two distinct men in me," he once said to Roederer. "The man of the head and the man of the heart. Do not think that I am not as tender-hearted as other men. I am really not a bad sort of fellow. But from my earliest youth I have trained myself to silence that string which has now ceased to give out any sound."

Idle boasting! He was still much more sensitive than he would admit or than he liked to believe. An extremely nervous man, he was a prey to every outward impression. True, he often feigned rages in order to intimidate others, but more often that anger was genuine and outrageously brutal. At such moments the nervous twitching of his face, his wild gestures, his occasional fainting spells caused his enemies to declare that he was an epileptic. He bullied his wife, Hortense, his brothers, his sisters, and often treated Eugène like a lackey. He was insultingly scornful to Berthier, his constant military collaborator. He would rebuke Talleyrand sharply, make terrible scenes with Fouché, burst into storms of abuse against Maret, Regnier, Decrès, even Cambacérès, rip up Josephine's and Hortense's gowns with his spurs because they were made of English muslin, knock down and smash anything he could lay his hands on— all marks of a man so overburdened with cares and responsibilities that he often lost all sense of balance. But the next moment he would regret his violences, would calm down in the twinkling of an eye, admit his mistake and atone with a gracious word or a favor granted.

"I make myself out worse than I am," he confided to Caulaincourt, "because I have noticed that the French are always ready to eat out of your hand. They lack seriousness and consequently that is what impresses them most. They think I am stern, even harsh. All the better: that relieves me of really being so. . . . Come, Caulaincourt, I am a man. In spite of what certain people say I, too, have compassion, I too have a heart—but it is the heart of a king. I cannot get upset over the tears of a duchess, but I am deeply moved by the ills of the people. I want them to be happy, and the French are going to be. If I live ten years more everyone will know what it is to be comfortable. Do you really think that I do not enjoy making people happy? It does me good to see a contented face, but I have to keep a firm check on that natural inclination of mine or people would take advantage of it."

His fundamental kindness was evidenced in the innumerable gifts he made and his extreme generosity. All the old friends he

CAROLINE BONAPARTE
QUEEN OF NAPLES
From the Portrait by Mme. Vigée-LeBrun

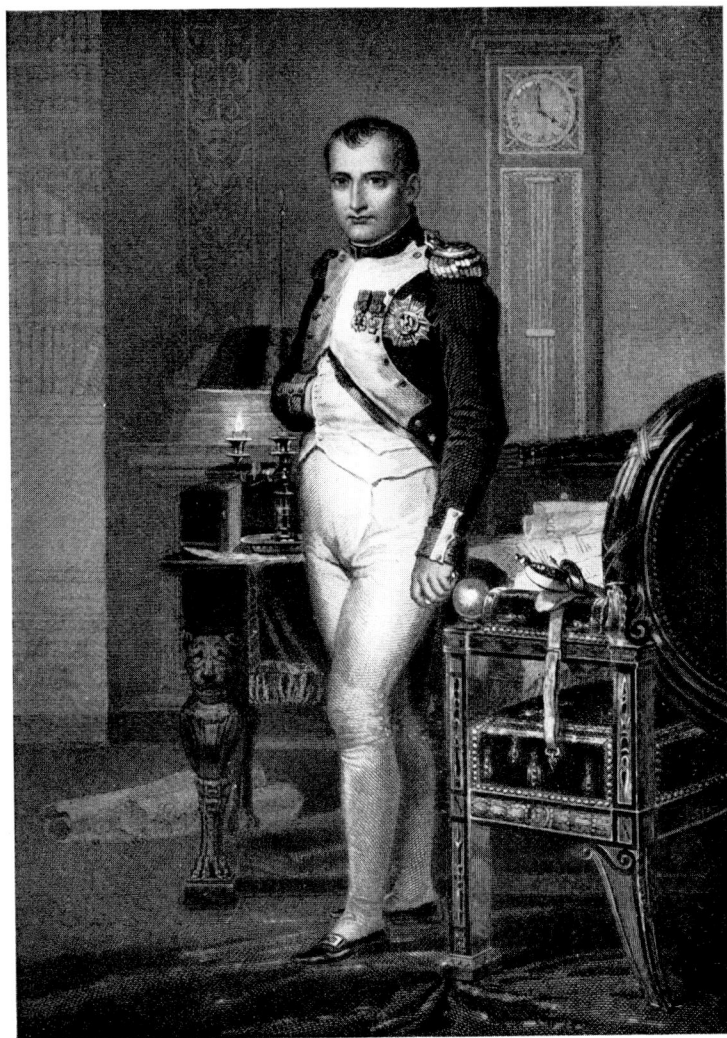

NAPOLEON I
After the Portrait by David

had known at the beginning of his career in Corsica, at Brienne, at Valence, at Toulon received posts, honors, pensions. Mme. de Marbeuf had lost her fortune: Napoleon bestowed another fortune on her, appointed her son as his orderly officer and, on his marriage, made him a present of a splendid mansion. Her daughter was married to an émigré, but in spite of the husband's Royalist opinions, Napoleon gave her a dowry and made him a colonel. The Boucheporns, children of the former tax collector in Corsica, were equally favored. He provided handsomely for the Marshal de Ségur, who had signed the little Bonaparte's commission of gentleman cadet in 1784. When the Marshal called to thank the First Consul the latter saw him to the staircase on the way out—a thing he never did as a rule. As the consular guard, which was drawn up on either side, presented arms and the drums beat a ruffle, the old soldier of the monarchy, pale with emotion at those forgotten honors, swayed and almost fainted. Napoleon pensioned the family of Kéralio and also Mgr. de Juigné. The latter refused the office of Archbishop of Lyons, but was made a canon of Saint-Denis and a count of the Empire though he had asked for nothing. As he was old, infirm and incapable of fulfilling any function, Napoleon said to him:

"I shall excuse you from any activities. The income of fifteen thousand francs which I am giving you is in honor of the chapter and in recognition of your ability."

Dupuy, his professor at Brienne who had corrected his History of Corsica, was made librarian at Malmaison; Berton, headmaster at the high school in Reims; Domairon, inspector-in-chief of schools. In spite of his turbulent life Patrault too was given aid.

When Duroc admitted the former writing-master at Brienne to Napoleon's presence, he was greeted with the following sally:

"For the hell of a hand you taught me, you certainly deserve congratulations!"

The old man got his pension all the same.

Mme. de Montesson, who had presented the young Bonaparte with the prize at Brienne, was provided with a "widow's dowry" of 160,000 francs. Laplace had examined him on his graduation from the Military School and had also been his companion in Egypt. He was made Minister of the Interior and, when he failed in that post, senator, count and chancellor of the Senate. Mlle. du Colombier, now Mme. de Bressieux, recalled herself to the memory of the lieutenant of the La Fère regiment. She was made lady-in-waiting to Madame Mère, and her husband was appointed administrator of forests. And, what was even more touching, Napoleon sent her a ring containing a miniature of a little man perched in a tree and tossing cherries to a young girl who held out her apron to catch them.

Nor did he forget his landlady in Valence, Mlle. Bou, whom he rescued from poverty and, in addition, set up her brother as a stockbroker in Paris. The First Consul summoned Montalivet to Malmaison and questioned him at length about their old friends. Bonaparte asked in particular for news of a woman who had kept a coffee shop where the young officers had been in the habit of meeting. Montalivet assured him that she was still alive.

"I am afraid," said the Consul, "that I did not pay in full for all the cups of coffee I drank at her place. Here are fifty louis. Please see that she gets them from me."

Montalivet was made prefect, then commissioner-in-chief, minister, count of the Empire. Napoleon was always to treat him as a friend. One day when the Emperor had been more than usually insulting, Montalivet offered to resign from the ministry. Napoleon promptly apologized.

"My dear Montalivet," he said, grasping both of his hands, "let us forget what has just happened, shan't we? You will stay with me, won't you?"

All his former schoolfellows and his brother officers were handsomely provided for. Des Mazis became master of the household and chamberlain, his brother, manager of the State lottery—an important post; Lauriston, general and ambassador; Lariboisier and Sorbier, inspector-generals of artillery; Villarceaux, prefect of the Guard; Boubers's widow, governess to Hortense's children; and Hédouville, minister plenipotentiary.

The latter's name had been struck off the list of émigrés and he had returned to France. When he appeared at the morning reception, Napoleon scarcely so much as glanced at him. But the moment they were alone, he took him by the ear:

"Good morning, chevalier! Where did you come from? Didn't I hear that you had emigrated?"

Hédouville murmured an excuse. Napoleon began to laugh: "You are lying. . . . I see that you will make a good diplomat." And he gave him a diplomatic post.

General du Theil, who had singled Bonaparte out at Auxonne, was now a decrepit old man, but he was put in command of the fortress of Metz. Commissioner Naudin became inspector at reviews. The family of Dugommier was given a pension in perpetuity. Even the incompetent Carteaux was made governor of Vincennes and manager of the lottery. "I knew him before Toulon," those words on Napoleon's lips always betokened a gift. Suchet, Marmont, Victor were to become marshals and dukes. Junot had made himself Duc d'Abrantès: the Emperor confirmed his right to that title. Only that young man's mad pranks were to prevent him from becoming a marshal. Mme. Turreau was now a widow and poverty-stricken. She was given a large pension.

As for Pontécoulant, who had saved him from despair by calling him to the geodetic bureau of the Committee on Public Safety, Bonaparte sent for him at the beginning of the Consulate.

"You are a senator," he said to him without preamble.

"The honor you wish to confer on me is impossible," replied the former member of the Convention. "I am only thirty-six years old and the required age is forty."

"Well, you shall be prefect of Brussels or of any other large city you choose, but remember that you are a senator and come and take your seat when you are old enough. I should like to show that I have not forgotten what you did for me."

Some time later Pontécoulant became financially embarrassed—so much so that he was on the point of selling his ancestral lands. At first he could not bring himself to appeal to the

Emperor, but finally he made up his mind to do so. Napoleon looked at him sternly:

"How long have you been in this condition?"

"For three months, sire."

"Well, those are three months wasted. . . . The first thing tomorrow morning you must see the treasurer of my civil list. He will pay over to you one hundred thousand écus."

In the midst of war with Russia, after Eylau, Napoleon learned that Berthollet, his companion in Egypt, was having financial difficulties. He wrote to him at once telling him that he was placing 150,000 francs at his disposal, and that he was delighted to have this opportunity to be of use to him and to give him proof of his esteem.

Even his enemies shared in the manna. Gohier, the ex-President of the Directory, became Consul General. Carnot, who had opposed Napoleon consistently and with dignity ever since the beginning of the Empire, was assigned a retirement pension of ten thousand francs as a former minister and a handsome sum representing "the arrears of his salary as a general." A delicate pretext in order not to hurt Carnot's feelings.

Nor did those at whose hands he had suffered have cause to fear his vengeance. The widow of the former minister, Aubry, who had removed him from his post in the artillery, was given a pension. Letourneur, who had stripped him of his rank, was appointed Prefect of the Loire, then councillor to the Auditor's Office.

It is true that Napoleon considered generosity indispensable to any ruler not born to the throne—he could make himself solid only by bestowing benefits. But many a time he gave with a generous hand when there could have been no calculation on his part. Economical where he himself was concerned—so much so at times as to remind one of his mother's avarice—it amused him to do things for other people, he loved to give. He would never allow anyone to thank him and always dismissed them abruptly as if he were steeling himself against emotion. That would make him too much like other men: he had to live on a higher plane.

His generosity to his marshals, his generals, his grand officers, his ministers, was stupendous. Their endowments, the extra bounties he granted them from his own privy purse often equaled the immense gifts he lavished on his brothers and sisters. Lasalle, Junot and Rapp were always hard up for money. All they had to do was to tell their troubles to Napoleon and he would pay their debts every time. They all had sumptuous mansions, castles, millions—even those he had the most cause to complain of: Bernadotte, practically an avowed enemy, Clarke, who had spied on him for the Directory, Davout, an unruly subject in Egypt, Masséna, an arrant plunderer, headstrong Soult, all lived, not like princes, but like kings. It was the same with Cambacérès, Talleyrand, Fouché, Lebrun, and even, though on a lesser scale, with Roederer, Maret, Daru. He insisted upon having them keep up a grand scale of living not only because the brilliancy reflected on his reign and dazzled Europe, but because industry, the commerce of the country, the life of the people benefited by it, with a resulting increase in general prosperity.

The audiences, which were supposed to last one hour at the most, frequently dragged on for two. Lunch would be kept waiting, the servants heating it over hot water. When the Emperor sent word that he was ready he was served alone in his own salon, on a little mahogany pedestal table. A palace chamberlain remained standing by Napoleon's side, while Dunan, the maître d'hôtel, hovered about him. The Emperor ate very rapidly and not at all neatly. He would pick up bits of food in his fingers, dip his bread in the sauces and spatter his coats copiously. He observed no order in the meal, passing from the roast to the hors-d'oeuvres only to jump back to the second course. His favorite dish was chicken fried with tomatoes— chicken à la Marengo. He also liked cutlets, breast of roast lamb, fried fish, beans, lentils and Italian *pasta*. He insisted that the quality of the bread must always be of the best. And as he was afraid of putting on weight, he often ate sparingly.

"Monsieur," he would say to his maître-d'hôtel, "you can

certainly see that you are giving me too much to eat. I do not like that. It upsets me. I do not wish to be served more than two courses."

Sometimes he would scold Dunan roundly, then flatter him to cheer him up.

"Ah! Dunan, you are luckier to be my maître-d'hôtel than I am to be Emperor."

As a beverage he drank a little Chambertin diluted with water. He was no more of a connoisseur of wines than of food. One day having invited Augereau to his table at the camp in Boulogne, Napoleon asked him how he liked his wine.

"Well, I have tasted better," Augereau ventured to reply.

After each meal Napoleon drank a cup of coffee. The haste with which he swallowed his food caused him severe stomach distress which usually ended in vomiting. At such moments he would fling himself on the floor and groan, for he was not very brave about physical pain. The Empress would be summoned: she would nurse him, encourage him and make him sip an infusion of herbs slowly.

Sometimes he would ask to have the children of Hortense, Caroline or Elisa brought to his luncheon table. His affection for little Napoleon was deep and genuine. He would take the little fellow on his knees and let him forage in his plate, teasing him, making him eat lentils one by one, smearing his little face with sauce. The child would shout with glee. His brother, Napoleon-Charles, was not so patient. One day the Emperor told him to look the other way and then stole his egg. Napoleon-Charles grabbed up a knife, shouting:

"Give me back my egg or I will kill you!"

"What, rascal, you would kill your uncle?"

The child repeated:

"Give me back my egg, or I will kill you!"

Napoleon put the egg back in the plate.

"You will make a fine gangster when you grow up!"

He gave him a sip of coffee. The little fellow made a face and spat it out.

"Ah! your education is not complete," said the Emperor. "You have not learned how to dissemble."

Achille Murat was a handsome lad bursting with health and beauty. He would not tolerate being teased. One day when Napoleon had tweaked his ears too hard before an infuriated Caroline, the little fellow flung himself at him, crying:

"You are a nasty, mean, bad man!"

Napoleone Bacciocchi was only five years old but she already had the airs of a young lady. Once the Emperor scolded her before a number of guests:

"Nice things I have been hearing of you, Mademoiselle! You did something in your bed last night!"

The little minx jumped to her feet and looking the Emperor haughtily up and down retorted:

"If you have nothing more sensible to say, Uncle, I shall leave you."

The Emperor was delighted and told the story to everyone.

That brief moment of relaxation and leisure was the time when Napoleon received his intimate friends, writers and artists: Talma, David, Isabey, Monge, Arnault, Fontaine, Denon.

As an old friend of the dark days, Talma was always cordially welcomed. Almost every week he spent an hour with Napoleon either at the Tuileries or at Saint-Cloud. He would bring him the gossip of the stage, all those theatrical rumors that the Emperor loved to hear, rumors that made a new man of him. In return Napoleon would advise Talma about his rôles and discuss their interpretation.

When Talma was playing Cæsar in *The Death of Pompey,* Napoleon told him:

"You wave your arms about too much. Rulers of empires are not so prodigal with their gestures. They know that a wave of the hand is an order, that a glance means death and they are therefore sparing of gestures and glances. . . . There is also one line where you miss the implication—you put too much sincerity into it: 'For I who hold the throne equal to infamy . . .' Cæsar is not saying what he really thinks there. Don't make Cãesar talk like Brutus. When the latter says he has a horror of kings, we have to believe him: but not the former. Notice the difference."

Talma followed the Emperor's suggestions. Soon afterward Napoleon saw him interpret the same rôle at Fontainebleau and declared that it was the first time he had really seen Cãesar.

Napoleon frankly admired his old friend. For that matter he was always ready to pay homage to talent.

"Do you realize," he said to Mme. de Rémusat, "that a talent, no matter what form it may take, is a real power, and that even I never receive Talma without taking off my hat?"

A regular butcher of money, Talma was frequently in difficulties. Though the actor never asked for help, the Emperor never wearied of paying his debts. He must have cost Napoleon several millions.

Others who appeared at the audiences were the official painters, and foremost among them, David, in whom Napoleon saw the man who was to portray the highlights of his reign. He examined his sketches for the great painting of the Coronation carefully, sometimes let him make a swift sketch of himself, as he also did with Isabey and Gérard for that matter. Canova succeeded in getting him to pose several times for a quarter of an hour for the colossal statue he was planning: the Emperor garbed in the robes of the ancients and bearing in his right hand a winged victory. Napoleon would become annoyed:

"What! Pose again! What a bore that is!"

Canova made a wax model and presented it to Napoleon as a sample. He kept it in his study two weeks. He was not particularly pleased with it—he thought it too naked—but he authorized the sculptor to cut it in marble.

He was always extremely kind to Isabey though more reserved than in the days of the Consulate. Mushroom monarch that he was, he could not run the risk of "seeing anyone put a hand on his shoulder." He had the same manner toward all his old friends. Duroc, Junot and Marmont easily accustomed themselves to it, but Lannes rebelled and persisted in using the familiar *tu* to the Emperor whenever they were alone. Napoleon disliked that familiarity thoroughly, but he put up with it. Others among his callers were Berthollet; Monge, to whom he talked science; Denon, with whom he discussed new purchases for museums and orders to artists; Fontaine, his favorite architect, who showed him his plans of triumphal arches, palaces, temples and explained his ideas on decoration; and also Barbier, librarian emeritus, who kept him informed on the most infinitesimal events in the literary world. Though Napoleon did not really like literary men and even mistrusted them, preferring by far "men who were occupied with positive things," he tried to keep in touch with all the new books, whether they were the works of Mme. de Staël, of Chateaubriand, or the platitudes of Népomucène Lemercier.

He would take leave of his callers and, before returning to his study, would descend the little staircase to Josephine's apartment. She would have dined with her ladies and perhaps played a short game of billiards, then have sat down to some tapestry work which served generally as a means of passing the time. The Emperor would break into the conversation, tease Josephine, make himself agreeable to Mme. de La Rochefoucauld or peevish to Mme. de Rémusat, talk clothes, fashions, ask about the latest gossip from the Faubourg Saint-Germain. He would be quite at ease, very gay. Then suddenly his smile would vanish, his eyes would wander: the thought of matters that awaited his attention would claim him again. Unable to stand it any longer he would mount the steps four at a time.

His study at the Tuileries had been the former bedroom of Marie-Thérèse, the wife of Louis XIV. The walls were almost entirely covered with four bookcases and a breast-high glass wardrobe that contained the folios and files habitually in use. The room was lighted by a single window in the corner. In the embrasure of that window Méneval sat at his desk with his back turned to the garden. A large mahogany table, ornamented in bronze, stood in the center of the room, and before it an armchair, shaped like an ancient bench, upholstered in green cashmere. The cloth was spotted with ink—Napoleon wiped his pens on it as well as on his coats—and the arms were scratched by his knife, a habit he had formed during the boring discussions at the Council of State. The Emperor sat in it only to sign papers. As a rule he settled himself at the right of the fireplace on a small sofa beside a pedestal table that held the day's mail. Flinging his sword and hat on a chair he would sit silent for several moments, biting his nails or tapping his foot. Sometimes he would close his eyes and think so intently that it almost seemed as if he had fallen asleep. "I meditate a great deal," he confided to Roederer. "The reason why I always seem to be ready for everything, to meet any contingency, is because I always think things over carefully before I make any move—in other words I have foreseen what might occur. It is not genius revealing suddenly and mysteriously what I should do and say in a given circumstance in which others would be caught unprepared: it is thought, meditation. I am always working, at dinner, at the theatre. I even wake up and work at night." That meditation entailed no little fatigue. "When I meditate," he said, "I am so disturbed that it is really painful. I am like a woman in labor."

Soon he would pull himself together, rise and begin to pace slowly back and forth, then faster and faster as he began to dictate to Méneval. He almost never made a correction, never repeated a sentence. Often, to emphasize his point, he would pull the cuff of his sleeves. Now and then he would take a pinch of snuff—more from habit than from any real liking for it—and spill it all over his vest. His secretary would jot down the principal sentences and the significant words as fast as his pen could fly, fitting the whole text together afterward. Precise, meticulous, Napoleon insisted upon looking over all his letters, and frequently corrected them. He had a mind "with compartments," a real miracle of an ordered memory, that considered one after the other the most divers questions—diplomacy, finance, naval affairs, legal questions, business.

His meticulousness, his attention to detail, was exaggerated. With the idea of founding a military school at Fontainebleau, he dictated a complete outline of 517 points without stopping for a second. When Josephine was obliged to go to Aix to take the waters, he said to Chaptal:

"The Empress is leaving tomorrow. She is a good woman, but easily influenced. We must draw up an outline of conduct for her to follow. Take this down." And he dictated twenty-one pages of large-sized folio. He provided for every eventuality, even to the questions and answers she should make to the authorities on the way.

His work tools were always close at hand. A geodetic office near by furnished him promptly with the maps and atlases he needed in planning his wars or in dreaming of the organization of Europe. His archives were kept with great care. He insisted upon having extensive summaries of everything written in several columns, where they could be seen at a glance. Everything was classified in categories. He carried on his person a note in which he had condensed the fortune of France into a few lines. Reports on his own army and on the armies of other countries were arranged on index cards in boxes. He went into business matters thoroughly, considering them in their detail as well as in their general scope, making all decisions with clarity, common sense, and an eye to the public interest. He annotated the reports of his ministers in an almost illegible handwriting, which Méneval however managed to read or rather to decipher. He revamped budgets, pared them down, reduced them, writing the figures himself. In addition to that he wrote articles for the *Moniteur,* outlines for speeches, proclamations. A born publicist, he knew the importance of phrases on a people as sensitive and nervous as the French and instinctively hit on the brief, strong, new formula that presents all the facts and at the same time sways minds. "I must touch the people's imagination," he said to Volney. "When that fails, I shall be nothing, and another will succeed me."

On another day, depressed by something that had gone wrong, he kept harping on the thought:

"Imagination is the nose of the masses and the masses can always be easily led by the nose."

Like Bourrienne before him, and perhaps even more so,

Méneval led a terrible life. Bending over endless dictations, obliged to straighten out innumerable pages of unfinished thoughts after the Emperor had left his study, two whole days would sometimes pass before he could go to his own home, see his family and change his clothes. The aides-de-camp, who occasionally took his place, were equally harassed. "A man would have to be made of iron to hold out on the job we are doing," said Rapp. Napoleon was severe, demanding with his subordinates. He considered that he had a right to be because he worked more than they did. In the field he wrote to Josephine: "I am a slave among men. My master is heartless, his name— the nature of things." His subordinates must sacrifice everything to the public good as he himself did. He once said in jest: "A man I make minister will have a bladder stricture inside of four years." He was all the more of that opinion because he himself had brought on a bladder trouble from overwork and was already beginning to suffer from it.

On certain days, rare it is true, he found that he was unable to concentrate on anything. A sort of sluggishness would come over him. He would wander around his study, chat with Méneval, stretch out to doze, get up again, pick up a book, leaf through it, perhaps read a page aloud. If the book struck him as poor or merely tiresome, he would fling it into the fire. Then he would go for a stroll about Paris with Duroc or an aide-de-camp, to look at a monument in course of construction, or to go window-shopping. Sometimes he even went hunting. He rode badly and would have had many falls if his horses had not been specially trained. He liked to pull them up short in the middle of a gallop. At reviews he mounted an Arab of a fine breed that looked average enough when it stood still. Let the drums beat a ruffle and the trumpets begin to blare, and the horse would rear proudly, paw the ground impatiently, and, once the Emperor was in the saddle, you would have thought it the most beautiful horse in the army. Hunting, which Napoleon considered a kingly obligation, gave him an opportunity for physical exercise. He would often spend a whole day at Rambouillet following a deer he never shot. Napoleon did not hold his gun tightly enough against his shoulder and as a result his arm was frequently very sore.

But those breathing-spells in his working life were rare indeed. As a rule he continued to work in his study until evening. Dinner was at six o'clock. Punctual as always, Josephine would be waiting in her drawing-room, dressed in a very low-cut evening gown and covered with jewels or pearls. She always wore too much rouge, but the Emperor was accustomed to it and scarcely noticed it any more. She would wait patiently, chatting meanwhile with her ladies. Seven o'clock, eight o'clock, nine o'clock—and still no Napoleon! He has forgotten dinner and no one dares to remind him. In the kitchens a chicken is put on the spit every quarter of an hour so that one may always be done to a turn when the Emperor is ready to be served. One day they roasted as many as twenty-three while waiting for the Emperor, who did not come down to dinner until eleven o'clock. At last the Emperor arrives, without having changed his clothes. He runs a critical and knowing eye over the ladies' gowns, drops a compliment or a criticism, and, offering his arm to Josephine, leads her into the room where the table has been laid.

At the Tuileries the sovereigns almost always dined alone. At Saint-Cloud, Compiègne or Fontainebleau, there were usually a number of guests present: the Court chamberlain, a minister or a general, frequently one of the Empress's ladies. The dinner was brief as a rule—Josephine was no more of a gourmand than the Emperor. Napoleon was even surprised that it took a quarter of an hour to get the business over.

After that Duroc came to report on the events of the day. A number of aides-de-camp, several orderly officers, brought despatches. Napoleon read them. That was also the hour when he had foreign newspapers translated to him and glanced through various pamphlets. He did not talk much—a few words to Josephine now and then. Seated opposite him she played her rôle to perfection, always smiling, always discreet, always attentive. She tried to please him in everything and was quick to sense his mood.

Napoleon then rose and, preceded by the Court Chamberlain, returned to his own drawing-room, where the Empress served coffee. After which Josephine withdrew to her apartments. Every other evening she held a circle. As she passed slowly along the line of her guests the Empress would have a pleasant word for each. She would then sit down to a game of whist or backgammon. In beautiful gowns of satin or moiré that left their high breasts bare, with their curls framed in *chérusques,* the ladies seated themselves at tables of lotto or, gathering in small groups, talked in low tones. Officers in uniform and men in court attire stood around looking excessively bored, the light from the chandeliers picking out their gold braid and the bright colors of their coats.

After an hour or two in his apartments, Napoleon would return to the drawing-room.

"The Emperor!"

All rose. They would hear his firm, rapid step. Then he would enter the room, acknowledging the bowed heads with a brief nod. Moving from one to the other he would stand rocking back and forth on his heels, with one hand under his coattails. At the approach of that simple little officer of the *Chasseurs,* generals, ministers, princesses, duchesses with names ancient and great, or newly created by a victory, felt their pulses quicken and pulled themselves together for a mumbled "Yes, sire!" or "No, sire!" which was all they could manage in reply to his questions.

Gone were the gay and intimate evenings of the Consulate. The Emperor did not joke these days or tell ghost stories or play at Twenty-one as at Malmaison. He insisted that his court must maintain "an impeccable form."

"The free and easy days are past," he kept repeating. "Things are solemn and serious now."

Moreover, that Court, which was so obviously new, was gloomy and stiff. Former members of the National Assembly were chilled by the ceremony, the rigid etiquette; generals, sprung from the people, turned an ironical eye on those aristocrats who had accepted the Republic. Napoleon himself did not feel at ease. His country-boy upbringing came to the fore again. He had always been shy with women and he now displayed a curtness, even a certain boorishness toward them. Now and then he would get a sharp reply, which, however, he did not seem to resent.

"Well, Madame," he once said to the Duchess de Fleury, who had just returned from her exile and whom he knew to be light of morals, "are you still so fond of men?"

"Why yes, sire," she replied. "When they are courteous."

To Mme. Regnault de Saint-Jean-d'Angély, whom he liked and who, in all the glory of her twenty-eight years, was one of the beauties of the Imperial Court, he said abruptly one evening:

"Do you know that you are looking very old, Mme. Regnault?"

She smiled and retorted blandly:

"What Your Majesty does me the honor to tell me would be very hard to hear if I were at an age to be annoyed by it."

Napoleon turned away amid a rising murmur of approbation.

To the wife of a general, he flung:

"Your husband's campaigns make fine holidays for you!"

At other times he displayed a certain good humor. The "bad-mannered lieutenant" (as Chaptal called him), had his moments of grace. When Laure Junot returned from Portugal, he welcomed her cordially:

"Well, Mme. Junot, one always gains by traveling. See how well you make a curtsy now, doesn't she, Josephine? She has quite an air, hasn't she? She is not a little girl any more, she is Madame the Ambassadress . . ."

Mme. Junot beamed with a pride that quite transformed her Arabian features. She looked almost pretty.

Another round of his guests and then Napoleon would return to his study again. But he never failed to appear when a play was presented on the stage he had had built at the Tuileries, as usual under Talma's direction. He also attended concerts given in the Salle des Maréchaux or in the Empress's apartments. He was particularly fond of singing—so much so that he decorated the eunuch, Crescentini, with the Crown of Iron—which gave evil tongues much cause for laughter. To those same people Grassini retorted amusingly one day:

"*Eh bien, oubliez-vous sa 'blessoure'?*"

He also accompanied Josephine to the Opéra or the Théâtre-Français for an act or two, sometimes even to the Feydeau. On rare occasions he would attend a reception given by his brothers, his sisters, or one of his dignitaries. At such gatherings when he was under another roof than his own and freed of the restraints of imperial etiquette, he enjoyed himself thoroughly—especially if it happened to be a masked ball. But many a time when he had promised to attend a reception, he would set to work on his papers while waiting for the appointed hour and would forget all about it. That occurred at a ball given by Decrès. The Emperor had announced that he would arrive at ten o'clock. He made an appointment with Gaudin for eight and sat down to revise the budget with him. At midnight the Empress sent a page to announce that they were waiting for the Emperor and that the ball was "very beautiful."

"In a little while," Napoleon replied. "Tell the Empress that I am working with the Minister of Finances. We shall soon be there."

Later on—another reminder.

Pen in hand, Napoleon was adding up figures. The clock began to strike. He raised his head abruptly.

"What time is that?"

"Three o'clock, sire."

"Ah! *Bon Dieu!* It is too late to go to the ball. What do you think?"

"Sire, that is exactly my opinion."

"Well then, let's each go to his bed."

And accompanying Gaudin to the door he added: "And most people think we spend our lives having a good time and, as the Orientals say, eating sweets! . . . Good evening, Excellency!"

As a rule he went to bed around eleven o'clock. He was not sharing the same bed with Josephine now—he needed more freedom in his work and in his thoughts, he said. But he still went down the secret staircase to join her fairly frequently.

MARIE WALEWSKA
From the Portrait by Lefèvre

JEROME BONAPARTE
King of Westphalia
After the Portrait by Mme. Kinson

Wearing a dressing-gown and preceded by Constant bearing a torch, he would go down to her room. The Empress would be delighted—each of those visits 'seemed to her a little victory. The next day, rubbing her pretty hands, she would tell everyone about it.

"I am late getting up today, but you see, that is because Bonaparte spent the night with me."

At such times she was gay, vivacious, bubbling over with laughter. That was a good moment to ask favors of her. "She rebuffed no one," wrote Constant, "and people could get anything they wanted."

As a rule Napoleon would rush back to his room like a whirlwind and pull off his clothes in great haste, flinging his coat on the floor, his hat on a piece of furniture, his decoration on the carpet. Then he would call loudly for Constant:

"Hullo there! Mr. Constant!"

The valet would hold out the bandanna which he wound around his head, and light his silver-gilt night lamp. Napoleon promptly got into his bed, which was always heated by a warming pan except during the great summer heat. Pungent fumes rose from an incense burner: pastilles of aloes, ambergris, benzoin and perfumed vinegar. Napoleon detested a musty odor and, even more, the odor of the human body. Josephine's extreme fastidiousness and the sweet, fresh perfume of her skin had always been a delight to him. Let a woman to whom he had taken a fancy be careless about her person or indulge too heavily in perfumes, and he lost interest at once.

If he could not sleep he would send for the Empress to read to him. She had a soft, low voice and the regular monotony of her delivery made him drowsy. After he had fallen asleep Constant would leave him and go up to his own room. Roustan and the manservant, who happened to be on duty, slept in the salon adjoining the Emperor's bedroom. Day and night his bath was kept in readiness: he had been known on occasion to call for it in the middle of the night.

Sometimes, after three or four hours of a deep sleep, he would get up and, slipping on a pair of trousers and his dressing-gown, return to his desk. That was the moment when he felt most lucid and in the best form. If he had anything to write, he would send for poor Méneval and have him wakened. Then, pacing back and forth, he would begin to dictate. The night would be broken by a light supper and day would dawn before he dismissed his secretary.

"What is the matter with you, Méneval?" he would cry. "Why! You're asleep on your feet!"

Then, laughing at the young man's swollen eyes and haggard face, he would give him a resounding thwack on the back to wake him up. He himself then got into bed again and dozed for an hour or two. In that way, according to Roederer, Napoleon often managed to get as many as eighteen working hours into his day.

Part Three

THE POLISH LOVE

I

Marie Walewska

ON OCTOBER 1, 1805, Napoleon set out from Strassburg to deal with the new coalition which England had entered into with Austria and Russia. He was deeply affected. He kissed Josephine, who was in tears, and embraced Talleyrand.

"It is hard," he said, "to say goodbye to the two people one loves best."

He had moments of those outbursts of tender feeling. This one was followed by a sort of nervous anxiety. He burst into tears, vomited. They made him sit down and gave him a little orange-flower water to drink. By degrees he recovered his composure and, wiping his eyes, called for his carriage. A moment later he was off.

On the 2nd of December, the sun of Austerlitz dawned bright and clear. A perfect victory reminiscent of the victories in the Italian campaign. Peace was signed almost immediately at Pressburg. On his return to Paris, Napoleon made out a list of promotions for kings. Among his allies first—the Elector of Bavaria and the Duke of Württemberg. Then—and this was the most important—those among his family. He took the throne from the Bourbon of Naples and gave it to Joseph. Murat became Grand Duke of Berg; even Pauline, who had been neglected so far, was made Princess of Guastalla. Eugène had been legally adopted by the Emperor. He was now married to the daughter of the King of Bavaria, with the promise of succeeding to the crown of Italy if Napoleon were to die without posterity. A few months later, Louis was to be proclaimed King of Holland.

He lavished favors and honors on his nearest and dearest, first of all because he was still imbued with the Corsican idea of the clan and because he saw in his brothers and sisters, his safest supporters, his most grateful vassals; but also—and this was per-

haps the real reason—because he loved them. Notwithstanding
his sudden changes in temper, his bluffness of speech—the Latin
method of blowing off steam—he tried in every way to please
them. Madame Mère was not pleased with the Trianon which
the Emperor had set aside for her? He bought her the château
of Pont. Was Pauline tired of her husband, the handsome but
incompetent Borghese? Napoleon took him off her hands by
sending him to the army. Elisa was greedy for money and lands
—he granted her slightest request. Jerome was waiting for the
Church—which so far had proved obstinate—to annul his marriage to Miss Patterson. In the meantime Napoleon made him
a captain in the navy, then a commodore. Soon he was to become
a French prince, an imperial highness, with an income equal to
his brother's. Seeing Hortense unhappy with the maniac whom
she had been forced to accept as a husband, Napoleon sought
to console her by lavishing courtesies and handsome gifts on her.
And to tame that difficult husband he gave him more than four
millions in the year 1805 alone! His Uncle Fesch had failed
in his embassy to Rome; moreover he was deliberately deceiving
the Emperor and supporting ultramontane doctrines—Napoleon
made him coadjutor to the Prince Primate (the Archbishop of
Prague), with the promise of a responsible post and enormous
revenues.

To please his wife Napoleon had been sending one of her
young cousins, Stephanie de Beauharnais, to Mme. Campan's
school for the past two years. An orphan and destitute, Stephanie had first been in the care of an Englishwoman, Lady
Bath. Now when Napoleon married Eugène to the Princess of
Bavaria, the latter was engaged to the hereditary Prince of
Baden. The Emperor could think of no better way to console
that young man for his loss than to offer him the hand of
Stephanie de Beauharnais. Who would dream of holding out
against the Emperor of the French? Certainly not that little
German princeling. On Napoleon's return to Paris, it was all
arranged before the future couple had even so much as had a
glimpse of each other. The Emperor thereupon took Stephanie
out of her boarding school and settled her at the Tuileries in

an apartment next to Josephine's to train her for Court life in the interim before the wedding. Stephanie de Beauharnais was just seventeen, with the loveliest figure in the world, a beautiful complexion and, above all, an irrepressible gaiety. From the very start she was the pet of the household and Josephine made much of her. Stephanie delighted the Emperor and amused him. She treated him like a favorite uncle, and he, who was so fond of youth, adapted himself to her roguishness so well that the Empress began to suspect an affair and was anxious to send the girl away. Napoleon's sisters raged against the intruder. What might not this new caprice lead to? Would not their own high stations be endangered? Rivalries of precedence are never so sharp as in a brand-new Court.

Those sisters lost no opportunity to snub and humble Stephanie, who retorted with gay jests and quips. Caroline in particular was outraged; she even went so far as to insult the girl openly. At one of the evening receptions, while the assembled guests were waiting for Napoleon to appear, Caroline sent a message to Mlle. de Beauharnais ordering her to rise—it was contrary to etiquette for anyone to remain seated "in the presence of His Majesty's sisters, the Princesses." Stephanie obeyed, but that time the insult had been too public and she burst into tears. At that moment the Emperor entered. Surprised to see the young girl weeping he asked Josephine what the matter was. The Empress was only too delighted to report Caroline's insolence.

"Is that all?" Napoleon said. Then, turning to Stephanie: "Well, come and sit on my knee. You won't be in anyone's way."

Caroline almost choked with rage. That whole evening the Emperor did not address a word to her. To teach his sisters a lesson, he decided to adopt Stephanie. The following day a notice appeared on the register of the Count de Ségur, grand master of ceremonies:

"Our intention being that the Princess Stephanie Napoleon, Our daughter, may enjoy the full prerogatives of her rank, she shall be placed at Our side at all levees, receptions and at table, and at such times as We are not present, she shall be placed at the right of the Empress."

Daughter of the Emperor, with precedence over all the princesses! The Senate, the high offices of State, sent delegates to congratulate her. Napoleon himself took charge of her trousseau. The young girl lived in a veritable fairyland until the day when her fiancé appeared.

Alas! Charles was nothing but a country bumpkin in body and in mind. He could neither talk nor smile—he was, as it were, transfixed by an excessive shyness. Stephanie disliked him at sight. She made fun of him to her friends. And yet—was it fear of the Emperor or ambition?—she went to the altar with him. A brilliant marriage! All Paris was ablaze with lights, all Paris danced. But that night when Charles tried to enter Stephanie's bedroom, she refused to let him in and, for greater safety, compelled her schoolmate, Nelly Bourjoly, to sleep with her.

Josephine insisting without effect, Napoleon took the young girl severely to task. She held out for a week, both at the Tuileries and at Malmaison. In vain did the prince have his hair cropped à la Titus to please her—Stephanie laughed in his face. Every night the unfortunate fellow found her door locked and was obliged to sleep in an armchair.

At first Napoleon controlled himself, but in the end he lost his temper and compelled Stephanie to accompany her husband to Karlsruhe. There, so he thought, the capricious minx would certainly be obliged to relent. Stephanie evaded, wrote plaintive letters to the Emperor. "I imagine that I am in France. I think I am near you and I even take pleasure in dwelling on my sorrow."

Napoleon answered in no uncertain terms.

"Be as charming as you can to the Elector. He is your father. Love your husband. He deserves it because of the devotion he shows you."

Tired of struggling, Stephanie finally yielded. She would put up with Charles, she would be a Grand Duchess and she was to lead the life of a German princess, always unhappy, always under observation. Her husband was to die of poisoning while still a young man. Their son, kidnapped from his cradle, a victim of a palace tragedy, was poor Gaspard Hauser. . . .

As is usual with husbands, Napoleon was never more attentive to the Empress than when he was deceiving her. Those were the moments when he closed his eyes most frequently to her extravagances, when he provided most amply for her protégées. The more numerous his extra-marital adventures, the more he exercised his wits to hide them from her.

When Mme. Duchâtel's reign came to an end, Caroline Murat looked about for another favorite. In that way she would get even with Josephine and make sure of her own interests. Though she was Grand Duchess of Berg, Caroline was not satisfied—she wanted to be a queen like Julie, like Hortense. When Napoleon called on her on his return from Austerlitz, she directed his attention to one of her ladies, Eléonore Denuelle, a former school friend of hers from Mme. Campan's.

Eléonore Denuelle de la Plaigne, daughter, it would seem, of Louvet de Couvray, the author of *Faublas,* had foolishly married a rascal named Revel, a former officer. Two months after the wedding Revel was arrested for forgery. While waiting for her divorce, Eléonore appealed to Caroline for aid. The latter took her into her household first as a sort of reception clerk, then as a reader. Napoleon's sister might be ambitious and as Talleyrand said "carry Cromwell's head on a pretty woman's shoulders," but she was also a loyal friend and enjoyed helping people. For that matter Eléonore was beautiful and charming—nineteen years old, tall, dark, with a fine figure, slender hands and feet, an exquisite neck, regular features and alluring black eyes. She had few morals or scruples. She had been brought up by a frivolous mother of rather questionable repute and she had one desire only—to shine.

Napoleon found her to his liking and let her know it: she yielded promptly. He received her the first time at the Tuileries, in his private apartment. Eléonore was one of those rare women who did not become attached to him. To her that liaison was merely a passing annoyance that would repay her in ample material compensations. She herself told the story that, even in the Emperor's bedroom, she often took advantage of a momentary distraction on his part to push the hand of the clock forward a half hour. Always in a hurry, always keeping track of the time, Napoleon once satisfied, would glance at the clock.

"So soon!" he would murmur.

And back he would go to work, leaving Eléonore to dress and disappear, well pleased at having shortened the interview.

No sooner had she received her divorce than she discovered that she was pregnant and promptly informed the Emperor. Napoleon was somewhat sceptical at first. He had heard from Fouché that Murat was also courting the lady. Nevertheless Duroc installed her in a fashionable apartment on the rue de la Victoire, where Napoleon visited her from time to time. On December 13, 1806, she gave birth to a boy. He was registered under the name of Léon "son of the demoiselle Eléonore Denuelle, age twenty years, of independent means, and of father unknown."

The news reached the Emperor at Pulstuck, at the height of his campaign against the Russians. Absorbed as he was by the cares of war, that news, nevertheless, moved him deeply. A son! He had a son! . . . So, Corvisart, Josephine, his brothers, even he himself, had been wrong! He could have children and so make certain of his dynasty. A new world seemed to open up before him. That was the moment when he thought of the "hoax" * Josephine had suggested—if he ever had a natural son, she would recognize it as her own child and, in consequence, as the heir to the throne. But Napoleon was far from France. Besides, he could not be sure enough of Eléonore and he dared not entrust her with such an important secret. His thoughts were soon to turn in another direction.

If he had had any doubts as to his paternity they were to vanish the moment he saw the child on his return from Poland. He was a strong, handsome boy, with Napoleon's shape of head,

* Napoleon himself used that term in speaking to Las Cases and Gourgaud at St. Helena.

his eyes and his mouth. He took the child in his arms and fondled him. Little Léon had been placed in the care of Mme. Loir, Achille Murat's nurse. Thenceforward Napoleon was to see the little fellow from time to time and he was to settle on him an income of thirty thousand francs, which would be increased on several occasions by important gifts.

As for Eléonore, she promptly committed a blunder that ruined her in the Emperor's eyes. One day accompanied by her mother she appeared at Fontainebleau where the Court was in residence and, going up to the Emperor's apartments, ordered Constant to announce her. Such audacity was too much for Napoleon. Through his valet he forbade Eléonore ever to appear before him without his permission and requested her to leave Fontainebleau at once. He never saw her again. The young woman wasted no time in consoling herself. Provided with a very ample dowry (half a million) she married a Lieutenant Augier the following year. After that officer's death during the retreat from Russia, Eléonore was to marry a third time—a Bavarian, Count de Luxbourg. She led a busy, turbulent life and did not die till the end of the Second Empire. Mistrusting a mother who was far too volatile and capricious, Napoleon appointed Baron de Mauvières, Méneval's father-in-law, guardian for little Léon. From time to time the Baron brought the little boy to the Tuileries or to Saint-Cloud.

That campaign of 1806-1807, launched first against Prussia and then against Russia, frightened Josephine. She was all instinct and she seems to have sensed the danger, not only for Napoleon, but for herself. The Emperor took a playful tone in trying to comfort her. What was she afraid of anyway? She had her daughter, her grandchildren, good news! From Berlin he wrote telling her of the pardon he had granted to Prince von Hatzfeldt, head of the Prussian municipality, who had been caught in the act of spying.

"I have received your letter in which you seem annoyed with me because I speak badly of women. It is true that I despise intriguing women above anything else in the world. I am accustomed to good, sweet, persuasive women. Those are the women I like. If I am spoiled, it is not my fault, but yours. For that matter you will see that I have been very kind to one of them who proved to be both appreciative and honest—Mme. von Hatzfeldt. When I showed her her husband's letter, she burst into tears and with deep feeling exclaimed naïvely: 'Oh! That really is his handwriting!' Her tone of voice as she read it, touched one's heart. I felt sorry for her. 'Well, Madame,' I said to her. 'Throw that letter into the fire. I shall not have the heart to punish your husband.' She burnt the letter and appeared to be very happy. Her husband is now much relieved. Two hours before, he was lost. . . ." (November 6th.)

However, Josephine was not wrong in fearing the effect of that war for herself. It was, in fact, to mark an essential turning point in Napoleon's mind and heart. In Poland he was to find the second love of his life, a calmer, deeper love that, coming after his youthful passion, was to touch him far more poignantly, to influence his policy, to orient his destiny.

On January 1, 1807, alone in his carriage with Duroc, Napoleon halted at Blonie on the road to Warsaw to change horses. In the delirious crowds that pressed against the wheels, two women, crushed, half-smothered, waved their hands. As Duroc got out of the carriage, he heard one of them call to him in pleading tones:

"Oh, sir! Get me out of here and do arrange for me to catch a glimpse of him if only for a second!"

A pair of enormous childlike eyes were raised to his. Beneath her black fur bonnet, she was small, blond, fragile and utterly charming. Emotion had dyed her transparent skin a deep pink. Duroc, ever courteous, pushed his way through the crowd, offered his arm to the young woman and led her to the carriage.

"Sire," he said to the Emperor who was leaning out of the window, "here is a young lady who has braved the dangers of the crowd to see you."

Napoleon took off his hat and started to say a few words, which the stranger did not let him finish. A look of ecstasy came over her face as she clasped her hands and, with bated breath, exclaimed:

"Welcome, welcome, sire! A thousand times welcome to this land of heroes who but await your coming to rise again!"

Napoleon was impatient to get on, but that welcome surprised him and he took a second look at her. He liked blondes and she was certainly the most ravishing one he had ever seen. The hint of Slavic accent in her speech delighted him. Seizing one of the bouquets with which his carriage had been filled on the way, he offered it to her.

"Keep it," he said with a smile. "Keep it as a guarantee of my good intentions. We shall see each other again in Warsaw, I hope."

Then the carriage drove off. The Emperor leaned out of the window and waved his hat in farewell.

Such was the first meeting between Napoleon and Marie Walewska. Born a Laczinska, of an ancient but impoverished family, at sixteen Marie had obeyed her parents' wishes and married Anastasio Colonna Walewski, a châtelain, in other words, a landed squire, a wealthy man of a noble house, but an old man, twice a widower and of a morose disposition. For three years he kept Marie locked up in his gloomy castle of Walewice, where she acted as secretary to him. A son was born to her, her only joy: she hoped to see him grow up a free man in a regenerated land. For Marie Walewska was, above all else, a patriot. Disappointed in her woman's dreams, she had transferred all the passion of which she was capable to unhappy Poland, that had been so cynically dismembered. If, since Jena, Napoleon's victories had caused her heart to beat faster, it was because she saw in him the natural enemy of the three voracious eagles, the giant who could force them to disgorge, the Messiah who would make her nation rise again from the oblivion in which for eleven years—eleven years only—it had languished.

As Napoleon drew nearer to the Polish frontier that nation did rise in truth. Never perhaps had such enthusiasm, such hope mounted toward him. Over the stretches of snowy wasteland he sped in his green berlin, lighted on the way by bonfires ablaze in every village, lulled to sleep by the sound of bells that rang out on the frosty air as if for the resurrection of Christ. Entering Warsaw with the thermometer at twenty degrees below zero, he passed on his way to the palace through streets where every window was filled with ladies in low-cut evening gowns, who flung him kisses and pelted him with flowers—come from who knows where, but they were the flowers of spring. Among so many others, Marie Walewska stood on the balcony of her house. He caught sight of her, recognized her and bowed.

She was too shy to attend any of the festivities at first. However, on the Emperor's order, Duroc made enquiries about her and requested Prince Joseph Poniatowski, the head of the provisional Polish government, to invite her to his ball. Countess Walewska declined the invitation. The Prince came to see her and insisted, somewhat clumsily:

"Who knows," he said, "perhaps Heaven will make use of you to restore our country!"

She would not give in. Her husband then urged her in his turn. Knowing nothing of the adventure at Blonie, Napoleon's attentions had not roused his suspicions. At last tired of pleading with her, he commanded her to go. Marie resigned herself: she would appear at the reception in honor of the Emperor.

When she arrived at the Blacha Palace, where all the Polish aristocracy had assembled, a flattering murmur followed her steps. She was dressed with the utmost simplicity—a white satin gown and over it an embroidered tulle tunic, no jewelry, but on her fair hair a wreath of myrtle. The moment she was seated Poniatowski hovered behind her chair. The Emperor, he whispered, had asked about her a number of times. He had glanced at Count Walewski and murmured: "Poor woman!" Finally, he had asked to see her dance.

"I do not dance," she replied, worried at so much homage.

A few moments later the orchestra stopped playing. The Emperor crossed the drawing-room. He looked preoccupied, almost sullen. He addressed a few words, distractedly, to the men and women who were presented to him. At last he came to

Marie Walewska. Pale and very straight she stood before him with lowered eyelids. In a hoarse voice he said:

"White does not go well on white, Madame."

As she did not reply, he added in a lower tone:

"This is not the welcome I had the right to expect. . . ."

Still she did not speak. He gave her a long look and passed on.

At once Marie was surrounded, questioned, flattered. She escaped and called for her carriage. At her home she found flowers and a note:

> You are the only one I saw, you are the only one I admired, you are the only one I desired. Send a prompt reply to calm the impatient ardor of
>
> N.

Those passionate words—too passionate—wounded her. What sort of a woman did Napoleon think he was addressing?

However Prince Poniatowski, who had brought the note in person, was waiting in front of her house for a reply. Mme. Walewska sent her maid to him:

"There is no answer."

He protested, he must see the Countess. She locked herself in. The Prince pleaded with her from the other side of the door at the risk of being overheard by the Count. In the end, worn out, he went away.

But the next morning, on awakening, the young woman received another message. She returned it to the bearer, unopened. All morning long her doorbell kept ringing. Callers followed one after the other: Joseph Poniatowski, the most important magnates, Duroc. . . . She refused to see them all. Her husband intervened, insisting that she should receive the Poles at least. They urged her to be present at a dinner the Emperor was scheduled to attend. She pleaded a headache. They made so bold as to remind her:

"Everything must yield, Madame, before circumstances of such vast import to our nation. We trust therefore that your indisposition will pass before the hour for that dinner which, as a loyal Pole, you cannot refuse to attend."

She yielded at last, poor child, surrounded by all those avid glances. Blind to the whole situation, her husband, sent her to a Frenchwoman, Mme. de Vauban, the mistress of Prince Poniatowski, who was to instruct her in the details of etiquette. That woman of the old régime was delighted with her rôle and overwhelmed Marie with flattery and praises. They read her the letter she had refused to accept:

> Have I displeased you, Madame? I had, however, the right to hope the contrary. Am I mistaken? Your eagerness has grown less, whereas mine has increased. You rob me of my rest! Oh! Bestow a little joy, a little happiness on a poor heart that is ready to adore you. Is it so difficult to obtain a reply? You owe me two.
>
> N.

And they gave her a petition to read, signed by the members of the provisional government, in which, crudely, they implored her not to thwart Napoleon's desires:

> Madame, little causes often produce great effects. Throughout all ages women have had tremendous influence on the politics of the world. . . .
> If you were a man you would give your life to the just and noble cause of the Fatherland. As a woman there are other sacrifices you can make and which you should force yourself to make, painful as they may be.
> Do you think Esther gave herself to Ahasuerus because she loved him? The terror he inspired in her was such that she fainted at his glance. Was that not proof that love had no part in that union? She sacrificed herself to save her nation—and she had the glory of saving it.
> May we be able to say the same for your glory and our happiness!

What emotions did that extraordinary petition from the great men of her country arouse in a young woman of twenty, alone, passionately patriotic and with no one to advise her? They treated her like a heroine, declared that she held the happiness or unhappiness of an entire people in her hands. She lost her head. Moving like an automaton she dressed and made ready to attend the dinner where the Emperor would appear, so they told her, only on condition that she herself were present.

Struck by Marie's beauty, Napoleon had been perhaps even more touched by her melancholy. The Polish woman's reserve, coming as it did after the impulse that had flung her at him at Blonie, whipped up his desire, made it more imperious. Accustomed to swift abandonments, her resistance inflamed him. The caprice of the first moment became a violent desire that roused him to a state of unusual perturbation. "The day after the ball," writes Constant, "he kept getting up, walking about the room, sitting down and getting up again. I thought I would never get him dressed that day." He was tormented by jealousy, which, in him, was never far from love. Because he had noticed that two of his aides-de-camp were overly attentive to Mme. Walewska at that same reception, he ordered Berthier to send Louis de Périgord to the front line on the Passarge, and Bertrand to Jerome's headquarters at Breslau.

Marie entered the drawing-room. The Emperor walked toward her.

"I thought Madame was ill," he said to her. "Has she quite recovered?"

Reassured by that discreet tone, she thanked him. They took their places at table, Marie next to Duroc and opposite the Emperor. She listened with beating heart while Napoleon talked of Poland and asked questions about its history. His glance often lingered on her. Suddenly he motioned to Duroc. The Grand Marshal leaned toward his neighbor. What had she done with the bouquet the Emperor gave her at Blonie? he asked.

She replied that she was saving it for her son.

"Ah, Madame," murmured Duroc, bending his handsome curly head toward her, "allow us to offer you something worthier of you."

"I prefer flowers," she answered curtly.

A moment's silence, then Duroc, embarrassed, managed to say:

"Well, we shall gather laurels on your native soil to offer to you."

The Emperor arose to take coffee in the salon. Again he approached Mme. Walewska, smiled at her and, touching her hand, murmured in a low tone:

"No, no, with such sweet, such tender eyes, with that kind expression a woman must let herself yield, she cannot take delight in torturing—or she would be the most coquettish, the cruelest of women."

She did not answer. What could she say? Napoleon moved off and the rest of the men followed him.

Marie spent that evening at Mme. de Vauban's house where the Poles maneuvered her, against her will, into a tête-à-tête with Duroc. He spoke to her respectfully, courteously, and tried to rouse her sympathies by telling her of the Emperor's anxieties, of the strain such a life as his entailed.

"Could you," he asked, "deny the request of a man who has never known what it was to be refused? Ah! His glory is beset with sorrow. It rests with you to brighten it with a few moments of happiness."

Bewildered, she burst into tears. As Duroc took leave of her, he placed a letter on her knees. Marie Walewska refused to break the seal. Someone opened it and read it to her:

> There are moments when too great responsibilities become a burden, and that is what I am experiencing now. How satisfy the need of a heart aflame with love that would cast itself at your feet but is restrained by the weight of high considerations that paralyze the most ardent of desires? Oh! If you only would! You alone can remove the obstacles that separate us. My friend Duroc will assist you with ways and means.
>
> Oh, come! Come! You shall have everything you wish. Your country will be dearer to me when you have taken pity on my poor heart.
>
> *N.*

And still Marie Walewska turned a deaf ear to that plea. But wily voices around her kept repeating that the fate of her country rested with her. In the end she told them:

"Do with me as you will."

They left her behind closed doors—and there she sat, shivering, disconsolate. Now and then she would move over to the window: behind the panes of glass in the half-darkened room, she could see Warsaw celebrating and the people dancing by torchlight.

A knock at the door! A man entered, or a woman, she did not know which. Her head was whirling. Someone wrapped a fur cloak about her, threw a scarf over her hair. Someone else offered his arm. She passed down the staircase and entered a carriage that rolled swiftly over the cobblestones and drew up before the Grand Palace. They led her along a gallery lined with portraits, then into a room. She sank down into an armchair. Someone was kneeling before her, kissing her hands—Napoleon.

He spoke to her tenderly, soothingly . . . she did not hear. Suddenly, he clasped her in his arms, kissed her on the lips. She sprang to her feet and rushed to the door. He was there before her. Throwing his arm about her, he half carried, half led her back to her armchair.

What could this revolt mean? He had not expected that. He did not know that she had been forced to this interview. Was the Polish girl just an artful hussy, trying to sell her surrender? But the tears that rolled down her blanched cheeks, the sighs that lifted that childish breast seemed so sincere that he was filled with compassion. Napoleon became all gentleness; he took an almost fatherly tone, questioned her about her family: where did they come from, where was she brought up, why did she marry an old man? At first she could not speak, then gradually growing calmer, she managed to stammer a few words that let him glimpse the emptiness of her life.

"What has been joined together on earth," she sighed, "can be severed only in Heaven."

He laughed . . . and she burst into tears again. Then he began to talk about himself. She listened to him and the hours passed. There was a knock at the door. Duroc entered.

"What, so soon!" cried Napoleon. "Well, my sweet and plaintive dove! Come, dry your tears! Go and lie down. Do not fear the eagle. With you he has only the strength of a passionate love, but a love that above all longs to win your heart. You will end by loving him for he will be all things to you. Do you understand?"

He wrapped her cloak about her, covered that lovely head with her veil and refused to let her go until she had promised to return the next day.

By that time she was almost reassured. Did she believe that the Emperor would be satisfied with a tender friendship? Her woman's vanity, infinitesimal as it was, was flattered by his attentions. Broken, exhausted, she fell asleep.

When she awoke they brought her a bouquet—a sheaf of laurel combined with rare flowers—two boxes and a letter:

> Marie, my sweet Marie, my first thought is for you, my first desire to see you again. You will come back, won't you? You have promised me. Otherwise the eagle will fly to you! I shall see you at dinner, my friend has told me. Deign therefore to accept this bouquet: let it be a mysterious tie, a secret understanding between us when we are surrounded by others. When my hand presses my heart, you will know that it is filled only with thoughts of you, and in reply you will touch your bouquet. Love me, my sweet Marie, and may your hand never leave your bouquet!
>
> N.

The boxes contained a bouquet of jewels, a garland of diamonds. Anger again seized Marie Walewska. Did the Emperor think he could buy her?

They crowded around her, tried to calm her. She sent the jewelry back to the Grand Marshal. Duroc met her later that day at a reception and ventured a light reproach. She replied that she would accept nothing from Napoleon. What she wanted from him was not diamonds, but the hope of seeing her country reborn.

"Has not the Emperor given you that hope?" Duroc asked.

And he explained that, after the war, Napoleon intended to restore Poland's autonomy. She shook her head. Duroc tried vainly to convince her. He was an honest man and he heartily disliked the task of go-between which the Emperor had placed on his shoulders. Moreover he pitied Marie and was worried about her. But Napoleon had appealed to his friendship. And when the Emperior took that tone, Duroc would have gone to the end of the world on his knees for him.

For a few moments Marie Walewska thought of flight. Flinging some clothes into a valise she sat down at her desk to write a farewell letter to her husband:

> Your first thought, Anastasio, will be to criticize my conduct when you learn why I am writing to you. But when you have read to the end, you will not blame me. I have done my best to open your eyes. Alas, you were blinded by a nameless vanity and, I realize, by your patriotism: you did not want to see the danger.
>
> Last night I spent several hours with ——. Your political friends will tell you who sent me there. I came out unharmed, promising to return this evening. I cannot keep that promise, for now I know too well what would happen.
>
> Some people will think that I am deserting: others will tell you so without a doubt. Tell those men that one's conscience and one's convictions come before sacrifice for one's country and that this alone has saved me from suicide.

Suddenly she experienced a revulsion of feeling. Desert— could she do that? Had she the right to betray the cause to which she had dreamt of devoting her life? What was her duty as a wife compared to her duty as a Polish woman? There followed a long and painful struggle with herself, from which she emerged utterly exhausted. . . .

That evening she allowed herself to be driven back to the Grand Palace.

The Emperor was apparently in a bad mood, disgruntled.

"So, here you are at last," was his welcome. "I thought I was never going to see you again."

He led her to a chair and, standing in front of her, poured forth wild reproaches. Why had she come to meet him at Blonie? Why had she pretended to welcome his attentions? Why had

she refused his gifts? Was she playing with him? And, flying into
a rage, he shouted:

"That's just like a Pole! You have merely confirmed my
opinion of your nation!"

Trembling, but courageous, since it was a question of her
country, she implored him:

"Oh, sire! Have mercy! Tell me what that opinion is!"

The Poles, he said, were proud and fickle. They were capable
of much enthusiasm, but their emotions were of short duration.
She was like that. She apparently offered herself to him and
when he reached out to take her—she had vanished. But he was
not the man to be discouraged.

"I am going to make—note that word well!" he exclaimed
violently, "I am going to *make* you love me! I have made your
country's name live again. Thanks to me the Polish race still
exists! I shall do even more. But remember that just as I hold
this watch in my hand and break it before your eyes, so the
name of Poland and all your hopes will perish if you cast aside
my love and refuse me yours!"

His strong voice rang out, vibrant with emotion. Poor Marie
stood there silent, motionless. But when he flung his watch on
the floor and crushed it under his heel, her nerves gave way and
she fell in a faint.

When she recovered consciousness, when she saw Napoleon's
anxious face and heard the words he murmured, she realized
that he had taken an improper advantage of her. He had committed that act of baseness under the impulse of a savage passion. . . . Now he was sorry and, confronted with her despairing eyes, he was afraid. . . .

A sad and heavy hour in which the man knelt silent and
abashed before his captive who sobbed softly, endlessly. At last
Duroc arrived. With the Emperor's help, he carried Marie to
the apartment that had been prepared for her in the same
palace, for she was not to be allowed to return to her own home.

In the days that followed Marie saw no one but Napoleon.
She passed the time in tears, prayers, meditation. In the eve-

ning she dined alone with the Emperor, each time reminding him of his promises, each time pleading her country's cause. In all her shame one thought alone comforted her: Napoleon would pay his debt to her by reawakening Poland. And, in fact, she learned that he was gradually building up again the various services of the nation. A Council of State was formed, a ministry, a nucleus of the Polish army composed of the élite of the country's youth. Now, under the leadership of Poniatowski, they were to fight under the glorious flags that had been hidden away since the partition of the country.

Count Walewski's eyes were open at last and he retired to his estates in Posnan. Marie breathed more easily. Between her and Napoleon a sort of tenderness, a real friendship had developed. The Emperor made every effort to soothe her, to reassure her, to present the future to her in the rosiest light.

"You can rest assured," he told her, "that the promise I made you will be fulfilled. I have already forced Prussia to surrender the part she usurped. Time will do the rest. It is not the moment. We must have patience. Politics is a string that will snap if pulled too hard. Meantime your statemen will be learning their profession. For how many of them have you? You are rich in loyal patriots; you have willing hands, yes, I admit that; honor and courage ooze from every pore of your men, but that is not enough. One must have a great unity."

He confided his deepest thoughts to Marie—undoubtedly the first time with any woman, for he had always found Josephine too frivolous for serious discussions.

"You know that I love your nation, that my plans, my political views, all lead me to desire its complete restoration. I intend to support its efforts, to protect its rights. Everything that does not interfere with French interests and my duties toward France I shall undoubtedly do. But remember that the distances between us are too great. What I may build up today can be destroyed tomorrow. My first duty is toward France. I cannot spill French blood for a cause foreign to her interests, or arm my people to rush to your aid every time you need help."

She ventured to disagree with him, thereby teaching him a

thousand things he did not know about the life, the history, the social world of Poland. They frequently differed in opinion. She never yielded: it was Napoleon who gave ground. He would pat her cheek or pinch her ear.

"My dear little Marie, you are worthy of being a Spartan and having a country. . . ."

He loved her so dearly that he took an interest in every detail of her life. He insisted that she give up her white, black and gray gowns and take to colors of which he was particularly fond.

"A Polish woman," she replied, "must wear mourning for her country. When you have brought it to life again, I shall wear nothing but pink."

The Empress lingered on in Mainz, where she was awaiting permission from the Emperor to join him. Polish women were so dangerous, people kept telling her. Napoleon quieted her fears as best he could.

"The beauties of Poland do not deserve the opinion you have of them," he wrote to her, as early as December 31st. "I received your letter in a wretched barn where the only bed I had was mud, wind and straw."

He was not lying: he had not yet seen Marie Walewska.

Josephine insisted upon joining him.

"My dear," he wrote to her on January 7th, "I am touched by all you tell me, but the weather is cold, the roads very bad and far from safe. I cannot therefore expose you to so much fatigue, so many dangers."

Now that the Polish idyl was in full swing he was anxious for the Empress to return to France without delay. She protested and complained. Napoleon replied good humoredly:

I laughed at your remark that you had married a husband to be with him. I had thought, in my ignorance, that the wife was made for the husband, the husband for country, family and glory. Forgive my ignorance: our beautiful ladies can always teach us something new. . . .

Josephine dared not disobey any longer. She was anxious not

to displease Napoleon for she hoped that the kingdom of Poland, once re-established, would go to Eugène and not, as the Bonapartes were already saying, to Jerome or Murat. In her drawing-room, surrounded by her intimate friends, she laid out the cards to discover what fate held in store for her and she played innumerable games of patience. She had learned of the Emperor's love affair with Mme. Walewska, and had even ventured to refer to it in writing to him. He evaded with a jest. But he could not refrain from confiding to his brother Joseph: "My health has never been so good, so much so that I have become even more of a lover than in the past. . . ."

At Napoleon's urgent request Mme. Walewska finally consented to attend the festivities that followed one after the other in Warsaw in the interim before the campaign was resumed. He would not enjoy them if she were not there. He liked to see her before him, under the gleaming lights, in all the brilliancy of her youth and frail beauty. Often he would motion to her, secretly, signs that she alone could understand. She admired his ability to think of her and at the same time neglect none of the duties that devolved on him. He answered her tenderly:

"Does that surprise you? Remember that I must be worthy of the high office that is mine. I have the honor to rule nations. I was merely an acorn: I have become an oak. I stand out in clear view. People see me and observe me from afar as well as from near by. That situation forces me to play a rôle that cannot always be natural to me, but which I must maintain in order to account, to myself more than to others, for the display which is forced upon me by the status with which I am clothed. For instance, with the eyes of all on us, how could I say to you: 'Marie, I love you!' And every time I look at you that is what I want to say, but if I so much as bend down toward your ear I am departing from custom."

Those about them, the General Staff, men and women in Polish social circles, became the accomplices of his love. Though she rebelled against it, Marie was received everywhere with the honors due a sovereign. A kind of discreet enthusiasm followed the steps of the new Esther. Her two sisters-in-law, Princess Jablonowska and Countess Birgenska, were the first to go to her side, to praise her conduct, not to defend her, for Marie's talent for self-effacement and the little that was known of her private suffering disarmed even the envious.

However, Russian troops under Benningsen were massing in East Prussia and the Emperor was obliged to return to the army. Every day he sent a messenger to Marie, who had left for Vienna with her mother. After a number of successes came Eylau, a battle partially lost, which left the end of the war in doubt. Napoleon was deeply moved by the spectacle of the vast plain on which the corpses lay buried under the snow.

"The country," he wrote sadly to Josephine, "is strewn with the bodies of the dead and wounded. It hurts one and the spirit is crushed at the sight of so many victims."

His disappointment brought on a severe and very painful stomach attack. In those moments of weakness he could not bear to be alone. Taking up quarters in the castle of Fincken-stein till spring when he could engage in a decisive action, he sent for Marie to join him. The sacrifice he was asking of her was very great. This time she was obliged to leave her family and her child openly, to publish her dishonor to all. She did not hesitate. The very fact that Napoleon was unhappy, made him irresistible. Was he not fighting for Poland? He sent her brother, Téodor Laczinski, a captain in the Lancers, to escort her to Finckenstein. There she lived like a recluse, with only Napoleon for company. In the morning he never left her side except to work with Berthier, Maret, or Savary; or to hold a review in the castle courtyard while Marie looked on through the shutters of her bedroom window. Afterward he would come back to lunch with her—Constant, his valet, would serve it on a small table. Then Duroc would appear to help the Emperor go over his mail from France. So the slow, tranquil hours passed. Marie read and embroidered. Napoleon annotated his ministers' reports, flinging the dossiers and pamphlets on the floor beside him. A big log fire would be burning on the hearth.

Sometimes, deep in thought, the Emperor would get up and push aside the litter of paper with his foot, pace up and down the room, wander over to the casement window to gaze out over the countryside still white with snow, and then come back to toast his feet at the fire.

He loved her more and more every day—he could not do without her. It was not the feverish, jealous love for Josephine that had tortured him, almost driven him out of his mind, but a more mature, tenderer passion, one that had deep roots in his spirit as well as in his flesh. Marie may not have loved him yet, but living in such close intimacy with him she had come to know him better. She felt particularly drawn to him in his moments of frequent melancholy when he would bewail the loneliness of men like himself, and their need—so seldom gratified—of a confidante they could trust, of an enduring affection. At times he even pretended to be more disillusioned than he actually was, for the sheer pleasure of rousing her sympathy and of seeing the Polish girl gaze at him with tender eyes.

So several weeks passed in a charming intimacy, broken only by the rare absences of the Emperor when he was obliged to visit some outpost or other. On May 15th, he received word of the death of little Napoleon, the son of Louis and Hortense. The little fellow had died in a few days as the result of the croup. Napoleon was deeply grieved for he had dearly loved that child. During the campaign he almost never closed a letter without an affectionate message for him: "Greetings to M. Napoleon" . . . "Don't forget M. Napoleon" . . . "I have received a letter from M. Napoleon" . . . "A kiss to little Napoleon." . . . He mentioned his grief to Fouché. And to his old friend of the Egyptian days, Monge, he wrote: "Thanks for your kind words on the death of poor little Napoleon. It was his fate."

Alas, thought Napoleon, Fate was master. Around him he saw his soldiers, his favorite officers dying. That was all there was to life: a narrow, difficult path on the road that leads to death. He wrote several letters to Hortense urging her to keep up her courage, even scolding her awkwardly:

My daughter, you have not written me a line in your great sorrow. . . . I am told that you take no interest in anything, that you are indifferent to everything—as I can easily perceive from your silence. That is not good, Hortense. . . . Your son was all in all to you. Your mother and I therefore mean nothing! Had I been at Malmaison I would have wept with you. . . . Farewell, my daughter, be *cheerful*. You must resign yourself. Keep in good health so that you may fulfil all your duties. (June 12th.)

He himself had no time to dwell on his grief. The campaign had begun again. On June 6th, Napoleon returned to the army. On the 14th, the anniversary of Marengo, he crushed the Russians at Friedland. Having lost his guards, his artillery, his flags, Alexander fled behind the Niemen.

A week later peace was to be concluded on the raft of Tilsit. To Marie Walewska it brought keen disillusionment. Out of consideration for Russia, Poland was restored in part only under the form of a grand duchy. Half of her former provinces remained Russian or Austrian. Deeply grieved, the young woman rejoined the Emperor at Königsberg. In those three days he spent with her, Napoleon tried to comfort her. He begged her to wait a little, to trust in him, not to give him up—she had told him that she would not go to Paris, that she would retire to her mother's house in the country to await happier days. Napoleon pleaded with her.

"I know," he said, "that you can live without me. . . . I know that your heart is not mine. . . . But you are sweet and kind; your heart is so pure, so noble! Would you deprive me of a few moments of joy at your side each day? That joy I can have only through you—and yet people think I am the happiest man on earth!"

Those pleas could not fail to touch her in the end. Marie promised that when he returned to France she would join him there.

II

Napoleon and Lucien

THE PEACE of Tilsit raised Jerome to the rank of king. Napoleon turned the Prussian provinces of Westphalia into a State and presented them to that young man of twenty-two. He married him to Catherine, daughter of the King of Württemberg. Catherine was certainly not a pretty girl and she was already far too heavy, but she was a princess and her kindness and loyalty were such that they would always redound to her undying credit. The marriage ceremonies at Paris were magnificent, and Jerome made his début as a sovereign by squandering three million francs in two months.

On his return to Paris after their long separation, Napoleon found Josephine restless and constrained. The death of her grandson had been a great blow to her—she realized that the strongest tie that bound her to Napoleon was now broken. More than ever in her heart of hearts she lived in terror of a divorce.

As a matter of fact he had been thinking of divorce ever since Tilsit. Why, he wondered, should he not strengthen his affiliation with the Czar by a family alliance? Alexander had a sister—it was rumored that he would not have refused to give her to Jerome. Could he refuse the Emperor of the French, for whom he professed such admiration and friendship? Back again at the Tuileries, Napoleon began to consider the matter more closely: he felt positively young in contrast to Josephine's haggard face. She was still exquisitely distinguished, but she had lost her beauty; and, tormented by her fears, she was often less gracious, sometimes even cold. People began to desert her drawing-room and flock to the Elysée, where Caroline Murat held the most agreeable of courts—also the most useful to ambitious souls.

There they conspired openly with Maret, Fouché and even Talleyrand, for the Empress' downfall.

Against so many enemies Josephine stood almost alone. Eugène was ruling Italy, Hortense was taking the waters in the Pyrenees and amusing herself with a number of young people. Fouché, the most active of the conspirators, chose this moment to crush her.

Fouché figured that the birth of little Léon and the new Polish love affair should have destroyed most of Napoleon's scruples. He himself would now free him of the last tie, that of the emotions—the Emperor, he was sure, would be grateful to him later on. It did not take him long to prime his guns. He allowed word to get about Paris that Napoleon had decided on a divorce. Then, hastening to Fontainebleau, where the Emperor had gone for the hunting, Fouché asked for an audience with Josephine and engaged battle.

The political future of France, he told her, would be compromised if the Emperor were to remain without an heir. Napoleon would never bring himself to ask the Empress to go. Moreover it was up to her to take the lead heroically and to immolate herself in the public interest.

That cruel blow stunned the Empress. But, quickly recovering her composure, she asked:

"Have you come at the Emperor's request?"

"No, of course not! But my devotion to the dynasty compels me to speak as I do."

The Empress drew herself up. Fouché had acted only on his own initiative. All was not lost.

"I do not have to account to you," she replied haughtily. "I shall talk with the Emperor."

Not in the least abashed, Fouché tried to press for an answer. She dismissed him. Before leaving he handed her a long letter in which he had enumerated the various reasons for his action.

Josephine promptly sent for Lavallette and M. and Mme. de Rémusat. She showed them the minister's statement.

They were unanimous in advising her to see the Emperor without delay.

"Let him read that letter," advised Rémusat. "Watch him
if you can, but whatever happens, pretend to be annoyed at
that indirect advice and tell him again that you will obey only
a definite order issued by him."

The Empress approved of that advice: tomorrow morning,
the first thing, she would go to see Napoleon.

But reflection or perhaps fear prevented her from keeping
that promise. She was so sure that such a step would be final.
Napoleon, for his part, seemed only too eager to avoid tête-à-
têtes. Then Mme. de Rémusat who liked to make herself important, decided to act on her own accord. She would go and
see the Emperor herself. One night, as Napoleon was coming
out of his study at one o'clock, on his way to bed, Constant
announced the lady-in-waiting. Surprised, Napoleon told him
to send her in. Mme. de Rémusat informed him of Fouché's
maneuver. The Emperor flew into a rage. How dared his minister interfere in his private life without his permission, mix
himself up in affairs and sentiments that were none of his
concern? He dismissed the officious lady-in-waiting, went down
to Josephine's apartments and that same night had a long
explanation with her.

To begin with he found fault with her incessant debts, then
the talk turned to topics of a broader scope. The question of
children came up. Napoleon again lamented the loss of his
nephew: he considered the possibility of having little Léon
legitimatized. Josephine offered no objection. She herself was
inclined toward that arrangement which would insure her own
position.

With an emotion that was not feigned, Napoleon disclaimed
Fouché and, at last, touched on the hypothesis of a dynastic
divorce for the purpose of a second marriage. And he added,
somewhat naïvely:

"If such a thing should happen, Josephine, you would have
to help me make that sacrifice. I should count on your friendship to protect me from all the disagreeableness of that en-
forced rupture. You would take the initiative, would you not?

And putting yourself in my place, you would have the courage to decide on your retirement of your own accord?"

The same thing, in short, that Fouché had proposed, but sugar-coated with affection. . . . Josephine was well aware of that and, fully mistress of herself, she faced the danger. She replied categorically, as Rémusat had advised.

"Sire," she said, purposely adopting the ceremonious form which as a rule she used only in public, "you are the master and you must decide my fate. When you order me to leave the Tuileries, I shall obey promptly. But the least you can do is to give me a definite command. I am your wife. I have been crowned by you in the presence of the Pope. Such honors are not to be thrown lightly aside. If you divorce me 'all France shall know that you are the one who is driving me away, as it will also know my obedience and my sorrow."

Far from wounding Napoleon, that refusal moved him—even to tears. The scene ended in passionate embraces and Napoleon spent the night with Josephine. He promised to give Fouché a good dressing-down. And in fact when the Minister of Police returned to Fontainebleau, he did "haul him over the coals." Fouché stood his ground and repeated his arguments. Josephine tried to have him dismissed, but Napoleon refused. However, as Fouché continued his campaign at Court and in public, Napoleon wrote to him on November 5, 1807:

> Monsieur Fouché, for the past two weeks I have been hearing of the indiscretions you are committing. It is high time for you to stop and to cease meddling directly or indirectly in a matter that does not concern you in any way whatsoever. Such is my will.

He embraced Josephine and repeated that Fouché had merely acted out of misplaced zeal:

"After all, one must not hold it against him. The important thing is that we are determined to reject his advice and that you really believe that I could not live without you."

There spoke habit, his old affection—certainly not reason. Reason as he well knew would command him to divorce her. But he did not have the courage. He was still too attached to

Josephine. Those incidents seem even to have drawn them closer. They were now spending almost every night together. Often during the day, in the presence of intimate friends, he would revert to the attentions of bygone days, wheedling her, flattering her, clasping her in his arms. He spoke to Duroc and Maret, his bosom friends, of his plan to legitimate Léon. They advised against it. These, they told him, were no longer the days when a Louis XIV could make the Duc de Maine and the Comte de Toulouse his heirs. What had been wrong for a monarch by divine right was impossible for a plain soldier who had won his title at the point of the sword. Then and there Napoleon renounced the idea and, whatever value she may have attached to it, Josephine followed the advice of her son, who considered such a plan unworthy of the Emperor, and did not remind him of it again.

She had recently received word of the death of her mother, Mme. de la Pagerie, in Martinique. That loss saddened her, though many years had passed since she had seen her mother. Napoleon was unwilling to announce the death—it would interfere with Court activities. The Empress even continued to wear colors.

Deprived of the presence of Marie Walewska, who was still in Poland, the Emperor began to amuse himself with Mme. Gazzani, a beautiful Genoese whom Josephine had engaged as a reader while in Milan where Mme. Gazzani had been attached to the Empress' staff of honor. Talleyrand and his henchman, Rémusat, were furthering her cause and had established her comfortably and discreetly at Fontainebleau. The lady surrendered with a right good will the moment Napoleon so much as intimated his desire.

Daughter of a dancer, Carlotta Gazzani had the face of a Madonna on a body that was a trifle too long and thin. She was a brunette with glorious eyes and dazzling teeth, but her hands were ugly and she always wore gloves. The Emperor's rare favors seem not to have turned her from her modest position in life. She was never to be more than a makeshift—and she knew it. Little by little she made a comfortable place for herself at Court. She had a salon which was crowded with distinguished people and, as her six-thousand-franc salary was obviously inadequate for that style of living, Napoleon added to it by numerous gifts. Better still he made M. Gazzani tax. collector for Evreux, an important post, in which he amassed a fortune. By her submissiveness, her compliance, the reader, to whom the Emperor returned only at rare intervals, became such a close friend of Josephine's that the latter even defended her. One day when he was in a bad humor, Napoleon asked the Empress to dismiss Mme. Gazzani.

"I do not want to see Mme. Gazzani around you any more," he said. "After this evening she must return to Italy."

"Don't take her from me," Josephine pleaded. "We two shall weep together—we understand each other very well."

He granted her request. As a matter of fact, Mme. Gazzani was to remain with the Empress to the end.

Never had Napoleon appeared so sprightly, so ready to have a good time. He showed it at that time by courting Mme. de Barral, one of Pauline's ladies-in-waiting. Mme. de Barral was as tall as a grenadier, and her pretty, childish face contrasted all the more amusingly with the freedom of her language. The Emperor met her at several hunt breakfasts and found her highly entertaining. They exchanged a few love letters and after that Mme. de Barral received the Emperor in her apartment at night. That affair was merely a passing fancy. Her husband, whom she led by the nose, was made a chamberlain and a baron.

The women were now flinging themselves at the Emperor. While many in his Court were afraid of him, many others would have been happy to be singled out for attention. So much adulation could not fail to turn his head. One evening in Josephine's apartment, to tease her, he began to boast of his successes with women.

"I have never found any women who were cruel," he said preening himself.

Hortense, who was present, replied with spirit:

"That's because you only tried the ones who were not!"

He laughed, tweaked her ear and remarked to the Empress:
"Do you hear how your daughter treats me! She thinks I
have never been anything but an old man!"

His sisters, Caroline and Pauline, vied with one another in
their efforts to provide him with mistresses, hoping that those
women might be of use to them later on and that, in any event,
they would undermine Josephine's influence.

Fouché and Talleyrand followed their example—Fouché,
who had tried vainly to give Mme. Récamier to the Emperor
as a mistress and had never forgiven the charming Juliette
for her refusal; and Talleyrand who, according to Napoleon,
always had "his pocket full of women." As a man of the *ancien
régime* Talleyrand hoped that the sovereign would amuse himself and work less, thus leaving him in control of affairs—and
through affairs, of profits.

To tell the truth neither Napoleon's heart nor his mind
was stirred by those physical "diversions": his thoughts, his
affections still turned toward that Polish woman, living in
retirement on her distant estate, to whom he sent many a brief
but tender message.

Still another "diversion" was Mme. Mathis—she, too, in the
group around the Princess Borghese. A blond little Piedmontese, she was plump and rosy and her legs were too short,
but she was high-spirited and winsome and she held the Emperor's attention for a brief moment. Of all his loves that was
the most fleeting. No sooner had Napoleon won her favor than
he set out for Italy, refusing to take the Empress with him in
order to have a freer hand.

He had undertaken that journey to Italy less for the purpose
of showing himself to his transalpine subjects than to make
arrangements for a divorce—which though still postponing, he
was considering more and more. He sent for the King of
Bavaria and his daughter, Charlotte, to come to Vienna. Charlotte was the sister of Augusta, Eugène's wife, a beautiful and
charming woman of whom Napoleon was very fond. If Charlotte should by any chance resemble her sister, he might marry

her. But one look at her was enough! He gave up that plan and promptly turned to another, that of a family alliance. At that point he summoned his brother Lucien to Mantua for a final interview.

Nearly four years had passed since Napoleon had last seen his brother—the efforts of Madame Mère, Fesch, Joseph and Elisa notwithstanding. To any tentative approaches Napoleon may have made Lucien had stubbornly refused to pay for his entrance into the imperial family by repudiating his wife or, at least, permitting his marriage to be regarded as morganatic. He had bought the Nuñez Palace in Rome, property at Canino, a number of villas and led a very pleasant life, busying himself with literature, excavations, the theatre and paintings. He had wormed his way into the favor of Pope Pius VII and had been made a Roman prince. When all Europe was bowing the knee before his brother's will, Lucien continued to hold him at arm's length—and all for love of a woman who, acccording to Napoleon, did not deserve it, but for that reason was undoubtedly better able to keep it.

Méneval was sent to Lucien's hostelry to fetch him. When Roustan announced him, the Emperor was seated behind a round table on which was spread a large map of Spain. He did not look up. Was he so absorbed in his plans that he had not heard? Lucien entered the room and waited. Napoleon, he thought, had changed—he was fatter, paler. The Emperor rang a bell, still without looking up. Lucien moved toward him.

"Sire," he said, "it is I, Lucien."

Napoleon rose and held out his hand. Lucien made a move to embrace him. Napoleon submitted, then, disengaging himself, he looked his brother over.

"Well, so it is really you? How are you? How is your family? Did you have a good journey? And the Pope, how is he? The Pope is very fond of you!"

That flood of questions was clear evidence of his embarrassment at seeing that brother who was so far superior to the others, to whom he owed so much and whom he had treated so harshly. Hesitant, suspicious, for he feared that Napoleon meant to keep him prisoner now that he had him in his hands, Lucien replied that his health was good and "that he was pleased to see that His Majesty's was also."

"Yes, I am well," said Napoleon slapping his stomach, "but I am getting too fat and I have to watch my weight."

He took a pinch of snuff and, looking at Lucien again, exclaimed. "Why! You are looking very well, you know? You were too thin before. Now you are really quite handsome."

He invited him to sit down. They drew up their chairs near the table and a moment of silence followed. Napoleon began nervously moving some pins with red, black, and yellow heads about on his map, then, with a sweep of his hand, suddenly knocked them over.

"Well, what have you to say to me?"

"Sire, you were kind enough to express a desire to see me. I shall not hide from you that our mother's reports and Joseph's too, have led me to feel that I might count on a return to Your Majesty's good graces."

"That depends entirely on you. Are you still so fond of Mme. Jouberthou?"

The duel was on again.

"Mme. Jouberthou is my wife," Lucien replied calmly, "and her son is mine."

"No, no, I do not recognize that marriage—therefore it is null and void."

"It was contracted according to the law—both civil and religious."

Retorts flashed back and forth with the swiftness of rapiers. Napoleon began to threaten:

"I have conquered Europe. I shall certainly not give way before you. It is due entirely to me that you are able to live quietly in Rome. . . . But I shall order them to throw you out. I shall force you to leave Europe."

"Suppose I do not obey?"

"I would have you arrested."

"Well, what of that?"

"Don't talk to me that way! Don't think you can bully me! . . . Get out of my presence! . . ."

The Emperor's eyes snapped fire, his nostrils quivered. Lucien replied coldly:

"I had no intention of displeasing Your Majesty by a remark that shows the high opinion I have of Your Majesty's greatness of soul."

Napoleon made a praiseworthy effort to control his anger. He lowered his voice.

"Talleyrand is right. In this whole business you have acted like a hot-headed Jacobin. . . . I realize that you were useful on the 18th of Brumaire, though I have had no clear indication that you actually saved me. But what I do know is that you have contested the unity of my power. . . ." A few minutes later he added: "But enough of all that! It is ancient history. Listen to me, Lucien, and weigh my words carefully. Above all let us not lose our tempers. You came here in full confidence. The Emperor of France cannot betray Corsican hospitality."

At that promise Lucien must have breathed a sigh of relief. They were both standing by that time, Napoleon pacing back and forth in the brilliantly lighted drawing-room. Coming back toward Lucien he seized his hand in a firm clasp.

"We are alone here. No one can hear us. On the question of your marriage I am the one who was in the wrong. I went too far. I should not have interfered with your wife. But what is certain, my dear Lucien, is that her beauty will fade. By the time you have lost your illusions about love, you will be an enemy of my system and I shall be obliged to persecute you in spite of myself. For, if you are not with me, I tell you, Europe is too small for us both."

As he talked he kept taking snuff and scattering it on the carpet. Hesitant, deeply moved, Lucien heard him out.

"What do you want of me?" he asked.

"What I want is for you to get a divorce, that is all."

And Napoleon continued his efforts to convince him. A divorce of course implied a recognition of Lucien's marriage.

He was not ready to end the interview just yet, so he changed
the subject and began to speak of his relatives. They were all
causing him worry and much disappointment. As to Josephine,
she was definitely growing old and was becoming more and
more unattractive and boring. He was sorry he had not
divorced her before. By this time he might have had grown
children.

"For you might as well know that I am not impotent as you
all said."

"But, sire, I never said so, and for the very good reason that
I have always thought the exact opposite."

Napoleon then confided to Lucien that he had had a child
by one of his mistresses. And launched on that subject he went
on to speak complacently of Mme. Walewska:

"There is a charming woman, an angel—"

Lucien smiled.

"You laugh because I am in love! Yes, that is true, I am,
but my policy always comes first and that policy would lead
me to marry a princess."

Who would take Josephine's place? He had not yet fixed on
his choice. Then abruptly he asked the age of Charlotte,
Lucien's oldest daughter.

"If you had come into my system," he said, "I would already
have affianced her to the Prince of the Asturias or to some other
great prince . . . even, perhaps, to an emperor."

He had, in fact, been considering that idea for several
months. A marriage with Charlotte would have many advantages. But she was so young! Lucien made no reply. Napoleon
again urged him to get rid of his wife. They would both get
divorces at the same time.

Lucien murmured wearily that he had not the same reasons
for divorcing that Napoleon had. His wife was young and prolific, whereas Josephine . . . Napoleon was not annoyed by
that parallel. On the contrary his tone was kindly as he assured him:

"There will be no difficulties about the children of your
first wife."

The children of Lucien's second marriage would be richly provided for; Mme. Jouberthou herself would receive a duchy. As for Lucien—with a gleam of pride in his eyes, Napoleon spread out a map of Europe and waved his hand over it:

"Look at that map! Come in with us, Lucien, and take your share! It will be a fine one, I promise you. The throne of Portugal is vacant—I have issued a proclamation that the king has ceased to rule. I will give it to you. You shall be in command of the army best fitted to conquer it easily. I shall make you a French prince and my lieutenant. Just say the word. You shall have whatever you wish, provided that your divorce is granted before mine."

Lucien did not answer. Napoleon flew into another rage, then asked him to send little "Lolotte" to their mother.

Lucien replied that he would gladly do so.

Day was almost breaking. . . . The interview had lasted six hours. The Emperor held out his hand to his brother. Lucien kissed him on the cheek and left the room. To win his brother, Napoleon had tried every means: he had been harsh, affectionate, imperious, confiding. He had dangled memories, ambition, before him. And all he had obtained was a vague promise to send Charlotte to Paris. Yet so eager was he to win that brother that he still cherished illusions. It was all in vain. Lucien would not agree to any arrangement.

The Emperor then turned to Eugène—he might not have a brilliant mind but he had never failed to show him obedience and devotion. At Milan, before the Estates, he made Eugène heir to the kingdom of Italy. Josephine would be pleased, for her son's future was still her greatest anxiety.

Two years were to pass before Lucien, at Joseph's insistent demand, made up his mind to entrust his daughter to Madame Mère. By that time Napoleon had renounced his rather hazy plan of marrying her. From the moment of her arrival in Paris, Lolotte showed an extremely independent, not to say, hostile, attitude. Her letters—censored by Napoleon's order—poked fun at the fiancés that were offered to her, at her grandmother's avarice, at Pauline's flightiness. The Emperor stood it patiently for three months, then sent her home to her father. From the day when Napoleon made the Pope a prisoner at Fontainebleau, Lucien realized that he was no longer safe in Rome and he decided to set out for America. He was stopped by a British cruiser and interned in England. There, under the beautiful shade trees of Thorngrave, he was to work at polishing his epic poem *Charlemagne,* the most boring perhaps ever composed by a man of brilliant mind.

III

Divorce?

TRUE TO HER PROMISE Marie Walewska arrived in Paris in the early days of 1808. With her came her brother, Teodor, and a maid. Despite his minor infidelities, Napoleon was still as deeply devoted to her as ever: to him she was "his Polish wife." Duroc was ordered to settle her first in the rue du Houssaye, then in an attractive house at 48 rue de la Victoire. There she lived in retirement, receiving the Emperor some-times of an evening, but more often going to his private apart-ments at the Tuileries. Henceforth there could be no fear of any intrusion on Josephine's part. Her position was now too precarious: she dared not endanger it. At the Emperor's re-quest Corvisart watched over Marie's health. Every morning someone waited on her to ask what orders she cared to give. She had very few: she had no desires, confident as she was that she was first in Napoleon's thoughts and sustained by the hope that soon, through love of her, he would restore Poland to its former glory.

She had only one French friend—Duroc. She had long since forgiven the Grand Marshal for the rôle he had played at Warsaw and had learned to appreciate that earnest, loyal man, the only one in a sycophantic Court who dared to tell the Emperor the truth. Duroc's influence was tremendous: he never abused it, never used it for himself, but only in good causes, to relieve misfortunes or for Napoleon's own good.

The winter of 1808 was a brilliant season: magnificent fes-tivities at Hortense's on the occasion of the marriage of her cousin, Mlle. Tascher de la Pagerie to Prince d'Arenberg; at Berthier's; and at Neuilly both at Pauline's and at Caroline's, the two sisters giving masked balls for the Emperor at his re-quest. The ball at Caroline's was the most elaborate since the days before the Revolution. *La Vestale* by Spontini, the Empress' special composer, being then much in vogue, some of the guests, costumed as vestals, danced a quadrille—among them, Hortense, despite the fact that she was already eight months with child. She made her entrance preceded by a Folly clad in attractive tights and twirling a fool's bauble in her hand. That Folly was one of Hortense's innumerable protégées, Mlle. Guillebeau—the daughter of a bankrupt—a lively, rather hoydenish girl who haunted the salons in search of lovers. She had already found two—Junot and Murat. Now, as a matter of policy, Caroline had for some months been on intimate terms with Junot. When she saw Mlle. Guillebeau enter her drawing-rooms she could not restrain her anger. That girl, with whom both her husband and her lover were betraying her, dared to appear in her house, before the whole Court! Marching straight up to the Folly, Caroline insulted her openly and ordered her out of the house. Hortense intervened: the two sisters-in-law exchanged a number of harsh words and the Queen of Holland left the ball in her turn. To avenge herself for that affront, she hit upon the idea of having her mother engage Mlle. Guillebeau as a reader and understudy for Mme. Gazzani.

Napoleon delighted in those reunions, Italian style, where, dressed in a domino he could circulate among the crowd, generally on Duroc's arm, and amuse himself by rousing the ladies' curiosity—his proposals were frequently far from proper —and tormenting the husbands with malicious and indiscreet comments on their home life. But try as he might to disguise himself, he was always recognized. His ambling gait, his habit of placing his hands behind his back, more particularly his voice, defied even Constant's ingenuity, though the valet did his best and gave him innumerable bits of advice. To his first question a domino would invariably reply with a "Sire." Napoleon would turn on his heel, disappointed. At a ball given by Marescalchi, the ambassador from Italy, he changed his costume as many as three times, and three times he was recognized. One evening he refused to go to the Opéra with

Josephine, but followed her there secretly to surprise her. Duroc and Constant were with him. They addressed each other by the familiar *tu* and used fictitious names: Napoleon was "Auguste," Duroc "François," Constant "Joseph." They looked everywhere for the Empress—in the auditorium, in the foyer, in the boxes. They spoke to as many as twenty dominos but could not find her. Finally a masked figure approached the Emperor and began teasing him with such freedom and spirit that Napoleon was taken aback. The figure then vanished into the crowd. The Emperor was annoyed and returned to the Tuileries. The next morning he remarked to Josephine:

"So you didn't go to the ball at the Opéra last night, eh?"

"Oh, yes, I was there."

"Oh, come now!"

"I assure you I was there. But what did you do all evening, my dear?"

"I was working."

"That is strange. I saw a domino at the ball who had the same size foot as yours and wore the same kind of boots. I thought it was you and talked to him quite familiarly."

Napoleon laughed heartily. The Empress confessed that, at the last moment, she had changed her costume, as the one she was wearing did not strike her as suitable.

"I am sorry for you," Talleyrand once remarked to Rémusat when the latter was appointed director of theatres. "You have to amuse the *unamusable!*"

A witticism that, like so many of its kind, was false. At forty Napoleon was still extraordinarily youthful. It was natural, however, that matters of state should occupy his thoughts more and more. At that moment he was worried about the Spanish situation. Talleyrand had persuaded him to dethrone the Bourbons; and a strong army under the command of Murat, who saw at last a chance of becoming king, had invaded Spain.

Caroline was all graciousness, all charm to the Emperor on whom that crown depended. Moreover by clever maneuvering she was also trying to win Talleyrand and Fouché. The Minister of Police had by no means renounced his campaign against Josephine. On the contrary he even went so far as to bribe mobs to stand under the windows of the Tuileries and shout for the Emperor to contract a new marriage. Talleyrand informed Napoleon as to the real motive behind that incident. At that hour he himself was not advocating divorce. Though he did not tell Napoleon, he knew that the Russian princess whom the Emperor was considering would not be given to him. The Spanish campaign was a serious matter. It was no time to embark on domestic worries. Napoleon was apparently of the same mind. . . . But he did not know what to do and wavered constantly from one side to the other. In that period of indecision Talleyrand seems to have been his chief confident.

"First of all," Napoleon told him, "if I divorce my wife, I shall lose all the charm she brings into my home life. I shall be obliged to study the tastes and habits of a new and younger wife. And finally, I should be showing rank ingratitude for all she has done for me. I am not much loved now and that would be even worse."

However, Talleyrand was well aware that some day policy would outweigh sentiment. One morning, meeting M. de Rémusat as he was coming out of Napoleon's study, he told the chamberlain that it looked to him as if the divorce were as good as granted.

"We will all do well," he added, "to consider it settled and to refrain from any useless opposition."

That same evening there was a Court reception, followed by a play. The salons were crowded with a throng of princes, ambassadors, dignitaries and bejeweled women in beautiful gowns, awaiting the entrance of the sovereigns. After a long delay a chamberlain announced that the Emperor was slightly indisposed and that their Majesties would not appear. The play opened before a room that emptied little by little. Talleyrand and Rémusat hurried to the Emperor's apartment and were told that "he has been in bed with his wife since eight o'clock and he has forbidden anyone to enter the room till the next day."

Turning on his good heel, Talleyrand exclaimed impatiently:

"What a devil of a man for always yielding to his first impulse and never knowing what he wants to do. Well, he had better make up his mind!"

The following day the Empress confided to Rémusat that Napoleon had dined with her at six o'clock. He had talked little and had seemed depressed. She had been waiting in her apartments for the hour of the reception when she was summoned to the Emperor who had been taken ill. She rushed to his rooms, found him in one of his stomach attacks that sometimes ended in actual convulsions. At sight of Josephine he began to weep and, pulling her down on the bed where he lay full length, he clasped her in his arms heedless of her Court gown and the tulle *chérusque*.

"My poor Josephine," he kept saying over and over again, "I shall never leave you."

It was a repetition of the attack he had had before the Coronation. But three years of fears and anxiety had made Josephine callous. This time she did not weaken.

"Do not get excited," she told him. "Make up your mind what you want and let us have done with these scenes."

She helped Constant nurse him, gave him some tea to drink and urged him not to appear in public that evening but to go to bed. He consented on condition that she would come to bed with him. And so insistent was he that she was obliged to take off her state robes at once and get into bed beside him. He continued to weep and, referring to his family and Fouché, he kept saying:

"They will come hanging around me and tormenting me. They make me so miserable. . . ."

It was a distressing night broken by restless dreams and exhausting embraces. In the morning Napoleon rose at the usual hour—to all appearances he had forgotten the entire episode.

Josephine continued to live in daily suspense. She confided to Mme. de Rémusat that she thought Napoleon was trying to wear her down, to disgust her, to make her ill, perhaps even worse. Entire days of coldness would be followed by violent reproaches for mere nothings—because she had been too gracious to Prince Mecklenburg, for instance. He would make scathing remarks about her age and her efforts to conceal it, and he would rage against her extravagances. Moreover she had the strain of always being on parade under the hostile eyes of the Bonapartes, who were openly predicting her downfall. . . . No wonder she sometimes felt as if she could not go on any longer. For several days she was seriously ill and it was with a sigh of relief that she saw the Emperor set out for the journey to the southwest where the trouble in Spain was about to begin. That was only a brief respite. She was obliged to rejoin Napoleon at Bordeaux and later at Marracq, a little château near Bayonne where he had taken up residence. Part of the Court accompanied her and among her ladies was the amusing Mlle. Guillebeau.

Josephine had deliberately chosen the Guillebeau to annoy Caroline, who was also with her on the journey. Unfortunately in the close quarters of Marracq, Napoleon's eye fell on the young dancer—he had not noticed her before. Mlle. Guillebeau raised her pretty gray eyes to his, fluttered her amazing eyelashes and lowered them swiftly. Napoleon wasted no time in sending Roustan to inform her that he would call upon her in her attic room under the roof. The little slyboots made no pretense of shyness or offense. A few seconds later she was in the Emperor's arms.

He visited her on several nights in succession and found her much to his liking, facile and of a loving disposition. However, since his marriage with a Beauharnais, Lavallette had become one of the Empress' most loyal partisans and he kept an eye on the Emperor's correspondence. Mlle. Guillebeau was far from discreet in the letters she wrote to her mother and her friends in Paris. Napoleon was promptly informed. Lavallette showed him a reply of Mme. Guillebeau's in which she coached her daughter, outlining the rôle she was to play and insisting particularly that she must by all means arrange for "living traces that might prolong his favor." The Emperor was disgusted by the cynicism of those intriguers. Mlle. Guillebeau was packed into a coach and, escorted by a trusty valet, promptly sent back to Paris. There was to be no more talk of the reader. Shortly afterward she married a M. Sourdeau, a man of few scruples, who was appointed tax collector in Florence and was to squander his income, a mistake which the Restoration would fortunately rectify.

During that sojourn at Marracq, Napoleon displayed the same dynamic activity as at the Tuileries. But he walked more, often strolling with Duroc along the Adour near the Boucau. Now and then his steps turned in the direction of a dovecote at the far end of the park whence he would descend to the river bank, cross the Nive and call on Caroline who was living in the village of Lauga.

Separated from Mme. Walewska, he was to all appearances once more under the influence of his wife, who did the honors of Marracq with such exquisite tact and grace. It even looked as if Napoleon had gone back to her altogether. That was because he had always been strongly influenced by the actual presence. The Empress made the most of it, though she was careful not to show her triumph. Napoleon even slipped back into his old ways with her, exhibiting a youthful playfulness: he would throw away Josephine's slippers to compel her to get into the carriage alone with him in her stocking feet, or chase her on the beach and laugh heartily when he pushed her into the water. No one knew what to make of him any more.

The King of Spain, Charles IV and his queen, Marie-Louise, arrived in Bayonne and dined at Marracq. The descendant of Louis XIV was heavy and stupid, with drooping eyes, a monstrous nose and a gargantuan appetite. Napoleon had given orders that the dinner should be prepared with great care. The King did ample honor to it, but refused the vegetables.

"Grass is fit only for cattle," he said.

Every time a dish was served, he would turn to the Queen: "Louise, do eat some of that. It is good."

Napoleon and Josephine could scarcely keep their faces straight.

The Queen was short and fat, as dowdy as a market-woman and she could drink like a trooper. Her eyes peered out of her red face like the hard, bright eyes of birds. She had an abrupt way of speaking, and a scornful manner when she addressed her husband.

At the suggestion of the Empress, who was as usual beautifully gowned, the ladies spent the afternoon in the hands of coiffeurs and beauticians—Duplan, Josephine's own hairdresser, attending the Queen and coming out of the test with flying colors. Marie-Louise emerged from his hands presentable at least—all but her face which no amount of attention could improve.

To Napoleon those princes were contemptible puppets of royalty, their son Ferdinand a hateful usurper. It would be a simple matter, and a just one, to dethrone them. But Murat, his lieutenant beyond the Pyrenees, had deceived him in every report. With complete confidence in his genius, his star, Napoleon plunged headlong into the capital mistake of his life.

As he could not annex such a vast state to France he must therefore have a man of his own to govern it. And that man, in spite of his defects of character—his laziness, his vanity—he thought he had found in Joseph. To him, notwithstanding the passage of time, Joseph was still the eldest of his race and the dear companion of his youth. The moment he sent Murat to the Ebro, he offered Spain to his brother. Joseph declined—he preferred Naples. Disappointed, Napoleon then thought of Louis, who had made such a failure in Holland and was always disregarding advice and complaining of the climate. He wrote to him: "If I make you King of Spain, will you accept? Can I count on you?" "No," replied Louis. "I am not a provincial governor. The only promotion for a king is Heaven." Would it have to be Jerome then? But his wife, the good Catherine, was a Protestant and a good one. To please her—but really because he was having the time of his life in Cassel—Jerome declined the offer. Napoleon then insisted on Joseph, and in the end he accepted.

The eldest of the Bonapartes immediately began to give himself the airs of a grandson of Charles V. Greeted by a Spanish deputation at Bayonne he talked down to his new subjects and calmly signed himself: *I, the King.* He gave up the idea of Naples with real regret, but not until he had had the pleasure of tying up the future sovereign by a constitution which, for that matter, the Emperor approved. Murat and Caroline were to go to Naples. Napoleon was really giving that throne to Caroline, for he was displeased with Murat's presumption and his intrigues. In his talk with his sister, Napoleon displayed much keenness and not a little suspicion. The contract he imposed deliberately made them his vassals. Moreover he took back the grand duchy of Berg and even seized everything the Murats owned in France: the Elysée, Neuilly, lands and castles. Caroline and Joachim I were to set out for Naples stripped to the bone. But what was the fortune they were renouncing compared to a kingdom?

Napoleon left Marracq on the 18th of July. Even before he was back in Paris, Dupont had capitulated at Baylén and Spain had risen. Austria was mobilizing. The Emperor immediately set out for Erfurt where he spent two weeks receiving the adulations of the German princes. To impress a terror-stricken Europe where so many fires were already smoldering, he made a display of his glory. "I am going to dazzle the Emperor Alexander by showing him my power," he said to Talleyrand. He sent the élite of his Guard to that quiet German town and with them the richest plate, the most beautiful pieces of furniture belonging to the crown. He had a theatre specially built for the Comédie-Française, which had been brought there almost in its entirety under the direction of Talma. The festivities were marvelous. The Czar, a tall, clean-shaven, fashionable young man, at once an autocrat and a liberal, flattered the Emperor and was jealous of him. He was conspiring with Talleyrand to bridle Napoleon's ambition, perhaps even one day to crush him, and therefore showed his future adversary all the more attention and deference. When the actor declaimed the famous lines of *Œdipus:*

The friendship of a great man is a favor of the gods,

the Czar grasped the Corsican's hand and, to the servile applause of the kings about them, declared:

"I count on yours."

That night Constant was awakened by muffled cries issuing from Napoleon's bedchamber. The valet roused Roustan, who lay beside him in the anteroom. Again the same cries, but louder this time. Constant pushed open the door and saw the Emperor lying outstretched across his bed with the clothes flung back. Inarticulate sounds came from his opened mouth. He was pressing his hands against his chest with all his strength. Constant called him. Napoleon did not answer. Then the valet shook him. The Emperor opened his eyes and stammered:

"What is it? What is it?"

He sat up, staring about him like a man in a daze. Constant explained that he had roused him because he thought he was having a nightmare.

"You did well," Napoleon replied. "I was having a terrible dream. A bear was tearing open my chest and eating my heart."

Constant had to change his nightshirt: it was dripping wet with perspiration. The impression of that nightmare was so strong that Napoleon had difficulty in going to sleep again.

In that troop of French artists was Mlle. Bourgoing, Napoleon's rebellious subject and avowed enemy. The actress seems to have caught Alexander's fancy for a brief moment. Napoleon revenged himself for her perfidy by an ungallant trick.

The Czar called on Napoleon informally as the latter was dressing and confided to him, man to man, that he was interested in the actress.

"I would not advise you to make any advances to her," Napoleon said.

"You think she would refuse me?" asked Alexander in surprise.

"Oh, no, but tomorrow is mail day and in five days all Paris would know every inch of Your Majesty's anatomy from head to foot. . . . Besides, I am thinking of your health. . . . So I hope you will be able to resist the temptation. . . ."

Alexander registered a doubt or two.

"From the way Your Majesty speaks, I am tempted to think you have a personal grudge against this charming actress."

"No indeed," replied Napoleon. "I only know what people are saying."

That was enough to dampen the Czar's ardor.

Goethe was first presented to the Emperor at one of the morning receptions. The next day, while he was at lunch, Napoleon sent for him and complimented him with a flattering abruptness:

"You are a man, Monsieur Goethe."

Napoleon announced that he was to be presented with the Legion of Honor and added a few words of praise for *Werther*.

"I don't like the end of your romance," he said.

"I am quite sure, sire," replied Goethe wittily, "that you do not like a romance to end."

The Emperor discussed the theatre with the poet. In tragedies, he explained, it was old-fashioned to bring about the solution through the intervention of Fate.

"Those times are past. What is the object of talking about Fate nowadays? Fate is policy."

And yet he himself believed so thoroughly in destiny—which was, perhaps, why he always denied it in public.

"You should write the *Death of Cæsar*, but in a nobler, grander style than Voltaire's. That would be the most beautiful work of your life, your *chef d'œuvre*. In that tragedy you would have to show how Cæsar could have made the happiness of humanity if he had been given time to carry out his vast schemes. Come to Paris, Monsieur Goethe, I insist upon it."

He was already annexing the great German in his mind. On another occasion he said to him, with his usual vanity:

"Come to *Iphigenia* tomorrow, Monsieur Goethe. You will see a goodly number of kings in my box. Do you know the Prince-primate? No? Well, you will see him asleep on the King of Württemberg's shoulder."

With that Prince-primate, Archbishop of Prague and a big sycophant, he discussed the Golden Bull at a dinner which the Grand Duke gave for him at Weimar and where only crowned heads were present. Napoleon cited the exact year.

"How does Your Majesty happen to know those things so well?" asked the prelate.

"When I was a second lieutenant in the artillery—" the Emperor began.

The kings stared at him, amazed at that proud simplicity. He stopped short, then insisted, with a smile:

"When I had the honor of being a simple lieutenant in the artillery I spent three years in garrison at Valence. I did not know many people and I led a very retired life. By good luck I found lodgings near a scholarly bookseller, one of the most agreeable of men, who let me read his library from beginning to end over and over again. I have not forgotten a word of it."

At the ball that followed he did not dance. "I attended the ball at Weimar," he wrote on October 9th to Josephine. "The Emperor Alexander dances, but not I. Forty years are forty years."

That former lieutenant who flung cherries at Mlle. du Colombier had not relinquished the idea of marrying a Russian princess. How could Alexander, whom he was sure he had won over completely, refuse to give his sister, Catherine, to the Emperor? He took the Czar into his confidence, explaining that his life was so empty: he needed rest and was living only for the moment when he could safely give himself up to the pleasures of home life.

That hint—and others even plainer—had no effect. Talleyrand, and his confederate Caulaincourt who had turned against the Emperor because the latter had opposed his marriage to Mme. de Canisy, worked on Alexander so well that the latter would make only a vague promise in reply. And, after the two emperors had embraced and parted, poor Catherine was to be married in all haste to a puny and scrofulous prince, George of Holstein, who at least saved her from the misfortune of marrying the French Cæsar.

Napoleon hurried back to Spain with all possible speed and soon managed to re-establish the situation there. War with Austria was now unavoidable and he returned to Paris to face that new danger. Moreover he had to square accounts with Talleyrand. During Napoleon's absence the Prince of Benevento had plotted with Caroline and Fouché to call Murat to the throne in the event that the Emperor should be seriously wounded or killed. Napoleon would allow no one to arrange for his succession but himself. He summoned Talleyrand to the Tuileries and blasted him with his wrath. Waving his arms angrily, his eyes sombre, his mouth twisted, he hurled bitter reproaches at the man he had thought his friend.

"You are a thief, a coward, a faithless cur! You have tricked and deceived everybody . . . you would sell your own father. . . . Today you are against the Spanish campaign when you were the one who first put that idea in my head! What are you scheming anyhow? What are you hoping for? I dare you to tell me. . . . Why haven't I had you hung to the gates of the Carrousel? But there is still time. Do you know what you are? *Vous êtes de la . . . dans un bas de soie!*"

Cambacérès, Lebrun, Fouché, Decrès were witnesses of that unchained virulence. They held their breaths in terror. The prince was silent: he did not even raise an eyebrow, there was not a gleam in his eye. In the end his impassive manner cooled Napoleon's wrath. But he hurled one final insult:

"You did not tell me that the Duc de San Carlos was your wife's lover."

In a tone of icy courtesy, Talleyrand replied:

"Really, sire, I never dreamed that that relation could be of consequence to Your Majesty's glory or mine."

The Emperor turned and left the room. One by one the dignitaries returned to the anteroom which was thronged with officers and courtiers who had heard every word. Talleyrand moved slowly through the crowd. At the door he was heard to remark distinctly:

"What a pity that such a great man should have such bad manners."

The following day Talleyrand appeared at the levee with his breast covered with all his orders. Napoleon turned his head away as he passed in front of him. Now that his anger had cooled he undoubtedly regretted having gone too far. Notwithstanding his vices Talleyrand was valuable to him. The fact is that Napoleon was still impressed by his minister. Moreover he was to handle him with gloves. Though he took the key of Lord High Chamberlain from him to give it to Montesquiou, he was to leave the minister his rank of Vice-Grand Elector, his pensions and the immense fortune he had made so brazenly. The day would soon come when Napoleon would again address him, their quarrel apparently forgotten. In August, 1811, he was to say to him at Trianon:

"What a devil of a fellow you are! I can neither keep myself from talking over my affairs with you, *nor from liking you*."

But the Prince of Benevento did not forget. He had been too deeply humiliated and never severely enough punished. From that day he was Napoleon's bitter enemy and never ceased to betray him and to plot against him.

In those three months when the Emperor was busy making ready for the campaign against Austria, he divided his time between the Elysée, Malmaison and Rambouillet. He had seen Marie Walewska again, but he was also seeing a young woman whom he had met at Lyons in April, 1805, and whom he had summoned to the Tuileries the following year. Mme. Pellapra was married to a speculator on the stock exchange who was suddenly made tax collector at Caen—a position Napoleon was fond of bestowing on betrayed husbands. Little is known of Mme. Pellapra but there is no doubt that she was more to the

Emperor than a passing fancy. Her youth, her charming face delighted him. From time to time, at fairly long intervals, he received her at the Tuileries. She was to have a daughter by him, Emilie, who became in later years the beautiful Princess de Chimay, a gentle, intelligent and charming woman.

1809

AUSTRIA WENT TO WAR. On the 13th of August Napoleon left Paris for Germany and in five days the enemy was driven out of Bavaria. At Ratisbonne the Emperor suffered a slight wound. He was standing beside Lannes, examining the defenses of the city through his field glasses when a bullet, fired from the ramparts, struck him in the right heel. While Yvan was bandaging the wound he remarked coolly:

"No one but a Tyrolese could have hit me at such a distance. Those fellows are wonderful shots."

He was in pain, for the bullet had touched a nerve; but he mounted his horse at once and set off at a gallop to show himself to his troops, who greeted him with wild cheers of enthusiasm. The next day, though running a temperature, he held a review of the army.

The road to Vienna was open. The Imperial family fled and Napoleon entered the beleaguered capital. Nine days later the French troops crossed the Danube and joined battle with the main army of Archduke Charles, which was intact at Essling. The losses on both sides were terrific. Napoleon exposed himself so constantly that General Walther, one of the commanders of the Guard, finally shouted at him:

"Go back! Or else I'll order my grenadiers to carry you off the field."

When a bullet hit the Emperor's horse on the flank, a furious clamor rose from the ranks:

"Let the Emperor withdraw at once or we will throw down our arms."

Napoleon obeyed that cry of love.

On the second day Lannes was about to batter the enemy's center when the Danube rose suddenly, carrying away bridges and cutting him off from the reinforcements he was expecting. The French were forced to withdraw to the island of Lobau. The Emperor was calm and collected as he followed the files of wounded that were being evacuated. Suddenly he caught sight of Lannes being carried past on a stretcher. An officer was supporting his head, which was drained of blood. The Marshal had had both legs broken. He was dying. Napoleon rushed to him, burst into tears and kneeling beside him, took him in his arms, regardless of the blood that dyed his uniform.

"Lannes," he kept repeating, "don't you know me? It is Bonaparte, your friend."

The wounded man looked up at him and murmured:

"Yes, sire, you are going to lose your best friend."

"No, no, you will live. Isn't that true, Larrey? You will pull him through, won't you?"

They pointed out that any emotion might be fatal to the Marshal. Napoleon rose and grasped his hands. Then mounting his horse he rode off, his faced bathed in tears. Suddenly he jerked his hat from his head and flung it on the ground. A soldier stooped to pick it up.

"Leave it!" Napoleon thundered and rode his horse back and forth over it until he had trampled it to bits.

His friend? Yes, Lannes was his friend, the one to whom perhaps he was the most attached. He respected him, he loved him. Moreover Lannes was an old war comrade who had witnessed his rise to glory, a good Frenchman, a great general. "His courage at first outweighed his intellect," Napoleon was to say later on, "but his intellect increased daily to make the balance.... I found a pygmy: I lost a giant."

Lannes was carried to Ebersdorff, where Larrey amputated. Gangrene set in and soon the Marshal lay dying. The Emperor went to see him every morning with Berthier. Against all reason he refused to give up hope.

"The Marshal," he wrote, "will come out of this with a wooden leg."

The evening before his death, Lannes, who was still clear in mind, spoke to him with his customary frankness:

"I need not recommend my wife and children to your care. As I am dying for you, your pride will compel you to protect them. You are surrounded only by sycophants. . . . You will be betrayed and deserted. Make haste to end this war as quickly as you can. The whole country wants peace. You will never be more powerful, but you can be much more beloved. Forgive these truths from a dying man who is deeply attached to you."

Napoleon's face was drawn with grief. He turned away without a word.

Lannes died the next day. Marbot went to meet the Emperor and urge him not to enter the room. The stench was unbearable. Napoleon pushed him aside, strode over to the Marshal's bed and leaning over, kissed the dead man. He remained there for an hour, deep in thought. Berthier tried to get him to come away but he would not listen. He kept murmuring like a tragic refrain:

"What a loss for France and for me!"

The checkmate at Essling was serious. All Europe rang with the news of Napoleon's defeat. The despoiled Pope excommunicated him. The Tyrol rose. The English prepared to invade the Low Countries. Napoleon saw the extent of his danger and worked day and night to avert it. For a short time he was ill. Reverses, which always reacted on him physically, had brought out an eruption on the base of his neck. When the celebrated Viennese physician, Franck, hesitated to use sulphur to absorb it, Napoleon sent in haste for Corvisart. Though he was confined to his bed, feverish and suffering from bronchitis in addition, he still insisted on carrying on his work. The men about him lost their heads. By the time Corvisart arrived the Emperor had already begun to improve. His physician applied leeches and finished the cure. He then made ready to return to France.

"What!" cried Napoleon. "Leaving so soon? What is the matter? Are you bored?"

"No, sire, but I would rather be in Paris than Schönbrunn."

"Stay with me. I am going to fight a great battle. You will see what that is like."

"No, sire, thank you, but I am not curious."

The Emperor smiled. He knew that Corvisart was a great lady's man. Undoubtedly he had torn himself away from some mistress or other to come to the Emperor.

"Oh, you are a good-for-nothing," he cried. "You want to go back to Paris to kill your poor patients inch by inch."

Corvisart would not give in and he left on the following day.

The Emperor spent the next six weeks in careful preparations for his revenge. The morale of his generals was at a low ebb: he brought it up again. He visited the island of Lobau almost every day to inspect work on the fortifications and to encourage the soldiers. He lived among them, even going so far as to undress one evening and bathe nude in front of the troops. He took an interest in the slightest details, had an eye to everything. On July 4th the French troops withdrew from the Island of Lobau at night under cover of a violent storm and massed on the left bank of the river. Two days later came Wagram—a perfect maneuver, a miracle of daring and discretion.

One more victory at Znaïm and Austria asked for an armistice. While waiting for peace to be signed the Emperor settled for three months at Schönbrunn and sent for Mme. Walewska to join him there. He could not do without her any longer. There in a charming villa at Meidling they led again the intimate home life of the days of Finckenstein. Once again Napoleon was all hers.

Every day there was a parade or a review in the courtyard of the castle. On October 12th, as Napoleon was descending the flight of steps in front of the castle, a well-dressed young man with a pleasant face approached him under pretext of handing him a petition. He was driven back and searched. A large kitchen knife was found hidden in his coat! Frederick Stapps, the son of an Erfurt pastor, had intended to kill Napoleon in whom, like most young Germans of his day, he saw the tyrant of his Fatherland. The Emperor insisted upon questioning him himself. He would have liked to pardon him.

"If I set you free," he said to him, "will you go home to your parents and give up your plan to kill me?"

"Yes, if we have peace. But if the war goes on, I shall try to do it again," replied the youth.

Napoleon shrugged his shoulders. Convicted by a military tribunal, Stapps was shot on the very day the bells of Vienna rang to announce the conclusion of peace.

To please Marie Walewska and to realize her dream at last, Napoleon would have liked to restore Poland as a whole. But he was afraid of alienating the Czar. On this point without any doubt, Marie had cause for discreet reproaches. But Napoleon explained the difficulties of a situation further complicated by bad news from Spain. Once more she resigned herself. She kept her trust in the future and in the man who had already performed so many miracles. Moreover an event, both grave and gay, distracted her mind from political anxieties. She was going to have a child. For some time she had been feeling ill, but had waited to consult Corvisart on his return to Vienna. The doctor had cleared up her doubts. At first she was desperately troubled, almost overwhelmed by the irregularity of her situation. Would the child that was about to be born bear the name of the Walewskis? What would the Count do? However her love for Napoleon was now so great that it outweighed any other consideration and her fears were swallowed up in joy. When Marie informed the Emperor, there was not the slightest doubt as to how he felt: he was beside himself with pride and happiness. A child by Marie Walewska! He was going to have a child!

He may have had cause to doubt Eléonore's virtue and to wonder sometimes whether little Léon really was his son, but he was sure of Marie. She was incapable of inconstancy. He knew too that she loved him now. So he was going to have another child outside of the line of succession at a time when his marriage was sterile, when an heir was so necessary if the Empire were to endure. It was now certain that he could have children—the proof was obvious. And today that confirmation did not come to him in the midst of the anxieties of war: today he had more time to think of himself. He made up his mind at once. He would get a divorce—and right away. He had already wasted too many years. He could not understand now why he had hesitated so long. When he was with Marie, young, beautiful, sweet, intelligent and cultivated, who did not intrigue and did not squander money, he saw the Empress' age and defects in a glaring light. Even during the campaign he had been deaf to Josephine's pleas. Now he answered her letters coldly. Once in a while a brief note signed with an absent-minded "Wholly yours."

Had Josephine been there with him at that moment the memory of their former tendernesses would have risen to her defense, her light voice would have touched the heart of the man she had held so long in the belief that their destinies were intertwined, their stars coupled. But she was not there. In her place Marie gave Napoleon the true intimacy, the affection he had always needed so greatly. From that moment the Empress was doomed.

Marie made ready to return to Poland, where she would wait for her child to be born. Moved by a spirit of patriotism as well as from kindness of heart Count Walewski had forgiven her. He was to do even more: soon he would invite her to Walewice that her child might be born on the family estate.

While still at Schönbrunn, Napoleon, knowing his weakness where Josephine was concerned, seized on the pretext of work that was being finished at Fontainebleau where he was to stay on his return and ordered his architect to wall up the communications between his apartment and Josephine's. So, by the time he arrived, the irreparable step would have been taken. A devious and brutal procedure! And yet not one of his entourage showed any surprise or rather no one raised a protest. Who would dare to? Méneval? He was too unobtrusive. Duroc was the only one who could have ventured a remonstrance. But that wise friend cherished an ancient grudge against Josephine. The Grand Marshal had not forgotten that she had opposed his marriage to Hortense. In that decisive hour, he held his peace.

Napoleon came home by way of Germany, as usual with seven-league boots. From Munich he sent Josephine a brief note announcing his return:

> My dear, I am leaving in an hour. I shall be at Fontaine-bleau from the 26th to the 27th. I suggest that you come there and bring some of your ladies with you.

On the morning of October 26th, his carriage drew up in front of the broad stone steps of the château. Duroc, who had preceded him by several posts, and a number of officers, were there to receive him. But as bad luck would have it, neither Josephine nor any of the Court had arrived. Napoleon sent off a messenger to Saint-Cloud to inform the Empress of his arrival. Then, while waiting for Cambacérès whom he had summoned and who, punctual as always, had appeared at the château at dawn, he inspected the new alterations inside the castle. He was very restless and kept repeatedly asking the time.

Cambacérès found the Emperor in a bad humor. Napoleon complained of the exaggerated alarms that had spread throughout France as a result of the campaign, he complained of the ineptitude the government had shown. He spoke of the dangers he had been exposed to and of his complete contempt of death. Finally he came to the matter of the divorce. Though it hurt him to do so, he had resolved to go through with it. Cambacérès was sufficiently a friend of Josephine's to feel sorry for her. He proffered a few timid observations. Napoleon replied haughtily. "He seemed to move in the atmosphere of his glory." The Arch-chancellor did not have the courage to insist.

The moment he was left alone the Emperor set to work, but his mind was not on it. He refused food, taking only some soup and a little chocolate. That continued delay on the part of a woman who usually anticipated his every desire, irritated him, but he was even more vexed at the thought of what he would have to tell her. It would be a battle royal, and for that battle he lacked the courage he showed when face to face with the enemy.

At last, at six o'clock, the Empress arrived. She went straight to the library, where Napoleon had secluded himself. He did not look up from his writing. It was the first time he had treated her that way. After what seemed an interminable delay he raised his head.

"Ah, so there you are, Madame," he said coldly. "A good thing too, for I was just about to leave for Saint-Cloud."

Then his gaze wandered back to his desk. Josephine was horrified at that reception after a separation of seven months. She stammered a few excuses and her eyes filled with tears. The Emperor then rose and embraced her. She retired to her own apartment to dress, returning an hour later for dinner. She wore a becoming white satin polonaise over her Court gown, with ornaments of silver wheat and blue flowers in her hair. Napoleon looked at her.

"I was not long in dressing, was I?"

He pointed to the clock: half past seven. Again a delay! Then he gave her his hand and walked toward the salon where the table had been laid. Meeting Decrès and Montalivet on the way he said:

"I shall be with you in five minutes."

Josephine was anxious to avoid a tête-à-tête.

"Those gentlemen have just come from Paris," she pointed out. "They certainly have not dined yet."

"Ah, that is right."

And he motioned to the ministers to join them at their table. They had scarcely time to unfold their napkins. The next moment the Emperor rose and returned to his study where they were obliged to follow him. Josephine then received a few friends in her own apartment. Napoleon joined her for a few moments and appeared so gay and charming that it seemed as if he were trying to make himself at home again.

The next day he received Fouché, whom he treated with considerable harshness. He was still angry with the Minister for having taken it upon himself to call out the soldiers of the National Guard during Napoleon's absence to repulse the English who had landed at Walcheren. Everyone had expected that

Fouché would be dismissed. But that astute statesman managed to get himself out of the hole with his usual cleverness. Moreover Napoleon was well aware of the value of his services. Fouché had done so much for him since Brumaire. He might be even more valuable in the coming struggle with the Church. A Napoleon, excommunicated and dragging the Sovereign Pontiff from jail to jail, might have need of the *Conventionnel* of '93 to influence public opinion. He therefore passed a sponge over his faults and ended by taking him back into favor. Catching sight of Talleyrand, he asked him: "What would you have done if I had been killed at Wagram?"

The death's-head above the high embroidered collar smiled: *"Nous aurions fait caca dans nos culottes."*

Napoleon laughed at the gross vulgarity. Then his brow darkened and he looked worried. He could think of nothing but the impending divorce. In Josephine's presence he was embarrassed, constrained. She lost her head and talked of her danger to everyone about her, to friends, physicians, even to servants and tradespeople. She questioned Bausset, the Prefect of the Palace, about the walling up of their apartments. He replied vaguely in some embarrassment.

"Monsieur de Bausset," Josephine said, "you may be sure there is something behind all that!"

Napoleon was showing her less attention now. When he went for a drive he took Pauline, not Josephine, with him in his barouche. Nor did she follow the hunts any more. Even the courtiers were beginning to neglect her, to be a little less obsequious. And yet Napoleon had not dared to have the decisive interview. He was afraid of Josephine's despair, of her tears. That silence of his frightened her. He had requested Lavallette, her nephew by marriage, to prepare the way for him. Lavallette declined. Fouché had spread the news of the divorce in Paris. No doubt he would be delighted to do the job. But the Emperor disliked that idea. If things ever came to that pass, he had promised Josephine that he himself and no other, would break the news to her.

V

The Divorce

ON THE 14TH OF NOVEMBER, Napoleon returned to Paris on horseback, instead of driving as usual in the carriage with Josephine. The kings of Bavaria, Saxony and Württemberg and the Napoleonides—Jerome and Catherine, Louis, the Murats— were arriving to celebrate the Peace of Vienna. Before that throng of monarchs and princes, the Emperor and the Empress forced a smile to their lips, but inwardly their tension, their anguish, was as great as ever. Josephine was losing weight: she could not sleep and the moment she found herself alone with her daughter she burst into tears. Hortense was not the comfort she had hoped for. Seeing her mother unhappy, the daughter had come to hope for a break, but she refused to lift a finger to bring it about. On two different occasions Napoleon had appealed to her in vain.

At last he made up his mind to speak himself. In rapid words, almost stammering, he explained that they would have to separate in the interests of the Empire. He hoped that she would be the one to request the annulment of their bonds. She groaned. It was not the loss of the Crown she mourned, but she could not bring herself to leave Napoleon. Distressed by her plaintive tones, he steeled himself.

"Do not try to move me," he said abruptly. "I still love you, but polity has no heart—it has only a head. I will give you five millions a year and the sovereignty of Rome."

She could not answer for weeping. He shrugged his shoulders and, as he was about to leave the room, turned and said:

"You might as well know that this divorce will be an episode in my life! What a scene for a tragedy!"

On the 22nd of November he ordered Champigny to have Caulaincourt make an official request for the hand of the Grand

Duchess Anne, the Czar's youngest sister. On the 26th he summoned Eugène to Paris. He was counting on him to pacify his
mother.

Josephine's despair was deep. This time she had no illusions.
The blow she had always feared, that she had gone to such pains
to avoid on his return from Egypt, that she had thought to ward
off by her religious marriage, that fatal blow had fallen at last
. . . and nothing could save her. She had not loved Bonaparte in
the beginning, she had betrayed him basely and she had never
understood him. But gradually, with the years, she had come to
have a feeling of genuine affection for him. She admired him for
having climbed to that extraordinary pinnacle, frail though it
seemed to her. She was even dimly grateful to him for having
connected her with it. As a younger woman she had been under
the spell of his heroic dominion; now, aging, she clung stubbornly to that vivid memory, that glorious testimonial of her
years of happiness. She appreciated its value at the very moment
when she was about to lose it: she mourned his glory, his trust,
his kisses.

One thing was certain: she mourned the loss of the "position"
(as she somewhat vulgarly called it) in which he had placed her
even more than she did the man. No longer to be an empress,
to squander millions, to be the object of the adulations of
France was a bitterer blow to her than to leave her husband. In
her silly head, vanity, self-interest, affection were mixed in a
confused jumble. What a degradation for her children! And
what a triumph for those Bonapartes she had always hated and
whom she had fought ever since her marriage! They were responsible, she thought—particularly the women. But in that she
was mistaken: as Napoleon had told her his policy, the necessity
for continuing his line, had doomed her. But she would not see
it. What was a necessity of State she represented as a palace
intrigue.

Escaping one day from so many hated festivities, she went to
Malmaison with Laure Junot. There, walking with her friend
in those gardens that held so many memories for her, she confided her torment, her bitterness of heart. In vain did the youth-

ful friend of "Puss-in-boots," the little Laurette who had become the Duchesse d'Abrantès, protest that neither Madame Letizia, whose lady-in-waiting she was, nor the princesses had mentioned the divorce in her presence. Josephine shook her head:

"Mme. Junot, remember what I tell you today in this garden, in this place which is a paradise and which perhaps will soon be a hell for me. Remember that this separation will kill me. I tell you, those women will be responsible for my death!"

The gay round of suppers, plays, concerts, receptions helped to distract the Emperor and he flung himself into them with a whole-hearted zest. But he could not avoid seeing Josephine at dinner. To both of them those meetings were a torture. She did not speak for fear she might faint, while to avoid that silence Napoleon read reports and cut the meal as short as possibile.

On November 30th the Empress appeared at table wearing a large hat tied with ribbons under her chin to hide her haggard, tear-stained features. The Emperor sat with lowered eyelids. Every now and then his cheeks twitched with a nervous tic. Neither of them touched food, except for appearance's sake. Not a word was spoken. There was no sound save the rattle of the plates, the low murmurs of the footmen, and the tinkling of the glass that Napoleon struck from time to time with his knife. Ten minutes passed in that manner. Then Napoleon uttered a deep sigh and turned to Bausset:

"What time is it?"

Without waiting for the Prefect's reply he rose and passed into the adjoining salon. The Empress followed him slowly, her handkerchief pressed to her lips. Coffee was brought in, a page presenting it on a tray as usual to Josephine for her to serve the Emperor. But Napoleon took his cup himself, poured coffee into it, dropped in a lump of sugar and looked at his wife, who stood motionless in utter bewilderment. He drained his cup and motioned for the others to leave them alone. Bausset and Constant lingered anxiously in the serving pantry. A few minutes later they heard loud cries from Josephine. A flunky started for the room. Bausset stopped him: the Emperor would call if he wanted him. . . .

At almost the same moment Napoleon appeared in the doorway and stood there swaying. The Empress lay outstretched on the floor.

"No, no," she was moaning, "I shall never live through it."

"Go in there, Bausset," ordered the Emperor, "and shut the door." Then he asked, "Do you think you are strong enough to lift Josephine and carry her down the inside staircase to her apartment where her women can look after her?"

Bausset was a huge man with the build of a stevedore. With the Emperor's help, he lifted the Empress, who, as soon as she was in his arms, let her head drop on his shoulder and closed her eyes as if she had fainted. Napoleon picked up a lighted torch and led the way. As Bausset was going down the narrow staircase, Napoleon handed his torch to the Prefect and seized Josephine's legs. Bausset tripped on his sword and stumbled. In his excitement he tightened his grip on the Empress. To his amazement she murmured in his ear: "You are squeezing me too hard. . . ." She had not lost consciousness for even a second!

As soon as they reached her bedroom Napoleon and Bausset laid her on the bed and the Emperor pulled the bellrope to summon her women. While they were hovering about their mistress he went into the boudoir and, pacing incessantly back and forth, burst out impulsively to the Prefect who stood mopping his streaming forehead:

"Divorce has become a harsh duty for me. The scene Josephine has just made distresses me all the more as she must have heard from Hortense three days ago . . . about the unhappy obligation which compels me to separate from her. . . . I pity her with all my heart. I thought she had more character . . . and I was not prepared for these paroxysms of grief."

He was so disturbed that he had difficulty in breathing. After he had sent for his stepdaughter and Corvisart, he returned to his own apartment, exhausted.

Hortense hurried to her mother and, taking her in her arms,

rocked her like a baby. When Josephine had grown a little quieter, Hortense went up to the Emperor's rooms. He came out to meet her and, undoubtedly to hide his agitation, remarked dryly:

"Well! So you have seen your mother. What did she say to you? My mind is made up. There is no going back now. Nothing can make me change, neither tears, nor prayers."

Hortense answered proudly:

"You are free to do as you please, sire. No one will interfere with you. It is necessary for your happiness—that is enough. We shall make the sacrifice. Do not be surprised at my mother's tears. Rather you should be surprised if, after a union of fifteen years, she did not weep. But she will submit to your decision—of that I am confident. And we shall all take with us the memory of your many kindnesses."

Stirred to emotion by the voice of that child he had seen grow up, Napoleon dropped his mask.

"What!" he exclaimed with tears in his voice. "You are not all going to leave me? You are not going to desert me? Don't you love me any more? If only my happiness were at stake I would gladly sacrifice it for you, but it is the happiness of France. Pity me rather because I am compelled to sacrifice my dearest affections."

That desertion frightened him. He realized that in spite of all his power, all his pride, he would not be able to endure it. Hortense was moved by his suffering and relented. Napoleon tried to win her over. He wanted her to live near him, to continue to be his daughter. But she refused. She was vexed with him and she blamed him for her marriage. She was not going to stand his harshness any longer.

"Sire, I must go with my mother: she will need me. We cannot live with you any longer. We are asked to make a sacrifice—and we shall make it."

However, she was soon to yield in the interests of her sons as well as on the advice of her mother. But in the pomp and splendor of those days—a reception at Malmaison for the German kings, a Te Deum for peace, a grand banquet at the

Tuileries, reviews, dinners, a ball at the Hôtel de Ville and a gala performance at Court, both mother and daughter found it hard to endure the curious glances of the courtiers and the triumph of the Bonapartes over the Beauharnaises who were crushed at last. Hiding her swollen eyelids, Josephine played her part as a sovereign unflinchingly. She appeared at all the ceremonies, all the assemblies, talking and welcoming guests, always smiling, always gracious.

At the bottom of her despair a last hope lingered. Eugène was hurrying up from Italy: perhaps he would save her. But when he arrived, on the 5th of December, that faint glimmer was extinguished. Hortense went to meet him and warned him. Accustomed to obey, he yielded. That same day all four of them, Napoleon, Josephine, Eugène and Hortense met at the Tuileries. The Emperor, deeply moved, explained his intentions. While Josephine was not to continue to reign, she was still to be the Empress and she would have a splendid establishment. Eugène would receive a princely endowment in Italy. Separated from a husband who had caused her too much suffering, Hortense would find that her future and that of her sons would be assured. Eugène replied, as his sister had done, that they would go with their mother. Napoleon protested with warm affection:

"Eugène, if I have been of any use to you in your life, if I have taken the place of a father to you, do not forsake me. I need you. Your sister cannot leave me. Your mother does not wish it. Those exaggerated ideas of yours would only make her unhappy."

And he added shrewdly, for sincere though he was, he was still shrewd even when deeply moved:

"Stay, if you do not want posterity to say, 'The Empress was driven away. Perhaps she deserved it.' Is it not a fine enough rôle for her to remain near me, to prove that it was just a separation of policy, that she desired it, so acquiring new claims to the esteem, the respect, the love of a nation for which she is making the sacrifice?"

Grasping his stepson's hand, he drew him toward him and embraced him. Eugène made no reply. Josephine was at the end of her strength. For the first time, quite frankly, she yielded. But, fearing that her children might be forgotten, she asked that Eugène be given the Kingdom of Italy. Her son interrupted her:

"Mother, I do not wish to be considered. Your son would not accept a crown at the price of your separation."

"There speaks Eugène's heart," said Napoleon. "He is right to rely on my affection."

Josephine did not attend the circle that evening, Napoleon doing the honors alone. But on the 11th she appeared again at a hunt which Berthier gave at Grosbois. She was late and they did not wait for her. The Marshal left behind only an aide-de-camp to receive her—a man she scarcely knew. He held out his hand, addressing her with a few words of simple courtesy. Seeing herself thus forsaken, Josephine could not restrain her tears. Grasping the colonel's arm she implored:

"You will not forget me, will you? No matter what happens to me?"

The party had been very gay before she appeared, but with her arrival, like a ghost at the feast, the merriment was quenched. The dinner was a funeral. A number of actors gave a performance of *Cadet Roussel,* a current succes at the Variétés, but a stupid choice for the occasion as the hero talked constantly of getting a divorce "to have descendants or ancestors." The audience was astounded. The Empress could scarcely control her emotion. As for the Emperor, he was so annoyed that, to teach everyone a lesson, he redoubled his attentions to the Empress, Hortense and Eugène, and ignored his sisters.

On December 15th, at nine o'clock in the evening, the Tuileries was ablaze with lights. Kings in gala uniforms, decorated with all their orders, queens, princesses in silken gowns and court trains, their heads starry with jewels and emerging from *chérusques* of gold or silver, marshals in dazzling uniforms, dignitaries, gathered in the throne room. As the clock struck the hour, the door of the Emperor's study was flung wide on both sides. Madame Mère, Louis, Jerome, Murat, Eugène, Julie,

Hortense, Catherine, Pauline and Caroline entered slowly one after the other in order of precedence. Napoleon and Josephine received them seated behind a large table covered in red-fringed velvet and embroidered with eagles. At a sign from the Emperor all took their seats in silence. The Empress was dressed in a plain white gown, no jewelry, and with only a ribbon in her hair. She was very pale, but calm. The Emperor had on the uniform of the Colonel of the Guards. His eyes stared sombrely and he kept twisting the braid on his coat. Cambacérès and Regnault de Saint-Jean d'Angèly, Secretary to the Imperial Household, were ushered in. Napoleon rose and taking a paper, read in a low but penetrating voice. He had thought the speech Maret had prepared for him too dry, too official and had re-written it himself. After explaining in a few brief words the political necessity of the divorce, he ended by paying a touching tribute to the woman he had once loved so dearly and from whom Fate now compelled him to part:

"God knows how much such a resolve has cost my heart! But no sacrifice is beyond my strength when I have been shown that it is for the good of France. . . . I have only praise for the devotion and love of my beloved wife. . . . It is my desire that she shall preserve the rank and title of a crowned Empress, but above all that she never doubt my affection and always consider me her best and dearest friend."

As he sat down, Josephine rose to her feet. She too had found the statement that had been submitted to her thoroughly banal. And with her own hand, on her paper edged with Roman designs, she had written a few sentences replete with all her easy grace and tact—and also her grief:

"With the permission of our august and dear husband, I must declare that being without hope of having children who might satisfy the needs of his policy and the requirements of France, it is my pleasure to give him the greatest proof of attachment and devotion that has ever been given on earth . . ."

At that point her strength failed. Choking with sobs she sank back in her chair. Regnault picked up the paper and continued reading:

"I owe everything to his kindness: with his own hand he crowned me and from the height of that throne I have received only evidences of affection and love from the French people. . . . The dissolution of my marriage will not change my affection: the Emperor will always find me his best friend. . . . We are both proud of the sacrifice we are making for the good of the country."

The unhappy woman listened, motionless. Napoleon leaned toward her and taking her hand, clasped it in his. A moment so poignant that even the Bonapartes, who had been triumphing a little while before, were moved. Madame Mère wiped away a tear. Pauline and Caroline looked abashed. Eugène, who was standing beside the Emperor, shook with a nervous chill. Hortense hid her face in her hands.

Cambacérès drew up the declaration of the divorce. Napoleon signed with a heavy flourish. Josephine wrote her name underneath his. Madame Mère then wrote hers, in a hand that trembled. Then came the kings and the queens. Josephine left the room on Hortense's arm, Eugène following them. A moment later she fell in a faint.

Napoleon had provided magnificently for Josephine's future. He had once mentioned Rome and an endowment of five millions. But at the crucial moment, his solicitude as chief of State and his personal sense of economy reduced that liberality. He gave Josephine simply the status of a dowager empress. As residences she was to have the Elysée, Malmaison, and another château of her own choosing. All her debts and a yearly income of three millions were to be paid.

As Josephine had feared, Napoleon gave Eugène nothing. He was to remain viceroy of Italy but without any guarantee for the future. Hortense received the assurance that she could stay in Paris as long as she chose, that she could have her children, her honors and also the freedom of which she was in such sore need. With her endowments, gifts and holiday funds, she would have three million francs a year at least. Not only did Napoleon tolerate her liaison with Flahaut, but he even promoted the latter, making him a general, a count and an aide-de-camp. Satisfied for herself and for her mother, Hortense was unhappy about Eugène. She never complained directly, but the Emperor sometimes felt the reproach in her eyes as they rested on him.

After the ceremony of the divorce the Emperor returned to his own apartments. He was depressed and, calling for Constant, got into bed. Suddenly the door opened and Josephine appeared, her hair falling about in wild disorder. She walked toward the bed like an automaton, stopped suddenly and burst into tears. Napoleon held out his arms and they clasped each other in a long embrace.

"Come, come, my good Josephine," he murmured. "You must be sensible. Come, be brave, be brave! I shall always be your friend. . . ."

Cheek to cheek they both wept. They were left alone in the secret flow of memories. An hour later Constant, who was waiting in the adjoining room saw Josephine pass out again. She motioned to him sadly. He then went into Napoleon's room to put out the light as usual. The Emperor made no sound. He was huddled so deep in his bed that his face was hidden by the covers.

The next morning Napoleon was dejected, miserable. As Constant dressed him he sighed heavily. No audience that day. He locked himself in his study, but he did not work. After a brief good-morning to Méneval he flung himself down on his little sofa and sat there for a long time with his head resting on his hand. . . . He had decided to spend the first days of the separation at Trianon. When they came to announce that the carriages were waiting, he picked up his hat and turned to his secretary:

"Come with me, Méneval."

Descending the private staircase, he entered Josephine's apartment. She was alone and apparently deep in thought. At the sound of his step she rose and, flinging herself into his arms, burst into tears. It was hard to make an end of the painful farewell. At last the Emperor put her down tenderly on a couch, and requesting Méneval to remain with her until he had left, he went out through the ground-floor rooms. Flinging himself into his carriage he ordered Duroc to get in with him.

Josephine begged Méneval earnestly to assure Napoleon that she would always love him and that she implored him not to forget her. When she had grown a little quieter, she too made ready to leave, but for Malmaison. Her luggage had already been piled up in the Cour du Carrousel. A group of officers, women, servants, stood about waiting in the grand entrance hall of the Tuileries to pay her a final tribute. She passed between them, her face covered with a thick veil, one arm flung around the shoulder of one of her ladies-in-waiting, and a low murmur of sorrow followed her as she crossed the threshold of the palace that had known her in the days of her happiness and power and to which she was never to return. The blinds of her berline were lowered, the horses set off at a gallop in the driving rain.

How mournful the Trianon was those winter days! Napoleon was disoriented, restless. He missed—and cruelly—the atmosphere with which Josephine had surrounded him, her artful caresses, her instinctive comprehension of anything that might please him. The very first evening he wrote to the woman he had sacrificed. The next morning he sent her another letter by his equerry d'Audenarde:

> They tell me you have lost courage since your arrival at Malmaison. And yet that place is filled with our affection which cannot and must not change—at least on my part. I long to see you, but I must be sure that you are strong and not weak. I am a little weak, too, and I suffer cruelly.

He passed the time as best he could, hunting at Satory in the mud, playing cards, drumming on the window-panes. All the Bonapartes were there. Caroline and Pauline tried vainly to amuse him. He was very short with them and paid no attention to Mme. de Mathis, whom Pauline had taken care to bring with her. He was bored and miserable. Unable to stand it any longer he hurried to Malmaison. Josephine was in very low spirits, despite the fact that her children were with her and she had been receiving numerous visits as the result of the Emperor's unspoken command. "Have you seen the Empress?" he kept asking. And the carriages began to roll along the road to Malmaison, Majesties, Highnesses, courtiers hastened to greet the sovereign who had been set aside, but not cast out. Grateful for those attentions, docile, uncomplaining, she moved everyone to pity. In that first visit Napoleon avoided seeing her alone to prevent a renewal of their painful farewells. But he was extremely attentive and as soon as he had returned to Trianon sent her a scribbled note:

> My dear, I found you weaker today than you should be. You have shown courage. You must continue to be brave. You must not give way to melancholy; especially take care of your health which is so precious to me. You sadly misjudge my affection for you if you imagine that I could be happy when you are not. . . . Farewell, my dear, sleep well. Remember that is my desire.

Not love certainly, but how much affection still and, from the bottom of his heart, what regrets! That note, delivered in the evening, caused her tears to flow again. Far from consoling her, such tokens only increased her suffering. Mme. de Rémusat urged her to walk, hoping that it would make her sleep. But the poor Empress returned exhausted from those strolls along the garden paths in that beautiful park that called up memories of a past still vividly alive.

"It sometimes seems to me," she said to her friend, "that I am dead and all I have left is a kind of vague ability to realize that I am no more."

On the 18th of December, Napoleon hunted deer at Saint-Germain under a heavy downpour. He needed physical exercise, muscular relaxation. Three times he sent some game to Malmaison and asked for news from there. And every day a note, to which Josephine replied with long letters.

> A thousand, thousand tender thanks for not forgetting me. . . . There are some affections that are life itself and that can end only with it. Be happy! Be as happy as you deserve! Those words come from my whole heart.

Poor Josephine, her fine handwriting was blurred with tears.
. . . On the 20th, Napoleon was detained by a Council of Ministers and sent Savary to her. On the 21st he wrote in the
evening:

> I hope you have been to look at your plants, the weather
> having been fine today. I did not go out except for a little
> while this afternoon at three o'clock to shoot a few hares.

On the 24th he paid her a surprise visit. For several days he
had been very surly, "in a dog's mood," Jerome's wife said,
but he laid himself out to be charming to Josephine and invited her to come to see him the next day at Trianon. The
King of Württemberg was there: it would be a change for her.
He insisted upon keeping Josephine, Hortense and Eugène
for dinner. Frivolous, empty-headed as Josephine was, for a
moment she could fancy herself a sovereign again as she sat
beside the Emperor at table. "She looked so happy and at ease
that one would have thought Their Majesties had never separated," noted Mlle. Avrillon.

On the 26th the Emperor returned to the Tuileries. But without the woman who for ten years had graced those rooms with
her charm that palace seemed cold and austere to him.

"I was very bored," he said, "when I returned to the Tuileries. That vast palace seemed empty and I felt as if I were
completely isolated."

That same evening in another letter he wrote with naïve
masculine egotism:

> I shall have to dine all alone.

During the month of January, which he insisted upon beginning with her, he went to see her five or six times, though he
was worn out; insisted upon having a daily bulletin of her
health; made her innumerable gifts; and racked his brains to
think of things that might please her. That man who had
tormented her so much because of her extravagance now actually forestalled her requests for money. After spending a few
hours with her at Malmaison one evening he wrote to her the
next day, Sunday, February 7th:

I was very happy to see you again last night. . . . I have set aside 100,000 francs for the year 1810 for extra expenditures at Malmaison. You are to use it as you see fit. Estève is to pay over 200,000 francs to you as soon as the contract with the Maison Julien is signed. I have ordered them to pay for your ruby necklace, which I shall have the appraisers value for I do not want any jewel robberies. That will cost me 400,000 francs. I have ordered that the million which the Civil List owes you for 1810 be put at the disposal of your lawyer to pay your debts. You should find from 500,000 to 600,000 francs in the desk at Malmaison. You can take it for your silverplate and your linen. I have ordered a very beautiful porcelain service for you: they will make it according to your desires so that it may be very beautiful.

Household details, but was he not at one and the same time the man of the most comprehensive dreams and the careful calculator of detail? He wanted Josephine to trust him and was anxious that she should not listen to false rumors, "not worry about idle tales." She ought to know him for that matter: "Josephine, I am vexed with you, and if I do not hear that you are cheerful and happy, I shall come and give you a good scolding. . . ."

He was still fond of her, he still thought of her often. But the press of State affairs had enveloped him again. Work, ever his panacea, was to help him gradually to overcome his sorrow. His religious marriage to Josephine had been dissolved on January 12th by the office of the archbishop, a rather shady arrangement to tell the truth, as the Pope should have been the one to officiate in such matters. However, the Emperor, so hurried and in such a hurry, was not above a little irregularity. Josephine was not obliged to appear. No doubt to her the rupture of that last bond by which she had tried to save herself meant nothing more than a customary formality.

Little by little, though she still wept—tears came easy to her —her grief wore itself out. She started to gossip with her ladies again. She took an interest in clothes. "Mourning is very becoming to me," she said. "I shall wear it for a year." Soon, as she dreaded the winter at Malmaison, Eugène obtained permission for her to live at the Elysée. Napoleon called on her there, but only brief visits. He was growing less and less attentive. Absorbed in plans for his remarriage, he was already eager for that ceremony to be over and done with. He was looking toward the future, dwelling in thought on the pictures his mind called up, lingering on them lovingly. He galloped in dreams. To his close friends, he was already speaking of "my children."

Part Four

MARIE-LOUISE AND
THE KING OF ROME

I

The Second Marriage

NAPOLEON HAD SECURED a divorce for the sole purpose of taking another wife and having heirs by her as soon as possible. "I am marrying a uterus," he had said. He had looked for that wife first in Russia. But, worried by the Czar's prolonged silence, he thought of Marie-Louise, the daughter of the Emperor of Austria. Josephine was anxious to have a hand in the arrangement and she recommended that choice, even going so far as to send for Mme. de Metternich, who was then in Paris. The latter wrote to Vienna: Metternich leapt for joy. A family alliance with Napoleon would open the way for him to obtain an amelioration of the last treaty which had been so rigorous. He requested the Emperor Franz to broach the matter to his daughter, and, without waiting for a reply, sent word to Josephine that Austria would be delighted to bestow the hand of its princess. He even added that the Hofburg would be enduringly grateful to her for her kind mediation.

After consulting his family and his Council, Napoleon made up his mind. He would marry Marie-Louise; he would send Eugène to Ambassador Schwartzenburg to request that the marriage contract be drawn up without delay.

What Marie-Louise was like and how she felt about it, he had not the slightest idea. He had seen a few portraits and miniatures of her—all far too flattering. The Archduchess was the eldest daughter of feeble Franz and his first wife, the Empress Teresa. She was just eighteen years old, a tall girl, with slender arms and legs, a heavy body, a billowing bosom, delicate joints, beautiful hands, and gorgeous blond hair as soft as silk. Her complexion, which was naturally fresh and high-colored, had been somewhat marred by the smallpox. China-blue eyes set flat in her face gave her a blurred, sheeplike expression, and her long, straight nose and her thick, sensuous lips were all Hapsburg. She was very shy, utterly lacking in grace, walked badly and had a childish giggle. Though she had been well educated, spoke six languages, played the piano, drew and painted, she appeared somewhat stupid. She knew nothing about life. In fact her innocence had been guarded to such a degree that she had never been allowed to have any male animals about her, only female dogs, cats and canaries. The books she had read were all expurgated and she had seen nothing more exciting than charades. She was, in short, an overgrown boarding-school miss, gentle, pious, loving and submissive.

She hated France which had put her aunt, Marie Antoinette, to death, dethroned her grandmother, Caroline of Naples, murdered priests and denied God. To her Napoleon, that "terrible Corsican" was a sort of Antichrist, born of the blood and dregs of the Revolution. He was a Turk, an atheist, who made his wife miserable and flogged his ministers. Three times he had conquered Austria; twice he had driven from Vienna the father she adored, deprived him of the crown of the Holy Roman Empire and brought him to his knees. The mere mention of that name made her shudder. After Wagram she wrote to her friend, Victoire du Poutet: "I assure you that just to see that person would be a worse torture to me than all the martyrdoms. . . . I should be consumed with rage if I were obliged to dine with one of his marshals." When the divorce became known in Vienna and she herself began to be talked of as a possible candidate, she wrote: "I let everyone talk and am not in the least worried. I am only sorry for the poor princess he will choose, for I am quite sure I shall not be the one to become the victim of his policy." At that very moment her father was already sacrificing her. Not daring to tell her in person, he wrote her a letter. Then he sent Metternich to her.

"What is my father's will?" the Archduchess asked simply.

The minister protested that the Emperor had no intention of forcing her. But such great interests were involved. . . . She made no demur; she submitted, not however without a certain nobility:

"I desire only what my duty commands me to desire. Where the interests of my father are at stake, he must be consulted and not my will."

However she raised a religious scruple. Had Napoleon's first marriage been annulled by the Church? Metternich interposed the Papal Nuncio to quiet her and calm her fears. Her brothers and her sisters pampered and cajoled her as if by order, congratulating her and talking of the happiness in store for her.

Napoleon had never doubted for a moment that she would accept him. But he was delighted with the eagerness Austria was showing. The thought of his marriage absorbed him completely. Pride—a pride such as he had never known—went to his head. "The little noble," the Jacobin soldier, was about to be united with the most ancient, the most illustrious ruling house in Europe. The daughter of the Cæsars in the bed of the little lieutenant of Valence! Never had he measured to such extent the full power of his genius and the magnitude of his fortune. Like a schoolboy he set to work to write a letter of thanks to Marie-Louise on his best paper. He made arrangements for her household, ordered Caroline to see to the marriage chest and the trousseau, which must be magnificent. And while waiting for Berthier, whom he had sent to Vienna as ambassador extraordinary to marry the Archduchess by proxy, he began lavishing sumptuous gifts on her. Generous by nature, Marie-Louise divided most of those gifts among her entourage. She had resigned herself to her fate, but she shed many a tear when she said goodbye to her father and stepmother at St. Polten. Then, accompanied by Caroline, whom Napoleon had chosen for that honor with the idea of reassuring and flattering the Murats, Marie-Louise set out for France by slow stages.

At that moment Josephine was almost forgotten. Now that Napoleon no longer saw her near him day after day, he had become accustomed to doing without her. He still wrote to her, but his notes were brief, his affection had cooled. The

Court had never been gayer or more brilliant: hunts and receptions by day, and in the evening, concerts, plays, balls. Napoleon went to visit Bessières at Grignon. At first he had thought that Josephine might join him there, but she tactfully found an excuse, which he promptly seized upon. "It might perhaps be rather unbecoming for us to stay under the same roof during the first year. . . ." He was very gay, playing hunt the slipper with the ladies, dancing the *Monaco,* and even, in jest, forcing Maximilian, the fat King of Bavaria, to dance. He had become a little second lieutenant again and he dashed about the park and played prisoner's base with as much zest as in his youth. He then went on to Rambouillet, where the festivities were continued.

His mind was already busy with thoughts of the son he would have and on whom he intended to bestow the title of King of Rome, so depriving Eugène of any hope of succeeding to the throne in Italy. To compensate him he was to have a grand-duchy in Frankfurt. Not that Napoleon showed any less interest in his stepson—he was even to consider the throne of Sweden for him—but his own Empire seemed too small to him to provide for the children he hoped to have, and he began to reach out jealously for everything at hand.

Fearful of opinion at the Court of Vienna, he ordered Fouché to forbid any mention of the discarded Empress in the newspapers. Her presence was beginning to embarrass him: he would have liked to send her away. He presented her with the property of Navarre, near Evreux, which he raised to a duchy and on the 12th of March invited her to retire to that estate. An order of exile under a gracious form.

"My dear, I hope that you have been pleased with what I have done about Navarre. I suggest that you go there around the 27th of March and stay through the month of April."

Sick at heart, disappointed, deserted now by everyone save her children and her personal retinue, Josephine obeyed. It was high time: the following day the new Empress was to arrive at Compiègne.

Those had been days of chafings, of feverish and chaotic preparations for the reception of Marie-Louise. Toward the last Napoleon's impatience had increased. He did not know what to do with himself. He questioned Corvisart feverishly as to his ability to have children.

"What is the average term of potency in regard to paternity?" he asked him. "For instance, can a man of sixty who marries a young woman still have children?"

"Sometimes."

"And at seventy?"

"Always, sire," retorted the facetious physician.

Napoleon was only forty: he felt reassured. But he was in a hurry to see his wife. He plied everyone who had seen Marie-Louise in Vienna with questions about her, he wore them out with his curiosity. He even kept some of the Hapsburg medallions on his table and compared them with a sketch that Lejeune, Berthier's aide-de-camp, had brought him.

"Ah, there's the Hapsburg lip!" he exclaimed rubbing his hands.

"Come now, tell me frankly," he asked the officer in Talleyrand's presence, "what do you think of the Archduchess?"

"Very charming, sire."

"Very charming! That does not tell me a thing. Come! How tall is she?"

"Sire, about the same height as the Queen of Holland."

"Ah, that is good. What color hair has she?"

"Blond, like the Queen of Holland's."

"And her complexion?"

"Very white, with fresh coloring like the Queen of Holland."

"Then you would say she ressembles the Queen of Holland, eh?"

"No, sire, and yet I have answered your questions truthfully."

Napoleon dismissed the officer. Turning to Talleyrand he shook his head:

"I can get nothing out of them. It is clear that my wife is ugly, for not one of those young rascals has been able to tell me she is a pretty girl. After all, if she is kind and gives me big boys I shall love her just as much as if she were a beauty."

He took refuge complacently in little signs. One of Marie-Louise's slippers had been sent to Paris as a model. Napoleon went into ecstasies over its small size. He tapped Constant lightly on the cheek with it.

"There is a slipper of good omen. Have you ever seen many feet as small as that? Why, you can hold it in your hand."

To make the time pass more quickly, he hunted, gave balls, suppers. His work was neglected. He posed for his portrait, conferred with Dreux-Brézé, Louis XVI's master of ceremonies, concerning details of etiquette—which he criticized with a captious formalism. He attended in person to the decorations of the chapel at the Louvre. As there was some question about where to put certain paintings that they were obliged to take down, he said simply:

"Well, the only thing to do is to burn them!"

At Compiègne he visited the Empress' apartments ten times, chose the draperies, furniture, little knicknacks. Eager to appear at his best he ordered a lavishly embroidered coat from Léger, Murat's tailor—but he was not satisfied with it and flung it down on a chair. The fashionable bootmaker of the day made him the finest shoes. One day, alone with Hortense and Stephanie of Baden, he said to them:

"I must learn to make myself more attractive. My stern, serious manner might repel a young woman. She probably likes all the things young people of her age enjoy. Come, Hortense, you are our Terpsichore. Teach me to waltz."

The two princesses laughed at him. He insisted and for two evenings in succession Hortense gave him lessons, humming the tunes herself. But he grew dizzy quickly, felt nauseated and had to stop. He laughed merrily at his own awkwardness:

"I am too old. I can see that I am not meant to shine as a dancer."

Stephanie consoled him with flattery:

"You will never be anything but a poor pupil, sire. You are born to give lessons, not to receive them."

Meanwhile, escorted by Caroline, Marie-Louise was approaching Compiègne by easy stages. Napoleon wrote to her every day, sent her gifts of rare flowers, and pheasants. She replied with vapid little notes which he read with pleasure. He complained that the messengers were too slow, though to please him they rode their horses to death.

On the 27th of March the Empress was expected at Soissons. Napoleon could not stand the delay any longer. He called his valet:

"Quick, Constant! Order a carriage without markings and then come and lay out my clothes."

He would surprise Marie-Louise by appearing before her unexpectedly, disguised as a simple officer. He was already enjoying in advance her astonishment. That morning he lingered over his dressing, donning his green uniform of the Chasseurs de la Garde and the long gray coat he had worn at Wagram —"in coquetry of glory," as Constant said. Above all, a gambler's superstition—for he owed Marie-Louise to Wagram.

Murat was there, waiting for his wife, too, so the Emperor invited him to accompany him. In his barouche under the steady downpour of rain, seated next to Murat, he kept looking at his watch impatiently, ordering the coachman to drive faster. At each change of horses he got out, tried to hurry the postilions. Arriving in the little village of Courcelles, in Champagne, they met a courrier who was riding a quarter of an hour ahead of the Empress' party. The Emperor leapt from the barouche and, to get out of the downpour, ran under the porch of the church. Soon the cortège appeared. Napoleon signaled to the Empress' coachman to stop and rushed toward the huge berline. But the Empress' equerry, recognizing him, lowered the steps and flung open the door with the cry:

"The Emperor!"

Napoleon flashed an angry glance at the fellow:

"Didn't you see me motion to you to keep quiet?"

Then, disregarding formalities, forgetting that his coat was dripping with water, he flung his arms about Marie-Louise, who was silent, overwhelmed. He sat down beside her and directed the coachman to drive to Compiègne without stopping.

Napoleon clasped his wife's hands in his, inquired about her health, for she had a heavy cold, asked for news of her parents—all very friendly, very bourgeois. And he joked and laughed like a lover of twenty. He was enchanted with the lady: her timid, awkward gestures, her embarrassment, her gown—a flaming red relieved with gold embroidery—all delighted him. She more than fulfilled his hopes. Every inch an archduchess and a Hapsburg! The first shock over, she grew tame quite rapidly. Napoleon's attentions, his devotion were an agreeable surprise to her. The Minotaur to whom she thought she had been delivered was a man, and not old by any means, with handsome features and, when he smiled, an air of charming frankness. Soon she was chattering away in her guttural French.

The berline dashed over the muddy roads past Soissons without stopping for the splendid banquet that had been prepared by the authorities there. It was dark night when they reached Compiègne. The Emperor alighted, offering his hand to the Empress. Young girls, their hands filled with flowers, were left with their songs unsung as Napoleon hurried Marie-Louise to her apartments. There, with only Caroline to keep them company, they dined alone, eating heartily and gaily.

According to the program the Emperor should have slept outside of the palace that night, at the Hôtel de la Chancellerie. But he refused to leave the Empress' room. He had decided to marry her then and there without waiting for the ceremonies.

"What did your parents tell you before you left?" he asked her.

"To place myself entirely in your hands and to obey you in everything."

To quiet her scruples—was she properly married in the eyes of the Church, she wondered?—Cardinal Fesch was immediately summoned and reassured her. Napoleon led her to her bedroom, telling her that he would return as soon as she was in bed. He instructed Caroline to give her the customary advice. Marie-Louise, so "nice," was sorely in need of it. He himself returned to his own apartment and, undressing, drenched himself in eau de cologne then, clad only in a bathrobe, he hurried back to the Empress' apartment.

The next morning, while he was dressing, Napoleon asked Constant "whether anyone had noticed the dent he had made in the program." The valet replied in the negative, smiling. Just then an aide-de-camp entered. The Emperor, beaming broadly, tweaked his ear and said:

"Marry a German girl, my dear fellow! They are the best women in the world! They are sweet, they are good-natured, they have everything to learn, and they are as fresh as roses!"

He returned to the Empress' apartments and, toward noon, ordered breakfast for two to be served at her bedside. All morning he was delightfully gay. Dinner that night was preceded by a concert at which La Grassini sang with Crescentini, Paer playing the accompaniments. Marie-Louise, in pink, looked radiant. Napoleon kept falling asleep in his chair at her side. She was amused and nudged him with her elbow to waken him. He roused, smiled, made a few pleasant remarks and fell asleep again.

The second night was a repetition of the first. Marie-Louise began to enjoy love. Lymphatic and voluptuous, before long she was to like it too well, so well indeed that Corvisart felt called upon to warn Napoleon.

Affectionate under an outward appearance of coldness the young Empress was delighted with the tokens of affection which Napoleon lavished upon her in public as well as in private. She wrote to her father:

> Ever since my arrival I have been with him constantly and he is madly in love with me. I am deeply grateful to him and I love him sincerely. . . . There is something very winning and very touching about him that is quite irresistible. My health continues to improve. . . . I assure you, dear Papa, that the Emperor is even more particular than you about making me take my medicines regularly. While I had a cough he would not allow me to get up before two o'clock.

On the 30th they set out for Saint-Cloud and the following

day the civil marriage was performed. On April 1st, in the Salon Carré of the Louvre, they were married by Cardinal Fesch. Marie-Louise was magnificent in a gown of silver tulle made by Leroy. The Queens of Spain, of Holland and of Westphalia and the Princesses Elisa and Pauline carried her heavy court train—awkwardly and with exceedingly bad grace, to tell the truth. The evening before Pauline had ventured a protest: Caroline had burst into tears. Napoleon settled the dispute by saying "That is my will." But he released Caroline from the irksome duty because she had gone to meet the Empress. She walked alone, after Madame Mère, casting scornful glances at her sisters.

Napoleon wore knee breeches and a coat of white satin, with a short cloak of the same material, and a black velvet cap, trimmed with white feathers, and glittering with diamonds. Staggering under the weight of her crown, embarrassed, crimson, the Empress moved forward slowly. Of the twenty-seven cardinals of the Empire who were to attend the ceremony, thirteen Italians were absent, a protest against the Emperor's conduct toward the Pope, then a prisoner at Savona. When he saw those empty chairs, Napoleon was filled with rage. He would take their pensions from them, their charges, he would send them into exile. From that moment he was to redouble his unjust and impolitic violences against the Church.

Marie-Louise's household was organized on an even more sumptuous scale than Josephine's. She retained most of the Empress' former ladies-in-waiting and as *dame d'honneur* Napoleon gave her Lannes' widow, the Duchess de Montebello. Young and beautiful, the Duchess de Montebello was rich, as the result of the Emperor's endless generosity, but she held it against him for not making her a princess. However she gladly accepted that important post in Marie-Louise's household and she was to rule her like a tyrant. The weak Viennese would soon be seeing only through the eyes of her lady-in-waiting.

In Marie-Louise's service Napoleon placed a large group of women called "red," "black," "white," according to the color of their uniforms. It was their duty to keep men away from the

Empress. Napoleon was jealous of his young wife and was determined to avoid any surprises in that quarter. He had no faith in the virtue of women: he had found them all too easy himself. "Adultery," he often said, "is all a matter of a sofa." In short, he had left Josephine perfectly free—he was not to use the same tactics with his young wife. He would not allow her to take a walk, to go to a play, or to receive guests unless he were present. When Mme. de Montebello made the mistake of presenting one of her young cousins to the Empress, she brought down a severe scolding on her head. Marie-Louise could not take music or painting lessons, could not have her hair dressed, unless one of her women was present. Napoleon even reprimanded a reader "who remained at the far end of the salon while the jeweler, Biennais, was showing the Empress a coffer for her papers."

Palace flunkies, workingmen were not to be admitted to Marie-Louise's apartment until she had left it. Metternich, who had lingered on in Paris, was the only one to find favor in the Emperor's eyes. He was to report to Vienna that Marie-Louise was happy. Napoleon himself summoned the Minister to the Empress' apartments.

"I want her to talk quite frankly with you," he said, "to tell you what she really thinks of her situation. You are her friend. Therefore she must have no secrets from you."

He locked them in the drawing-room. An hour later he returned.

"Well," he said, "have you had a good talk? Did the Empress say many bad things about me? Did she laugh or cry? I won't ask for a report. Those are your secrets—yours and hers."

How could Marie-Louise help being happy? That loving solicitude, that thoughtful affection in which she could detect a basis of deep respect, could not fail to touch her. Was it love? Perhaps not, but a warm conjugal affection strengthened by that feeling for the home he had always had. There was perhaps a touch, too, of the complacency and the protective vanity of a man of forty toward a young woman of twenty. For her sake, during the first months of their married life, Napoleon transformed his manner of living. He began to neglect his work. In the morning he lingered in his wife's bedchamber, took an interest in her clothes and the way she wore her hair, chatted with her of little nothings, listened to her when she sat down at the piano to play, posed patiently while she sketched his profile. His old friends did not recognize him any longer. The man who had bolted his luncheon in six or seven minutes now tarried at table with her over a groaning board and never thought of rising before she did. If she expressed a desire to take a walk afterward, he waited for her. He played long games of billiards that bored him to death. To avoid leaving her in the hands of a groom, he made himself her riding master and ran behind her, without his shoes, in silk stockings, in the sawdust of the riding ring. He refused audiences, neglected his correspondence. In the midst of a meeting he would rise and close the debate because a chamberlain had come to summon him to Marie-Louise. To tell the truth, affairs of State seemed to bore him now. He spent entire afternoons with his Louise, catching cold because she always insisted upon keeping the windows open. He ordered informal balls given for her entertainment, at which he frisked like a boy, and plays, no longer of the serious type such as he enjoyed, but vapid pastorals, schoolgirl farces. At her request he gave much thought to dress, began to wear tight-fitting coats and gave up taking snuff. In April Metternich was able to write to his master:

"The Emperor is madly in love with her and, from all signs, I am convinced that she understands him thoroughly. He is so obviously in love with her that he cannot hide his feelings; and he subordinates all his habits to her desires."

That unaccustomed leisure, that idleness, was a sort of interlude in his tremendously active life. Later, in reviewing those years, he was to say, "I have been accused of losing my head over my alliance with the house of Hapsburg, of believing that I was more truly a sovereign after my marriage, in a word, of thinking that I was Alexander, son of a god . . . What can you expect? I had just married a pretty and charming young woman. I should certainly have been allowed to show a little joy!"

For her part Marie-Louise was becoming deeply attached to

him. "I should not like to cause him the least little annoyance," she told her uncle, the Grand Duke of Würzburg. If two or three hours passed and Napoleon failed to put in an appearance, she would become restless.

"What is my naughty lover doing anyway?" she would say in her Germanic jargon.

Her wardrobe, her jewel coffers were filled to overflowing. "I am well on the way," she confided to her brother, Anton, "to being the person with the richest trappings in our old Europe." For her wardrobe she had a thousand francs a day, for her privy purse twelve thousand francs a month, which caused her to remark: "The Emperor keeps his women well."

Napoleon's family did not like Marie-Louise; they compared her to a "big battered doll." Her spineless, listless manner often shocked them. But she was a real Empress. Through their brother's second marriage they were allied with ancient thrones. Moreover they were respectful and attentive to her, at least on the surface. "That princess," wrote Elisa, "has neither the beauty nor the wit of poor Marie Antoinette. Suitors of the type of Fersen will never venture to tell her stories. We find her peculiarities very amusing. She has the failing or the stupidity of repeating words she does not understand. For instance in speaking of Duroc she said: 'He's a queer fish!'—a remark she had heard from one of the valets. But one must admit that she has one quality: for an archduchess of Austria she is really very democratic and she always kisses us full on the mouth. We shall gradually become accustomed to her whining ways. Just so she makes the Emperor happy!"

Marie-Louise herself did not feel any real friendship for her new relatives. She was intimidated by Pauline's elegance, offended by Caroline's headstrong ways. As for Elisa, she preferred her little girl, Napoléone, a chubby-cheeked, rosy, charming child for whom she bought innumerable toys. Madame Mère, reserved, austere mother-in-law, frightened her. The only real friendship she formed was with Catherine, Jerome's wife, a German princess like herself and distantly related to her, with whom she had many tastes in common.

Such a complete and sudden change in his manner of living could not fail to affect Napoleon's health. He suffered from boils, and he had a bad cough. Corvisart tried vainly to make him listen to reason. At forty-one he could not live like a young man: he was too fond of the table, too devoted to his wife—he was wearing himself out. The Emperor shrugged his shoulders and refused to listen. Shortly afterward he set out on a fatiguing journey to introduce the Empress to the departments in the North and Belgium. Jerome, Catherine and Eugène went with them, Louis joining them at Antwerp. In a drenching rain the carriages dashed over the endless, muddy roads. At each change of horses, committees, speeches, children carrying flowers. The Court was worn out. Marie-Louise acknowledged the compliments awkwardly and showed her boredom at the receptions. The people of the towns found her "very red, very embarrassed, with a face utterly lacking in expression." The Emperor urged her to spare herself, but she insisted upon following him everywhere. "I cannot bear to be separated from him for a day," she wrote to Caroline from Antwerp. Moreover she thought that she was pregnant. Napoleon was tremendously elated at that news and showed her even greater solicitude if possible than before.

They returned to Saint-Cloud on the 1st of June and plunged into a round of Court festivities again: state reception at the Hôtel de Ville, followed by fireworks and a ball. The Emperor danced a quadrille. Afterward, while Marie-Louise stood stiffly on her dais, he walked about the room conversing with the spectators.

There was a gala performance at the Opéra and a magnificent fête at Pauline's, at Neuilly, where Marie-Louise recognized her own Schönbrunn reproduced in her honor. Napoleon was deeply touched.

"Your fête was enchanting," he told Pauline.

The Empress, however, was as impassive as a statue. She was paralyzed by timidity. Many people thought her unsympathetic.

Fêtes at the Minister of War's, for the Imperial Guard, and finally on July 1st a fête at the Austrian Embassy that ended in a tragedy. A large ballroom had been erected in the garden out of stagings and canvas and hung with tulle, taffetas, flowers and paper. Bugles blew a fanfare to announce the arrival of the Emperor and Empress, who made the rounds of the salons between two lines of twelve hundred guests. Suddenly a draft blew a gauze curtain against one of the wall lights filled with candles. Instantly the whole place was ablaze. Eugène hastened to inform the Emperor. The latter crossed the room with unhurried step and leaning over Marie-Louise, took her arm.

"We must leave at once," he said in a low tone. "The place is on fire."

They went down into the garden. Napoleon led the trembling young woman to her carriage and, to reassure her, drove with her as far as the Champs Elysées, whence she returned to Saint-Cloud. He then went back to the scene of the conflagration. It was nothing but a vast brasier from which rose cries of agony. With a crash the chandeliers fell on a panic-stricken crowd that rushed, in a primitive instinct of self-preservation, to the only entrance that was still free. Hortense, Caroline and Pauline were among the first to escape. Eugène rescued his pregnant wife from the crowd. Catherine of Westphalia rushed out onto the terrace and, losing her head, thought she was still in danger and flung herself into the rue Taitbout, where she was picked up by a passer-by. Soon the frail scaffolding collapsed. Cries arose from a great crowd gathered outside. Thieves began slipping in, snatching off jewels from bodies that lay in heaps and piles, even taking bits of a finger or an ear with them. The Emperor directed the rescue in quick, concise orders, and tried to comfort the ambassador, whose sister-in-law, Princess Schwartzenberg, had perished trying to rescue her daughters. The number of the dead ran into scores.

Napoleon returned to Saint-Cloud in the middle of the night and hurried to the Empress' apartments to inquire whether she had recovered from her fright. His face was dirty, his clothes disheveled, his shoes and stockings scorched. Entering her bedroom he dropped exhausted into an armchair.

"My God!" he exclaimed sadly, "what a fête!"

His emotion when he told Constant about the disaster, was

still so great that he trembled. He had been deeply affected by the tragic death of the Princess Schwartzenberg—in which he saw an unlucky omen. He was to refer to it again during the Campaign of France when he found the victim's husband, Schwartzenberg, facing him as Commander of the Allies.

II

March 20th

NAPOLEON WAS EXPERIENCING a serious embarrassment. He had been obliged to dismiss Fouché from his post. The Minister of Police had been negotiating secretly with England. Then, on July 6th, came the news that his brother Louis, who had fled from Holland because he wanted to be king and not prefect, had abdicated. The Emperor flung the dispatch on his desk and leapt to his feet. He was white with rage.

"How could I know," he said to Méneval in a voice choked with tears, "that a man to whom I have been a father would do such an outrageous thing? I brought him up on my slender pay as a lieutenant in the artillery: I shared my bread and the mattress from my bed with him. . . . And where does he go? To strangers, to give the impression that he is not safe in France!"

He informed Josephine, who was then taking the waters at Aix, that Hortense was at last freed from Louis' whims and hypochondria: "I have joined Holland to France, but the good thing about that is that it sets the Queen free and that that unlucky girl will come to Paris with her son, the Duke of Berg. . . . I shall look forward with pleasure to seeing you this autumn. Remember that I am always your friend." That friendship continued though he avoided any outward display, for Marie-Louise was extremely jealous. He would have liked to arrange a meeting between his two wives. The Austrian would not consent. At all events he allowed Josephine to go to Malmaison, where callers flocked to pay their respects. He himself spent two hours with her there on the 13th of June.

"Yesterday I had an hour of happiness," she wrote to Hortense. "The Emperor came to see me. . . . The whole time he was with me I had courage enough to restrain my tears, for I was on the verge of weeping; but after he had gone, I was very unhappy. He was kind and charming to me as usual, and I hope that he could read in my heart all the love and devotion I bear him."

Barante, the Prefect of Leman, displeased her by his lack of attention: he was removed from office. On hearing the rumor of Marie-Louise's pregnancy, she wrote to congratulate Napoleon. The Emperor, thanking her in a letter of September 14th, wrote: "The Empress has been pregnant for four months. She is well and is very devoted to me."

He was wrong by one month: the pregnancy anticipated during the journey to Belgium did not materialize. Marie-Louise, it seems, took baths that were too hot. But at the end of June a new hope was given them and this time there was no mistake. "The Emperor is in a state of good humor that beggars description," Metternich wrote to Vienna. Napoleon was in fact radiant. He never left the Empress' side. No more long journeys, no more exhausting receptions, no more horseback rides. They lived quietly, comfortably, at Rambouillet, at Trianon, then at Saint-Cloud and later at Fontainebleau. Château life in the country, informal concerts, informal plays, informal suppers. Marie-Louise enjoyed jugglers' tricks, magic-lantern shows and the trained animals of the Brothers Franconi, who held their circus in the open air. With Napoleon at her side she posed for Canova for her statue. She watched the Emperor play at prisoners' base. Twice he fell as he was chasing Duroc and picked himself up, laughing heartily. They played a joke on Prince Borghese on his birthday, sending him bouquets of nettles and at night putting bristles pulled out of brushes between his sheets. Napoleon's happiness, his impatience drove him to a restlessness that he relieved somewhat by hunting and reviewing his troops. Marie-Louise almost always followed him in her barouche. She wanted to go everywhere with him. Now and then, feeling in need of a little freedom, he would suggest that she send for some musicians, or go and visit a few museums or some textile works with Hortense. She would answer like a spoiled child:

"No, not unless you come with me."

"But I have no time."

"Then I would rather stay at home," she would reply. And, seeing her sulk, he would give in at once.

In his eyes, as in the eyes of all the Court, Marie-Louise had assumed an inordinate importance. On her rested the safety and the future of the dynasty. No one laughed now at her Teutonic accent, which she had never lost, at her ignorance which forced the Emperor to explain to her that there was no vulgarity in the words "a putative mother," at her trifling and puerile remarks. Instead, people admired her gift for "turning her ear almost in a circle without moving a muscle in her face!"

On November 4th there was a grand christening. Twenty-six children were brought to the font—the sons of Berthier, Duchâtel, Turenne, the daughters of Beauharnais, Caffarelli, Lagrange, Maret and, leading them all, little *Oui-Oui*, Louis Napoleon, Hortense's youngest son. The Emperor stood godfather to all twenty-six; Marie-Louise, godmother.

Josephine was not pleased to have her favorite grandson the godson of the new Empress. But that displeasure was nothing to the anguish caused by a letter from Mme. de Rémusat and written, obviously, at Napoleon's request. Employing a thousand circumlocutions her lady-in-waiting advised Josephine not to return to Paris. Marie-Louise's jealousy had been aggravated by her condition. Let Josephine go for a few months to Milan with Eugène, to Florence, even to Rome, and then return to Navarre in the spring. And—veiled threat—by so doing she would prevent an embarrassing situation from which the Emperor might extricate himself readily if he were less fond of her.

Josephine was panic-stricken. After so many promises was Napoleon now condemning her to exile? She implored Hortense, she besought the Emperor. Once more the latter weakened, changed his plan. He left Josephine free to choose: she could go to Italy, she could go to Navarre. "I approve whatever you do, for I do not want to inconvenience you in any way." Josephine was triumphant. So he still cared for her a little! And

she announced her return to Navarre, where she intended to
pass the winter.

Before returning to that vast, damp castle, she appeared at the
Elysée and lingered for a while at Malmaison, where she gave
a reception that was all the more brilliant because crowded with
malcontents and members of the opposition—all those in fact
who had sprung from the Revolution and who saw with anger
the imperial salons thronged with duchesses from the Faubourg
Saint-Germain and the "light horsemen" of the emigration. So
far did she forget her promises that Napoleon was obliged to
send Cambacérès to remind her that Navarre was waiting for
her.

Aside from a few attacks of nausea, Marie-Louise suffered but
slight inconvenience from her condition. Her figure thickened
early. In the past Napoleon had always had an aversion to pregnant women, but he now admired complacently that woman
who was so soon to give him a son. Not for an instant did he
doubt that the expected child would be a son. Fate owed him
that, he thought. And he set about making ready for that son
with passion. The King of Rome! Such the title which a *senatus-
consultus* conferred in advance upon the child, a resplendent
name linking the youthful glory of the French Empire to the
ancient empire of the West. As governess he named a woman of
irreproachable reputation and noble lineage, Mme. de Montesquiou. He modeled the King of Rome's entourage after the
household formerly established for the Dauphin. Court physicians chose as wet nurse Mme. Auchard, a jolly woman who was
always laughing. The child's quarters were to be next to Marie-
Louise's, apartments which Duroc had formerly occupied. The
high-ceilinged rooms that looked out on the Carrousel were re-
painted and refurnished throughout; and to prevent the baby
from hurting himself when he bumped a wall or fell the Emperor had them upholstered with a padded strip three feet in
height.

Marie-Louise was scarcely consulted. She took no interest in
anything, not even in the trousseau for her confinement nor the
baby's layette, both of which were magnificent. Napoleon pre-

sented her with Gobelin tapestries, Sèvres china, furniture,
jewels—and she in turn was to pass them on as heirlooms to her
family. She aired her happiness with the greatest naïveté. To
Mme. de Crenneville, her childhood friend, she wrote: "You can
imagine that in a great city like Paris we are not lacking in
amusements, but my happiest moments are those I spend with
the Emperor." To her father she wrote urging him to visit her:
"You will understand him perfectly when once you know the
Emperor personally. Then you will see how kind and affectionate he is in his family, what a noble heart he has, and I am convinced that you will adore him. I can never thank God enough
for having granted me such great joy."

On December 31st, accompanied by the Countess Potocka,
Mme. Walewska was officially "presented" to the Emperor in
the private apartments by Mme. de Luçay, Mistress of the Wardrobe. She was then received by Marie-Louise—the latter knew
nothing about her and greeted her with complete indifference.
Napoleon had expressed a desire to have "his Polish wife" take
her place at Court. In that way he could more easily provide
for her son's future. That son had been born on May 4, 1810, at
the Château of Walewice and had been given the name of Alexandre Colonna Walewski. The Emperor seems to have entertained the definite plan of making him king of a restored Poland
one day. Marie was banking all on that hope.

Napoleon still loved Marie Walewska, but the love of former
days had softened into a tender attachment in which the physical
played small part. He was too fearful of rousing suspicions in
his young wife. He visited the rue de la Victoire now and then
incognito, and with even greater secrecy Marie and her son
were brought from time to time to the Tuileries. Méneval,
Constant and Roustan were the only ones who knew of those
visits. But Duroc and Corvisart held themselves as before at the
Countess' orders. She had a box at all the theatres, a place at all
public ceremonies. The Emperor set aside a pension of ten
thousand francs a month for her—no doubt she had not wanted
more.

He made her son a Count of the Empire, and two years later he was to grant him an important entailment. Little Alexandre was a beautiful child: the bone structure of his face, his forehead and his mouth were like the Emperor's. Napoleon was deeply attached to him and sent almost daily to inquire for him.

Marie continued to lead the life of seclusion which she preferred generally in the company of her sister-in-law, Princess Jablonowska, at Paris or at Boulogne, where she had taken over Metternich's former mansion, or finally at Brétigny-sur-Orge, where she spent the summer, entertaining a few personal friends, chiefly Poles. The world of society scarcely knew her name and that was as she wished it to be. She was eager to avoid anything that might bring her into the limelight, or reveal her liaison with the Emperor.

In that period Napoleon was slipping into casual infidelity. Captain Lebel, assistant to the governor of Saint-Cloud, had a stepdaughter, a vivacious brunette with a beautiful figure who was something of a flirt. Through an officious friend her mother offered her to the Emperor. One day, yielding to curiosity, he sent Constant to fetch her. "The young woman," the valet relates, "was resplendent in person and attire and the mother beamed with delight at the thought of the honor in store for her daughter." At eleven o'clock that evening, young Lise was brought to Saint-Cloud and led through the Orangerie to the Emperor's private apartments. Napoleon detained her for several hours and, though he may have found her very charming, sent for her only two or three times thereafter. The mother was much disturbed. She tried to rouse Constant's sympathy: "Just look at my poor Lise, how red her face is! That is from chagrin at seeing herself neglected. The dear child! It would be so kind of you if you would only arrange to have her sent for!" Constant did his best, but it was no use. The master's whim had passed. And though Lise made such eyes at him during mass at Saint-Cloud as would have "made a Guard regiment blush," Napoleon showed no inclination to renew his interest in her.

On the evening of March 19, 1811, toward eight o'clock, the

Court was waiting for Marie-Louise, who was scheduled to attend an informal *opéra comique* in honor of her uncle from Würzburg, who had come to Paris to be present at her accouchement. Suddenly the Duchess de Montebello, who was by then the Empress' closest friend, hurried out of the private apartments, dressed in an ordinary street gown and announced that the Empress had suffered her first pains. At once the salons blazed with lights; pages hastened to inform the dignitaries whose duty it was to be present at the birth of the imperial child. While the palace was filling little by little with a throng of gentlemen in uniform and ladies in evening dress, Napoleon walked Marie-Louise slowly back and forth in her bedroom, murmuring words of encouragement. She was frightened and imagined that she was going to die. Now and then he handed her over to Mme. de Montebello and went into the Salon des Graces, where the family and physicians, bored and weary, were gathered. He made no effort to hide his anxiety: his face was drawn and solemn. At two o'clock he went to the accoucheur Dubois, who was standing before a little table examining his instruments.

"Well, monsieur, what about it?"

"Sire, we are waiting."

Gradually the pains lessened. Marie-Louise fell asleep. The Court then dispersed. Napoleon went to his apartment and got into the bath. Suddenly Dubois entered without knocking.

Napoleon imagined the worst.

"What is it?" he cried. "Is she dead?"

Later he was to explain to Gourgaud:

"I am so used to great crises that they have no effect on me at first . . . my reaction comes later. You might come and tell me the worst news imaginable and I would not feel a thing. But an hour later I would suffer from it."

Dubois explained his difficulty: the pains had begun again, the accouchement was at hand. But the child was presenting itself in a bad position, feet foremost.

"What are you going to do?" cried Napoleon. "Oh, *mon Dieu!* Is there any danger?"

"Sire, we must consider one of them—either the mother or the child."

"The mother," replied Napoleon without a second's hesitation. "The mother! It is her right." And he added: "Don't lose your head, Monsieur Dubois. Treat her as if she were a shopgirl from the rue Saint-Denis. Forget that she is the Empress."

He jumped out of the bath, dressed hastily and hurried down at once to her apartment. Marie-Louise was moaning piteously. Napoleon tried to reassure her: so did the Duchess de Montebello and Mme. de Montesquiou. With the help of Corvisart, Bourdier and Yvan, Dubois inserted the forceps. The Emperor took refuge in the adjoining room. He could scarcely breathe. His suspense was dreadful. At last Yvan appeared.

"Sire, the Empress is delivered."

Napoleon rushed into the room, knelt beside the bed and embraced Marie-Louise. The child lay forgotten on the floor. Napoleon thought it was dead. Mme. de Montesquiou laid the baby out on her knees and began rubbing his body from head to foot with hot cloths: she then blew a few drops of brandy into his mouth. Finally after seven anguished moments, came a faint little cry. Napoleon gave a violent start and rushed from Marie-Louise's bed to his child.

He took him in his arms, kissed him very gently on the forehead and carried him over to his mother's side. His emotion was such that he staggered.

"It is over," he told Hortense. "She is saved."

"Is it a boy?" his stepdaughter asked.

He gave a great sigh:

"Yes."

Hortense embraced him. But he pushed her away:

"Oh, I cannot stand all this happiness! The poor woman suffered so much."

While the cannon boomed one hundred and one times and the windows rattled, Napoleon wept. His anguish had been so great that for the rest of the day he was grave, almost sad.

He sent Eugène to Navarre to inform Josephine of the birth

of the King of Rome. She was pleased at that attention and congratulated him. He replied promptly:

"My dear, I have received your letter. I thank you. My son is a big child and in excellent health. I hope that he will turn out well. He has my chest, my mouth and my eyes. I trust that he will fulfil his destiny."

Those words expressed his pride, his joy, his confidence in the future and also the tenderness he felt for that little boy who had just been born.

In the weeks that followed he could talk of nothing but that little child; it seemed as if he thought of him only. Several times a day he went to lean over his cradle and question Mme. de Montesquiou and Corvisart in detail about his health. He made them take off his shirt so that he could see the child naked and admire his plump little arms and legs. He would laugh at the little fellow's impatient cries, hum a tune and make faces to amuse him and he was already tweaking his ear—but oh! so gently.

Marie-Louise loved her son, to be sure; but she did not and never would give him those little attentions that absorb mothers and bind them closely to their children. She let the governess carry him. She scarcely dared to clasp him in her arms and caress him, for fear of hurting him. That the child should be brought up by another woman she took as a matter of course. She had been brought up that way, at a distance from her mother, in the sole charge of her *ayah*. She seems to have had some regrets, however, for she complained of it to Mme. de Luçay. But she made no move to break that royal custom. She spent her leisure hours in the company of the Duchess de Montebello, reading, munching cakes and bonbons, drinking Viennese chocolate, writing, embroidering, taking piano lessons from Paer or painting under Isabey or Prud'hon. The rest of the time she was on official parade or else traveling with the Emperor.

Ever since Marie-Louise's accouchement Napoleon had reverted to his former way of life. He was sleeping and breakfasting alone and devoting almost all his time to matters of State, audiences, councils, reviews. His "profession" had him in its grip again: he would often work the greater part of the night. For that matter the times were disquieting. Notwithstanding so much outward brilliancy the Empire was passing through a dangerous phase. Business and industry were dull, famine threatened. The Spanish Campaign was continuing to devour the flower of the army and there was no doubt but that war with the Czar would soon break out.

Several months before the Emperor had said to Abbé de Pradt:

"In five years I shall be the ruler of the world. Russia is the only country left, but I shall crush it. Paris will reach to Saint-Cloud."

That vision of a new Paris had been germinating in him ever since the creation of the Grand Empire in 1806, but it had been strengthened by success, had become vital and urgent. To his mind it would be the tangible image of his glory. All the kings of Europe would have their palaces in Paris. The Pope would be chief almoner there. Napoleon would have liked to move St. Peter's bodily from Rome to Paris. Notre-Dame seemed mean and gloomy to his eyes, accustomed as they were to spaciousness and light. To him nothing could be noble enough, nothing stupendous enough for his capital. Paris must be the mother city of the world.

He was a poet and that gift raised his human talents to the superhuman. Splendid as reality was, it was merely a starting point for his dreams. Out of State, treasury, army, nations, he forged the material of his epic poem. Let a subject interest him and he began to talk with a colorfulness, a sharpness and a conciseness that were altogether surprising. His imagination ruled him now. He had lost all sense of the possible. And that poetic enthusiasm of his was to lead him into blunders that were to be the cause of his downfall.

On April 20th he went to Saint-Cloud, where Marie-Louise felt happier than in Paris and where he enjoyed the green fields and the waters. But soon he was obliged to keep the promise he

had made of a journey to the west, an exhausting journey.
Marie-Louise, who had not fully recovered from her accouchement, suffered from fever, grew thin and began to lose her hair.
She talked seldom and appeared to be sad when she was really
worn out. As for Napoleon he was in the best of spirits. At Caen
he met Mme. Pellapra, the pretty Lyonnaise, secretly. She presented him with her little daughter, named Emilie after her;
a charming child with long curls who bore a startling resemblance to Pauline Borghese at that age. Napoleon delighted in
caressing the little girl. He promised the mother not to forget
her.

He did his best to rouse the Empress' interest in the provinces
through which they traveled, even resorting to jests in order
to cheer her. At Cherbourg, while they were visiting on board a
ship, he seized her in his arms and made as if to throw her into
the sea.

"If you want to," she said listlessly.

Every day they received a report of their child from Bessières,
Captain of the Guard, and one from Mme. de Montesquiou.
They were delighted to find him looking extremely well on their
return. When Napoleon questioned the doctor, Bourdois de la
Motte, the latter assured him:

"The King of Rome will be a strong little fellow."

The public baptism, at which Cardinal Fesch officiated, was
celebrated at Notre-Dame on the 9th of June—the most magnificent spectacle of the Empire. It cost the treasury nearly two
millions. The godfathers were the Emperor of Austria and King
Joseph; the godmothers, Madame Mère and Queen Hortense.

Shortly afterward the Court moved to Rambouillet, then to
Trianon and finally to Compiègne. It seemed as if Napoleon
could not keep still. He craved change and, in that, he was
imitating the kings of old. Whenever the weather was fine the
Emperor lunched out of doors. They would bring him the "little king." He would take the child on his knees, swing him, toss
him up in the air, let him play with his crosses, with the hilt of
his sword, smear his lips with gravy, offer him a sip of Chambertin lightly watered. And he would kiss him, tickle him, tease

him until Mme. de Montesquiou was forced to protect her charge. He was still too young, she remonstrated. A little sheepish, the Emperor would hand him back to the governess.

Toward his son's governess Napoleon showed a real respect which Mme. de Montesquiou well deserved. Upright, pious, unbending, she may not have liked either the Emperor or the Empire. She was too much of the "Old France" for that. But when she accepted a duty, she devoted herself to it entirely. Napoleon knew that and realized that he could trust his son to that Royalist at heart. He showed her a delicate consideration and granted all her petitions. She need only have said the word and he would have made her a duchess. But she was too proud for that.

Another journey soon took the Imperial couple away to Holland and the borders of the Rhine, but on their return to the Tuileries the round of Court life began again. The Court was growing dull, tired. In those last weeks of 1811, France, in fact, all Europe, was tensed in a sort of anxious expectancy. One felt that great events were in the offing. Many wondered whether that vast and magnificent façade of the Empire might not give in a storm and come crashing down to bury them under its folds. One day, looking at the little king, the Emperor himself murmured:

"Poor child! What a mess of confusion I shall be leaving you!"

Among so many burdens that would have crushed another man, Napoleon was obliged to straighten out Josephine's affairs. She had continued her usual complacent, extravagant way of life, buying without counting the cost, giving to all who asked and gathering about her a personnel that throve on waste—as well as on an extreme laxness of morals. For all those demands not even her enormous dowry sufficed. The Emperor had warned her that she must economize, but in vain.

"Do not spend more than 1,500,000 francs and put the same amount aside every year. That will give you a reserve of fifteen millions in ten years for your grandchildren. It is sweet to be able to give them something and to be of help to them. . . . If

you want to please me, show that you have a large fortune. . . ."
(April 25, 1811). A fortune . . . the poor woman had already
contracted over a million in debts! Napoleon lost his temper.
He instructed Mollien, the Minister of the Treasury, to audit
Josephine's accounts. He granted her a dower of an additional
million, but in the future she would have to keep strict account.

"She cannot count on me to pay her debts any more," he said
to Mollien. "I have no right to add to what I have already given
her. Her family's future must not rest on my head alone. . . . I
am only mortal, much more so than other men."

Mollien assured him that Josephine was repentant: when he
had had his interview with her she had been moved to tears.
Napoleon exclaimed:

"You should not have made her cry!"

He took back the Elysée which was of no use to him, and gave
her in exchange the Palace of Laeken. If Josephine had to cut
her pension list, he would assume responsibility for paying it.

"Give me the names of her officers and tell her that I do not
want her to cry. . . ."

Marie-Louise gave him no such anxieties. Her orderliness,
her meticulous care delighted him. She had developed an interest in clothes and was fond of dressing beautifully—but she
never exceeded her budget. She needed no lingerie, for her
trousseau was still sufficient. In four years she bought only
twelve chemises. She hoarded her old clothes to the despair of
her women, who were thus deprived of the usual gifts. She was
a born accountant, writing down, noting, classifying every little
item, and all in her own hand.

On January 1, 1812, the King of Rome came into the Emperor's study, carried by Mme. de Montesquiou. He held in his
hand a little bouquet. The child had had a difficult time cutting
his teeth and he was a little pale. But his features were beautiful.
He had a large head, with a high, rounded forehead, eyes like
Marie-Louise, but of an even brighter blue, a turned-up nose
and the Hapsburg mouth, full-lipped but in the child exceedingly pretty. He was a lively little fellow, noisy and vigorous.

Napoleon never tired of studying his face, admiring his manly little ways.

To restore public confidence the Emperor gave a series of entertainments for the Court at the beginning of 1812: on February 6th, a grand court ball at the Tuileries. The Empress led the contradance with Berthier, Hortense with Duroc. Afterward they gave a sort of mythological allegory. Gowned in a tunic of India muslin, with a gold helmet on her head, and wearing the handsomest of the Borghese cameos, Pauline represented Rome. France was depicted by Caroline in a purple cloak, her proud head bedecked with tricolor plumes. All the youth of the Court, dressed as gods, goddesses, genies, hours, stars, capered and frolicked in dances arranged by the famous Despréaux. Countess Duchâtel looking very elegant, figured prominently among the Nymphs. Napoleon was so delighted with the pageant that he gave the dancers a prize of a hundred thousand francs. At Mardi-gras there was a masquerade ball at which Marie-Louise dressed as a native of Caux, in a high red velvet bonnet trimmed in silver, a blue corselet with gold buttons, lace fichu and sleeves, a red skirt and a gauze apron. At midnight she changed her costume, appearing this time as a peasant from Capri in a net dress embroidered in gold and covered with a coat of green satin. Mme. de Montebello was dressed as a peasant from Campania; Mme. de Bassano as a Tyrolese; Mme. de Rovigo as a Landaise and Mme. Duchâtel as a Basque. Mme. Philippe de Ségur represented an Alsatian; Mme. de Montmorency a peasant from Hamburg; Mme. de Castiglione a Pole; Mme. de Mortemart a Corsican. Hortense was in charge of a Peruvian pageant which was supposed to depict an episode in the conquest of America. Flahaut, her lover, and Canouville, Pauline's cicisbeo, were very handsome in their brilliant Inca costumes of gold and feathers.

Napoleon wore a blue domino and a gray mask. Followed by Marie-Louise, Mme. de Montebello jostled him in the throng.

"Monsieur," she said, disguising her voice, "do not stand in the way of a poor Italian girl."

HORTENSE DE BEAUHARNAIS
QUEEN OF HOLLAND
After the Portrait by Gérard

MARIE-LOUISE
EMPRESS OF THE FRENCH
From the Drawing by Prud'hon

"You are the one who pushed me, Madame," replied the Emperor speaking through his nose. "I have to protect myself."

And he gave her a slight shove with his shoulder.

"Aren't you looking for a lady from Milan?" asked the Duchess.

"No, signora, io adoro una donna di Firenze."

Marie-Louise then took over:

"Ah! So Monsieur has visited those beautiful lands of the sun?"

"Madame, I spent two years there in my youth."

"Tell me about your adventures."

"That would take too long. . . ."

The Empress and the Duchess began to push the domino back against the fireplace. Duroc ran to his aid:

"Ladies, let this stranger continue on his way."

Caroline in the costume of a Dalmatian peasant then attacked him:

"Is not Monsieur a subject of King Murat?"

"In that case," cried Mme. de Montebello, "he must dance the tarantella for us."

At a loss how to get out of his predicament, Napoleon answered in his own voice:

"Duchess, I could not dance with anyone but the Empress and I know that she would rather go about mystifying people."

At two o'clock, supper was served in the Salle du Conseil d'Etat. Marie-Louise was highly entertained. She wrote to her sister Leopoldine: "We have many amusements in Paris. No one in Vienna has the slightest idea of the gaiety here and of how the people love masked balls and good food."

And yet war with Russia was now inevitable. Napoleon gathered together the vast army that was to push forward to the Conquest of Moscow. He was always deep in thought now and had very little to say. Often at a play or at receptions his head would fall forward on his shoulder and he would nod. Marie-Louise appeared not to notice it.

The Emperor was seized with a fancy to live at the Elysée, which Josephine had recently vacated. The Tuileries depressed him: he was too much in the public eye there and he had no garden of his own. But he caught cold in that palace, which had been uninhabited for some time and was too cramped in size. They returned to the Tuileries on Sundays for mass and the Emperor's audience, with the presentations that followed. By the end of March the Court was back again at Saint-Cloud. No more fêtes now—a few concerts, one or two plays, several hunts where Napoleon rode hard to work off some of his nervous tension. The King of Rome, who was somewhat indisposed, had been taken to Meudon to the former château of the Grand Dauphin. Two or three times a week his parents went to see him or he himself came to Saint-Cloud.

On the 8th of May in the afternoon, the child was brought to Saint-Cloud by his governess. The next day Napoleon and Marie-Louise were to leave for Germany. The Emperor held the child in his arms a long time. He scolded him gaily because he could not yet say "papa" and "mamma."

"Lazybones, at your age I was already giving Joseph a thrashing!"

He tossed him up and down and the little fellow crowed with delight.

He began counting the child's features complacently:

"Eight teeth, sir, you have eight teeth."

"And his mamma's eyes," added Marie-Louise.

"Very beautiful eyes," said Napoleon. "Come, Mme. de Montesquiou, we are trusting you with our treasure."

He carried the child out to his carriage himself and watched him drive away. Moncey saw the Emperor's eyes fill with tears and his hands tremble.

Before leaving France Napoleon received Mme. Walewska at the Tuileries. He handed her an order establishing an entailment for little Alexandre of 170,000 francs income from property in the Kingdom of Naples. Soon thereafter she left for Warsaw, where she hoped to witness the complete liberation of Poland.

Accompanied by a magnificent retinue, the Emperor and the Empress reached the Rhine, then traveled through the little

German principalities, where they were received with highest
honors by the princes. In every town cannons roared, bells
pealed, priests chanted Te Deums, troops were drawn up on
parade. At night every house blazed with lights and the good
folk danced on the public squares under garlands of green. At
Dresden, Marie-Louise found her parents waiting for her. As
soon as the Emperor Franz was alone with his daughter he
asked: "Are you happy?" She smiled, showed him her jewelry
and her handsome gown which put the somewhat dowdy frock
of her stepmother, Marie Ludovica, in the shade. That stepmother was a spiteful soul. She hated Napoleon, but she overwhelmed him with flattery. In the morning she went nosing
about in Marie-Louise's finery, begging for jewels, gowns, a
thousand feminine objects. Her stepdaughter gave them to her
good-naturedly, confident that she would always have all she
wanted.

Fêtes followed fêtes, one more sumptuous than the last. Napoleon sent for Paer and his musicians. But a haze of anxiety
hung over everything. On May 29th, at four in the morning,
the Emperor set out to join the army. He embraced Marie-
Louise tenderly. That was their first real separation. "I am sad
and unhappy," wrote the young wife. "I try to get hold of myself but I shall not be any better till I see him again." To console
herself she went to spend a month at Prague with her parents,
returning by easy stages to Saint-Cloud. The little king was
there to welcome her. He had grown and was beginning to
walk now. The Empress ordered Gérard to paint a portrait of
the child. As soon as it was finished, M. de Bausset, Prefect of
the Palace, rushed off by coach to carry it to the Emperor.

III

Disaster

O N THAT ENDLESS ROAD that led him toward the Russia of Charles XII, Napoleon traveled under a burning heat, broken every now and then by drenching rains. Not a day passed that he did not write to his wife. From a château in Poland or in Lithuania, sometimes when he was fighting, from the army bivouac, he sent her brief but affectionate letters in which he tried to comfort her, advised her as to her conduct in Paris and in thought lingered near her and the little king of whom he always spoke with touching gentleness. After telling her that he had just won a battle, that he had taken so and so many cannon and flags, Napoleon would caution Marie-Louise not to yawn at the Council of State, to be sure to address the Pope with more formality and especially—especially—to kiss their little son for him. A bourgeois tone—but he was a husband, a father, and never had he felt more so than in that hour that took him farther and farther away from all he loved. For that weak and credulous child he hid his anxieties that gathered thicker about him the farther east he went. He kept repeating untiringly: "My health is good, everything is going very well." But he now realized the enormity of the risk. At Narbonne he explained his plan, as if to excuse, or perhaps, to deceive himself: "Alexander went as far as Moscow to reach the Ganges. That is what I have been saying ever since Saint Jean d'Acre. Today I have to go to the other end of Europe and conquer Asia in reverse in order to invade England." The Russians were still retreating and his army melted away from post to post. He himself often felt ill. He had lost the almost super-human endurance of past years, his vitality had diminished.

On the morning of the Battle of Moscow he received the portrait which the Empress had sent him. He was delighted with it. "It is a masterpiece," he exclaimed. Calling his generals he showed it to them proudly where he had had it placed on a campstool in front of his tent. "Gentlemen, if my son were fifteen years old, you may believe that he would be here otherwise than in oil." But a little later, as if seized by a secret fear, he said: "Take him away: he is too young to see a battlefield!" From then on he kept the portrait constantly with him. It hung in his bedroom wherever he went.

During that night of the 6th to the 7th of September he was taken ill. He had a heavy cold and was suffering, moreover, from an attack of dysuria. He shivered with chills and fever and kept drinking water incessantly. Every other moment he would ask the time. He had seldom been so restless. When the first light of dawn broke his aide-de-camp found him sitting on the side of his little bed with the green curtains, holding his head in his hands. He was deep in thought.

"What is war?" he was murmuring. "A barbarian's profession in which the main thing is to be stronger than the other fellow at a given point."

Was his luck about to leave him? He seemed to fear so. He asked Rapp whether he thought they would have a victory.

"Yes," replied the general, "but a bloody one."

At daybreak that fear was dissipated.

"There is the sun of Austerlitz," he said to his officers.

The battle began—a long, indecisive struggle. Napoleon walked slowly along a ravine slashing at the grass with his riding whip. He did not speak. He refused to throw in his Guard, and left Ney, Murat and Eugène to get out of the hole as best they could. There was no doubt that he was suffering: his eyes lost their sparkle, his will-power its edge. All through that campaign, for that matter, he hesitated, wasted time, relied too much on his generals.

Then came the entrance into a deserted Moscow and the fire that destroyed that colossal village of wood in three days. Napoleon hid his anguish from all, but especially from Marie-Louise. On the 24th of September he wrote to her: "I implore you to keep well. Be happy and kiss the little king fondly for me. What! That little rascal did not recognize his nurse! He is a little wretch." On October 6th: "I am glad to learn that you are getting about a little . . . Write often to your father and send the letters by special messengers."

Let Marie-Louise show herself to the Parisians, let her have a good time, let her give as many receptions as she pleased! He had firm faith in her character, her courage! What conception had he formed of the Austrian princess? He was judging her less on her own personality than on her race. He saw her only as the daughter of an Emperor.

At the Kremlin he began to work with furious intensity. He had offered peace to Alexander. While awaiting his reply, to show how calm he was, he signed a decree reorganizing the Comédie française. But the Czar was silent, winter was coming on and the cold was increasing. It was high time to begin the retreat. What was left of his army set out on the road to Poland, marking the line of its march with an endless trail of corpses. Napoleon often got out of his sleigh to march by the side of his soldiers. Muffled up in his furs, he would say a few words to them now and then, then lapse again into silence for hours.

He had not told Marie-Louise that he had been obliged to fall back to Germany. He minimized his disaster, saying merely that he was on the way to take up his winter quarters. He insisted that the "weather was superb." He thought of sending for her to come to Poland. On November 3rd he wrote: "I expect to hear from you at any moment that my son has cut his teeth and that the little crisis his health has suffered is entirely over. . . . My health is perfect. I have never seen such an autumn as this . . . it makes the march beautiful and less fatiguing. . . ." Alas, in that blood-stained sky the crows were falling frozen in mid-flight. He was lying, lying as a matter of policy and out of affection for her. A little later, however, he wrote, with what was almost a complaint: "The cold is very intense."

General Malet's surprise revolution, a mad plot which, however, threw the fate of the Empire in the balance for one whole morning, decided Napoleon to leave the army at Smorgoni.

First, however, he sent the following admission to Marie-Louise: "I am distressed at your anxiety, which will last at least two weeks. However, my health has never been better. *Things are going very badly*. At this moment the cold is severe."

Accompanied by Caulaincourt he set out by sleigh and galloped his horses over the vast white plain. He was fleeing his disaster and running to Paris to stop the echo of it. Wrapped in his furs, that man of the sun, whom only the snow had been able to conquer, talked to his companion, who was grave, paralyzed with cold. Napoleon unburdened himself on the most varied subjects, with that interest in himself which stirred him to seek out the hidden motives of his own acts and explain them in their detail and in their objectives, unpretentiously for that matter, without trying to excuse himself, in a sort of detachment that, in spite of all, was very simple, very human. In long monologues he demonstrated the technique of his policy, criticized his past actions, anticipated the future. He suffered keenly from the blow he had just received, but could not believe it fatal. When Caulaincourt ventured to contradict him, he flung at him:

"You are too young. You do not understand."

Then he tried to tweak his ear, but the fur cap was in the way.

"People are mistaken," he said. "I am not ambitious. Those long watches are too much for a man of my age. I like my bed and rest better than anyone. But I am going to finish my work. In this world there are only two alternatives, command or obey."

Rest? Yes, that was what he wanted at that moment, the rest in which he would be able to enjoy his wife and his son. But his power was threatened: he must first build it up again. Afterward he would ask nothing better than to grow old in peace and quiet. He still had many illusions. Malet had been executed with his accomplices. There were only the guerrillas left in Spain. Germany was not stirring. Come! Nothing was lost! He was full of projects.

"I can hardly wait, Caulaincourt, for peace to be general so that I can live as I choose. Every year we shall travel four months throughout France. I shall go by slow stages on horseback. I want to visit the departments where there are no means of communication. I intend to build canals, roads, to encourage trade and industry. In ten years I shall be as much blessed as I am, perhaps, hated today."

On leaving Warsaw, where, incognito, he received the Polish ministers, Napoleon wanted to turn off his road to see Marie Walewska, who, he thought, was still at the château of Walewice. Caulaincourt advised against it. Time was too precious. Besides, as they were soon to learn, the Countess had already left for Paris.

At Dresden he was the guest of the French Minister and while still in bed received the King of Saxony. He discarded his sleigh, which was so dilapidated it could go no farther and accepted a berline on runners which the King offered him.

In Prussia he became more aware of the danger he was running. If they were arrested, he and Caulaincourt "would be taken to London in iron cages perhaps." But he laughed at the idea. He seemed to believe that a mysterious power was protecting him.

Driving along the road in the landau which had replaced the berline at Erfurt and in which he could lie outstretched, the Emperor read letters from Marie-Louise and Mme. de Montesquiou aloud to his equerry.

"Haven't I a good wife?" he asked, complacently.

He bought rings, necklaces of glass beads for her and gave half of them to his companion "for the lady of his thoughts," that Mme. de Canisy whom he had so far prevented Caulaincourt from marrying.

Thirteen days of that breakneck pace that killed horses and stupefied men! On the 18th of December, shortly before midnight, the Empress had retired after attending a play at the Tuileries theatre. With great difficulty the Emperor and Caulaincourt identified themselves and hurried to Marie-Louise's apartments. Napoleon was still wearing his fur coat and sable cap, his chin was blackened by a beard of several days.

As Marie-Louise leapt from her bed in fright, he seized her in his arms.

He was at work again the first thing the next morning. He realized at last how frail was the edifice he had built. Malet had only to announce his death and the whole Imperial system had all but collapsed. He was dissatisfied, bitter. To stabilize his dynasty, to oblige France to think in the future of his wife and son, he could devise but one means: he would make his son Associate Emperor after the manner of the Cæsars, and have the Empress crowned by the Pope. With that in view he visited the old captive at Fontainebleau, embraced him, caressed him almost to the point of apologizing. But the cardinals were on the watch and shortly afterward the Pontiff withdrew his promise.

Napoleon could at least appoint Marie-Louise Regent. He thought by that move to hold Austria "which would not dare to make war on its own blood." While he was gathering his forces, building up his army again, he began to give an increasing number of balls and receptions. The Faubourg Saint-Germain made fun of his "wooden-leg balls." The Emperor was trying to fool France and Europe, but he did not succeed. Even in Paris angry murmurs followed him as he drove past. And England, making the most of Prussian treachery, formed a new coalition to crush him in the spring.

In those gloomy days, his only real joy was his son. He was a lively little fellow, affectionate, quick to anger but very tenderhearted. He was now wearing boy's clothes. Napoleon sometimes took him walking on the terrace along the water to show him to the Parisians. He made him appear at his windows during a review. Riding with the child in his arms he himself went out on the Carrousel at the head of his Guards. To please him he had him fitted with several little uniforms. The child was already showing military tastes. His favorite toys were flags, trumpets, drums, a great horse which he used so much that it had to be repaired innumerable times. Mme. de Montesquiou had given him a companion, little Froment, the son of a "red woman," his elder by ten months: and the two of them played

and fought on a perfect equality. That was what the Emperor
wanted. His son must be brought up as a real boy.

The little king had for that matter much natural charm. One
day when the child arrived at the Emperor's study, the Council
of State had just adjourned. The ministers were still standing about in little groups discussing matters of policy. The child
ran straight to his father with eyes for no one but him. Napoleon
stopped him and remarked gravely, almost sternly:

"Sire, you have not saluted. Come, make your bow to these
gentlemen."

The child turned around and, bowing to the ministers with
a grace that came natural to him, put his fingers to his lips and
blew them a kiss.

Beaming with delight the Emperor caught him up in his
arms and, parading him in front of the line of ministers as
though in a military review, said to them, laughing:

"I hope, gentlemen, no one will ever say I am neglecting my
son's education."

Now that the boy was growing up he often carried him off for
entire afternoons to his study, where he would get down on the
carpet and play with him, letting him build huts and little
towers out of the pieces of mahogany saw-toothed in such a way
as to identify battalions, regiments and divisions, with which
Napoleon worked out some new combination of ingenious
maneuvers for his coming battles. Sometimes the child would
fall asleep on his knees.

Shortly after his return, Napoleon went to see Josephine at
Malmaison, but secretly. Marie-Louise might be courteous
enough to Hortense, but she was still very hostile to the Creole.
Josephine had dreamt of coming to Court again, of playing a
second rôle there. That was impossible and Napoleon refused
her permission. At least, on her urgent plea he would allow
the King of Rome to be taken to Bagatelle. She could not restrain her tears on seeing Bonaparte's boy enter her drawing-
room. Controlling herself with difficulty she took him up on her
lap, kissed him passionately, tried to interest him in this and
that. When Mme. de Montesquiou was obliged to take him

away, Josephine delayed the moment of parting as long as she could. And with a heavy heart she bade goodbye to that child who owed his existence to her and whom she was never to see again.

She had always been fond of children. In default of Napoleon's official son she could at least receive young Alexandre Walewski frequently. She had persuaded the Countess to visit her at Malmaison and she lavished sweetmeats and toys on her son. Her jealousy of bygone days had vanished. Through a strange reversal, whatever concerned the man who had raised her to such extraordinary heights, to whom she had been unfaithful in the past and who had now sent her away from him, touched her and attracted her. She loved Marie Walewska because Napoleon had loved her and because, like herself, she too had been sacrificed to the daughter of the Hapsburgs.

The German Campaign which was to decide the fate of the Empire, opened on May 1, 1813. Weissenfels was a victory, but honest, loyal Bessières was killed there. Napoleon mourned that death keenly. He wrote to Marie-Louise:

"It is a great blow to me. He had gone over to the sharpshooters for no good reason, partly out of curiosity; the first bullet killed him dead. Send some word of consolation to his poor wife."

But the greatest blow, the one that crushed him, was Duroc's death. When, after Bautzen, he was told that the Grand Marshal had also been wounded during the pursuit of the Prussian rear guard, he refused to believe it.

"Duroc? Oh, no! You are mistaken. He was right here beside me just a moment ago."

An officer confirmed the sad news. Napoleon's one thought was to reach Duroc's side. General Drouot came up at that moment to ask for orders for the battle that was about to begin —and that battle was Leipzig! Napoleon pushed him nervously aside:

"Leave everything till tomorrow!"

Entering the hut where Duroc, wounded in the abdomen,

lay dying, he embraced him and tried to comfort him. The Grand Marshal was fully conscious. He thanked the Emperor, asked him to look after his daughter, and wished him victory and peace. The Emperor was distressed. Unable to speak, he clasped Duroc's hands tightly. At last Duroc begged him to let them give him some opium, and he added:

"Go now, sire, leave me. This sight is too painful for you."

Napoleon rose stiffly and, with drooping shoulders, moved toward the door.

"Goodbye, my friend," he said, "We shall meet again . . . perhaps soon."

At the threshold he staggered: the tears he had held back until that moment rolled down his cheeks.

He walked over to a bunch of faggots and sat there motionless, so dazed that he was not even aware that a dog that belonged to one of the Guard regiments came up and licked his hand.

For several days he was deeply despondent. He confided his grief to Marie-Louise: "For twenty years he has been my friend. Never have I had cause to complain of him. His death is an irreparable loss, the greatest I could have in the army." He bought the house in which Duroc died and ordered the pastor of the village to have a monument erected there.

Almost daily as during the preceding campaign he wrote to the Empress and with the same affection. He now began to associate the Regent with his policy, urging her to bring influence to bear on her father to keep Austria from joining the Coalition. From Erfurt: "Please write to Papa Franz and tell him he must not allow himself to be dragged in." From Borna: "Papa Franz is not behaving any too well. He has withdrawn his support from me. . . . If he listens to the Empress' tittle-tattle he will be building up a lot of trouble for himself. . . ." At Dresden, in the Marcolini Palace, the day after his interminable and furious interview with the Austrian Chancellor, who had become his personal enemy, he wrote: "I have had a long talk with Metternich and am worn out. My health, however, is good. I laughed at what you tell me about the little king's jealousy. How I wish I could see him. Kiss him for me. Have

you seen the elephant in the Jardin des Plantes? I hope that
peace will be signed in a few days now. I want peace, but it
must be an honorable one. *Addio, mio bene.* Wholly yours!"

The young Empress followed his instructions docilely. But
what could she do against the deep hatred of adversaries who,
now that they saw the colossus tottering, thought that this time
they would surely crush him! Napoleon imprudently permitted
a long armistice and so gave his enemies time to concentrate.

In Dresden he worked under a terrific strain. "We saw him,"
said Constant, "falling asleep over his maps again and again."
As a relaxation in the evening he often attended the theatre
that had been set up in the Orangerie of the Marcolini Palace.
He sent to Paris for Talma, Mlles. George, Mars and
Bourgoing. The whole city wore a holiday air. Napoleon and
his ally, the King of Saxony, gave dinners, balls, concerts, the
Emperor returning afterward to his apartment to work till late
into the night. On several occasions he invited Mlle. George
to visit him privately. And in their frank talk together he
relaxed, recovered something of his old spirit.

At the beginning of August, Napoleon joined Marie-Louise
at Mainz. It looked as though a rupture with Vienna were inevitable. The Emperor hoped, however, that the meeting with
his daughter would make Papa Franz pause. For that matter,
should Austria go against him, Napoleon was anxious to assure
Marie-Louise that his affection for her would not change. He
accompanied her to Wiesbaden, to Cassel, to the banks of the
Rhine. He pretended a gaiety he was far from feeling, but at
moments his mask slipped and he turned grave. He knew that
courage was at a low ebb in Paris, that treason was in the wind.
The tragic death of Junot affected him deeply. Junot had gone
mad and thrown himself from the window—Junot . . . another
friend of his youth. . . .

He set out again for Dresden where, the moment he arrived,
things began to happen. Austria declared war. Henceforth Napoleon would have to fight half a million men.

At that moment he was nothing but a gambler, reckless and
unrestrainable. Fortune had turned against him—very well, he

would use force. He flung everything he had onto that cloth crisscrossed with plains, rivers, woods. His strategy of 1813 was lumbering and weak. He won at Dresden where Moreau, his former rival, was killed by a French bullet. But his last allies betrayed him, his harassed officers were defeated one by one and at Leipzig, that gigantic "double or quits" which caused the downfall of the Empire of the West, the enemy vise closed on him.

Napoleon retreated toward the Rhine. During those last twenty days he had written to Marie-Louise only once and then not frankly. He wanted to spare her until the end and it was not till Gotha (October 25th) that he murmured: "The bulletins will tell you how things stand with me." At that supremely critical hour when Murat was planning to desert him, Napoleon also had to defend himself against Louis, who had come back to France to reclaim his kingdom of Holland. The Emperor sighed: "It is not very generous of him to force me to deal severely with him at a time when I have so much to do. But that man is crazy." "Pity me for having such a wretched family," he wrote to the Empress, "—and I have lavished everything on them." Ordering his marshals to hold the enemy he left the Rhineland to try to bolster up France. On November 9th he arrived at Saint-Cloud. Marie-Louise met him at the entrance and fell on his breast, weeping. He clasped her in his arms. The little king, handsome and glowing with health, recognized his father in spite of the latter's long absence and held out his little arms to him. Picking up the child, Napoleon entered his study.

During those four winter months in which he was preparing his defense against the threatened invasion he worked as perhaps he had never worked before. He saw little of Marie-Louise. Scarcely half an hour at luncheon, sometimes an hour in the afternoon. But at night he went to her apartment, except on those occasions when some gigantic task detained him too late at his desk. Then he slept in his own apartments. That tension, those heavy burdens, his failure, seemed to have made him harder. One day, seeing Laplace, of whom he was very fond, he said to him abruptly:

"You have changed and are much thinner."

"Sire," replied the scholar sadly, "I have lost my daughter."

"You are a mathematician. Work that out in calculus and you will see that it equals zero."

And yet he was gentle with his wife and son, kindly to those about him. At moments, however, his nervousness got the upper hand and he burst forth in terrible words.

New Year's Day, 1814, was gloomy. The Austrians had crossed the Rhine at Basel, the Prussians near Coblentz. Murat was negotiating. Joseph had been driven from Spain and had taken refuge in Paris, where he had resumed the titles and prerogatives of the premier French prince. At odds with the legislative body, Napoleon blasted the members who came to greet him:

"You have been trying to spatter me with mud. Know that I am a man who can be killed, but not insulted. You will have peace in three months or I shall perish!"

On the 23rd of January he entrusted Marie-Louise and the little king to the officers of the National Guard. "You will be responsible for them, will you not? You will defend them?" Cries of fidelity rang out enthusiastically. He was deeply moved by their sincerity. However, he apparently had no illusions when he set out to push back the invader. "Do they think I still have an army?" he said to Pasquier. To Mollien: "If the enemy should come to Paris that will be the end of the Empire." However that lack of hope in no way lessened his capacity for action.

The last afternoon he spent at the Tuileries he kept his son in his study with him while he sorted and arranged his maps and private papers, burning bundles of them. The little boy trotted about the room, pulling his wooden horse by the bridle and singing to himself. Now and then Napoleon turned and looked at him.

On the evening of the 24th he bade Marie-Louise a sad and tender farewell. He was never to kiss her soft pink cheek again; he was never to clasp her frail hand in his. According to Mme. de Montebello, the only witness present, the Empress murmured:

"When will you come back?"

Napoleon hesitated a moment. At last he said in a grave voice: "My darling, that is God's secret."

A little later he went stealthily tiptoeing to the little king's room. The child lay sound asleep in bed, his fists tightly closed, his mouth open, under the rays of the night lamp. Mme. de Montesquiou sat up, frightened. Napoleon put a finger on his lips. Careful not to wake him, he brushed his lips to his son's forehead. Then, without a word, he went away, forever, from what he held dearest in all the world.

This time he had to drive the enemy from the country or die. But could he drive him out with that army of conscripts, those discouraged generals who thought only of saving their fortunes and titles from the catastrophe they now looked upon as inevitable? His influence was so strong, however, that he put new life into those unhappy men. His plan seemed elementary enough. He was going to attack the enemy armies one by one and defeat them. And defeat them he did indeed. He defeated Blücher at Brienne, that same Brienne where he had gone to school, the one he had said would make such a fine battlefield. That was the moment when he learned of Murat's betrayal. He was greatly troubled.

"All this," he murmured, "will end with a Bourbon."

However he did not weaken. He wrote twice as many letters to Marie-Louise, in which he tried to cheer her. On February 7th from Nogent he wrote to her three times: "Your letter made me very sad. I see from it that you have lost courage. I hope that my affairs are going to take a turn for the better. Farewell, my good Louise, be brave."

He knew they were losing their heads in Paris, that Joseph, who had been left there as Mentor, was giving a coward's advice, that Talleyrand was merely biding his time to betray him. He himself had to withstand the entreaties of Berthier, Maret and Caulaincourt, who were urging him to make peace at any price. The thought of his wife and his son never left him. He gave orders to Joseph that, if the enemy arrived before Paris, he was

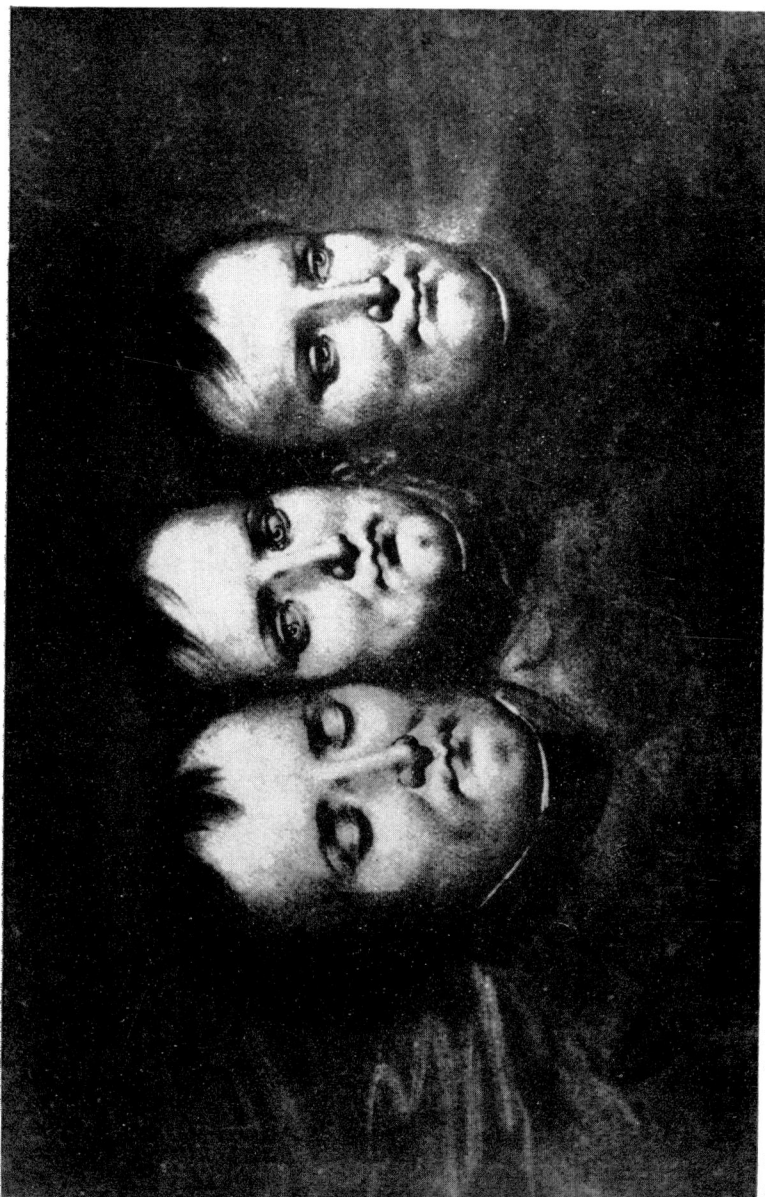

NAPOLEON AT ST. CLOUD, 1812

From the Sketch by Girodet

PAULINE BONAPARTE
Princess Borghese
From the Portrait by Mme. Kinson

to take them to safety: "The fate of Astyanax, prisoner of the Greeks, has always seemed to me the saddest in history. I would rather my son had his throat cut and were thrown into the Seine than to see him in the hands of the Austrians and taken to Vienna." Strange premonition! And all the while he was fighting. . . . He was still fighting. . . . At Champaubert, at Montmirail, at Vauchamps, Mormans, Montereau. And winning everywhere. Something perilously like hope stirred in him again. "I am closer to Vienna," he said, "than the Emperor of Austria is to Paris." However, certain matters had roused his jealousy. He advised Marie-Louise not to trust Joseph. "He has a bad reputation with women." A thoroughly unscrupulous fellow, Joseph was indeed hanging about his sister-in-law. "Keep the King far from your trust and your person if you care anything about my happiness," Napoleon wrote. "All that makes me a little sad. I need consolation from my family, but I am accustomed to nothing but irritations. From you, however, such a thing would be both unexpected and unbearable." On March 23rd, at Bar-sur-Aube, he informed Marie-Louise, with an extraordinary imprudence that can be explained only by his anxiety for her, that he was moving toward the east in an effort to draw the Allied armies away from Paris. Like a deer turning on its tracks to attract the dogs. . . . That letter was intercepted by Blücher. It showed him that the capital was undefended. The Allies rushed forward: Paris fell. Warned too late, Napoleon galloped all the way to Juvisy—to learn of the surrender.

At first he was crushed to earth. Then, almost immediately, at Fontainebleau where he had taken refuge, imagination, his will-o-the-wisp, raised its head. The Senate could manage to vote him out of power, but he was sure of his soldiers. They would follow the Little Corporal wherever he chose to lead them. But in a frightful scene his marshals rose against him. Then at last an immense weariness descended on the man who had carried such a heavy burden for so many years. "Those men," he said sadly, "have neither heart nor entrails! I have been beaten less by fortune than by the egotism and ingratitude of my brother-officers!" He made up his mind to abdicate, first, in favor of his son, then when Marmont went over to the Allies, unconditionally. Marmont, one of the best loved, one of the most favored among the comrades of his youth! That was a cruel heartbreak for him. "I treated him as if he were my own child," he said to Caulaincourt. "I counted on him. Ambition ruined him."

IV

The First Exile

AROUND NAPOLEON the desert was spreading. His ministers, his generals, had gone over to the Bourbons. His wife and son at least were left him. He still thought that he might live quietly with them in a dignity worthy, after all, of a prince, on the island of Elba or in Italy. They told him that the Empress, for whom he was waiting at Fontainebleau, had gone to Rambouillet, where she would find herself in the hands of the Allies. In that she had yielded to the advice of those about her—in particular of Mme. de Brignole, that scheming woman, an intimate of Talleyrand. Napoleon knew how weak Marie-Louise was. He foresaw that she would soon be restored to the Austrian fold. He would never see her again, nor their child. . . . Then, for the first time, he gave up. For a fortnight now each day had been swallowing up another one of the hopes that had sustained him in his disaster. He had resigned himself to disappearing from view that his son might be king in his stead. His son was not going to be king! He had been sure that he would not be separated from him—and they were taking the King of Rome away. His soldiers had thrown away their *cocardes;* the sovereigns of Europe were breaking their promises to him. He was at the mercy of his conquerors—and those conquerors were determined to humiliate him, to drag him in the dust, perhaps to murder him. His heart was wrung by the baseness of men. What could be left but death?

Ever since the retreat from Russia he had been wearing around his neck a little black sachet containing a poison of opium, belladonna and hellebore that Yvan had put up according to a formula of Cabanis. During the night of the 12th to the 13th of April he got up, poured out a glass of water and sprinkled a little of the powder in it. He drank it and went to bed again in the belief that he would never awake.

The drug was slow in taking effect. Napoleon sent for Caulaincourt, who had been his closest confidant in all that trying period. He handed him a little portfolio of red Morocco leather that contained Marie-Louise's letters and a note addressed to the Empress. On it he had written in a hand that had not faltered: "It is well that you went to Rambouillet. I approve of it. . . . Your father has been misled and has behaved badly toward us, but he will be a good father to you and your son. Goodbye, my good Louise, you are the one I love most in the world. I regret my misfortunes only because of the harm they do to you. All your life you will love the most devoted of husbands. Kiss my little son for me. Goodbye, dear Louise. Wholly yours, Napoleon."

In the faint glimmer from the nightlamp in the bedroom, Caulaincourt had difficulty in distinguishing his face. But the few orders which the Emperor gave in a feeble voice, and his stifled groans, warned the duke and, cold-hearted though he was, he shed tears. Napoleon drew him down and embraced him.

"Be happy, you deserve it, my dear Caulaincourt."

He was interrupted by hiccoughs. His skin was dry and icy cold. The first equerry wanted to send for help. The Emperor refused and held him back by his coat-collar "with an irresistible strength." His head was getting heavy, he said; at last he was going to "fall asleep." Out of pity Caulaincourt obeyed. But soon the hiccoughing increased, his limbs stiffened. Napoleon gritted his teeth to keep from vomiting. Once, between spasms, he ordered Caulaincourt to give his large dressing-case to Prince Eugène as a souvenir and to keep for himself the Emperor's handsomest sword and his cameo portrait.

"Tell Josephine," he added, "that I have thought of her often."

Josephine, his great love, the companion of his glory! He knew nothing about her now. And it was just as well. On her return from Malmaison on April 9th she had written to

Eugène: "As for you, you are free and released from any oath of fidelity. Anything you might do for *his* cause would be useless. You must look out for your family." Having received so much, she considered that disaster freed her from gratitude.

Speaking in a low voice, Napoleon thanked Caulaincourt for his services. For a second he lost consciousness, and the Duke, who thought he was dying, escaped at last from the room to summon the valet on duty. When he came back the Emperor reproached him gently for not letting him die in peace.

"How hard it is to die!" he said.

By that time he was so nauseated that he could not keep from vomiting. At last Marshal Bertrand hurried in with Yvan, who had been roused from his sleep.

"Doctor," Napoleon begged the physician, "give me another dose, a little stronger. . . . It is your duty. . . . If you care anything for me you must do this for my sake."

Yvan refused: he was not a murderer. The Emperor insisted, and the physician, losing his head, took to his heels like a coward. Napoleon pressed his hand to his stomach—he was apparently in great pain.

"Oh," he groaned, "why did I not die at Arcis-sur-Aube!"

But he was going to live. The poison was old and had lost its strength. Besides he had got rid of most of it by vomiting. Caulaincourt and Constant carried him to an open window and he fell into a prolonged doze. When Caulaincourt saw him again the next morning, he found him calm and resigned.

"I am condemned to live," he said. "Even Death has betrayed me. It will take courage to endure life after all I have been through. I shall write the history of the brave. . . ."

He urged his attendants not to mention the events of the past night. An unsuccessful suicide would only make him ridiculous and might harm his son. Maret then had him sign the ratification of the treaty which had been concluded with the Allies. Napoleon asked nothing for himself as the price of his abdication, but he stipulated in detail his desires for his family and for all with whom he was concerned, even including his servants.

Marie-Louise and her son were to receive the Duchy of Parma. Josephine would still have an income of a million, all the princesses and princes of his family were handsomely provided for. Eugène was to have a sumptuous estate outside of France. At the instance of his representatives, Macdonald and Caulaincourt, and the "generosity" of Alexander, Napoleon was to be ruler of the island of Elba, with an allowance of two millions: a battalion of his Old Guard would accompany him as an "escort of honor and security."

Countess Walewska had not seen the Emperor for months, but she was still devoted to him. At word of the disaster she hastened at once to Fontainebleau, arriving on that same evening. Constant informed Napoleon that she was waiting in a gallery for him to send for her. The Emperor was exhausted and half asleep . . . and he forgot all about her. Wrapped in her cloak the poor woman sat there for hours in the silent palace.

At dawn, worn out and despairing of seeing him, she rose and, taking care not to be seen—if the Empress were to learn of her visit she might turn against Napoleon—went out to her carriage. Not long afterward the Emperor suddenly remembered her and asked for her. Constant replied that she had gone.

"Poor Marie," said Napoleon, "she must have thought I had forgotten her. . . . I am deeply sorry. But," he added, pointing to his head, "I have so many things inside here!"

She wrote to him and he replied promptly with a warm, friendly letter. If, after she had arranged her affairs, she should go to Lucca or to Pisa to take the waters he would be glad to see her as well as her son.

That same morning an affectionate letter from Marie-Louise gave him fresh reason for living.

"All I wish," she wrote to Napoleon, "is to be able to soften your misfortune and to be of use to you. . . . I am so unhappy at being separated from you that I shall never be really myself again until you are with me. . . . I think of you only. . . . Your tragic situation tears my heart. I implore you never to doubt the loving affection of your faithful Louise."

So, after all, his wife loved him . . . she would not consent to be separated from him! He took courage again, began to look forward to happier days. Living with her on the island of Elba he would bring up his little son in his own way and prepare him for the day when France, regretting her vanished glory, would again turn toward her Emperor. At that moment Napoleon ceased to regret that he had not died. He began to discuss policies, to make plans and to arrange for his departure.

He sent for books on Elba and for maps and made inquiries about the climate.

"The air is very healthy and the inhabitants first-rate," he said to Bausset, the Prefect of the Palace. "I shall not be too badly off there and I hope that Marie-Louise will not dislike it either."

Walking on the terrace outside of the Galerie de François Ier, he remarked to that same Bausset who knew nothing of his attempted suicide: "If, in my despair, I were to kill myself, that would be an act of cowardice. . . . I am condemned to live." He was silent a moment, then, smiling bitterly, he added: "Between you and me, they say that a live cad is better than a dead emperor."

Did he still think that he might return to France one day? Perhaps. . . . When Bausset left him, the Prefect apparently thought so.

Those new hopes were soon shattered. The Emperor Franz, his father-in-law, informed him that he was offering Marie-Louise the hospitality of his family "for several months." So! She was going to Vienna with her child . . . what he had feared above all! To be sure it would have been impossible for the young Empress to hold out against the paternal will for long. Frightened by the menacing attitude of Napoleon's brothers, who would have liked to hold her as a hostage, Marie-Louise had listened to Mme. de Brignole. To separate her from Napoleon, that scheming woman sent for the valet Constant and the Mameluke, Roustan, as witnesses of the Emperor's infidelities. Moreover, Corvisart, duly prodded, dissuaded the Empress from visiting the watering-places of Tuscany or the island of Elba, which, he said, would be injurious to her health. Nevertheless she was still writing to Napoleon, and he still believed that in time she would join him in his "island of Sancho Panza."

During those anguished days at Fontainebleau not one of his near relatives whom he loved so dearly and whom he had loaded with honors, had lifted a finger to come to him: neither his mother, whom Fesch had dragged off to Rome, nor Joseph, nor Jerome, nor Pauline, nor Hortense. At the moment of disaster they had thought of themselves only. Even his servants deserted him, certain of them, like Constant, after robbing him. A few faithful souls were still left: Maret, Caulaincourt, Drouot, Bertrand, Cambronne. The last week was a ghastly void. Finally, on April 20th, Napoleon descended the great horseshoe staircase and took leave of his soldiers of the Old Guard, who were drawn up in the courtyard. He kissed their flag and their general; then, covering his eyes with his hand, he flung himself into his carriage and was driven rapidly away.

Through Briare, Nevers, Roanne he sped. In nearly every town the inhabitants turned out to greet him with respectful cheers. He was calm, almost cheerful. At Salvagny, not far from Lyons, he walked along the road while the horses were being changed. Meeting the curé of the parish, he pointed out to him a brilliant star in the heavens, perhaps the very one he had chosen as his own and to which, in the most significant moments of his life, he had always turned. He had forgotten the name . . . did the curé know it? The priest did not and apologized.

"What a pity, monsieur le curé," said Napoleon with a smile.

After Lyons he was received everywhere with hostile shouts. At Valence he met Augereau, who had basely denied him in a proclamation to his troops. Napoleon did not hold it against him.

"Where are you going in such a hurry?" he cried, taking him by the arm. "Are you off to Court?"

Augereau replied that he was going to Lyons.

They walked a little way along the road to Valence, then Augereau began to reproach the Emperor for sacrificing everything to his ambition. Napoleon doffed his hat to him and left him abruptly. Augereau did not even return the salute.

At Avignon the populace mutinied, and the Emperor was in danger. The cortège therefore made a detour away from the Rhône toward Aix. But all Provence was Royalist. At Orgon he was greeted with shouts of "Down with the tyrant!" and the Allied commissioners were forced to shield him with their bodies. Yielding to who knows what advice, perhaps even out of fear—for brave as he was under fire he had frequently shown fright before the mob and its noisy violence—he borrowed a coat from one of the couriers and mounting a post horse, galloped over the road for several miles. Near Aix he drew rein, exhausted, at the inn of the Calade. The innkeeper's wife who did not recognize him informed him that Napoleon would be killed before he could reach the coast. In all the towns the people were already hanging or burning him in effigy. It was dark night before he dared to enter Aix. He took a little food, but refused wine in fear of poison. Then he retired to a small bedroom at the back of the house, whence he could hear the angry clamor of the mob that had gathered in front of the inn. That was one of the most painful hours in his life. Those same wretched people had acclaimed him in his glory: now in his disaster they were trampling him underfoot. His heart was heavy when at last he fell asleep from sheer exhaustion. Not till shortly before midnight could he continue his journey and then only in disguise, by borrowing a uniform from the Austrian Commissioner Köller, a cloak from the Russian, Schouvalow, a helmet from the Prussian, Waldburg-Truchsess. A supreme humiliation to which, unquestionably, he should never have consented! But his mind was so numb . . . and he was really afraid.

At last on the 26th he arrived at the château of Bouillidou near Le Luc, where Pauline was waiting for him.

That house he knew well, having stopped there on his return from Egypt. With tears streaming down her face, Pauline came running to meet him and kissed his hands. They spent the whole evening together. Pauline insisted upon joining him in Elba, and he consented, happy to know that he would have a heart to whom he could unbosom himself, a loyal presence in his exile. The next day, minus the disguise which he gave up at Pauline's request, he set out for St. Raphael, where he embarked with his suite on the frigate *Undaunted*. The winds were variable and he was four days in reaching Portoferraio. There he was welcomed enthusiastically by the entire population. They thought he was bringing great treasures with him and that he would make their island a paradise.

To the man who had ruled Europe and lived in its most beautiful palaces, the island of Elba was but a miserable rock jutting out into the sea. And yet in those first days Napoleon seemed to be content. He organized his little state, cleaned up the port, fitted out a fleet, built himself a town house at Portoferraio and a country house at San Martino, made roads, directed the development of iron mines and kept his battalion of eight hundred *grognards* well in body and mind by exercises, reviews, maneuvers. On horseback from break of day, he could be seen galloping over all the paths on the island, followed by a few officers. Seldom had he ever been so active. The smaller the stage, the more he moved about on it. "It seems," said Sir Neil Campbell, the English Commissioner, "that he delights in perpetual motion and in seeing those who accompany him fall with exhaustion." He established an official entourage, appointing Bertrand grand marshal, Drouot military governor, Cambronne captain of the Guard, Peyrusse controller-general. Four chamberlains were selected from among the notables of the island: Foureau de Beauregard was named physician to the Emperor. In addition there were thirty-five servants and one hundred horses.

Ten days after his arrival Napoleon gave a reception which was a pale imitation of those at the Tuileries. Though society on the island was somewhat heterogeneous, some fifty women from the bourgeoisie as well as from the business world had been invited—all of them badly dressed and extremely awkward, but some of them quite pretty. Campbell recognized a number of embroidery workers to whom he had given his uniform to be mended only a few days before. Affable and cheerful, Napoleon gravely passed before that phantom court, pausing here and there to chat with men and women.

He was expecting Marie-Louise and her son and was having their apartments prepared for them. He wrote to the Empress urging her to come as soon as possible. "Elba is a very pretty island," he assured her. Marie-Louise was still answering his letters, but at greater and greater intervals. She was already completely under the sway of her German family, already absorbed in her new interests. Napoleon waited patiently. He suggested that she come to take the waters in Tuscany—in that way they would be nearer each other. But Vienna was opposed: they were determined to isolate Napoleon. Marie-Louise listened to Corvisart's advice and allowed herself to be persuaded. Embracing her son, whom she left as a hostage in Metternich's hands, she set out with Mme. de Brignole for Aix in Savoy. There she found her dear Montebello, who had come from Paris to join her. Marie-Louise had not entirely given up the idea of going to Elba; she was still thinking of Napoleon with friendship, with regret. But she would go later on. . . .

Napoleon was not deceived by those excuses. He knew how much Marie-Louise's affection had cooled. From the hermitage of the Madonna at Marciana where he went to escape the dog days, he expressed indignation at the way he was being treated. Then his affection came to the fore. Writing calmly now, he urged her to come and bring their child and he added, because she liked to paint: "There are some very beautiful landscapes to sketch here."

Poor man! He had no idea that Neipperg was already hovering about the Empress. That general had been assigned as her *chevalier d'honneur* and had waited upon her at Geneva. Marie-Louise received him coldly at first. But he was so amusing, so charming, so considerate! At Aix he was constantly paying her little attentions, such as thinning out her paints for her, carrying her shawl when she went to walk, accompanying her on the piano when she sang. Intelligent and cultivated, he knew all Europe and had friends in every court. He talked well, was full of life and had exquisite taste. Moreover he had had much experience with women. That one-eyed man was in fact a virtuoso in love. Marie-Louise was soon to allow herself to be caught in the meshes of a clever net.

For all of that she still suffered a few twinges of conscience. She sent Bausset to Elba with a little bust of the King of Rome. And on the 15th of August, the Emperor's birthday, she confessed to Méneval that she was very unhappy. Before long that unhappiness was to vanish into thin air; once again she would sing and laugh and chatter and be coquettish. Neipperg's devotion had won her. At the same time Napoleon's insistence, his effort to get her to come to him, antagonized her. He had sent Captain Hurault de Sorbée to help her make ready to leave for Elba. Faced with a decision, Marie-Louise rebelled and, with Neipperg's connivance, refused to see the messenger. That same day Hurault was denounced to the Prefect by Mme. de Brignole. He was arrested and sent to Paris.

Now that Marie-Louise had made her choice, she had no desire to see Napoleon again. In place of husband and honor she chose the easy life of the Austrian Court and General Neipperg. Instinctively she gravitated to the lesser position, the baser happiness. Before returning to Vienna she wrote to Mme. de Montebello, who had gone back to Paris, that Napoleon was compromising *her* with her family by his insistent messages: "I shall never go to the island of Elba (you know better than anyone that I have no desire to go) but the Emperor is really extraordinarily indiscreet and careless."

That was the end. She was never to write to Napoleon again except on New Year's Day, 1815, and then only a short note, courteous but cold. He, poor fellow, had never suspected her of bad faith, much less of infidelity. He thought she was a prisoner of Metternich. But from that moment an idea was born in him and it was to grow little by little until he forgot entirely his resolve to be discreet and to lead a quiet life. A few months more and he would be unable to resist that idea.

Toward the middle of June he received word of Josephine's death—not in a letter from Hortense or from Eugène, who had neglected that elementary courtesy, but through a newspaper that someone had brought from Genoa. That death was a great blow to him: for two days he remained indoors, refusing to see anyone but Bertrand and his wife. When they came to offer their condolences he said: "Poor Josephine, now she is happy!" He did not go into mourning, out of consideration for Marie-Louise, but it was plain to all that he grieved deeply. That woman had held a unique place in his life. To his dying day he was always to retain a tender memory of her. He never knew that Josephine had been unfaithful to him again and that she had died as it were, in the midst of and as the result of that infidelity.

When the Empire fell Josephine was living with Hortense. She had only one thought in her mind: what the future might hold in store for her. She received the Emperor Alexander at Malmaison and implored his protection. The Czar was captivated by her grace and by Hortense's elegiac charm, even going so far as to request the King of France to give the latter the title of Duchesse de Saint Leu. Josephine held a veritable court much frequented by foreign princes. Napoleon's first wife attracted to her house and entertained all those English, Germans and Prussians who had conquered him. She used her influence at the Tuileries to have Eugène appointed constable. Louis XVIII granted the ex-viceroy of Italy an audience and received him cordially, but there could be no question of making him constable. For that matter Eugène was not in the least interested. He preferred to be a prince, either in Italy or in Germany. Thanks again to the Czar, he was to be given the Grand Duchy of Leuchtenberg at the price—but what was that to Eugène?— of his status as a Frenchman.

Alexander became the official host, the house guest at Malmaison. Josephine presented him with the beautiful cameo which the Pope had given her at the Coronation. To entertain the Grand Dukes, they sang, they danced, they played prisoners' base. But of the fallen Emperor, not a word. However the Czar alone was not glamour enough for ambitious Josephine. Tired and ill as she was she insisted upon entertaining the Emperor of Austria and the King of Prussia. On May 24th, after a large banquet, she opened the ball with Alexander. Then in her low-cut evening gown, over which she had flung a light scarf, she strolled with him in the chilly night air beneath the shade trees in the park. Two days later, she was stricken with pneumonia and was delirious with fever. On May 29, 1814, Josephine, one-time Empress of the French, breathed her last. That beautiful body that had known so many pleasures, so many vanities, was laid to rest in the church of Rueil.

On August 2nd, Madame Mère arrived at Portoferraio from Livorno, bringing with her a modest retinue including old Saveria, who had never left her, and Abbé Buonavita a Corsican almoner who was somewhat short on intelligence. . . . The Emperor was delighted to see his mother again and lavished attentions on her. He lodged her in a house near his residence of the Mulini. In the evening he took her driving in his barouche along the sea. He dined with her and forced himself to play *reversi* with her. On Sundays she presided over his little court with that nobility of manner, that reserve which made her equally at home in good fortune or in bad.

On hot days, when he moved up to the hermitage of Marciana, she went with him and took lodgings in the village, two hundred meters down the hillside. Her presence was a great comfort to him. That old woman with the stern features, the motionless eyes, was the only one who really understood him. But she could not give him the life, the gaiety he needed. Sparing of words and gestures, she seemed always to be "attended by silence."

Marie Walewska sent her brother, Colonel Laczinski, to the Emperor to ask permission to come to the island. Napoleon was touched by her request: he still regretted that he had not received her at Fontainebleau. But he cautioned her to use the greatest discretion lest the Empress take offense. To receive Marie where prying eyes could not spy on them he moved up to Marciana on the 20th of August.

On the 1st of September at ten o'clock in the evening, she arrived outside of the harbor. With her were Laczinski, her sister and young Alexandre. Bertrand was waiting for her with a barouche and a number of saddle horses. Through a beautiful moonlit night the little company drove up the mountainside. At the peak of Procchio they saw the Emperor coming to meet her on a white horse. He kissed the Countess' hand gallantly, complimented her sister, embraced the child. Then on horseback, for there was only a steep mountain path before them now, the travelers rode up to the hermitage. "There is my palace," Napoleon cried gaily to Marie. He had assigned the little rooms in the cottage to his visitors and he himself went to sleep in a tent under some giant chestnut trees. During the night a storm came and it rained in torrents. Napoleon could not sleep. Toward dawn he called Marchand, now his valet since Constant's flight. Marchand told him that, in spite of all precautions, a rumor had spread at Portoferraio and even at Marciana, that Marie-Louise had escaped secretly from Vienna and had arrived on the island with the little king. Dr. Foureau de Beauregard had already come up to the hermitage to offer his services.

As soon as he was dressed the Emperor came out of his tent and went to speak to the physician. The weather was now beautiful and clear. Flecks of brilliant sunlight speckled the motionless treetops. A beautiful little boy was playing on the velvety lawn. Napoleon called him and caressed him.

"Well, Doctor," he said to Foureau, "what do you think of him?"

"Sire," replied the physician, "I find that the King has grown quite a lot."

The Emperor laughed: little Alexandre was a year older than the King of Rome, but there was strong resemblance between them. Alexandre's eyes, however, were like his mother's, perhaps a trifle darker. He had yellow hair that fell in curls on his shoulders. From Napoleon he had inherited the Greek shape of his head, the pale complexion, the pure, firmly cut mouth of the Bonapartes. Son of such a gentle mother, the little fellow had a determined character, and was quick of mind and speech. The day before, General Bertrand had asked him if he would not say how-do-you-do to him.

"No," the little boy had replied, "not till I have said how-do-you-do to the Emperor."

Napoleon made him come into his tent. The flag of the velites of honor and the sword Desaix had used at Marengo, hung above the camp bed. The Emperor sat down and took the child on his knees.

"How old are you, Alexandre?"

"Four and a half."

"Where were you born?"

"In Poland."

"Then you are Polish?"

"No, I want to be French, like Napoleon."

"What are you going to do when you grow up?"

"I am going to make war, like Napoleon."

The Emperor gave him a long look.

"Do you love Napoleon?" he asked almost in a whisper.

"Oh, yes indeed!" exclaimed the child.

"Why do you love him?"

"Because he is my papa, and Maman told me to love him."

Napoleon embraced him tenderly and, Mme. Walewska appearing at that moment, dismissed the child and sent him back to his games.

The Polish woman had changed. She was twenty-eight years old now and no longer the fragile fairy of the North whom her country had sacrificed to the conqueror of 1807. Less frail in appearance, she was more a woman now and her once-delicate face had grown fuller, wore an expression of calm assurance. She talked even less than before. Her affection for Napoleon had changed, too: today her love was tinged with a deep compassion. Disaster had bound him to her more effectually than his glory had ever been able to do. Forgetful of self, forgetful even of Poland, she thought only of the fallen hero.

Luncheon was served in the shade of the chestnut trees. The dishes were furnished by Madame Mère's kitchen, though the latter avoided seeing her son for those two days. Napoleon was gay, buoyant, exhilarated. In the afternoon he walked with Marie, her sister and little Alexandre. But on their return to the hermitage, the Emperor and Marie retired to one of the rooms in the cottage and there they remained alone for a long time. Marie pointed out the mistakes the Bourbons were making and assured him that France had recovered from its discouragement and was beginning to rebel against the new rulers. The Emperor smiled, but was careful not to speak the words that might give the Countess too much hope. She would have liked to stay there near him, but he refused to consider the idea. Her presence on the island would cause a scandal. That same evening she was to leave for Naples. The Emperor gave her messages for Murat, with whom Pauline had effected a reconciliation. Napoleon bore his brother-in-law no grudge: he knew too well the foibles of men. He also knew that Murat might still be very useful to him. But let him wait for his orders—an imprudence would ruin everything.

Marie had brought all of her jewelry with her, some of it of great value. She had intended to leave it with Napoleon, but he would not have it—he was not so poor as she thought. He even insisted that she take with her an order of 61,000 francs to cover the expenses of her journey. The Countess refused at first, then yielded: she was hoping to return before long.

At dinner, which was served in the tent, Napoleon insisted that little Alexandre, who had not lunched with him, should sit by his side this time. His mother demurred, fearing the child's high spirits; but the Emperor countered with stories of his own youthful years, of adventures he had had with Joseph, of his escapades on the *maquis*. The little boy was greatly excited and began to take liberties with Napoleon. The latter pretended to look very stern and asked:

"Aren't you afraid of the whip? Well, I advise you to be afraid of it. I was whipped only once in my life but I have never forgotten it."

And he told him the story of the thrashing he had received for making fun of his grandmother Fesch.

"But I do not make fun of Maman!" replied the little fellow in a frightened voice.

"That is well answered," cried the Emperor, and he seized him in his arms and kissed him.

At nine o'clock, after night had fallen, the travelers rode down the hill to the beach of Marciana. Just before they came to the village, Napoleon bade Marie farewell. He clasped her son in his arms and held him against his breast.

"Goodbye, dear child of my heart!" he said.

Then, deep in thought, he rode up the mountain path again. Getting out his long telescope he scanned the coast anxiously. The sky, which had been brilliantly clear only a little while ago, suddenly darkened. Then the storm broke. Napoleon was sorry that he had hastened Marie's departure and he sent an aide-de-camp hurrying after her to urge her to wait. By the time the officer reached the shore the Poles had obediently put to sea. That night the Emperor was so worried that he refused to undress, and not till daybreak, when the storm slackened, did he fling himself down on his bed. He was not fully reassured till a week later when Marie sent him word that she had come safely into port.

Then Pauline arrived in her turn. That "queen of baubles," who had been so frivolous, even so lax in morals throughout the whole reign, now sacrificed her pleasures in Italy to come and sit in boredom at Portoferraio. She loved and admired her brother—she was satisfied to share his misfortune and to place herself again under his rule, which was often harsh. He forbade her to wear her diamonds—they were too beautiful for the women of Elba. If she appeared in black or white he would make her change her gown, for he liked only color. She was the life and soul of the Emperor's intimate parties; she organized plays and costume balls, at which she danced till dawn. She allowed Drouot and innumerable others to pay court to her, even letting them go so far on occasion that Napoleon was obliged to call her down sharply. But at bottom he was pleased with her: she freed him from his solitude, she was the true consolation of his exile.

The old accusation of incest was to be revived. To please Louis XVIII police agents invented letters that purported to be written by Pauline to two colonels, her lovers, in which she spoke of herself as her brother's mistress, called the Emperor "the Old Rotter" and asked them to send her a remedy for syphilis. Napoleon was supposed not only to have taken advantage of his sister, but to have contaminated her! . . . That was just so much idiotic filth! The Emperor never suffered from syphilis and his relations with Pauline as with Caroline and Hortense were those merely of a brother and a friend.

Several passing fancies, for that matter, served to satisfy the brief recrudescence of sensuality which that idle, lazy life induced in him. The first to arouse his interest was the wife of an Italian captain, at that time stationed at Elba. Mme. Colombani was a native of Capri, a good-natured, easy-going person. Napoleon gave her to Pauline as a companion; but his affair with her did not amount to much and lasted only a short time. The Emperor then singled out Mme. Bellini, a Spanish woman. Though not pretty, she was charming and vivacious and she could dance *fandangos* and *jotas* to perfection. Finally one morning the beautiful Lise, the ephemeral favorite of Saint-Cloud, landed at Portoferraio. She was now styling herself Countess de Molo. The Emperor gave her a post in Pauline's entourage and began to visit her again—but always observing a thousand precautions. He knew that he was surrounded by spies of all sorts and he feared that any gossip might reach the Empress' ear.

His wife, his son—he thought of them constantly. That he received no news from them seemed to him an outrage, and rightly so. He begged the English Commissioner Campbell to transmit his protests to London. "One could scarcely cite in modern times," he said, "another example of such barbarity, such injustice. . . . My son has been taken from me as in days of old the children of the vanquished were carried off to adorn the triumphal processions of the conquerors."

He liked to talk to his close friends of various little traits in the child that amused him or struck him as unusual, of his reluctance to leave the "big house" of the Tuileries for Rambouillet. He always used a snuffbox adorned with a portrait of the little king. When, one day, it slipped from his hands, he flung himself on his knees and, in spite of his obesity, picked it up, saying over and over "that he would have been very grieved if his little darling's features had been spoiled by his awkwardness." Sometimes he called him his "poor little devil." He was all regret, all tenderness for that child. "There is something of a mother's love in my feeling for him," he confessed. "I even have quite a bit of it and I am not ashamed."

Toward the end of December General Bertrand's brother came to the island with some engravings he had bought in Rome. The Emperor had them brought to San Martino and spent some time looking them over. Suddenly, he stopped short, turned red and, with a sort of shiver, exclaimed: "That is Marie-Louise!" That cry was so poignant that those who heard it scanned his face anxiously. He noticed their anxiety, made an effort to control himself and began to praise the artist's talent. He picked up the next engraving—one of the little king. "My son," he murmured softly, and the tenderness in his voice was heartbreaking. He bent over as if he were about to kiss the little face in the engraving. "My son," he said and the word was almost a sob. Those about him held their breath. After a moment of deep silence Napoleon put down the picture, went into his study, locked himself in, and stayed there for half an hour. When he came out his face was pale and drawn. Without a word to anyone he got into his carriage and drove off. For several days after that he went about in a deep gloom, never smiling and scarcely uttering a word.

He had other causes for anxiety and they increased with the weeks. Royalists were planning to kidnap him or even to murder him. He was aware of this and called the matter to Campbell's attention. So far none of the stipulations of the treaty of Fontainebleau had been executed. The Bourbons had

not paid the Civil List as they had promised. In spite of Napoleon's economy, his personal funds were diminishing. Soon he
would be unable to pay or feed the last of his soldiers. Were
they trying to force him to let those soldiers go that he might be
entirely at the mercy of the Powers? There had been open talk
at the Congress of Vienna as well as at Paris of snatching that
miserable island of Elba from him and deporting him like a
common criminal to the Azores or to St. Helena.

To Napoleon that thought was unbearable.

"I am a soldier," he said to Bertrand. "Let them come to
kill me and I shall bare my chest, but I do not wish to be deported."

In France the blundering monarchy had been unable to recover its strong old roots again. The Restoration trampled on
consciences, upset moneyed interests. Maret sent young Fleury
de Chaboulon, a former assistant prefect of Rheims, to Elba to
assure Napoleon that minds were in a ferment and the army
champing with impatience. After considering the matter all
night long, Napoleon came to a decision. He would tempt Fate
once more. It was the only way he could protect himself and
win back his wife and his child. For several days he kept his
secret. Then he took Bertrand and Drouot into his confidence.
The former approved of the plan. Like all those who had followed the Emperor, he and his wife were bored to death on the
island of Elba. Drouot, who was more intelligent, considered
the move dangerous both to Napoleon and to France. But he was
deeply loyal and allowed himself to be persuaded. Napoleon did
not tell his mother till the last moment. The old Corsican
woman was numb with fear, but all she said was:

"Go, my son, and fulfill your destiny."

Later, in Marchand's presence, she could not restrain her
tears.

Pauline had not expected anything of the sort. She was planning a fête and she seems to have been overwhelmed. She could
foresee nothing but disaster. Weeping she handed Marchand a
necklace of diamonds:

"If the Emperor is unlucky he may need this. Oh! if that

should happen, Marchand, never leave him. Take good care of him. . . ."

Napoleon urged his mother and sister to wait at Portoferraio till he should send for them and their attendants. Then, on February 26th, taking advantage of the absence of the English Commissioner, who had gone to Livorno on a holiday, he embarked his soldiers on the slender flotilla he had gathered together, and at sunset he himself went on board the brig *Inconstant*. At first there was no wind. The Emperor paced feverishly back and forth on deck, waiting for the wind to rise. At dawn a light breeze sprang up and carried him toward one of the last chapters in his life, the one in which he would try to arouse a world—less to regain his throne than to recover Marie-Louise and his son.

The next day a number of Englishmen visited the deserted house of the Mulini and noticed on the night table in the Emperor's bedroom a volume of the life of Charles V. It lay open at the page of the abdication. . . .

V

The Hundred Days

ESCAPING BY A MIRACLE from the English and French war-ships that followed in his wake, Napoleon landed on the Juan Gulf near Antibes. He was anxious to avoid any violence: through his prestige alone "the eagle with the national colors must fly from bell-tower to bell-tower till it came to rest on the towers of Notre-Dame." Shunning the road along the Rhône, of which he had such bad memories, he followed the more difficult and still icy route of the Alps through Digne and Gap. The people were still loyal and greeted him with loud acclaim as he passed. On foot as a rule, a stick in his hand, with the tails of his gray great coat flapping in the mountain breeze, he marched by the side of his little troop. Riding tired him quickly. He had grown heavier on the island of Elba and the white cashmere vest under the uniform of the Chasseurs de la Garde was beginning to bulge. His color was jaundiced, his hair had thinned out, but when he smiled his face looked young and clear again and one felt as if a supernatural aura hovered around him.

At the Pass of Laffrey he risked his life as he faced the battalion of the line that had been sent to stop him. Baring his chest, he showed them his heart. The muskets were lowered. Soldiers flung themselves at his feet, kissing his coat, his hands. At that moment, perhaps, he experienced the strongest emotion of his life. His knees trembled, his eyes filled with tears.

"It is all over," he said to Bertrand and Drouot. "In ten days I shall be in the Tuileries."

He was sure of that now. France could not hold out against that man who had dared to invade her alone. France had a king, she had princes, ministers, generals, prefects; but let Napoleon appear and all that powerful machine collapsed! Generals handed over their regiments to him, mayors their towns. Soon there was nothing left for the descendant of St. Louis, the gouty king, but to flee like a poor abashed creature before the Ghost of glory.

With the addition of all the troops that had been sent against them, Napoleon's column soon formed a sizable army. He marched into Lyons amid a veritable tumult of joy. He had already written to Marie-Louise from Grenoble. From Lyons, on March 11th, he called her to him: "When you receive this letter, I shall be in Paris. . . . Come and join me there and bring my son. I hope to hold you in my arms before the end of March."

That letter, Marie-Louise refused to read. She gave it to her father, who joked about it with the sovereigns at the Congress of Vienna.

At Lyons the Emperor sent Marchand to Mme. Pellapra's house. There was so much excitement around him at the archbishop's palace where he was staying, he had so many matters to settle—for it was at Lyons that he actually took over the power again—that he was not able to receive the charming Emilie till late in the evening. Theirs was not a lovers' meeting, but a conversation between friends.

On the 13th he set out again on the road for the North. Ney had been assured that he would be welcomed "as on the day after the Moskowa" and he could not resist that appeal. At Auxerre Napoleon clasped him in his arms and refused to let him apologize. Two days later at nine o'clock in the evening, Napoleon entered Paris. A wildly cheering crowd surged forward to snatch him from his carriage and carry him on their shoulders into the Tuileries. His heart beat as if it would burst and he closed his eyes. Besides him he could hear his old friend Lavallette saying over and over again as he walked backwards to clear a path: "It's you, it's you, it's you!"

Most of his former ministers had rushed to his side and now crowded about him. Cambacérès, Davout, Decrès, Maret—they were all there. Even Fouché, who had not been in the least surprised by the turn of events. The Emperor talked with them as if he had just left that study the evening before. And, outside, the cheers of a great city filled the air. That same evening at the

Théâtre-Français, warmhearted Mlle. George appeared on the stage wearing a gown covered with violets, to the rousing applause of the parterre. Of the women who had formerly been close to him, the first to resume her old post as lady of the palace was Mme. Duchâtel. Napoleon was delighted to see her again. He was less gracious to his sister-in-law, Julie, and to Hortense, whom he received coldly, especially Hortense. He was vexed with her for her cowardly desertion, for her silence during his year of exile. He gave her an appointment for the next day. She appeared, timid, fearful, with her two children to safeguard her.

"I should never have believed that you would desert my cause," the Emperor told her.

She apologized—and rather cleverly. She had been obliged to remain with her mother who was all alone. . . . Also she had been afraid her husband might kidnap her sons.

"You did not have to stay in France. A crust of black bread would have been better. . . . You have acted like a child. When one has shared a family's greatness, one is in obligation bound to share in its misfortunes."

Hortense wept. Napoleon was so moved by her tears that he forgave her. And in the days that followed, touched by her humble attitude, he took her back into his favor.

As for Josephine, he cherished a curious belief about her that no one had dared to correct. He believed that she had been unable to survive his disaster. He insisted upon knowing all the details of her death.

"So you let my poor Josephine die!" he said to Corvisart, reproachfully.

He sent for Moreau, the physician who had attended her, and questioned him.

"What was the cause of her death?"

Moreau lied out of shame and pity—and no doubt also with an eye to his own interest.

"Sire, anxiety, grief."

"Grief, what grief?"

"At what was happening, at Your Majesty's misfortunes."

"Ah, so she used to speak of me?"

"Often, sire, very often."

"Good woman! Poor Josephine! She really did love me."

He was so moved that he could scarcely speak. He went on to question Moreau in detail as to the remedies he had given her, the marks of interest the Czar had shown her. A few days later, he went to Malmaison where he lunched alone with Hortense, strolled with her through the château and wandered about the park.

He flung himself into his work with all the zest of former days. He realized the enormity of the task that confronted him and he had no illusions about the men who served him. "They let me come back," he said to Mollien, "just as they let the others go." In vain he tried to drive a wedge between the Allies, to win over Talleyrand, to bribe Metternich. Having failed in that, he could at least seek to galvanize France into action. But France was very tired, and, the first excitement over, fell back again into a sort of inertia.

The cruelest disappointment of all came to him from Marie-Louise. Driven out of Vienna, Méneval returned to tear the bandages from Napoleon's eyes. Speaking in careful terms, with the greatest tact, but at the same time making no effort to color his statements, he told the Emperor that Marie-Louise had placed herself under the protection of the Allied sovereigns, that she had turned her son over to her father and that she herself was now completely under Neipperg's sway. He added that in dismissing him, the Austrian woman had instructed him to request the Emperor to consent to a friendly separation, which had become imperative. Napoleon emerged from those talks in a state of extreme perturbation, his eye distracted, his face the color of ashes. His son a prisoner! His wife seduced—what now was the use of playing that terrible game any longer? And yet he clung to it in the secret and tenacious hope that as conqueror he could compel the Allies to relinquish their prey. Meanwhile with an eye to the future, and also from a sense of shame, he carefully hid the Empress' dishonor, speaking of her only with consideration, affection, respect. If Marie-

Louise had not hastened to his side, it was merely because her family had refused to let her come. Not a word of bitterness—he did not want to show that he knew the truth. And never, throughout the rest of his life, was he to belie that attitude.

But he suffered moments of terrible anguish in that struggle of a hundred days and a hundred nights with the impossible, in his efforts to instil courage in hearts that wavered, to collect money that melted away, to hurl terrified conscripts into the fray behind his delighted Old Guard on the frontier. To Mme. Bertrand he said: "Let us hope that we shall not have cause to regret Elba."

Hortense was now doing the honors of his Court. The Emperor had taken up residence at the Elysée—he found the Tuileries too vast and gloomy now that he was alone. Joseph and Jerome had returned to Paris no longer as kings, but as simple princes. Joseph had effected a reconciliation between Napoleon and Lucien. The latter was living in the Palais Royal with a brilliant entourage and had immediately taken his place as a political leader. The Emperor was to rely more and more on the President of the Brumaire, on the clever orator who knew how to handle legislative assemblies. Louis continued to sulk in Florence. On leaving Elba Madame Mère had gone to Naples and then returned to Corsica, whence she had finally come to France and to Paris accompanied by Fesch. Less fortunate than the others, Pauline had been made prisoner by the Austrians at Viareggio, while Elisa had been taken to Brünn in Moravia. At a time when the Treasury was carrying so many burdens, Napoleon was providing handsomely for the upkeep of his family. Not even Louis was forgotten.

As for Murat, the Emperor was again urging him to soft-pedal, to avoid giving the Coalition any excuse to attack. But the hot-headed, scatter-brained fellow did not obey. Threatened by the Austrians and fearful of losing his kingdom, he invaded Central Italy. In the end he had been defeated at Tolentino by Neipperg. He was now nearing the coast of Provence on a *chebek* as a fugitive. Napoleon was furious at his conduct and forbade him to come to Paris. Murat dug in near Toulon, while his wife and children were interned by Austria at Trieste. His brother-in-law's blunder cost Napoleon one of the trump cards in his pack.

The moment Mme. Walewska learned of the Emperor's return, she hastened to Paris. Napoleon received her privately two or three times at the Elysée. With Mme. Duchâtel, Mme. Ney, Mme. Lavallette and Mme. de Turenne, Marie Walewska graced the few receptions that were given to show France and all Europe that the régime was firmly in the saddle again. There was no jealousy, no pettiness between those women, who smiled bravely to hide their fears and paid even greater honor to the menaced sovereign than they had paid to the Emperor in his glory. Mme. Pellapra, it seems, never came to the Elysée, but she saw Marchand and, through him, informed Napoleon of Fouché's intrigues, which she had discovered. Mlle. George requested an audience for a similar purpose, but the Emperor was too busy to receive her. He sent Marchand to her and, learning that she was hard up, gave her twenty thousand francs from his private purse. Just before leaving for Waterloo, he entrusted his servant—never did he have one more trustworthy—with a large package, sealed with his arms, for the Countess Walewska, and a similar package for Emilie Pellapra. Both contained money, negotiable bonds, shares in canal stocks and a very beautiful bracelet. He had given a thought to those women who loved him and to their children on the eve of hastening toward those muddy fields of Flanders where his eagle, already wounded, was to fall, never to rise again.

His disaster at Waterloo stunned him. For that matter he was physically exhausted. All during those eight days he had slept only a few hours. Deprived of his relaxing baths, he had begun to suffer from dysuria and in particular from an attack of hemorrhoids which made riding extremely painful. On several occasions his generals, Reille among others, and Turenne, had taken fright at his apathy. They saw him fall asleep over his maps. On the evening of the defeat, he tried again to die. But again Death, which expected more of him, would have none of him. And he allowed himself to be swept along on the terrible tide of that disorderly retreat.

Should he go back to Paris? At first he hesitated. He would be safer among his soldiers. He was afraid of mutinies: "If I return to Paris," he said to Bertrand, "and if I dip my hand in blood, I shall have to plunge it in up to the elbow." However he did not forget the mistake he had made in 1814 and he did not intend to repeat it. From Laon, at a gallop, he returned to the Elysée. Immediately he got into his bath, in the presence of Caulaincourt and Lavallette. He complained of Ney, of Grouchy. . . .

"What a strange fate," he said. "To have seen France's triumph slip from my hands several times."

He went into his bedroom and shaved as usual: Marchand helped him to dress. Joseph and Lucien were there, warning him that he had everything to fear from the Chambers. The Emperor shrugged his shoulders. He entered the Council of Ministers with a remnant of hope: he came out of it a doomed man. His abdication was a matter only of a day.

He strolled for a while with Benjamin Constant in the gardens of the Elysée, then dined with Hortense. Neither of them had much to say—just a few unimportant words.

The following day he renounced the throne. This time there was no revolt left in him: he was resigned. Hortense urged him to think of his safety. He lingered as if he were expecting some event to reverse the situation. Then, yielding to Fouché's insistence, he set out for Malmaison.

So his last resting-place on French soil was to be the one that had witnessed his youthful triumphs. To receive him, Hortense had set her mother's house in order. Many of his loyal friends gathered about him that first day: Madame Mère, Joseph, Lucien and Jerome were all there. That evening Hortense's salon was crowded with ladies. The Countess Walewska and Emilie Pellapra were each received separately by the Emperor.

The next day he walked alone in the park in the dazzling summer sunlight. Every turn in those garden-paths called forth a memory. On that smooth lawn he had played prisoners' base in the happy days of the Consulate; sitting in that bower with his friends of the Institute, his ministers, his generals, he had talked of the future he intended to build for France. Above all, everywhere he went, a shadowy figure followed him—Josephine. Her presence, her charm obsessed him. He sent for Hortense and sitting beside her on a bench, said to her:

"Poor Josephine, I cannot get used to living in this place without her. I always feel as if she were just about to step out of one of those paths, to pick one of the roses she loved so well."

Hortense wept. The Emperor continued in a level voice as if he were dreaming aloud:

"For that matter she would be very unhappy now. There was only one thing we ever quarreled about—her debts, and I scolded her soundly enough. She was a real woman in every sense of the word, changeable, vivacious, and with the best of hearts. . . . I should like you to have another portrait of her made for me, in a medallion, perhaps . . ."

Corvisart came up to introduce his pupil, Maingault, who was to accompany the Emperor to America, for Napoleon saw no freedom or safety for himself save in the New World. When he returned to his apartment, he called Marchand. Handing him a little flask filled with a reddish liquid, he said:

"See that I always have that on my person. Pin it either to my vest or to some other part of my clothing so that I can get at it easily."

The valet fastened the flask under the Emperor's left brace in a little leather bag.

"That is good," said Napoleon and gave him a light tap on the cheek.

Four days of suspense in which the Allies were drawing nearer and nearer to Paris, days in which the all-powerful Fouché kept procrastinating, delaying the Emperor's departure that he might hand him over to the enemy, days in which Napoleon, hearing the cheers of his Old Guard as they passed on the road from Reuil, felt the blood throb in his veins again. He still hoped that France would make use of his sword to put the invasion to rout. Four long and heavy days. . . .

On the 27th, before luncheon, Napoleon received the Baron de Mauvières, Méneval's father-in-law. The Baron had brought his ward, little Léon, who was at boarding school in Paris. The child was nearly nine now, a well-built little lad, with a charming face. Hortense chanced to come in at that moment, and the Emperor said to her in a low tone:

"Look at that child. Whom does he look like?"

"He is your son, sire. He is the image of the King of Rome." Napoleon looked pleased.

"I did not think I had a tender heart," he said, "but I was deeply moved. . . . I confess I have been doubtful for a long time as to whether he were really my child. I was eager to see him, and, like you, I was struck by his resemblance to my son."

Hortense replied that she would gladly keep little Léon with her, but she was afraid there might be gossip.

"Yes, you are right," said the Emperor. "I should have liked to know that he was with you, but people would be sure to say that he was your son. When I am settled in America I shall send for him."

Hortense then went up to the child and embraced him. She asked him questions: Was he happy in his boarding school? What did he do to amuse himself? Not in the least shy, the little fellow replied that he and his schoolmates played mostly at fighting and that they formed two sides, one called Bonapartists, the other, Bourbonists.

The Queen asked him which he had chosen.

"The King's side."

As she wanted to know why, he answered:

"Because I like the King and I do not like the Emperor."

Surprised and disappointed, Hortense pressed him further. Why did he not like the Emperor?

"I have no reason," said the little fellow, "except that I belong to the King's party."

Napoleon then embraced the child and dismissed him. He

sent the child's guardian a number of recommendations for the little boy's future training.

That evening a number of people came from Paris to say farewell. Mme. Duchâtel was received privately and spent some time in the library, where the Emperor had entrenched himself as in bygone days. Pale, dignified, that faithful woman who had followed the ascent of the meteor as well as its downfall, managed to control her grief. Mme. Pellapra followed her, but remained only a few seconds. The next day Mme. Walewska appeared with little Alexandre. She wept in Napoleon's arms for a long time. He tried to comfort her, to give her strength. No doubt he promised to call her to his side if some lucky event should change his fate. But she did not believe it, nor did he. Blinded by her tears, Marie left him, confident that she would never see him again. Hortense met her in the gallery and taking pity on her, led her to her apartments where the two women lunched alone to escape curious glances.

Fouché had finally promised Napoleon that two frigates would await his orders in front of Rochefort. The Emperor hastened his preparations for departure. He had already conferred with Peyrusse his treasurer and Noël, his notary, the successor of the famous Raguideau. He ordered three millions in gold removed from the Tuileries to Laffitte and handed over eight hundred thousand francs in bank notes and his large collection of medals to the banker in person.

"I do not know what is in store for me," he told him. "I have fifteen years more before me. . . . For that matter it does not cost much to feed me. With a louis a day I shall live extremely well anywhere. We shall see."

He provided for his brothers and sisters to the best of his ability. Joseph received 70,000 francs; Lucien 250,000 in cash and two millions in notes, which would never be paid; Jerome, 100,000 francs; Madame Mère, the same sum in addition to shares in canal stocks. Hortense was very rich, much richer than she would admit. She insisted upon giving Napoleon a diamond necklace, which she sewed into a ribbon belt. He made her take a note for the equivalent, and he did even more: he gave her a touching remembrance—Josephine's wedding-ring.

That evening as Hortense was sitting in the garden with Mme. Bertrand the Emperor joined them. The day was drawing to a close in a soft golden haze.

"How beautiful Malmaison is," Napoleon said softly. "How happy we would be to stay here, wouldn't we, Hortense?"

She could not trust herself to answer. All three sat on in silence for a long time.

On the 29th, his offer to serve as a simple general having been rejected, Napoleon gave orders for his departure. In the library he bade farewell to Joseph, Fesch and Talma (the latter had come to Malmaison every day wearing the uniform of the National Guard). Lucien and Jerome had already left. He embraced Hortense, clasped Mme. Walewska's hands and then Caulaincourt's. Madame Mère, the last of his family, then came forward. Slow tears trickled down her wrinkled cheeks.

"Goodbye, my son . . ." was all she said.

"Goodbye, *ma mère,*" replied the Emperor.

They clung to each other while those about them looked on in sorrowful respect. Then Napoleon went up to his own apartment. He took off his uniform and put on a pair of blue trousers, a maroon-colored coat, riding boots and a round hat with a wide brim.

After that he went down to Josephine's room alone. It had been left just as it was when she died. For several moments Napoleon stood lost in thought before that bed shaped like a seashell and supported by two swans. At length he tore himself away and went on down the stairs. A closed barouche, drawn by four horses, was waiting at the entrance to the little park. With a firm step Napoleon walked to the gate. He was followed by Bertrand, Savary and General Beker. A last glance for Malmaison, and the Emperor flung himself into the carriage and was driven off rapidly in the direction of Rambouillet.

There, a woman, dressed in men's clothes, was waiting for him. La Bellini from the island of Elba had hurried from Paris in a transport of love and pity to implore him to take her with him into his exile. He declined gently. The poor woman left in despair. Bertrand gave her several thousand francs, with which she sailed for America where she hoped to meet the Emperor again. Later on she was to settle in Lima, where she opened a boarding school for young girls and ended her days basking in the exalted memory of Napoleon.

Epilogue

EXILE AND DEATH

St. Helena

ROM ROCHEFORT, the Emperor expected to go to the United States, where he would live for some time at least as a traveler, perhaps even as a colonist, till changes in Europe permitted his return. But the English cruiser, warned by Fouché, blockaded the port. Urged by the chance companions who had cast in their lots with his, Napoleon decided to appeal to the generosity of the English Cabinet. He found only its vengeance. On August 8, 1815, the *Northumberland* carried him away to the island of St. Helena.

Tossed by wind and waves, at the caprice of long swells, that hapless soul was to float for weeks on the Atlantic before his ship dropped anchor in the harbor that was finally to engulf him. As he sailed toward a new hemisphere, Napoleon slowly paced the deck, his hands under his coattails in the characteristic gesture. Now and then he would stop to touch an anchor or a bit of rope, to listen to the song of a sailor, the cry of a sea gull, the endless soughing of the waves. Days dawned, ran their course and died. The sun appeared above the horizon in that east that had known the youthful glory of Bonaparte, soared aloft in a milky sky so hot that the planks of the deck burned his feet, only to sink again veiled in a red mist, in the direction of those vast forests of America where, had he said the word in time, Napoleon would have been free.

A bell rang the dinner hour. The Emperor's companions and the English officers assembled in the saloon. Admiral Cockburn bowed before his prisoner. Mme. Bertrand and Mme. de Montholon eyed each other's gown. The Emperor ate very little. After dinner they would play cards or he would talk and laugh a little. But more often he would stroll forward to the prow and sitting on a cannon, scan the heavens, in which every day new stars appeared.

On October 16, 1815, the *Northumberland* dropped anchor in front of an immense rock of black basalt against which the blue sea dashed and broke into spray. In a fault in the rock one could see a humble, straggling yellow village with here and there a few tufts of palm trees. With anxious hearts the French looked across at Jamestown and the crumbling volcano that was to be their prison.

Longwood lies on the eastern end of the island on a plateau that can be reached only by a sort of isthmus. There the Emperor would be guarded by soldiers a gunshot away at the camp of Deadwood. While Cockburn's sailors were setting the house at Longwood in order, Napoleon lived for several weeks at The Briars, the home of the merchant Balcombe, in a small pavilion overlooking the entrance to a gorge lush with tropical vegetation. The host's daughter, Betsy, a girl of fourteen, was still an enfant terrible. Napoleon was highly amused at her pranks—which sometimes went too far—and would tease her and play with her as if he were her own age. "I feel as if I were at a masked ball," he said. It was with genuine regret that he left The Briars to settle at Longwood.

Longwood—a little low farmhouse with a slate roof stained by rains and beaten by the winds. And round about, tawny bluffs, wrapped in mists, stubbly fields bordered with cactus and aloes on which a few sheep, a few scrawny horses grazed.

The Emperor's apartment consisted of six rooms. First, a parlor, paneled in wood, which was reached by a flight of five steps and a trellised verandah, served as an anteroom. Later a billiard table was set up there. Napoleon never played on it, but he used to spread his maps and plans on the cloth. There in that room he would pace back and forth, dictating for several hours each day (especially in 1816) to his companions—generally to Las Cases, the most devoted of them all—notes which he intended as a first draft of his *Memoirs*.

From the anteroom, one passed into the drawing-room, which was lighted by two windows to the west. There Napoleon re-

ceived visitors of distinction. And there in the first days of the
Captivity, the Emperor would wait every evening for dinner to
be announced. Bertrand, Las Cases, Montholon, Gourgaud
would join him. As a rule he would invite one of them to a
game of chess on a table set up in a corner. The ladies would
sit near-by, while the men stood and looked on in silence.

In that drawing-room, too, the Emperor and his suite usually
spent the evening. He would read aloud from a history or a
scientific book, a tragedy of Corneille or of Voltaire, perhaps
the Bible or maybe Virgil, or Ossian. The ladies would yawn
from sheer boredom. Sometimes he caught them at it and, with
a malicious twinkle in his eye, he would hand the volume to
one or the other of them and ask her to continue reading. Those
were dull evenings unless Napoleon, who had become more
loquacious in his idleness, chose to relate some episode in his
life, an anecdote of the Revolution, a stirring incident from
the days of the Empire. To those officers, all of whom, even
Bertrand, were ignorant of the details of his life, he would
open his memory like a well-stored cabinet, for hours at a time,
referring to the days of his youth with real emotion and talking
of his love affairs, unblushingly, with the bluntness of a soldier.
At other times he would go over his campaigns, sometimes
pointing out an error in strategy—Italy, Egypt, the wars with
Prussia and Austria, the retreat from Russia, that marvelous
and desperate campaign of France and, finally, the return from
Elba and Waterloo. He criticized his ministers, his generals,
his relatives, his two wives. He spoke freely of the lepers of
Jaffa to whom, out of sheer pity, he wanted to give opium, and
of the death of the Duc d'Enghien, for which he assumed entire
responsibility.

When he became excited he would wave his arms and gesture
with his hands. His companions could have spent the whole
night listening to him, and it was with regret that the little
court of exiles separated when, with a nod or a word of farewell,
the Emperor bade them good night and dismissed them.

Back of the drawing-room was the dining-room, a gloomy
apartment where the only ray of daylight filtered through the

high glass in a door. To the left was the library, a room so cold that in winter Aly, the valet and librarian, was obliged to blow on his fingers to keep them from growing stiff. While the thermometer at St. Helena never went below fifty degrees Fahrenheit, the humidity from May to December was much harder to endure than the winter frosts of northern climates.

To the right of the dining-room lay Napoleon's private apartment—his "interior" as he called it—in which he was to spend all his time during the last days of his life: two small rooms about four yards square, each lighted by two windows facing north (in other words, toward the sun, for St. Helena lies below the equator). He used the first room as his study, the second as his bedroom. Both rooms were hung in an ugly yellow nankeen that was badly mildewed. Each contained a portable camp bed of iron, and the Emperor used these in rotation. On one of those beds he had slept on the eve of Austerlitz, the other had gone through the Campaign of France with him.

There was no fireplace in the study and Napoleon never sat in it during the rainy season, preferring his bedroom, where there was a grate with a wood fire burning constantly. There in that narrow, modest room, so like the bedroom of a small-town businessman with its green-painted cane furniture, its muslin curtains, its worn carpet, the Emperor placed his dearest souvenirs. Above the mantel Marchand hung the portrait of the King of Rome, one of Marie-Louise, and one of Josephine, a medallion of Madame Mère and, last booty of war, the alarm clock of the great Frederick, brought from Potsdam. . . .

In front of the house lay close-cropped lawns of dried, yellow grass while to the east a gumwood forest of small trees with pale-green foliage and flowers like asters, their trunks gnarled and bent by the trade winds, gave only a miserly shade. In the beginning Napoleon often used to walk there.

Six small buildings, a few offices and outhouses surrounding an unpaved courtyard that was always damp—and that was all Napoleon had in which to lodge nearly fifty persons, including the Montholon children. Accustomed to the rigors of camp life himself, Napoleon was not the man to suffer from poor lodgings. But he was compelled to keep within narrow bounds, and as time went on those bounds were to be even more restricted. Moreover he was forbidden to communicate with anyone; his most private letters were opened and he was subjected to espionage every moment of the day and night. Not a move, not a gesture of the French which was not immediately reported. An orderly officer was quartered at Longwood to guard the Emperor. Fifteen visual signal posts were set up on the hilltops. On all sides—sentries. At night they drew so close around the house that they could touch it. After nine o'clock anyone entering or leaving was challenged—the Emperor as well as the lowliest valet.

Not only was Napoleon's freedom restricted, but his dignity was assailed. No one was permitted to address him other than as General Bonaparte. His enemies denied him the imperial title which clerks in every chancellory in Europe were trying vainly to efface. That wretched pettiness was the cause of many difficulties, much unhappiness. Everything had been taken from him—he had only his name left! For those six years Napoleon had had one thought only—to remain Emperor. Not out of vanity, but for his son's sake, for the future he hoped to prepare for him . . . for that reason, if for no other, he could not consent to be only the general of the campaigns in Italy. One cannot erase history and glory is not prescribed.

From that moment he waged a bitter and stubborn conflict with the English authorities, a conflict without hope of issue, that was to be aggravated by the arrival of the new governor, Hudson Lowe, at St. Helena.

Lowe was not a torturer: he was merely a subaltern bewildered by a responsibility beyond his capacities. He was, in short, just an official afraid of losing a highly lucrative post. Moreover, imbued with a keen sense of his patriotic duty he thought it a matter of honor to guard Napoleon closely, to prevent him from corresponding with the outside world, to discourage any inclination, as well as any possibility of escape. A formalist with a petty mind, and ignorant to boot, he was prodded to action by a general staff that detested the French.

The Emperor's entourage was composed of very mediocre souls. Napoleon had passed the better part of his life in the company of men of eminence, and he suffered at finding himself tied to companions who scarcely knew him and who had been induced to share his exile only out of fear or self-interest.

Grand Marshal Bertrand had gone through the campaign in Egypt. The Emperor had married him to a distant relative of Josephine's. Bertrand was an upright soul, of modest intelligence and somewhat timid at heart. He was faithful to the end in spite of the incessant struggle he was obliged to wage against his fellow-companions.

General de Montholon was thirty-two years old, a man of ancient lineage, with charming manners which ill-concealed his emptiness of mind and heart. He had had diplomatic posts and had been in the imperial armies. For the time being he was in disgrace because of his somewhat reckless marriage. He was an extravagant man and a born intriguer, but little by little he was to work on Napoleon till the Emperor who became really fond of him would end by making him his principal heir.

The Marquis de Las Cases was an older man but also of an old family. He had lived in London, but had returned to rally to the Empire. A sailor by profession he had transformed himself into a man of letters and had followed Napoleon whom he served as chamberlain to take his dictation and become the historian of the reign, so assuring himself enduring fame. Worn out by the animosities around him, he was to leave St. Helena in 1816, returning to Europe in the hope of making himself Napoleon's mouthpiece on the Continent.

General Gourgaud was much more intelligent and better educated than Montholon, but he was woefully lacking in the graces that make a courtier. Vain, restless, hot-tempered and capable of the most violent conduct, he was passionately devoted to Napoleon! His was a jealous, possessive love and he was sensitive to an extreme degree. Napoleon did not take the trouble to handle him in the right way and he was often unjust to his aide-de-camp. The most interesting of the four men who accompanied the Emperor in his exile, Gourgaud was also the loneliest and the most unhappy. In March, 1818, he was to return to Europe, embittered and disgusted by the machinations of the Montholons.

Mme. Bertrand was half creole and wholly English by instinct and training. She did not like the Emperor and the latter returned her aversion cordially. Back in the days on the *Bellerophon* when the French learned that they were to be deported to St. Helena, the excitable woman had tried to throw herself into the sea. Since their arrival at St. Helena she had managed to keep to herself and spent her time plotting to desert Napoleon and escape from exile.

Mme. de Montholon was a woman of the world, a coquette eager to please, who made the most of a remnant of real beauty. Her position in Paris being none too sure, she had agreed to grace Napoleon's little court without too much regret. That move, she thought, promised notable advantages to her husband, herself and her children. Should the Emperor return to power—and with a man like that did one ever know?—there was the certainty of a great position which would amply repay her for all her sacrifices. Her patience, her sweetness, her charm and her social grace were to be a real comfort to Napoleon. To Mme. de Montholon, more than to anyone else, he owed the few moments of ease and relaxation he was to find at St. Helena. She was to be the last smile of the Captivity.

Those two women who had nothing in common, neither birth, ideas, nor habits, were openly antagonistic from the first. They were jealous of each other, they quarreled and they involved their husbands in their animosities. For that matter the entire colony lived on a footing of mistrust and hostility, an atmosphere aggravated by the Emperor's thoughtless jests, by the cruel words that showed his utter contempt for men, his certainty that they were influenced solely by fear or by calculation.

Because his enemies had contested his title, Napoleon sought to preserve in the midst of that miserable household an etiquette that was perhaps too reminiscent of his reign. He had a firm belief in the necessity of state etiquette for fallen monarchs: without that they would sink back into the status of private individuals. But what a sad and poignant contrast to those wretched walls, those low ceilings, that musty furniture, those worn carpets, were the flunkies in imperial livery, those generals in gala uniform who dared not enter their ruler's presence till they had obtained an audience, who sat down only with his permission, who addressed him always with the words, Sire or Majesty. . . .

Too many servants cluttered up the household, which they robbed systematically. Some few were faithful—Aly and Marchand in particular, showing a touching loyalty. But most of the others were thinking only of lining their pockets and returning to France as soon as possible. So great was the slackness in the management and the waste in the kitchen that, notwithstanding the huge sums which the English allotted for expenses at Longwood, the French frequently lacked meat, fruits, and even wood for fire.

Napoleon was keeping more than ever to his little suite of rooms. Now that the boundary lines had been drawn closer, he gave up riding horseback, confining himself to a short drive in a barouche around the plateau of Longwood or a few turns in the woods to the southeast of the house. Most of the time he stayed in his own apartment, reading a great deal, dictating to his officers, as the spirit moved him, accounts of his campaigns, notes on Alexander, Caesar, Turenne, Frederick II, documents also intended to defend his cause in Europe. He worked irregularly, by fits and starts, often dropping one subject to take up another. He would toss off an idea on the wing, as it were, depending upon subsequent reading to furnish him material for completing his notes, developing them. One would think he had vast spaces of time before him and that into them he was flinging stones out of which he would gradually make a highroad. He did his best to kill time. And time was hard to kill on that island of capricious climate, where the sun was almost always drenched in rain or drowned in fog, on that plateau perpetually swept by the relentless trade winds. . . .

Napoleon had lived dangerously. He was a gambler, he loved risk. He did not try to make capital out of his misfortune as the Montholons would have liked to do. From that desert rock, unarmed save for his pen, he hurled defiance at triumphant England, threatened her, thundered at her. Spurred on by the complaints and bitter reproaches of his companions, he broke off relations with Hudson Lowe, whose awkward, even irritating, attempts at conciliation he was to rebuff to the end.

To that little handful of men and women so sadly lacking in character, life at Longwood around a fallen giant who too often recalled better days, quickly became intolerable. That fiction of sovereignty transported to the desert imposed terrible obligations on them. They had not the same reasons as Napoleon to endure the isolation, the quarreling, the poverty. They were thinking not so much of posterity, of the judgment of history as of their children, their own interests, their future. Obliged day in and day out to burn incense before that difficult and exacting master, they ended by displaying only the weariness, the weakness, the selfishness of men. . . .

Napoleon's principal resource lay within himself, in that essential quality that was the very foundation of his genius—his tremendous imagination, the inspiration of his most brilliant deeds, the cause of his greatest blunders. Now in his misfortune that imagination was to come to his aid. It was the buoy that upheld him, a swimmer lost in the infinite waste of the sea, and prevented him from drowning. "I believe," he said, "that Nature made me for great dreams: they found a granite soul in me. Thunderbolts could get no hold upon it and simply slipped off."

Misfortune might crush him for a moment: it could not break him.

Some few regrets he had and he expressed them with simple dignity. His thought reverted again and again to the power he had wielded, never to the pleasures of detail. "I had the instinct of the founder," he said one day, "not of the proprietor." He thought he was creating a world, but if that world escaped from him, he could get along without it. That attitude made him appear insensitive. He was not insensitive: he suffered like other men. "It takes more courage to suffer than to die," he once said.

Once before he had sought death, but the thought of suicide now repelled him. Such an end would not be compatible with his legend, as he well knew. He must drain the cup of adversity. Only so would he gain the respect of his enemies, only so would he conquer the future. He himself had forgotten his blunders, the blood he had spilled, the tears he had caused to flow, and he had no doubt that the world, dazzled by his glory, would forget them too. "Every hour," he said, "helps to rid me of my tyrant's skin. My memory will grow day by day." After the material reign, the reign of the spirit. What did it avail him to have conquered Europe if he could not reign century after century over the soul of the universe?

During the first three years, the life of those exiles was not always empty and sad. They still had hope. As late as 1818, Napoleon and his companions believed that a change in the English cabinet or some political crisis in France might give them back their freedom. But at the end of 1818 the Allied monarchs met at the Congress of Aix-la-Chapelle and agreed that if the net about him was not to be drawn closer it was at least to be held as it was. With this decision the Emperor's hopes began to fade. His companions, losing all hope, had now but one idea —to leave him and as soon as possible.

The terrible monotony of St. Helena, from the firing of the cannon at sunrise to the gun at sunset that brought the sentries in close about the garden, was beginning to weigh on those poor souls. It was the dullness of uniform hours, of a petty environment, of limited interests, of an unstable climate, of a wind that never went down, of faces that were always the same, of no news or bad news, of necessaries that were lacking or else worn out, of living in a foreign country under perpetual suspicion, of never feeling sure of others even among the French, of tasks set by the Emperor, of everlasting chess games where His Majesty had to win regardless of his poor play and, worst of all, of those evenings of four to which the absence of the Bertrands, in a sulk as usual, almost always reduced them.

His mother and his brothers wrote him cautious letters at rare intervals, but those letters were censored by the English Cabinet and by Lowe. The Emperor did not read them any more. What was the use? He knew that his wife was unfaithful, though he pretended to know nothing about it, for the sake of the dynasty, for the sake of his little son of whom he thought constantly. He had had no news from that little boy. In five years not a line from the child, not a sign to show the father that he was not entirely forgotten. Through the pity of a humble woman, Mme. Marchand, the mother of his valet, he had been allowed to twine around his fingers and kiss a little curl of golden hair. Through the imposture of a merchant he had received a miserable bust which he had placed on the mantel in the dreary salon. The Emperor showed it to all his visitors with pride. His son! He imagined him growing up in the palace of the Hapsburgs, educated as a German by a family eager to remove every memory of his origin. That thought must have been a bitter grief to him. However he was still convinced that the King of Rome would one day be released from the Hapsburg trap and, recalled by France, would restore the Empire. The father's crucifixion would crown the son. "If I die here," he kept repeating, "he will reign."

In those days he had no feminine distractions—at least no relations in which the senses played a part. Because of her resemblance to Marie Walewska, Napoleon noticed a young girl, Miss Knipe, who was known on the island as "Rosebud." But he met her only twice and then only to exchange a few words with her in front of her garden gate. Nor did he see much more of the little country girl, Mary-Ann Robinson, who offered him bouquets in the Valley of the Fisherman and whom he called "the Nymph." She was to marry a captain in the merchant marine and to leave the island with her husband.

Nor is there any evidence that Napoleon had intimate relations with Mme. de Montholon. He spoke of her to Gourgaud so freely, and even more he permitted Gourgaud himself to treat her so outrageously that a liaison between them would seem to have been impossible. Moreover, after two years of living together in the same place, Gourgaud and Mme. Bertrand, avowed enemies both of Mme. de Montholon, were still wondering in 1817 whether she really had become the Emperor's mistress. In those close quarters to which the exiles were reduced, such uncertainty in the two witnesses most antagonistic to Mme. de Montholon would seem to be decisive. Other commentators of the Captivity, both French and foreign, do not even suggest it. Even Lowe's papers that abound in gossip and tales of backstairs spies, are silent on that point. The Austrian Stürmer was the only one of the Allied Commissioners to make an insinuation that might be counted as mere gossip. That the Emperor and Mme. de Montholon were on a familiar footing there is no doubt. But it was a familiarity that was wholly natural in that solitude, a friendship sustained by the gracious manners and courtesy—by no means disinterested— of the "beautiful Albine," who was no longer beautiful and whose faded charms were scarcely qualified to arouse desire.

Moreover the Emperor's virility was exhausted: he had lost all interest in sex, as his remarks to Gourgaud (which must remain unpublished because of their crudeness), clearly show. Marchand reports that the Emperor also said to Montholon on one occasion:

"Oh, my dear fellow, when a man is fifty and in my poor health it is no use to talk of women. ..."

He was only fifty years old, but he was worn out from hard work and his meteoric career. His forehead was free of wrinkles, but he was an old man. The Consul with the sharp, clear-cut features, the razorlike mouth, had degenerated into a fat man with a soft, pudgy face. Napoleon's obesity made him old. No doubt he had already begun to suffer from that affection of the pituitary gland of which the first symptoms (as the autopsy later verified) were an abundance of fatty tissue, disappearance of hair on the body, atrophy of the genital organs and an extreme fineness of the skin. The result was total sexual frigidity.

During the first two years Napoleon's health was good—save for colds, congestions, headaches and attacks of low fever to which he had always been subject. But in October, 1817, he began to suffer from a liver complaint which the English always tried to deny, but which was confirmed by the medical reports of O'Meara and of Stokoë. He had long had a tendency to hepatitis. Even as Emperor he had suffered frequently from liver trouble. He was born with it, like his mother, like all his brothers and sisters.

St. Helena developed that tendency. The climate of the island was damp but not really tropical and perhaps not unhealthy. However the sanitary conditions of that period were deplorable. Water was scarce and foul: mosquitoes bred dysentery and swamp fever. A number of soldiers quartered in tents at Deadwood succumbed. All of the Emperor's companions suffered from it at one time or another. The Emperor's malady was aggravated by extremely poor hygiene: he was continually shutting himself up in his overheated little rooms, taking baths so hot that his valet could not put his hand in the water, eating too rapidly at irregular hours and not enough vegetables. Moreover the Emperor was wretchedly treated by the physicians that followed one after the other—O'Meara, Stokoë, Antommarchi, every one of whom persisted in applying the most corrosive drugs to an organism already appreciably weakened.

II

May Fifth

IN JANUARY, 1819, when Napoleon learned of the protocol of Aix and realized that he could no longer hope to return to Europe, he gave up the struggle and retired into the silence and solitude of his apartment. Most of his companions had left him: after Las Cases, Gourgaud had gone and after Gourgaud, Mme. de Montholon. The Bertrands were more or less in disgrace and living in their own home. This left Napoleon alone with Montholon and his servants. And Montholon was eager to leave too. The Bertrands had repeatedly asked permission to return to France. Napoleon held them as best he could, appealing to their pride, their sense of duty, showing them that it would be to their interest. . . . He tried to bribe those wretched souls who were not great enough to play the hero day by day, to get them to give him a few more months of their lives by telling them that he "had not much longer to live," if they would only wait a little while he would make them rich. But was he really ill? They did not think so. With a horrid eagerness they watched for signs of weariness, scanned the pallor of his face. Sometimes they despaired. Bertrand was the most respectful of them all, but one day he reproached his master: "The Emperor will bury us all!"

With a household so reduced in number the life at Longwood necessarily changed. The seclusion Napoleon had imposed on himself in answer to Lowe's pinpricks made the days drag out endlessly. The better to shorten them he tried changing the hour for meals, the hours for reading, or he took naps during the day. He had long ago given up any intensive work, but on certain nights he would still sit up to dictate a note—which he would then destroy the following morning.

At dawn, about six o'clock, he rang for his valet. Marchand, or Aly, whichever was on duty, would enter and throw open the shutters. Napoleon would then jump out of his camp bed and dress in haste: trousers of white fustian or duffel, a long padded coat, red leather slippers and a bandanna which he tied on his head himself. He then drank a cup of coffee and, if the weather was fine, went out into the garden humming some tune or other from his youth. Montholon would be sent for to accompany him. If it rained, or if the weather was foggy, he would go into the salon and the parlor, walking back and forth through the two rooms, talking and stopping now and then to look through his glasses—the fieldglasses of Austerlitz—from the little openings that had been made in the shutters. Those openings were generally closed to prevent the English officer detailed to guard him from seeing the Emperor. He still received his young Corsican physician, Antommarchi, in whom he had not the slightest confidence and whom he scolded severely for his frivolity and his disrespectful remarks. He would then receive Bertrand, who was always punctual, always meticulous and almost always in a taciturn mood. Napoleon thought Bertrand neglected him and devoted too much time to his wife and children.

About ten o'clock the Emperor breakfasted with Montholon in a tent in the garden or in his study, depending upon the weather. He had lost his appetite and ate only one dish now—eggs, a chicken wing, or a slice of ham, always preceded by a soup which he insisted upon having served boiling hot. The food was only mediocre: cattle and sheep were brought from the Cape and their meat was thin and tough. Hogs, fowl and fish, on the other hand, were good, the vegetables abundant and varied. But the bread was poor and made from flour that was musty or mildewed. A few fruits from Europe, and plenty of tropical fruits: but the mangos, guavas, avocados and grapefruit did not take the place for the French of the cherries, strawberries and peaches of which they were deprived. Napoleon enjoyed the bananas and he drank a little Bordeaux wine, the English having refused to let him import his Chambertin.

Montholon then went back to his own house and the Emperor lay down on his old sofa or on his bed. Marchand would read aloud until he saw that the Emperor had fallen asleep. Toward

three o'clock Napoleon rose and dressed. He was just as meticulous about his appearance as ever, though he shaved only every
two or three days now.

Since coming to Longwood he had given up wearing his
famous uniform of the Guard, choosing instead an old hunting
coat of green cloth which he had had turned and on which he
always pinned his two crosses. With this he wore a quilted waistcoat, white cashmere trousers, silk stockings and low-heeled
shoes with gold buckles.

He would send for Montholon again and walk with him in
the garden. All through the year of 1819 he took a great interest
in that garden, making his entire household dig ditches, turn
the soil, make pools, plant trees, tend to the vines and sow vege-
table and flower seeds. He himself used a pick and shovel. The
work had amused him and the exercise had given him back a
semblance of health. Often he would sit beside the little pools.
One of them had been made from an old bathtub from which a
thin trickle of water flowed. Napoleon's love of nature, always so
alive in him, had deepened. "A tree is what I want," he said in
almost plaintive tones to his last English visitor, Ricketts, a
cousin of Lord Liverpool. He also asked him to see that he was
not compelled to live in the new house where there were no
shade trees, which Lowe had built at great expense. He hated to
give up his little terraces. The man who had created a new
world, now devoted himself to that futile and ephemeral creation—a garden. But nothing is more vital and Napoleon loved
life. He may even have found a greater pleasure in designing
those squares, those paths of his humble rose garden than he
had ever experienced in helping his architects decide on improvements at Compiègne or Fontainebleau.

And yet even that distraction palled in the end. He had less
energy these days. With the aid of the little Bertrand children
he still watered his garden, but more frequently he would
wander through the covered paths or beside the flower beds outside of his bedroom. Musing, he would lean over a plant, pick a
passion flower or a carnation and hold it in his hand for a long

time. Or sheltered from prying eyes he would sit on the green-
sward and watch the flame-colored cardinals imported from
Brazil or those *avedavats* as big as bumble-bees, that go through
the fields at St. Helena in clouds in the harvest season, as they
pecked at the ground or flew from branch to branch. As a rule
he dined again with Montholon—alone when he was tired.
There was always a great deal to eat—now that his wife had gone
Montholon had only the pleasures of the table left, but the
Emperor took even less than at luncheon. On Sundays the
Grand Marshal and Mme. Bertrand came to dinner, which was
then served in the dining-room with formal elegance. Those
dinners of four were too sad, reminding them too forcibly of
their absent friends, and the Emperor discontinued them at the
beginning of 1820.

After dinner Napoleon returned to his private apartment, undressed quickly, throwing his clothes on the floor, and got into
bed. Marchand would come in and read to him, the Emperor
interrupting him every now and then to chat with him. Napoleon called him: "My son." And he was right. That young man
who had been educated above his station in life, had a generous
and loyal heart. He was the most patient, the most trustworthy
and certainly the most devoted friend the Emperor could have
had.

Often unable to sleep at night, he would wander from one to
the other of his camp beds. At times a sharp pain would shoot
through his side. Then he would wake Marchand and ask him
to prepare a bath. Those baths which relieved him also exhausted him. He would stay in them for two or three hours
at a stretch, and insist upon having them kept piping hot.
O'Meara, in his time, and later Antommarchi, both advised
against them. But the Emperor would not listen to his physicians: he did not believe they could help him. It is true that
at times he seemed to recover the strength of his former robust
constitution. And yet death was nearer than his friends or than
he himself had any idea—Death the only order of release that
could free him and his attendants, as long as he could not and

did not wish to escape, as long as Europe hated him, France had forgotten him, and even his family, for whom he had done so much, had virtually forsaken him.

In September, 1819, Cardinal Fesch sent out two priests, Abbé Buonavita and Abbé Vignali, along with the young physician Antommarchi. As soon as they arrived Napoleon ordered a chapel to be arranged in the dining-room at Longwood, where Mass would be celebrated every Sunday. The Emperor attended regularly. When he was too ill, the door of his bedroom was left open and he could hear the service from his bed.

On religion as on all subjects he expressed highly contradictory theories. "What makes me think there is no avenging God," he would sometimes say, "is to see that good people are always unhappy and rascals happy. You just watch—Talleyrand will die in his bed. . . . There is nothing but matter. Besides, if I had ever believed in a remunerating God, I would have been afraid in battle. . . . I know very well that death is the end of everything."

However, he was still sympathetic toward Catholicism. He admired the Christian religion and considered it a moral force and a necessary social tie. He spoke with respect of good priests. Of the Bishop of Nantes he said: "He was a holy man. Priests like that are useful to the country." Sometimes the words seemed to be forced from his lips by an inner compulsion: "The notion that sins can be remitted is a very beautiful one. That is why religion is beautiful and will never perish. . . . No man can say that he does not believe, or will not some day. Only a madman could say that he will die without confession. There are so many things that one does not know, that one cannot express in words. . . ."

The celebration of Mass at Longwood marked a milestone in Napoleon's career. No doubt he felt that it was now time for him to connect himself again with that religion which he had re-established in France and whose leader, the admirable Pius VII, so nobly forgiving of insults, was protecting his family. If not for his own sake, at least he should do it for the sake of his glory, for the sake of his son. First the politic motive, but little by little it was to lead him to a supreme acquiescence. . . .

However, the mysterious disease within him was progressing. He who had always been so prompt to rise in the morning, now lingered in bed. He complained to Antommarchi of "pains, as sharp as a knife-thrust in his right side." No one paid any attention, his physician less than anybody. It mattered not that he would put his hand on his side and say: "Gentlemen, you think I am joking! But just the same it is true that I feel something in there that should not be there." They were still sceptical. He began to wonder whether he might not have inherited his father's pyloric ulcer, that cancerous ulcer of which Charles Buonaparte had died at thirty-nine. On several occasions he told Antommarchi that, if he died, he wanted them to perform an autopsy so that his son might be forewarned, if that were possible, against an inheritance of the disease.

He still received Bertrand almost daily, but he refused to see Mme. Bertrand. By her stubborn determination to return to France she had become quite estranged from him. Let her go! He saw no harm in that, but she would have to take her children with her and Napoleon was devoted to them. Their departure would leave an irreparable void at Longwood. The children, for their part, loved him too. They would run to meet him the minute they saw him in the garden. They took all their little quarrels to him and made him their arbiter. Napoleon delighted in their fresh young affection. "Nothing devious about them," he kept saying. "They come right out with everything that enters their heads." He lavished presents on them: to Napoleon Bertrand, the eldest, a gold watch for reciting the multiplication table correctly, to Hortense a pair of earrings—he had Antommarchi pierce her ears so that she could wear them. He bought little Arthur, his favorite, whose pretty face may have reminded him of the King of Rome's, a pony from Java which the child had expressed a wish for. And he was constantly order-

ing his cook to make cakes and bonbons for them. Now at the
end of his Captivity, those children were the companions he
would miss the most. . . .

In the period between October, 1820, and March, 1821, Napoleon's condition became rapidly worse, with now and then a few
remissions of shorter and shorter duration.

Montholon wrote to his wife:

> Each day is like the next, or nearly so. At half-past eight
> or nine o'clock, the Emperor sends for me: often I breakfast
> with him, that is when he takes breakfast. At half-past eleven
> he lies down again. At one o'clock he receives Bertrand whom
> he keeps for a more or less lengthy visit, rarely longer than
> two o'clock when the latter comes to my house. At three I
> dress for walking and accompany the Emperor when he goes
> out. . . . At five o'clock I dine alone with the Emperor and
> stay with him till eight, nine or ten o'clock. Three-quarters
> of the time he has his dinner served in bed. He has not worked
> for several months. Last week he was extremely ill and gave us
> two days of great anxiety. He asks me to tell you to send him
> some books. He has someone to read to him, for his eyes tire
> very quickly.

Napoleon refused to take the remedies Antommarchi wanted
to give him. He had only contempt for that vain and irresponsible fool. His limbs were growing heavy now, he was always cold.
Light hurt him and he insisted upon having his bedroom her-
metically sealed, with blinds and curtains drawn. Montholon
and Marchand wandered about groping in the dark. The slightest noise brought an ejaculation of impatience from him. He
was taking practically no food . . . most of the sustenance caused
him nausea.

Montholon warned Lowe on several occasions, but the latter
refused to believe that the Emperor was really ill. Not only that
but he even imagined that Napoleon's seclusion concealed a
plan to escape. The officer on guard had to resort to all sorts of
ruses to catch a glimpse of the sick man and then seldom succeeded. Moreover the governor insisted, brutally, on sending an
English physician to Longwood. The Emperor held out against
it for a long time. In the end, yielding to the entreaties of his

companions who feared that Hudson Lowe might resort to extreme measures, he consented to receive Dr. Arnott. That army surgeon was just another fool. He insisted that there was nothing the matter with Napoleon—he was a hypochondriac. . . . The French, for that matter, were not far from agreeing with him. Only the Emperor recognized the nature of his disease and realized what it held in store for him. "The machine is worn out," he said. "It refuses to run. It is all over. I shall die here."

On the 10th of April he was confined to his bed—he was never to leave it again. Summoning all his strength he wrote his testament . . . an exhausting task of nearly eight days in which he dictated first to Montholon, then recopied in his own hand carefully, in order to make his handwriting more legible. That was essentially a political document, his last report, the most admirable of them all. But it was, moreover, a profoundly human document, evidence of his constant thought of his little son, his touching remembrance of his old soldiers and of France, and finally his pathetic gratitude to all those who had helped him and had devoted themselves to him. With a real anxiety he searched the hidden corners of his memory, went over his life again for a last time, asking himself whether he might not have forgotten someone to whom he owed recognition: the Corsicans of his youth, men of the siege of Toulon, his companions in Egypt, his friends of the Consulate, generals and ministers of the Empire.

He left remembrances to all the members of his family, even to Marie-Louise, to whom he commended his son urgently. And he divided the sums at his disposal at St. Helena and in France among the companions of the Captivity, reserving the largest share for Montholon, to the detriment of Bertrand. However, in the calm that precedes death, Napoleon showed more gentleness to the Grand Marshal, and even consented to receive Mme. Bertrand, who thereafter spent a few moments each day at his bedside.

He received Extreme Unction from the hands of Abbé Vignali. The ceremony was performed behind closed doors, Marchand being instructed to forbid everyone entrance to the room. When Vignali came out of the bedroom he said to Marchand:

"The Emperor has just been given Extreme Unction, but the condition of his stomach prohibits another sacrament."

Why all that mystery? Napoleon had never liked ritual and undoubtedly objected to having the sacrament administered in public. To Bertrand, the unbeliever, he was even to say that he had done it "for form's sake." At heart he was a deist, but in the face of death, he submitted respectfully to the last rites. "One ought to die in the religion in which one is born," he said to Marchand.

The Emperor was in a state of semi-consciousness for the last three days. To the very end he persistently refused to admit any English doctor other than Dr. Arnott. All that day of May 5th, in the salon where they had carried his bed, he lay dying peacefully. He suffered no convulsions, no pain. The French were all there, even the Bertrand children, gathered around his bed, waiting for the end. In the afternoon he began to breathe more slowly. The day was clear and warm. Through the two windows that had been thrown half open, one could see the ocean shimmering like a mirror in the sunlight. Suddenly, Alarm Signal, the sunset gun that daily heralded the approach of twilight, shook the windowpanes. Antommarchi leaned over the bed. Without a sign the man of battles had breathed his last to the roar of the cannon. In a few moments the swift tropic night would fall.

The young physician closed the Emperor's eyes. Surrounded by his companions who now, perhaps for the first time, understood his greatness, he lay on his little camp bed, a peaceful smile on his pale lips. The magic of death had given him back the youthful face of the First Consul.

What had been the cause of his death! Was it an abscess of the liver that had pierced the walls of the stomach near the pylorus? Two reports of the autopsy, the one signed by Dr. Shortt, an extremely honest surgeon, the other by Antommarchi, and drawn up the very day the body was opened, both reject that theory.

They reported the liver enlarged, perhaps swollen, but without visible alteration, whereas the stomach was gangrened and riddled with perforations. There is no doubt that Napoleon died of a cancer as his father had died before him and as Caroline and Pauline, not to mention Fesch, were to die after him. That cancer would have killed him at the Tuileries as well as at Longwood. But its development was indubitably hastened by the humid climate of St. Helena, as well as by the depression that overwhelmed the Emperor, particularly toward the end.

Though Sir Hudson Lowe, by his petty fears, may have interfered with the funeral ceremonies, the obsequies of the Captive were not without a certain nobility. The Governor even called out all the military forces at his disposal. Foreseeing that the English would not permit the return of his body to Europe, Napoleon had expressed a desire to lie in that narrow Valley of the Geranium where once, shortly after his arrival at St. Helena, as he was returning from Bertrand's house, he had rested beside a little stream. Every day since then his two Chinese servants had gone to fetch water from that stream for him.

The Emperor was laid to rest in the shade of three willow trees. Hudson Lowe had a grating built around the grave and placed a sentry-box near-by where an English soldier would continue to mount guard as if the Great Prisoner were still alive! There Napoleon was to sleep for twenty years!

For twenty long years he was to sleep beneath that simple headstone, visited only by rare travelers and those broad wings that fly from ocean to ocean at every return of the seasons. Then France, mourning his glory, was to carry him back at last and bury him under the dome of the Great King. The Return of the Ashes was to be an apotheosis without example in the history of all times.

Cleansed by his anguish, crowned by legend, Napoleon was thenceforward to undertake the conquest not only of Europe but of all the world, and this time with an invincible weapon—Thought. That abiding conquest was achieved more by the man than by the Emperor. By a strange sort of magic his physical image is more visibly present to us today, more familiar than it was even to our elders. Studying him dispassionately, with an open and unbiased mind, we probably see him more or less as he really was, in a close approximation to the actual truth.

For all of the brilliancy of a career that overturned space and devoured time, for all of his military genius, his civil talents, all the splendor that trails like star dust after his name at the distance of a hundred years, he strikes us not as the demi-god that some saw in him, not even as the hero—if by hero one mean a coherent personality that never wavered or weakened. To us he is a man, a very great man, a being of flesh and blood, a sensitive soul with countless irregularities and shortcomings, hard, capricious and excessively ambitious, but also, energetic and generous, with a sense of justice and a passion for orderliness and work, with finally a superb confidence in the destiny of France.

Knowing the man in his private life we can better understand the Emperor. Admiring him none the less, we love him the more for being so human like ourselves. He knew all the hardships of life, but he embodied a number of the highest qualities with which a child of this earth may be honored. To those who can rise above times, parties, even nations, those qualities assure Napoleon an exceptional place in the history of mankind.

Index